Gender Studies and the New Academic Governance

Heike Kahlert
Editor

Gender Studies and the New Academic Governance

Global Challenges, Glocal Dynamics and Local Impacts

Springer VS

Editor
Heike Kahlert
Bochum, Germany

ISBN 978-3-658-19852-7 ISBN 978-3-658-19853-4 (eBook)
https://doi.org/10.1007/978-3-658-19853-4

Library of Congress Control Number: 2017962071

Springer VS

Printed on acid-free paper

This Springer VS imprint is published by Springer Nature
The registered company is Springer Fachmedien Wiesbaden GmbH
The registered company address is: Abraham-Lincoln-Str. 46, 65189 Wiesbaden, Germany

Content

Introduction: Gender Studies and the New Academic Governance

Heike Kahlert

1 The Advent of Neo-liberalism in Higher Education and Research

Neo-liberalism is an economic theory and a social reform movement at the same time; its interconnected position as a knowledge technology and a political practice precisely contributes to its all-pervasive significance. Neo-liberalism positions itself in the tradition of Enlightenment through the actions stemming from its scientific and social configurations. It refers to the dominance of scientific rationality, or to be more exact, economic rationality. Thus, neo-liberalism can be considered as an escalation of the Protestant ethic, a nearly total and globalising regime of economic rationality. It aims at transforming capitalist societies in the direction of an all-encompassing market. In the 1980s, the strengthening of neo-liberalism in the era of Reaganomics and Thatcherism was initially called a 'neo-conservative revolution'. This term led to a clearer awareness of the tradition of the appropriate theory and politics than the (actually) misleading term 'neo-liberalism'.

Nowadays, 'neo-liberalism' is used as an umbrella term for principles such as the expansion of the market regime, the re-valuation of 'output' orientation, and the promotion of competition and individual freedom. Neo-liberalism has become the hegemonic narrative of the present age. However, its reach from governmental techniques all the way to daily modes of life is hardly perceived. The neo-liberal hegemony extends from the growing importance of the finance sector for all societal subdomains into the indicator-supported allocation of resources in the public sector into the strengthening of consulting, accountings and counselling up to the formation of a 'neo-liberal self' which optimises a technology of governing the self, according to market rules such as efficiency, performance and hard work. Thus, the neo-liberal hegemony is subtle, and this contributes to its power as both an economic theory and social reform movement.

The advent of 'new public management' in the 1980s as an approach of running governments, public service institutions and agencies, at both subnational and national levels, is part of the strengthening of neo-liberalism. This contributes towards making public service more 'business-like' and towards improving its efficiency by using private sector management models and performance criteria (e.g. Ferlie et al. 2009). This is also the case in academia. The neo-liberal transformations create a new 'academic governance' (Lewis 2013) and lead to the formation of 'entrepreneurial universities' (Clark 1998). Since the introduction of this new, market- and performance-oriented governance into academia, higher education and research are challenged by new regulation techniques, which go hand in hand with the implementation of managerialist tools, such as target agreements, rankings and evaluations; the demand for scientific excellence and its measurements; and the marketisation of knowledge production and transfer (e.g. Paradeise et al. 2009). Thereby, the relationship between science and society is changing: scientific knowledge is not only expected to be usable and useful for social demands, but it also has to prove its usability and usefulness to society. This is also the case for gender studies and gender research,[1] the focus of this book.

2 Gender Studies and Gender Research within Current Transformations

Since the beginning of gender studies and gender research in so-called modern Western societies, a high potential for innovation in science and society has been attributed to gender studies and gender research by gender scholars themselves and also in the rhetoric of science policy. This potential includes epistemic and organisational impulses for the system of higher education and research as well as for societal and political developments: gender studies and gender research have very often been introduced and valued as 'better (scientific) knowledge' with respect to the inclusion of the marginalised or excluded perspectives of women and gender relations in the academy.

With respect to the history of science, gender studies and gender research are new- and latecomers in academia. This reflects the history of science and academia which is built on a long tradition of the dominance of men and the exclusion or marginalisation of women as subjects and objects of scientific knowledge. This might

1 In this introduction, both terms are used as umbrella terms for studies and research dealing with gender, gender relations and gender orders.

explain why the field of gender studies and gender research has been feminised since its beginning; at all levels, it is mainly women who engage in this field, for example as students, research associates and professors. Men are in the minority. Accordingly, the development and promotion of gender studies and gender research has had, since the beginning, a twofold aim and meaning: supporting the implementation of gender equality for women in higher education and research, and promoting the development of scientific knowledge from a gender perspective with respect to contents, theories, methodologies, and corresponding organisational and cultural structures in academia.

However, the institutionalisations of gender studies in scientific organisations are often precarious and marginalised. Additionally, gender studies' disciplinary status is still evolving and at stake: it varies among being a subdiscipline in traditional disciplines, an inter- or transdiscipline, or a discipline of its own. Both the unclear disciplinary status of gender studies and its uncompleted institutionalisation are interconnected and still contested. Whether the history of the institutionalisations of gender studies in higher education and research can be seen as a story of success or of failure depends on the perspective.

What is happening to gender studies and gender research as an emerging but contested field of scientific knowledge in the conditions of the new academic governance, and which role gender studies and gender research play in the current transformations in academia, for example in research funding, university development and careers of the next generation of scholars, has interestingly not yet been well investigated. Of course, there are some publications dealing with these questions, for example special issues of international journals (cf. Davies and O'Callaghan 2014; Nash and Owens 2015; Camus et al. 2016; Liinasson and Grenz 2016). However, these publications consist mainly of theoretical reflections and field reports. That might be characteristic for this field of knowledge and the precarious status of gender studies in the academy, but it also makes clear that empirical and comparative research on these issues is still lacking. On the one hand this is astonishing, because the introduction of the new academic governance naturally has impacts on gender studies and gender research which should be analysed. On the other hand, this observation might reflect the problematic material conditions of gender studies and gender research in higher education and research in the 2010s.

3 About This Book

The idea for this book was generated during the final stage of my project *Gender Research and the New Academic Governance*, which analysed the organisational structures and organisational cultures in German higher education and research in order to foster the potential for innovation in gender studies in current conditions of transformations.[2] The project focused on analysing how much importance is ascribed to gender studies and gender research in the conditions of the new academic governance in contemporary transformation processes of the academic system, considering scientific, organisational (cultural and structural) and politically administrative perspectives. The project also investigated what kind of promotion gender studies and gender research receive in this process by different stakeholders and gatekeepers in higher education, science and research policy. In addition, the project also asked what the starting points are to deepen and broaden the field of gender studies and gender research in the conditions of the new academic governance (cf. Kahlert 2016). These research questions and engaged discussions with the participants in the final international conference of the project, which took place in September 2015, formed the starting point for this book. The contributions for this collection were recruited by invited articles from conference participants and additionally by an international call for articles.

All articles focus on gender studies and gender research in times of the new academic governance and consider current developments in higher education and research from different geopolitical perspectives. The articles make clear that the impacts of the new academic governance have global, glocal[3] *and* local dimensions which have to be taken into account in analysing the state of gender studies and gender research at the end of the 2010s. The authors are located in different regions of the world, including various parts of Europe, covering Northern, Eastern, Southern and Western perspectives, and also Brazil and South Africa, and thus they represent diverse geopolitical and sociocultural views on the abovementioned questions. They simultaneously draw a multifaceted picture of the current situation with respect to the global challenges, glocal dynamics and local impacts; criticise

2 This project was funded by the German Federal Ministry of Education and Research with the promotional reference 01FP1306 and was conducted at the University of Hildesheim in Germany. More information can be found online at http://www.genderforschung-governance.de/en/.

3 With this term I refer to ideas first introduced by Roland Robertson (1995) who states that the multidimensional process of globalisation has global and local or regional impacts simultaneously. Thus, 'glocalisation' focuses on the level of local or regional effects of worldwide globalisation.

the widespread tendencies of the marketisation of scientific knowledge, capturing not only the natural sciences and engineering but also the social sciences and humanities, including gender studies; suggest strategies for resistance against the neo-liberalisation of higher education and research; and identify starting points for further and optionally comparative studies on these issues. These contributions emphasise not only the need for more theoretical reflection and empirical research and for critical exchange on the current transformations, but also the need for political action to challenge, resist and change them.

3.1 Interventions: Gender, Gender Studies and Academic Feminism

The first three articles analyse the neo-liberal dynamics taking place in many different systems of higher education and research all over the world with respect to gender, gender studies and academic feminism, revealing how the discursive, material and emotional technologies of neo-liberalism influence research in general and feminist studies and gender research in particular on the macro-, meso- and micro-level. The articles make clear that on the one hand the global, glocal and local impacts of the neo-liberalisation of academia seem to be quite similar all over the world and on the other hand are particular in their manifestations, depending on the specific historical, geopolitical and sociocultural contexts and developments in different areas. Drawing on these analyses, the authors emphasise the need for critical interventions in the neo-liberal transformations and elaborate on possible strategies to challenge them.

In her article entitled *Gender in the Neo-liberal Research Economy: An Enervating and Exclusionary Entanglement?*, *Louise Morley* discusses the gendered implications of the global neo-liberal research economy. She explores the complexities and contradictions of neo-liberal discourse and how it has become entangled with higher education in general, and with the research economy in particular. Her argument is that neo-liberalism has been installed via material, discursive and affective means and thus influences, for example, not only funding and employment regimes, but also the daily work, including the emotional reverberations, in academia. Research, Morley shows, is now a major vehicle for performance management and a product or service valued for its commercial, market and financial benefits. Of course, these developments are inclusive: they affect both women and men. However, because of the ongoing misrecognition and under-representation of women as research leaders, the neo-liberalisation of research tends to be highly gendered and exclusionary. As Morley concludes, neo-liberalism is not essentially male, but it has reinforced the male dominance of the research economy by valuing and rewarding the areas and activities in which certain men have traditionally succeeded.

Kadri Aavik and *Raili Marling* focus on the impact of the neo-liberalisation of higher education on gender studies and feminist research in post-socialist settings in their article entitled *Gender Studies at the Time of Neo-liberal Transformation in Estonian Academia*. By using the example of Estonia, Aavik and Marling explain the status and developments of gender studies and feminist research and consider how feminist scholars in these conditions both accommodate and challenge the corporatisation of universities. Because of the discursive and material dimensions of neo-liberalism identified by the authors, it becomes obvious that feminist scholars in Estonia (and probably also elsewhere) are largely complicit in the neo-liberalisation of academia, playing by its rules rather than offering resistance. Neo-liberalism thus not only affects the scientific discourses and interventions but also has an impact on the precarious working conditions of feminist (and other) scholars. Therefore, the authors emphasise the need for revitalising academic trade unions and organising resistance to neo-liberalisation collectively. They conclude that advancing intersectional perspectives in feminist scholarship and forming intersectional coalitions might be a way forward.

In her article entitled *Neo-liberalism and Feminism in the South African Academy, Desiree Lewis* affirms that neo-liberalism's effects on academic feminism are more or less similar in the global North and the South. According to her, neo-liberalism also augments and redeploys core-periphery relations, creating market-based and developmentalist knowledge-producing networks that pose distinctive challenges for feminists in different geopolitical spaces. By analysing the location of current feminist work in South African universities, the author is concerned with two related aims. She unpacks specific challenges for feminists that both constitute and are constituted by global streams of capital and knowledge, and reflects on the possibilities for radical feminist responses to the neo-liberalisation of the academy. Thereby, Lewis considers how an analysis of globalisation's effects in specific contexts can help deepen transnational feminist critiques of the neo-liberal academy. In her view, transnational feminism can challenge the entrenched power relations that global neo-liberal research and knowledge production reproduces by self-reflexivity, regaining radical perspectives, networking, and rebuilding research and activist communities between the global North and the South.

3.2 Interactions: Gender Research, Academic Feminism and Society

The articles in the second part deal with a central expectation of the new academic governance, namely active and engaged interactions between research and society and the involvement in transdisciplinary problem-solving in those collaborations with various social actors. With respect to gender research and academic feminism, the authors elaborate on this expectation by analysing different types of relationships between gender research and society and identifying various social actors participating in these interactive relationships. The case studies from different contexts and regions of the world reveal that gender research and academic feminism are not only scientific endeavours but also at all times interconnected with social influences and movements with the aim to change or improve science and society. However, this improvement might originate from the call for putting social justice into action and/or the call for innovation.

In her article entitled *The Relationship between Gender Research and Society in the Norwegian Brainwash Controversy of 2010–2011*, *Pia Vuolanto* analyses a recent public controversy in Norway that unveiled different social actors' definitions and expectations of gender research. The object of the empirical study is the popular science series *Brainwash* which was produced by the Norwegian broadcasting company and comprised seven programmes on topics from gender research, such as gender equality, gender identity issues and violence, and raised a lively public debate. Through a close reading of newspaper articles, articles in scholarly journals and blog posts, the author focuses on the different views and perceptions that different actors had of the relationship between gender research and society during this unusually large public controversy. In order to analyse diverse understandings of the relationship between gender research and society, she describes the idea of 'research markets' in different social worlds and their connected reference groups and distinguishes five of them, namely the markets of gender research itself, social sciences and humanities, natural sciences, policymaking, and anti-feminism. The analysis concludes that in the conditions of the new academic governance, the mission of universities and also gender research as change makers and allies of society has to be taken into account as more interactive.

Amélia Augusto, Catarina Sales Oliveira, Emília Araújo and *Carla Cerqueira* analyse the relationship between gender studies and gender equality policymaking in the conditions of the neo-liberalisation of academia in Portugal. In their article entitled *The Place for Gender Research in Contemporary Portuguese Science and Higher Education Policies within the Context of Neo-liberalism* they argue that gender studies is central to the objectives, direction and social purpose of both education and science, as both a driver for the future and for the transformation of societies. Using the European policy context as a guideline, as well as some Portuguese specificities, the authors discuss the impacts of neo-liberal policies of science and higher education on the prioritisation of scientific fields and scientific outputs, on the privilege of some modes of production of science, on the depolitisation of gender issues in the university, and ultimately on the possibilities and constraints for the affirmation and consolidation of gender studies. They reveal that although gender studies has a considerable history within science and academia with a growth of work and publications, gender studies' contributions in several fields are either kept invisible or just voided. In this context, the emergence of gender mainstreaming policies is identified as both part of the solution and part of the problem, because of the danger inherent to gender mainstreaming of losing the critical and transformative standpoint on gender as a historical and sociocultural construction and not as a given reality represented by gender studies.

Sigrid Schmitz focuses on another aspect of science and technology policies, namely the international top-down initiatives of demanding and promoting the integration of 'sex' and 'gender' into the governance of all fields of science and technology, from funding to research and development to publication policies, and to the assessment of the impact of scientific knowledge and technical products in society. In her article entitled *On the Use of Innovation Arguments for Getting Gender Research into STEM*, she examines the project *Gendered Innovations in Science, Health and Medicine, Engineering, and Environment*, which was initiated in 2009 by Londa Schiebinger from Stanford University, based on her collaboration with scholars Ineke Klinge and Martina Schraudner. This project is a main source of information and guidance for various governmental activities in international science and technology policies on how to integrate 'sex' and 'gender'; for example, it was co-opted by the European Union in 2012. Schmitz elaborates on contents and concepts of this project in relation to the findings and scope of knowledge available from feminist science and technology studies and questions the strategic invocation of 'innovation'. In order to strengthen the original perspective of gender for scientific knowledge production, she finally offers approaches to include feminist epistemologies and postcolonial perspectives in science, technology, engineering and mathematics.

In their article entitled *Academic Feminism and Exclusion in Brazil: Bringing Back Some of the Missing Voices*, *Cristiano Rodrigues* and *Mariana Prandini Assis* point to the fact that feminist knowledge production itself may undermine its contribution to social usefulness. By investigating the constitution of gender and feminist studies in Brazil, they claim that throughout its development and particularly in its struggle with so-called mainstream academia and science governance to contest its scientific marginalisation, this portion of the feminist field ended up producing some other exclusions of its own. Thus, and unintentionally, according to the authors, it contributed to perpetuating part of the marginalisation that is characteristic of hegemonic modes of thinking and knowledge production. More specifically, besides attaching itself to rather reductive notions of what its political subject is, it also did not create the conditions and the space within which voices articulated from the far margins, such as those of Black women, could flourish. Along these lines, the authors claim that in the Brazilian context, one of the ways for gender studies and gender research to continue to be asserted as scientifically and socially useful and relevant is to continuously confront the exclusions that it itself produces and to commit to radical inclusion, for example of Black feminist knowledge production.

3.3 Institutionalisations: Gender Studies' Epistemic and Organisational Statuses in the Academy

Finally, the last four articles focus on how conditions, patterns and strategies of how gender studies is institutionalised in the neo-liberalised academy. In doing so, the authors deal with different epistemic statuses of gender studies between being a particular perspective of knowledge and a discipline among others, and belonging to the fields of social sciences and the humanities. Additionally, the authors reflect on different organisational statuses of gender studies, depending on the epistemic value given to this perspective of knowledge or discipline. Undoubtedly, it is not a coincidence that all authors state the misrecognition and disqualification of gender studies as proper scientific knowledge, a knowledge which must be taken seriously within the many-voiced academic concert of disciplines. Also, all articles reveal that the new academic governance has ambivalent impacts on gender studies: on the one hand, it profits from a tailwind that appreciates interactions between gender studies and research and societal demands such as putting gender equality into action, but on the other hand gender studies has to succeed within the market conditions of neo-liberalism and is subjected to performance measurements and evaluations in spite of its precarious material conditions.

In her article entitled *The Institutionalisation of Gender Studies and the New Academic Governance: Longstanding Patterns and Emerging Paradoxes, Maria do Mar Pereira* first reviews the literature feminist scholars have been producing on processes of institutionalisation of women's, gender and feminist studies (WGFS) for several decades. With regard to the new academic governance, she systematises some of its key findings by differentiating macro- and micro-level patterns of institutionalisations. She then draws on an ethnographic study of academia to argue that, in some contexts, established patterns in the institutionalisation of WGFS are being transformed by the emergence of new models of academic governance. Pereira identifies the situation as paradoxical because of simultaneous trends of continuity and change and discrepancies between more recognition at the institutional level and in official discourse and the dismissing of the field at the epistemic level and in everyday 'corridor talk' and unofficial discourse. She concludes that this coexistence of continuity and change, of recognition and marginalisation of WGFS, is a key mechanism of the contemporary governance of science. Thus, an analysis of gender studies in times of the new academic governance must consider both the 'new' aspects of the scientific governance and the 'old' inequalities that it covertly reproduces.

Farinaz Fassa and *Sabine Kradolfer* investigate the institutionalisation process of gender studies in a Swiss French-speaking university, with a particular focus on its articulation with local social demands. In their article entitled *Gender Studies: A 'Cheeky Knowledge' Renormalised?*, they focus on questions of the inter-, trans- and postdisciplinarity of gender studies that were initially seen as an undeniable advantage for this field of knowledge. The authors argue that in the conditions of the new academic governance which introduces managerialist tools into scientific organisations and the demand for scientific excellence mainly rooted in a quite traditional disciplinary approach, gender studies is now faced with three dimensions of accountability, which are in in tension with one another, namely the professional, the political, and the institutional/managerial dimensions. According to Fassa and Kradolfer, a comparison with the changes that have occurred over the past 25 years in other interdisciplinary fields of knowledge, such as area studies and cultural studies, suggests that the social resistances and new scientific objects offered by gender studies, area studies or cultural studies tend to be diluted under the joint influence of new social demands, fragmentation and globalisation, paving the way for new academic disciplinary definitions that bring back to normal the 'cheeky knowledge' built by these studies.

With respect to German academia, *Heike Kahlert* focuses on the link between gender studies and gender equality policies which form another social demand on gender studies. In her article entitled *Gender Equality as a Boon and a Bane to Gender Studies in the Conditions of the New Academic Governance*, she discusses the strong but ambivalent link between gender studies and gender equality policies. Based on case studies on the significance and consideration of gender studies in university development processes, the author examines first how and in what conditions gender studies are taken into consideration in university development processes, especially when universities can profit from gender studies in order to fulfil the legal requirement to put gender equality into practice. Second, she shows what constellations of factors and actors support or hinder the development of gender studies in universities and how these mechanisms function in practice. Thirdly, she discusses how the relationship between gender studies and gender equality policies is shaped in the organisational practices of the universities and how the partly implicit connection of gender studies with gender equality policies is made explicit. The conclusion is that gender studies profits from the legal pressure to put gender equality into action but suffers from the disqualification as non-academic because of its link with gender equality.

Finally, *Blanka Nyklová* focuses on some of the intersections of geopolitical location and the position of gender studies as a discipline in the Czech Republic. In her article entitled *Gender Studies in the Czech Republic: Institutionalisation Meets Neo-liberalism Contingent on Geopolitics*, she first describes the establishment of gender studies and its institutionalisation in this particular context which started after 1989. She then analyses the intersection of geopolitics and neo-liberalism and how it affects local gender studies. Based on semi-structured interviews with scholars and activists, and observations and practice as a gender studies researcher in Czech academia, the author explores how the specific geopolitical setting impacts the field of gender studies and scholars navigating it. She argues that gender studies as a discipline has profited from the massification of higher education, which she considers as part of neo-liberal higher education reforms, and from the incorporation of gender, e.g. in the European Research Area and in other EU policies. However, this positioning of gender studies is identified as at least partly problematic: it both strengthens the local focus on institutionalised (rather than grassroots) activities and may undermine the perceived local relevance of the discipline that resonates with early post-1989 anti-feminist discourse that has not been effectively challenged so far.

4 Acknowledgements

This book was made possible by many actors, first of all the Federal Ministry of Education and Research in Germany for funding the research project *Gender Research and the New Academic Governance* and thus enabling deeper empirical investigations on this emerging field of knowledge with respect to German academia. I am also indebted to Dr Cori Antonia Mackrodt from Springer VS, who immediately indicated a great deal of interest when I introduced the idea to her and who provided a lot of help. I am very grateful for their support! Furthermore, I would like to thank several anonymous international reviewers who carefully commented on previous versions of the articles and thus helped sharpen the arguments elaborated in the texts. For the careful work on all the formal and invisible aspects of the book, such as consistent references, I would like to thank Vivian Sper and Katharina Haßlinghaus. I would also like to thank Elizabeth Meyer zu Heringdorf for her professional English-language review of all the articles. Finally, I am much obliged to all the authors who agreed to reflect on these complex topics in order to improve the understanding of ongoing global challenges, glocal dynamics, and local impacts to gender studies and gender research in the conditions of the new academic governance, and for their patience and professional communication during the completion of the manuscript.

References

Camus, Céline, Katharina Kreissl and Aline Oloff. Eds. 2016. *Universitäten im Wandel – Innenansichten aus der reformierten Hochschule*. Feministische Studien, Special Issue 34 (1). Berlin: De Gruyter.

Clark, Burton R. 1998. *Creating Entrepreneurial Universities: Organizational Pathways of Transformation*. Paris, Oxford: IAU and Elsevier Science.

Davies, Helen, and Claire O'Callaghan. Eds. 2014. *Feminism, Academia, Austerity*. Journal of Gender Studies, Special Issue 23 (3). Abingdon: Routledge.

Ferlie, Ewan, Christine Musselin and Gianluca Andresani. 2009. The Governance of Higher Education Systems: A Public Management Perspective. In *University Governance, Western European Comparative Perspectives*, ed. by Catherine Paradeise, Emanuela Reale, Ivar Bleiklie and Ewan Ferlie, 1–19. Dordrecht: Springer.

Kahlert, Heike. 2016. *Genderforschung und die neue Governance der Wissenschaft: Stand und Perspektiven. Forschungsergebnisse und Handlungsempfehlungen*. Hildesheim: Stiftung Universität Hildesheim. http://www.genderforschung-governance.de/images/inhalte/Broschuere_Genderforschung_2016.pdf. Accessed: June 24, 2016.

Lewis, Jenny M. 2013. *Academic Governance. Disciplines and Policy*. New York, Abingdon: Routledge.

Liinasson, Mia, and Sabine Grenz. Eds. 2016. *Women's/Gender Studies and Contemporary Changes in Academic Cultures: European Perspectives*. Women's Studies International Forum, Special Issue 54 (January–February). Amsterdam: Elsevier Science.

Nash, Jennifer. C., and Emily A. Owens. Eds. 2015. *Institutional Feelings: Practicing Women's Studies in the Corporate University*. Feminist Formations, Special Issue 27 (3). Baltimore: John Hopkins University Press.

Paradeise, Catherine, Emanuela Reale, Ivar Bleiklie and Ewan Ferlie. Eds. 2009. *University Governance: Western European Comparative Perspectives*. Dordrecht: Springer.

Robertson, Roland. 1995. Glocalization: Time–Space and Homogeneity–Heterogeneity. In *Global Modernities*, ed. by Mike Featherstone, Scott Lash and Roland Robertson, 25–44. London, Thousand Oaks, New Delhi: Sage.

I

Interventions: Gender, Gender Studies and Academic Feminism

Gender in the Neo-liberal Research Economy: An Enervating and Exclusionary Entanglement?

Louise Morley

Abstract

In this article, I discuss the gendered implications of the neo-liberal research economy. I explore the complexities and contradictions of neo-liberal discourse and how it has become entangled with higher education in general, and with the research economy in particular. Drawing on critical literature, questionnaires and discussion data from women at diverse academic career stages gathered in British Council seminars in Hong Kong, Tokyo and Dubai, I argue that neo-liberalism has been installed via material, discursive and affective means. This includes funding and employment regimes and the stimulation of a range of emotions including fear, shame, competitiveness and pride. A focus will be on how academic research is aligned with the political economy of neo-liberalism. In the context of unbundling and the *uberisation* of higher education, research is now a major vehicle for performance management and a product or service valued for its commercial, market and financial benefits. When this is added to the ongoing misrecognition and underrepresentation of women as research leaders, there are dangers of a highly gendered and exclusionary research economy. I conclude that neo-liberalism is not essentially male, but that it has reinforced male dominance of the research economy by valuing and rewarding the areas and activities in which certain men have traditionally succeeded.

Keywords

Gender, Neo-liberalism, Research Economy, Feminist Knowledge, Global Academy

1 Nebulous, Normative Neo-liberalism: The Uberisation and Unbundling of Academic Life

Neo-liberal is a ubiquitous and polyvalent ideology in the knowledge economy of the global academy today. The conceptual apparatus and reason of neo-liberalism have been applied to and have transformed higher education policies, practices and priorities in diverse geopolitical regions. The political economy of neo-liberalism is associated with rolling back the state and rolling out financialisation, marketisation, globalisation, privatisation, deregulation, inhumanity, austerity, injury, disposability and philistinism, i. e. the dominant value of academic work is economic, rather than intellectual (Brown 2015; Collini 2012). It can be not only a catchphrase, empty signifier or framing device, but also a potent condensate to express frustration at the rapidly changing value base of higher education in general, and of research in particular.

The neo-liberal transformation of higher education has been both discursive and material, shaping what it is possible to do, say and be, and is linked to funding and employment regimes. It has both ontological and epistemological consequences, constructing academic identities, priorities and knowledge creation itself. As a discourse, it is seen to offer both creative and oppressive potential. For some, neo-liberalism represents progress, modernisation and a type of creative destruction that purges archaic practices and date-expired people. The future of higher education is often theorised using disaster and crisis metaphors, including tsunamis (Popenici 2014) and avalanches (Barber et al. 2013). In this analysis, higher education is broken and needs to be disrupted and reformed in order to avert further crises. Disruption is often undertaken through neo-liberal practices such as audit, privatisation and its related unbundling that is the fragmentation of components of higher education that are then outsourced to other, often private providers (Macfarlane 2011). The unbundling is also applied to audit and the identification of areas of academic life that can be subjected to metrification and review, e. g. publications, citations, research grants, doctoral completions and more recently research impact (Colley 2014). Accountability and metrification are seen as welcome interventions to discipline what was often perceived as a formerly unruly profession that traditionally had too much independence and autonomy. Measurement, or management by numbers, represents a concretisation of academic labour and productivity that counters the immaterialisation and abstraction of academic life. Metrics impose the *law of value* through which the labour of higher education workers is quantified and compared, managed and disciplined (De Angelis and Harvie 2009). However, metrics can also be reductive and simplistic, or an ideology posing as a technology (Lynch 2014; Ozga 2008). They also imply norms. Butler (2006) observed that the multiplicity and continual changes in academic norms require us to ask which norms are evoked in judging any piece of work, and how they are interpreted.

Neo-liberalism has had a profound impact on academic identities and promotes particular forms of subjectivities and citizenship. In the neo-liberal knowledge economy, academic labourers are no longer employees resourced by their institutions, but are now autonomous entrepreneurs responsible for their own investment decisions and income generation for their organisations. Neo-liberalism is both fixed and fluid, producing winners and losers. As Lemke (2001) argues, neo-liberal society is characterised by the fact that it cultivates and optimises differences. Neo-liberalism is also performed through a disarticulation of structural inequalities. It is about individual enterprise, agency and endeavour. Cognitive capitalism means that there are rich rewards for those academics who are servile to the demands of the market, including lucrative leadership positions, large research grants, performance pay increases and gatekeeper power in decision-making fora. There are severe penalties for those who fail to meet the performance indicators. For example, accounts of the suicide of Professor Stefan Grimm, who worked at Imperial College, University of London, UK, reveal how he was about to be dismissed for failing to meet financialised research targets, despite several grant applications (Morley 2015; Parr 2014). It would be erroneous to suggest that it is a question of a simple binary with winners and losers positioned in direct relationship to their acceptance or rejection of neo-liberal values. The nebulousness, fluidity, capriciousness and contradictory nature of neo-liberalism means that in the course of one professional lifetime, it is possible to both win and lose. Winning can be temporary as the clock keeps being reset (Gill 2010). In the research economy, one's dominant academic value is the size of the latest grant. Furthermore, the emphasis on relentless competitive individualism and entrepreneurship means that the collective often loses out. Harvey (2007) contends that neo-liberalism is a project that sets out to restore class dominance to sectors that saw their fortunes threatened by the ascent of social democratic endeavours in the aftermath of the Second World War. This process, he argues, has entailed the dismantling of institutions and narratives that promoted more egalitarian distributive measures in the preceding era. Competitiveness in higher education is central, with the reconstruction of students, employers and the state as consumers of an expensive higher education product and its outputs.

Universities are being driven to act as for-profit businesses in order to compensate for the withdrawal of public funding by neo-liberal governments. The term *uberisation* (Goldberg 2016; Hall 2016) has crept into the lexicon, suggesting that any service can be flexibly provided at any time by a series of micro-entrepreneurs (who often lack employment rights), and is digitally mediated. This capitalism masquerading as democratisation relies heavily on customer satisfaction surveys and evaluative data to unbundle or customise the 'service' and promote the product in increasingly competitive markets. It could be argued that this precarity has always been part of the research economy, with its reliance on adjuncts who lack job security. Research projects have traditionally drawn on the uberised labour of (often female) doctoral and post-doctoral scholars (Reay 2000). This short-term strategy of contractualised and disposable academic labour and a popularist approach to students and research funders as customers contrasts with longer-term aims of developing critical citizenship and knowledge and bringing social justice issues, including gender equity, into intellectual projects and organisational cultures.

2 Resisting Resistance and Investing (in) Oneself

Deconstructions of neo-liberalism and denunciatory analyses have become a central occupation of counter-hegemonic scholars (Connell 2013; Ferguson 2009; Holmwood 2014; Lazzarato 2009; Lynch 2014; Radice 2013). Critical engagements are as diverse as the concept itself, and are often saturated in affect. I receive a range of responses whenever I speak about neo-liberalism at academic conferences and seminars. A conundrum is why, if critical knowledge is the *raison d'etre* of the global academy, do academics comply so readily with procedures that often work against them, and represent the interests of dominant groups, i.e. the same groups that are dismantling, privatising and uberising the academy? A common *cri de coeur* is: why has the academic profession failed to resist (Leathwood and Read 2013)? This is often followed by questions about whether opportunities for resistance are differentially distributed in an increasingly asymmetricised, casualised or uberised profession. For example, do academics at the bottom of organisational hierarchies such as early-career researchers, part-time researchers, ethnic minorities or the many non-promoted women academics have the capital to create alternative structures (Angervall 2016)? Another response is that we just need to get on with it, perform and stop mourning a fictitious golden age. A further familiar engagement is that it is a local, rather than global phenomenon, and that it exists mainly in the UK, Australia and the USA, but not in socially progressive economies such as the Nordic countries, an argument disputed by studies of neo-liberalism that suggest that it has "swept across the world like a vast tidal wave of institutional reform and discursive adjustment" (Harvey 2007, p. 23). Peck and Tickell (2007) argue that the temporal and spatial edges are always blurred, i.e. it is not always clear when and where neo-liberalism has developed, or how it has travelled or transferred. While the tidal wave, or stealth revolution (Brown 2015), has resulted in a fairly uneven taking up of its rationalities and practices, neo-liberalism is a subject of critical analysis in diverse geopolitical regions, including East Asia (Lin 2009; Mok and Lo 2014; Ong 2006), New Zealand (Roberts and Peters 2008; Shore 2010), Britain, Chile, Mexico and France (Fourcade-Gourinchas and Babb 2002), Australia (Weller and O'Neill 2014), Latin America (Sader 2008), Sweden (Edenheim and Rönnblom 2012) and in wider Europe, including Germany (Marazzi 2010). It is both a constituent of globalisation and is conveyed via global vectors.

One form of academic resistance, it seems, is the desire to interrogate the concept. The term 'neo-liberalism' appeared in nearly 1,000 academic articles annually between 2002 and 2005, and was "used to characterize an excessively broad variety of phenomena" (Boas and Gans-Morse 2009, p. 137). It is frequently a synonym for capitalism and assaults on the poor and vulnerable, or a "straw man of anti-statism" (Plehwe and Mills 2012, no pagination). It has both rhetorical and analytical power. The term, however, is invariably pejorative and used mainly by its critics, rather than its advocates (Newman 2013). Boas and Gans-Morse (2009, p. 140) suggest that "virtually no one self-identifies as a neoliberal, even though scholars frequently associate others – politicians, economic advisors and even fellow academics – with this term." Stiglitz (2008, no pagination) describes neo-liberalism as a "grab-bag of ideas" based on the fundamentalist notion that markets are self-correcting, allocate resources efficiently and serve the public interest well. For many, it has become a form of abuse, with explanatory power to signify all that is wrong with the political economy of higher education, and indeed the broader context of global economics. Weller and O'Neill (2014, p. 110) argue that:

> "The word neoliberalism gets power too from simultaneously pulling on a theoretical framework to apprehend the world, while talking directly about the materialisms allegedly produced by that framework."

For the purpose of this article, I wish to offer the definition that it is a type of market fundamentalism and an ideology that seeks radical changes in the relationship between state and society. Davies (2013, p. 37) suggests that neo-liberalism might be defined as "the elevation of market-based principles and techniques of evaluation to the level of state-endorsed norms." Neo-liberalism involves society being regulated by the market, rather than vice versa. Scholars suggest that neo-liberalism means that social relations and individual behaviours are deciphered using economic criteria and within economic terms of their intelligibility, thus eliding any difference between the economy and the social. Brown (2015, p. 9) has fastidiously examined neo-liberalism in her latest book on the topic. She argues that it has become "a normative order of reason developed over three decades into a widely and deeply disseminated governing rationality."

Market principles frame every sphere and activity and *Homo Oeconomicus* is foundational to the rationality of neo-liberalism, she claims:

> "All conduct is economic conduct; all spheres of existence are framed and measured by economic terms and metrics, even when those spheres are not directly monetized." (Brown 2015, p. 10)

In this analysis, academic labour in general and research in particular are valued in terms of possibilities for income generation and wealth creation, e.g. innovation and enterprise.

Thomas Lemke (2001, p. 203) also believes that neo-liberalism is a political rationality that tries to render the social domain economic and to link a reduction in (welfare) state services to the call for "personal responsibility" and "self-care". The economic matrix, argues Lemke (2001), is also programmatic in that it enables a critical evaluation of governmental practices by means of market concepts. In the neo-liberal approach the market is no longer the principle of self-delimitation by the government, but instead the principle against which it rubs, or as Foucault (1979 quoted in Lemke 2001, p. 198) puts it, "a kind of permanent economic tribunal". Why does this matter? It attacks democracy, as Brown (2015, p. 9) suggests: "Neoliberalism assaults the principles, practices, cultures, subjects and institutions of democracy understood as rule by the people." Neo-liberalism achieves this by privileging the individual over the collective, or *demos*.

Investment is key to the understanding of neo-liberalism. The neo-liberal subject constantly calculates and adds value to her/himself. The financialisation agenda produces subjects who are managers of their own portfolios seeking investment and maximising their value. The discourses of networking, employability and higher education as a private, positional good, i.*e.* concerned with individual economic investment rather than socially responsible, critical citizenship are all about attracting investors and making oneself more marketable. As Brown (2015, p. 22) suggests, individuals need to see different aspects of their lives in terms of investments in themselves for which they are entirely responsible:

> "Both persons and states are construed on the model of the contemporary firm, both persons and states are expected to comport themselves in ways that maximize their capital value in the present and enhance their future value, and both persons and states do so through practices of entrepreneurialism, self-investment, and/or attracting investors."

In this analysis, the good citizen is the effective market competitor. Competition requires comparators such as scores, grades and indicators of worth. Everything requires an exchange value, and nothing is worth doing if it cannot be quantified and rewarded in the context of key performance indicators. In other words, all academic labour, activity and productivity need to be made intelligible via dominant metrics and norms. The neo-liberal aim is to transform society itself into a mode of enterprise, of entrepreneurial and productive activities, of creative and competitive subjects. Work is valued as economic conduct, with an economic calculation of endless self-enhancement (Winnubst 2012, p. 92).

3 Entangling Neo-liberalism with Higher Education

Neo-liberalism has travelled from global economic governance to global education governance, resulting in a technical rationalist approach to knowledge (Patrick 2013). Higher education has been placed within a system of accounts (McGettigan 2013). It has been "hollowed out", lacking an ethical or social function (Cribb and Gewirtz 2013, p. 339). Everything, as Roger Brown (2013) argues, is for sale, and the market can provide anything. In the UK, this has justified the introduction of high tuition fees (currently up to £9,250) on the basis that graduates will get a good personal return on their educational investments when they cash them in in the labour market. It is also now possible to buy rather than meritocratically gain entry to universities, as the world is filling up with for-profit diploma mills (Morley 2014a) that make no claims for developing critical or socially responsible citizens. It is also possible to commission and buy academic assignments, essays and even doctoral dissertations online in the rapidly developing phenomenon of contract cheating (Lancaster and Clarke 2012). Students are being reclassified as consumers or commodified subjects, who must be kept happy, satisfied and positive about their university experiences in order to evaluate their institutions with high scores. In the UK, teaching quality is being submitted to market metrics. The *Higher Education Act* (2017) in the UK introduced the *Teaching Excellence Framework* in September 2017 (BIS 2016) which converts students' positive evaluations of their teaching into the possibility of their universities demanding even higher tuition fees. Preoccupation with the happiness of students is in marked contrast to the intense unhappiness of the academic labour force – many of whom feel overregulated, subjected to mindless surveillance and bureaucracy, and held to account via reductive and infantalising performance indicators (Collini 2003; Gill 2010; Warner 2015). Will Davies (2014, no pagination) suggests that neo-liberalism thrives on governing through unhappiness, or "heating up the floor to see who can keep hopping the longest". This enervating virility culture and the construction of academic identities via metrics and management by numbers (Ozga 2008) results in an assemblage of discursive, symbolic and material rewards for those servile to the priorities of the market. On the other hand, the *losers* are subjected to precarity, short-term or zero hours, and sometimes teaching-only contracts, with limited opportunities for tenure or promotion (Butler 2013). Competitive measuring is the essence of the global prestige economy (Blackmore 2015). If individuals are unable to contribute to their institution's high scores, they are seen as having no right to employment security. Paradoxically, they cannot contribute to high scores while their labour is so precarious, e.g. research time is often absent from the contracts of casual academic labourers who are paid an hourly rate for their teaching or employed on short-term contracts.

One of the most invidious effects of the neo-liberalisation of the global academy has been that research has been submitted to market metrics (Roberts and Peters 2008). It is now more about quantifiable outputs than pursuing an intellectual project. Monbiot (2009, no pagination) observes that universities "are being turned into corporate research departments. No longer may they pursue knowledge for its own sake: the highest ambition to which they must aspire is finding better ways to make money."

The financialisation of research has become a truth about its quality. Research is now conceptualised as income-generation, commercialisation, utility, knowledge mobilisation and impact, i. e. demonstrating that research funding results in economic and policy benefits, and performance management. It is not about criticality, scholarly independence or the production of counter-hegemonic knowledge. The political economy of research is part of the shifting values of academic life.

Table 1 The Values Shift in Higher Education

From	To
Scholarship	Entrepreneurship
Intellectual	Income Generation
Knowledge Creation	Knowledge Mobilisation
Policy Analysis	Policy Compliance
Criticality/Citizenship	Employability

I developed Table 1 to attempt to map out some of the values that are embedded in the new vocabularies of higher education today, and how the endless repetitions of the new lexicon install new identities and priorities – all offering new possibilities for competition and self-promotion.

4 Resisting Resistance: Stepford Colleagues

Explanations for the academic profession's failure to resist include consideration of the potent affective economy entangled in neo-liberalism. As Ball (2015) argued, it captures both money and minds. Neo-liberalism's incitement to become an entrepreneur of the self is registered and lived out emotionally (Winnubst 2012). Shame, fear, pride, guilt, desire and joy are crucial to the ways in which neo-liberalism becomes internalised and reproduced. By monetarising desires it makes us desire what is monetarised, e.g. large research grants and high institutional rankings in the global league tables. The interiority of neo-liberal discourse is enabled via performative repetition (Butler 1990), and the TINA (There Is No Alternative) effect (Marcuse 1964), and relentless naturalisation, or common sense, taken-for-granted understandings (Harvey 2007). The hegemonic hold of neo-liberalism involves a form of common sense that revolves around the naturalness of the market. This closing of the political universe and the erasure of intelligible, legitimate alternatives to economic rationality means that to oppose is to self-isolate, or even self-destruct (Morley 2015).

A further explanation for neo-liberalism's hegemonic grip on the academy relates to how it has been introduced, i.e. by stealth, rather than by revolution, often via audit regimes and funding mechanisms (Morley 2003; Brenneis et al. 2005). Brown (2015, p. 35–36) argues that it is generally more "termite-like than lion like". It is a form of capillary power in so far as it is everywhere and nowhere, evocative of Foucault's (1991) theory of governmentality, suggesting that we regulate ourselves. The economic rationalism infusing neo-liberal educational policy tends to act upon individuals through the use of specific discourses aimed at governing the self (Patrick 2013). The neo-liberal subject and actor is not only autonomous and self-managing, but also obeys commands, e.g. how much and where to publish. The competition involved in neo-liberal employment and funding regimes has also transformed forms of resistance as it has eroded solidarity, or any sense of the collective. Resisting takes one out of the game, leaving the path clear for voracious competitors. Playing the game is central to survival for individuals, organisations and nation states (Colley 2014). Resistance has also been curtailed through temporalities and the increasing demands on academic time. The accelerated academy means that time pressures reduce deliberation about political circumstances and priorities. Carrigan (2015, no pagination) has developed this idea in his use of the term "cognitive triage". We attend to what is immediate, to the relentless bureaucratic demands and accountability, to deadlines, performance indicators, needs of students, funders, colleagues and line managers, and delay reflection on longer-term considerations. There is a powerful ethos of sacrifice and austerity (Gill 2010). To complain suggests vulnerability and that one is not up to the challenges of cognitive capitalism in the modern entrepreneurial university. Critique can merely serve to produce more competition and opportunities for academic boasting. For example, often when I attempt to name the quotidian neo-liberal processes in my profession, I am met with a chorus of robotic voices performing the discourse and positioning me as the 'other'. Neo-liberalism intersects nicely with ageism, and counter-interventions are easily disqualified by positioning critics as date-expired. 'Stepford'[1] colleagues wishing to ascend the hierarchy or gain reputational and material advantage in the research economy will do and say whatever it takes to succeed. Often, neo-liberal regimes are all that they have known. In her high-profile resignation from academia, Marina Warner compared UK higher education with Chinese communist corporatism, "where enforcers rush to carry out the latest orders from their chiefs in an ecstasy of obedience to ideological principles which they do not seem to have examined, let alone discussed with the people they order to follow them, whom they cashier when they won't knuckle under" (Brown 2014, no pagination).

Warner was inundated with responses to her resignation from around the globe. In 2015, she summarised some of the injuries that colleagues reported in their correspondence:

> "Others wrote to say that once they had contributed significantly to the *REF* [*Research Excellence Framework*[2]], their posts were terminated: their usefulness was over. Some had obtained large grants, and found themselves pushed out when the funding ended. Some have agreed to contracts that require them to obtain x amount of grant money if they are to keep their jobs or look forward to any kind of promotion. Some had

1 This term is borrowed from the fictional suburb of Stepford, Connecticut, in Ira Levin's 1972 novel *The Stepford Wives*, later made into movies (in 1975 and 2004). In the story, men in this seemingly ideal town have replaced their wives with attractive robotic dolls devoid of emotion or thought. The term 'Stepford Wife' is used to describe a servile, compliant, submissive wife who happily does her husband's bidding and serves his every whim dutifully.

2 The *REF* is the successor to the *Research Assessment Exercise*. It assesses the research of British higher education institutions via disciplinary panels of peer reviewers. It focuses and grades publications, research culture and research impact. It was used in 2014 to assess UK research during 2008–2013, and is currently under review for 2021 at the time of this writing (spring 2017).

> been told to change their research topic to something that lay outside their expertise entirely." (Warner 2015, p. 8, author's emphasis)

Exit can be forced or sometimes chosen, as a form of resistance. A body of "quit lit" is emerging (Flaherty 2015, no pagination). These are testimonies from academics who have decided to leave the academy and who have applied their critical skills to an analysis of the neo-liberal employment and research regimes that they could no longer tolerate or could not tolerate them. These affect-laden narratives have been compared with the end of the relationship rancour – full of the vocabulary of disappointment, loss and resentment. Many academics experience a passionate attachment to their disciplines and to their professions, and feel impeded, contaminated and frustrated by the shifting values. The quit lit accounts suggest that neo-liberal reforms can be experienced as intolerable amounts of surveillance and performance management, creating increasingly toxic and unhealthy workplace cultures (Thornton 2014).

The circulation of affect in the neo-liberal academy enables and produces self-governing subjects and actors. Recently, when speaking in Germany of how neo-liberalism had become entangled with gender in the global research economy, I was accused by a young woman academic of depressing her. She wanted positive ways forward, without the incremental critique of the concept. Deconstruction of dominant discourses is often perceived as destruction, leaving participants feeling that they lack hope or aspirational frameworks. It is not a happiness formula (Ahmed 2010), as criticality sets one against the juggernaut of the status quo (Danvers 2015). This response, I believe, illustrates part of the problem. Neo-liberalism has become so naturalised and has so harnessed desires and aspirations to the needs of the economy, that to challenge it can sometimes leave people without direction. Neo-liberal practices and values in higher education demand a silencing of critical engagements, and a performance of positivity. The imperative is to (rapidly) comply, not reflect. Equally, critique of neo-liberalism is so much a part of counter-hegemonic scholarship that there is rarely the space to imagine or posit alternatives (Ferguson 2009). Bozalek et al. (2013) have argued that we need a theory of critical hope. That is, we need to stay connected to our critical faculties, while not collapsing into despair. We need to keep working towards an inclusive and gender-just society, despite the barrage of neo-liberal diversions.

5 What Does Neo-liberalism Have to Do with Gender?

Gender intersects with neo-liberalism in multiple ways (Scharff 2014). Feminist research has suggested that women, and in particular young women, have been constructed as ideal neo-liberal subjects in so far as they are reported as aspirational and capacious. McRobbie (2009, p. 15) suggests that young women have become "privileged subjects of social change". Some young women, especially from privileged socio-economic communities, have hungrily engaged with new opportunities, including access to higher education and the labour market and control over reproduction. Other critics suggest that feminism itself has been co-opted, appropriated and incorporated into the neo-liberal project (Rottenberg 2014). The imperative to 'lean in' (Sandberg 2013), suggests that gender equity is about individual cognitive and behavioural restructuring and agency, rather than socially structured change. However, there have been some perverse consequences of neo-liberalism's intersections with feminism. For example, some feminist journals have high citation indexes (a key indicator of value in the research economy). Women are enrolling in higher education in most regions of the world (with the exception of sub-Saharan Africa and North Asia) in greater numbers than their male counterparts, prompting a global panic about the feminisation of higher education and women as the advantaged sex (Gill et al. 2017; Hillman and Robinson 2016; Leathwood and Read 2009; Morley 2011). However, there is still a global gender pay gap (Currie 2012), an absence of women in senior leadership positions (Morley 2014b; Morley and Crossouard 2016a, 2016b), and the depressing continuation of widespread misogyny and violence against women – even in the academy itself (Phipps and Young 2015).

Neo-liberal feminist subjectivity involves becoming an entrepreneurial actor rather than a social activist. Rottenberg (2014, p. 422) argues that neo-liberal feminism is replacing liberal feminism by creating a new feminist subject who is fully responsible for her professional success, well-being and work/life balance, "oriented towards optimizing her resources through incessant calculation, personal initiative and innovation". The emphasis on individual investment is predicated on the erasure or dismissal of the issues that concern the overwhelming majority of women globally, e.g. violence, poverty, health, housing and employment rights. Including more women in existing structures and systems has long been the liberal feminist success criterion for gender equity, e.g. in professions, institutions and leadership positions and including them in political opportunities. Neo-liberal feminism takes this a step further by celebrating and promoting the individuals themselves. Feminism is often co-opted or cited by individually successful women such as celebrities and entrepreneurs, to promote their achievements. This type of girl power is rarely linked to any political analysis of patriarchy and injustice. Rather, it cites asymmetrical gender differences to justify the need for enhanced opportunities for certain women to advance. Any female success is coded up as a feminist intervention and is used as an indicator of progress, political superiority and market distinction. It is also highly essentialised, implying that the insertion of any woman, regardless of her values, is a victory for feminism. The convergence of contemporary feminism with neo-liberal capitalism favours recognition of economic achievement rather than recognition of social identity or redistribution of resources (Fraser 2013). Fraser (in Leonard and Fraser 2016, no pagination) suggests that neo-liberal feminism simplifies, truncates and reinterprets feminism in market-friendly terms, e. g. we think of women's subordination in terms of discrimination that prevents talented women from rising to the top. This version of feminism, argues Fraser, "provides an emancipatory veneer for neo-liberal predation". The emphasis is on women changing or advancing themselves, rather than changing or advancing society, and women's advancement relates to alignment with the values of the market.

Neo-liberalism tends to represent the interests of the dominant groups in most societies. The global elite has traditionally controlled the research economy, deciding who and what is fundable, publishable and promotable. Resources flow into elite institutions, thus reinforcing their hegemonic gatekeeping roles. The gendered monopoly of the research economy is a major cause for concern, with epistemological hierarchies frequently reflecting social hierarchies (Rees 2011; Wickramasinghe 2009). Markets, in neo-liberal theory, are said to disrupt monopolies and producer interests (Holmwood 2014), but this does not appear to have happened in relation to women and research. While gender has gained some research policy attention, for example in the European Union (European Commission 2008, 2011), researchers have repeatedly questioned and exposed how women's capital, particularly feminist capital, has little value (Code 1991; Morley 2015; Walby 2011). Most women, it seems, suffer a credibility deficit in the research economy.

It is pertinent to ask what happens when the neo-liberal apparatus meets women's research capital. An immediate response is that the capital is rendered unintelligible, inaudible and invisible. Accountability, that beloved concept of the neo-liberal project, does not seem to apply to gender equity. Globally, men have the edge as researchers by an enormous ratio of 71 men to 29 per cent women (UNESCO 2012). Currently, approximately four out of five professors in Europe and nine of 10 of the heads of European universities are men (Husu 2014). The prestigious European Research Council, which is endowed with €13.1 billion between 2014 and 2020, offers grants for different career stages. In 2007–2013, men's success rate for the starting grant level was 30 per cent and women's 25 per cent; for advanced grants, 15 per cent for men and 13 per cent for women (Husu 2014). Husu (2014) reported that the knowledge-intensive Nordic countries, with globally some of the most progressive gender equality policy frameworks, had only 12 per cent female leaders in their research centres of excellence in 2011. In the UK, only two of the seven research councils reported an equal proportion of female applicants and academics (Else 2015). The European Science Foundation report *Research Careers in Europe – Landscape and Horizons* also noted:

> "Although the number of women entering universities and achieving academic degrees has exceeded the number of men in many European countries during recent years, there is still a significant gender gap as far as career advancement and the higher level of the research career ladder are concerned." (European Science Foundation 2009, p. 7)

Research authority does not stick to women, it seems. Feminist scholarship has explored how women have been traditionally cast as unreliable knowers (Code 1991). Walkerdine's (1998) early work emphasised how femaleness is invariably positioned on the devalued side of the archaic Cartesian binary. Women's lack of authority as knowers could also account for the catalogue of absences and exclusions from the research-based prestige economy. Women are less likely to be journal editors or cited in top-rated academic journals (Tight 2008; Wilson 2012); women are also less likely to be principal investigators and are underrepresented on research boards and peer review structures that allocate funding (European Commission 2008, 2011). They are also awarded fewer research prizes (Nikiforova 2011), and are less likely to be keynote speakers at prestigious academic conferences (Schroeder et al. 2013). Without wishing to homogenise or essentialise women by suggesting that increasing their participation results in more gender-sensitive processes and practices, or espouse a neo-liberalism feminism that claims that the presence of any woman, whatever her values, is a victory for gender equality, it could be argued that there is a circular relationship between the exclusion of certain groups from prestigious relay points in the knowledge economy and the reproduction of the norms that define the field. For example, women's research authority is often insufficiently recognised to allow them to be peer reviewers and gatekeepers in influential positions, and peer reviewers continue to misrecognise women's research. A classical study of the peer review system of the Swedish Medical Research Council revealed that female applicants for postdoctoral fellowships had to be 2.5 times more productive than their male colleagues to get the same peer-reviewed rating for scientific competence (Wennerås and Wold 1997). The situation is continuing today, with questions about who acts as gatekeepers of precious research resources. Husu's (2014) research found how the excellence-marked initiatives that have been established across Europe have been more beneficial for male than female researchers and that female researchers are losing out in excellence funding even in the systems that are formally in favour of gender equality. She reports an "unspoken antagonism between gender equality, as defined in funding bodies' policy aspirations, and the outcomes of their decisions on what they defined as excellence. In short, excellence, at least as it is currently operationalised, is creating new gendered stratifications in our research landscapes." (Husu 2014, p. 2)

Exclusions raise questions about who is defining the field of social research, who are the standard makers, and what are the performance indicators. A related question is whether the exclusion of certain social groups, ideologies and methodologies produces epistemic exclusions, normative reproduction and intellectual closures in a global knowledge economy.

To address some of the above challenges, the British Council organised seminars in 2012–2013 in Hong Kong, Tokyo and Dubai under the title *Absent Talent: Women in Research and Academic Leadership* (Morley 2013, 2014b, 2015). The seminars brought together women at diverse career stages to discuss women's participation in higher education leadership and research (Forestier 2013). Participants from South and East Asia, the Middle East, North Africa, Australasia and Europe were invited to share experiences and knowledge of gender-related issues in higher education, including enablers and obstacles to women's progression as leaders. In advance of the seminars, 40 questionnaires were circulated to academic women working in Australia, China, Egypt, Hong Kong, Indonesia, Japan, Jordan, Kuwait, Malaysia, Morocco, Pakistan, Palestine, the Philippines, Singapore, Thailand and Turkey, and 20 were returned. The sample was constructed to include current and previous vice chancellors, deputy vice chancellors, deans, research directors, and mid- and early-career academic women located in social sciences, humanities and STEM (science, technology, engineering and mathematics) disciplines. They were asked for their views on what enables and supports women, what interventions exist to encourage women, their personal experiences of being enabled or impeded from entering research and leadership positions, and what makes leadership attractive/unattractive to women. Panel and group discussions and presentations were recorded, transcribed, analysed and coded in order to capture formal and informal narratives about how gendered power is relayed in the global academy, and to identify key themes, patterns and discontinuities across the national boundaries.

In Hong Kong, the panel included six senior women academics from Australia, China, Hong Kong, the Philippines and Thailand. In Japan, the panel comprised three senior academic women from Japan, Thailand and the UK. Additionally, in Tokyo, four papers were presented from the Philippines and Malaysia and two from Japan. In Dubai, the seminar preceded the 2013 *Going Global* conference and provided the opportunity for papers to be presented from Egypt, Hong Kong, Jordan, Kuwait, Malaysia, Morocco, Pakistan, Palestine and Turkey. There were

22 seminar participants in Hong Kong, 25 participants in Tokyo and 25 in Dubai. From this relatively small sample, policy, statistical and often visceral knowledge was shared and co-created.

6 The Gendered Global Research Economy

Some of the key themes narrated by the women in my study included terms that are often used in discussion of the neo-liberal academy: precarity, unbelonging, gendered unbundling and exclusion. These were compounded by gendered readings of power and privilege, including lack of authority, the affective economy, gendered career pathways and networks, and the overwhelming lack of sponsorship for them at crucial stages in their careers (Morley 2015). The terms are associated both with the political economy of neo-liberalism and the competitive global research economy. However, the gendering of both domains, and their interaction with inequality regimes, reveals the subtle and damaging ways in which research merit is gendered, evaluated in market terms and associated with particular embodiments (Davies et al. 2005). A common observation made by women in this research was that research authority does not stick to women, and that differential values are culturally assigned to women and men. Additionally, informal relays of power in the form of gendered networks, opportunity structures and norms disrupt the logic of meritocratic progression. Women reported how gendered networks suggest that some people are rendered invisible and inaudible in the neo-liberalised knowledge economy. A common complaint related to attribution and that women's underrepresentation in powerful positions in the research economy was attributed to their lack of talent, competitiveness, commitment, agency, or their caring responsibilities and perceived career interruptions, rather than to structural social and institutional discrimination. Their frequent observations about how they were excluded from research opportunities and diverted more to precarious or teaching-only contracts and low-level, high-volume bureaucracy suggest that research capacity is not a neutral entity that already exists to be talent spotted, but is co-created by contingency, context and opportunity structures. It is the gaze of the observer, loaded with sociocultural meanings and power relations that identifies who is to be developed as a potential research leader (Morley 2015).

My research suggested that the neo-liberalised optic or evaluative gaze that was used to identify research leadership potential was not seeing many women. Differential value was accrued and attributed to different types of knowledge workers in the neo-liberal economy. Women reported how they either were not on or had not been encouraged to get on to research career pathways, including membership on key decision-making research committees, journal editorial boards and teams for large-scale projects. If they were not located in appropriate research spaces, this meant that they were less likely to develop research capacity. A barrier that was reported by all respondents was the interplay between horizontal and vertical segregation and the gendered division of labour, with many women (and some men) invariably tasked with inward-facing domestic labour. This positioning materialised academic identities that were not conducive to success in the global research economy, producing yet another circularity. As 'failed' academic capitalists, they were less likely to get promotion or tenure (Coate and Howson 2014). Women described how the unbundling of academic services meant that they were often deployed in less prestigious areas of academic life. This positioning interacted with a lack of opportunities to apply for research grants and produced research-inactive academic identities. The failure in grant capture in today's financialised global academy means that they are more likely to be deployed in less prestigious areas of academic life, and so the gendered unbundling continues. Their academic identities were constructed as losers. This was discussed by Winnubst (2012, p. 86):

> "Consequently, as the neoliberal ontology of human capital takes root through this social rationality of enterprise, questions of identity slide into the question of success."

The academic 'winners' in the sample, such as women vice-chancellors, deans and directors of research centres, frequently reported how they had had to work excessively to achieve their positions, invariably with no structured support, mentoring or professional development. In other words, they had succeeded as enterprising individuals. Some, however, came from socially and/or economically privileged backgrounds, or academic dynasties that had provided them with important opportunity structures and social capital. This did not mean that their leadership was problem-free, as many narrated quotidian encounters with gendered relays of power that stripped them of their authority and often left them feeling undermined and devalued (Morley and Crossouard 2016a). Women also discussed how the concept of merit, as defined in higher education, operates to reinforce male advantage by rewarding those characteristics that men do well, i. e. having a single-minded focus on research and publication over an extended period of time to the exclusion of other responsibilities such as care work and diverse career experiences, and with important sponsorship and developmental opportunities. Women often found that their academic capital was misrecognised and marginalised in financially driven research markets. If certain social groups are persistently and structurally excluded via precarity and hierarchy, this represents a form of distributive and epistemic injustice.

7 Summing Up

Neo-liberalism is not an external, material entity or seamless monolithic apparatus that is easily identified and resisted. Neither is it nonhuman or essentially male. It is not just about injury or subjectification. However, it is a policy and affective installation that has been absorbed into academic identities. The obsession with competitive individualism, income generation and profit means that it can be highly beneficial for those who comply with the market-driven and metricised performance indicators. As Coate and Howson (2014) argue, prestige comprises the accumulation of esteem indicators. If women are being discriminated against by not gaining power and prestige in the research economy, this places them in a weaker position in the hierarchy of winners and losers in the global academy, e.*g.* they are less likely to be leaders (Morley 2014b; Morley and Crossouard 2016a, 2016b), will earn less (Currie 2012), and will be more likely to be part of the uberised and unbundled academic precariat (Butler 2013), that is, on short-term and part-time or zero hours contracts. While not all academic women are injured personally, and some are most definitely neo-liberal winners, neo-liberal values damage women as a group, in so far as they reinforce individual investment and gains, rather than collective struggles to overcome social injustices and exclusions. Knowledge production, custody and dissemination processes purport to be neutral and objective, but overlap with social and policy hierarchies. The issue is not just about employment opportunities for relatively privileged academic women, but also about knowledge itself. Narratives of social justice and inclusion have been dismantled in favour of economic growth. Inequality, it seems, is essential to stimulating market competition.

A question that remains is what is to become of counter-hegemonic knowledge in general, and feminist knowledge in particular, in a research ecology based on monetarised values. A further question for critics of the neo-liberal political economy of higher education is what is desired, rather than what is contested. How can feminists produce different knowledge and produce knowledge differently (Lather 2013)? One challenge is that feminism is frequently perceived in the global research economy as date-expired, or as an opportunity for commercial enterprise, e. g. expensive courses to empower women to become leaders. A further issue is the extent to which the value base of neo-liberalism has been internalised by researchers themselves. McNay (2009) talks about the economisation of subjectivity. Neo-liberalised entrepreneurial subjects relate to themselves as if they were a business (Scharff 2016). It is questionable whether complex and nuanced feminist explorations have a market value in societies that want quick fixes and quantitative change, e.g. more women on boards. It is important not to reify feminism but to see it as dynamic and open to transition and transformation. However, can gender be kept on the agenda in a way that does not incorporate, colonise, re-purpose, neutralise or co-opt it into the tedious taxonomy of performance indicators that silence rather than enliven debates on the university of the future? A range of options have been identified at various seminars and conferences that have discussed these topics, including crowdfunding of feminist scholarship, the creation of more feminist space in learned societies and more accountability measures for funders. A *Manifesto for Change* was co-constructed at the British Council seminars in Hong Kong, Tokyo and Dubai (Forestier 2013). In a cultural context of post-feminism that individualises failure, this intervention attempted to identify structural, rather than personal impediments to women's research achievements. Desires for change were directed to opportunity structures in the socio-political sphere rather than turned inwards to the entrepreneurial self.

Manifesto for Change:
Accountability, Transparency, Development and Data

- Equality as Quality – Equality should be made a key performance indicator in quality audits, with data to be returned on the percentage and location of women professors and leaders, the percentage and location of undergraduate and postgraduate students, and gender pay equality. Gender equity achievements should be included in international recognition and reputation for universities in league tables.
- Research Grants – Funders should monitor the percentage of applications and awards made to women and to actively promote more women as principal investigators. The application procedures should be reviewed to incorporate a more inclusive and diverse philosophy of achievement.
- Journals – Editorial boards, and the appointment of editors, need more transparent selection processes, and policies on gender equality, e.g. to keep the gender balance in contributions under review.
- Data – A global database on women and leadership in higher education should be established.
- Development – More investment needs to be made in mentorship and leadership development programmes for women, and gender needs to be included in existing leadership development programmes.

- Mainstreaming – Work cultures should be reviewed to ensure that diversity is mainstreamed into all organisational practices and procedures.

A task is to ensure that the above change interventions are not neutralised or co-opted into the neo-liberal project by institutions taking them up in order to strengthen their market position, e. g. diversity as a commercial enterprise. Nor should they be unbundled and executed on separate trajectories from core academic leadership.

Neo-liberalism is not essentially male, but it has reinforced asymmetrical power relations and the male dominance of the research economy by valuing and rewarding the areas and activities in which certain men traditionally succeed. It has restored the gender order that was beginning to be challenged by feminist academic work. The existence of neo-liberal feminism is a warning that it would be erroneous to construct all women as feminists or committed to the collective good. However, with research priorities increasingly determined outside of epistemic communities and the utilitarian rationality that links research to economic growth rather than social responsibility, it is imperative that feminists keep troubling and disturbing the common-sense norms and rationalities of the neo-liberal research economy. It is a policy assemblage, and as such can be dismantled.

Acknowledgements

The author would like to thank the British Council for enabling and facilitating the empirical research, the 72 women participants in this study, and Heike Kahlert for inviting and editing this article.

References

Ahmed, Sara. 2010. *The Promise of Happiness*. Durham: Duke University Press.

Angervall, Petra. 2016. The Academic Career: A Study of Subjectivity, Gender and Movement among Women University Lecturers. *Gender and Education*. doi:10.1080/09540253.2016.1184234.

Ball, Stephen. 2015. *Neoliberalism – How It Travels, and How It Can Be Resisted*. https://reclaimingschools.org/2015/09/11/neoliberalism-how-it-travels-and-how-it-can-be-resisted/. Accessed: July 25, 2016.

Barber, Michael, Katelyn Donnelly and Saad Rizvi. 2013. *An Avalanche Is Coming: Higher Education and the Revolution Ahead.* London: Institute for Public Policy Research.
Blackmore, Paul. 2015. *Prestige in Academic Life: Excellence and Exclusion.* London: Routledge.
Boas, Taylor C., and Jordan Gans-Morse. 2009. Neoliberalism: From New Liberal Philosophy to Anti-Liberal Slogan. *Studies in Comparative International Development* 44 (2): 137–161.
Bozalek, Vivienne, Brenda Leibowitz, Ronelle Carolissen and Magan Boler. Eds. 2013. *Discerning Critical Hope in Educational Practices.* New York: Routledge.
Brenneis, Don, Cris Shore and Susan Wright. 2005. Getting the Measure of Academia: Universities and the Politics of Accountability. *Anthropology in Action* 24 (1): 1–10.
Brown, Jonathan. 2014. Marina Warner Compares UK University Managers to "Chinese Communist Enforcers". *The Independent,* September 3. http://www.independent.co.uk/news/people/novelist-marina-warner-compares-uk-university-managers-to-chinese-communist-enforcers-9709731.html. Accessed: September 5, 2014.
Brown, Roger. 2013. *Everything for Sale? The Marketisation of UK Higher Education.* London: SRHE.
Brown, Wendy. 2015. *Undoing the Demos: Neoliberalism's Stealth Revolution.* New York: Zone Books.
Butler, Judith. 1990. *Gender Trouble.* London: Routledge.
Butler, Judith. 2006. Academic Norms, Contemporary Challenges: A Reply to Robert Post on Academic Freedom. In *Academic Freedom after September 11,* ed. by Barbara Doumani, 107–142. New York: Zone Books.
Butler, Sarah. 2013. Universities Twice as Likely as Other Employers to Use Zero-hours Contracts. *The Guardian,* September 5. https://www.theguardian.com/uk-news/2013/sep/05/universities-colleges-zero-hours-contracts. Accessed: July 25, 2016.
Carrigan, Mark. 2015. *Cognitive Triage.* http://markcarrigan.net/tag/cognitive-triage/. Accessed: July 25, 2016.
Coate, Kelly, and Camille K. Howson. 2014. Indicators of Esteem: Gender and Prestige in Academic Work. *British Journal of Sociology of Education* 37 (4): 567–585.
Code, Lorraine. 1991. *What Can She Know? Feminist Theory and the Construction of Knowledge.* Ithaca: Cornell University Press.
Colley, Helen. 2014. What (a) to Do About "Impact": A Bourdieusian Critique. *British Educational Research Journal* 40 (4): 660–681.
Collini, Stefan. 2003. HiEdBiz. *London Review of Books* 25 (21): 3–9.
Collini, Stefan. 2012. *What Are Universities For?* London: Penguin Books.
Connell, Raewyn. 2013. The Neoliberal Cascade and Education: An Essay on the Market Agenda and Its Consequences. *Critical Studies in Education* 54 (2): 99–112.
Cribb, Alan, and Sharon Gewirtz. 2013. The Hollowed-Out University? A Critical Analysis of Changing Institutional and Academic Norms in UK Higher Education. *Discourse: Studies in the Cultural Politics of Education* 34 (3): 338–350.
Currie, Jan. 2012. Gender Pay Equity Reviews in Australian and Swedish Universities: Are They an Impetus for Change? *Journal of Critical Studies in Business & Society* 3 (1): 129–157.
Danvers, Emily. 2015. Criticality's Affective Entanglements: Rethinking Emotion and Critical Thinking in Higher Education. *Gender and Education* 28 (2): 282–297.
Davies, Will. 2013. When Is a Market Not a Market? "Exemption", "Externality" and "Exception" in the Case of European State Aid Rules. *Theory Culture & Society* 30 (2): 23–59.
Davies, Will. 2014. *Governing Through Unhappiness.* http://potlatch.typepad.com/weblog/2014/12/governing-through-unhappiness.html. Accessed: May 10, 2017.

Davies, Bronwyn, Jenny Browne, Susanne Gannon, Eileen Honan and Margaret Somerville. 2005. Embodied Women at Work in Neoliberal Times and Places. *Gender, Work and Organization* 12 (4): 343–362.
De Angelis, Massimo, and Davis Harvie. 2009. "Cognitive Capitalism" and the Rat Race: How Capital Measures Immaterial Labour in British Universities. *Historical Materialism* 17 (3): 3–30.
Department of Business, Innovation and Skills (BIS). 2016. *Higher Education: Success as a Knowledge Economy: Teaching Excellence, Social Mobility and Student Choice.* https://www.gov.uk/government/publications/higher-education-success-as-a-knowledge-economy-white-paper. London: Department of Business, Innovation and Skills. Accessed: July 25, 2016.
Edenheim, Sara, and Malin Rönnblom. 2012. Tracking Down Politics and Power in Neo-liberal Society. *NORA: Nordic Journal of Feminist and Gender Research* 20 (4): 227–229.
Else, Holly. 2015. *Subjects' Gender Balance Not Reflected in Grant Applications.* https://www.timeshighereducation.co.uk/news/subjects-gender-balance-not-reflected-in-grant-applications/2019454.article. Accessed: May 5, 2015.
European Commission. 2008. *Mapping the Maze: Getting More Women to the Top in Research.* Brussels: European Commission.
European Commission. 2011. *Structural Change in Research Institutions: Enhancing Excellence, Gender Equality and Efficiency in Research and Innovation.* http://ec.europa.eu/research/science-society/document_library/pdf_06/structuralchanges-final-report_en.pdf. Accessed: July 13, 2016.
European Science Foundation. 2009. *Research Careers in Europe – Landscape and Horizons.* http://docplayer.net/5677579-Research-careers-in-europe-landscape-and-horizons-a-report-by-the-esf-member-organisation-forum-on-research-careers.html. Accessed: December 22, 2016.
Ferguson, James. 2009. The Uses of Neoliberalism. *Antipode* 41 (s1): 166–184.
Flaherty, Colleen. 2015. Public Good-byes. *Inside Higher Ed*, September 9. https://www.insidehighered.com/news/2015/09/09/essays-academics-fed-higher-ed-mark-resurgence-quit-lit. Accessed: September 25, 2015.
Forestier, Katherine. 2013. "Manifesto for Change" for Women in Higher Education. *University World News*, March 16, Issue No: 263. http://www.university worldnews.com/article.php?story=20130313132344590. Accessed: April 5, 2013.
Foucault, Michel. 1991. Governmentality. In *The Foucault Effect: Studies in Governmentality*, ed. by Graham Burchell, Colin Gordon and Peter Miller, 87–104. Hemel Hempstead: Harvester Wheatsheaf.
Fourcade-Gourinchas, Marion, and Sarah Babb. 2002. The Rebirth of the Liberal Creed: Paths to Neoliberalism in Four Countries. *American Journal of Sociology* 108 (3): 533–579.
Fraser, Nancy. 2013. *Fortunes of Feminism: From State-managed Capitalism to Neoliberal Crisis.* London: Verso Books.
Gill, Rosalind. 2010. Breaking the Silence: The Hidden Injuries of the Neoliberal University. In *Secrecy and Silence in the Research Process: Feminist Reflections*, ed. by Róisín Ryan-Flood and Rosalind Gill, 228–244. Abingdon: Routledge.
Gill, Rosalind, Elisabeth K. Kelan and Christina M. Scharff. 2017. A Postfeminist Sensibility at Work. *Gender, Work and Organization* 24 (3). doi:10.1111/gwao.12132.
Goldberg, David. 2016. *Can We Resist the Onslaught of the "Uber-isation" of Universities Through a Stronger Social Pedagogy?* Talk at the Centre for Humanities Research, Univer-

sity of Western Cape, South Africa. http://heltasa.org.za/can-resist-onslaught-uber-isation-universities-stronger-social-pedagogy/. Accessed: July 14, 2016.

Hall, Gary. 2016. *The Uberfication of the University.* Minneapolis: University of Minnesota Press.

Harvey, David. 2007. Neoliberalism as Creative Destruction. *The ANNALS of the American Academy of Political and Social Science* 610 (1): 21–44.

Hillman, Nick, and Nicholas Robinson. 2016. *Boys to Men: The Underachievement of Young Men in Higher Education – And How to Start Tackling It.* http://www.hepi.ac.uk/2016/05/12/3317/. Accessed: December 22, 2016.

Holmwood, John. 2014. From Social Rights to the Market: Neoliberalism and the Knowledge Economy. *International Journal of Lifelong Education* 33 (1): 62–76.

Husu, Liisa. 2014. *Research Funding Gap: Her Excellence Dwarfed by His Excellence.* http://euroscientist.com/2014/06/research-funding-gap-excellencedwarfed-excellence/#sthash.aMIyrJ3S.dpuf. Accessed: July 8, 2014.

Lancaster, Thomas, and Robert Clarke. 2012. *Using Turnitin as a Tool for Attribution in Cases of Contract Cheating.* York: Higher Education Academy.

Lather, Patti. 2013. Methodology-21: What Do We Do in the Afterward? *International Journal of Qualitative Studies in Education* 26 (6): 634–645.

Lazzarato, Maurizio. 2009. Neoliberalism in Action: Inequality, Insecurity and the Reconstitution of the Social. *Theory, Culture & Society* 26 (6): 109–133.

Leathwood, Carole, and Barbara Read. 2009. *Gender and the Changing Face of Higher Education: A Feminised Future?* London: SRHE/Open University Press.

Leathwood, Carole, and Barbara Read. 2013. Research Policy and Academic Performativity: Compliance, Contestation and Complicity. *Studies in Higher Education* 38 (8): 1162–1174.

Lemke, Thomas. 2001. "The Birth of Bio-Politics": Michel Foucault's Lecture at the Collège de France on Neo-Liberal Governmentality. *Economy and Society* 30 (2): 190–207.

Leonard, Sarah, and Nancy Fraser. 2016. Capitalism's Crisis of Care. *Dissent* (Fall). https://www.dissentmagazine.org/article/nancy-fraser-interview-capitalism-crisis-of-care. Accessed: January 5, 2017.

Levin, Ira. 1972. *The Stepford Wives.* London: Random House.

Lin, Angel. 2009. The Narrowing of Intellectual Space by Western Management Discourses: Higher Education in Hong Kong. In *Higher Education in East Asia: Neoliberalism and the Professoriate*, ed. by Gregory S. Poole and Ya-chen Chen, 107–121. Rotterdam: Sense Publishers.

Lynch, Kathleen. 2014. Control by Numbers: New Managerialism and Ranking in Higher Education. *Critical Studies in Education* 56 (2): 190–207.

Macfarlane, Bruce. 2011. The Morphing of Academic Practice: Unbundling and the Rise of the Para-academic. *Higher Education Quarterly* 65 (1): 59–73.

Marazzi, Christian. 2010. Neoliberalism Is Destroying Europe. *The Guardian*, September 14. https://www.theguardian.com/commentisfree/2010/sep/14/neoliberal-europe-union-austerity-crisis. Accessed: December 22, 2016.

Marcuse, Herbert. 1964. *One-Dimensional Man.* Boston: Beacon Press.

McGettigan, Andrew. 2013. *The Great University Gamble: Money, Markets and the Future of Higher Education.* London: Pluto Press.

McNay Lois. 2009. Self as Enterprise: Dilemmas of Control and Resistance in Foucault's *The Birth of Biopolitics. Theory, Culture & Society* 26 (6): 55–77.

McRobbie, Angela. 2009. *The Aftermath of Feminism: Gender, Culture and Social Change.* London: Sage.
Mok, Ka Ho, and Yat Wai Lo. 2014. The Impacts of Neo-liberalism on Higher Education in China. In *Neo-liberal Educational Reforms: A Critical Analysis*, ed. by David Turner and Yolcu Huuseyin, 139–163. London: Routledge.
Monbiot, George. 2009. These Men Would've Stopped Darwin. *The Guardian*, May 11. http://www.guardian.co.uk/commentisfree/2009/may/11/science-research-business. Accessed: July 25, 2016.
Morley, Louise. 2003. *Quality and Power in Higher Education*. Buckingham: Open University Press.
Morley, Louise. 2011. Misogyny Posing as Measurement: Disrupting the Feminisation Crisis Discourse. *Contemporary Social Science* 6 (2): 163–175.
Morley, Louise. 2013. *Women and Higher Education Leadership: Absences and Aspirations.* Stimulus Paper for the Leadership Foundation for Higher Education. Ms. http://www2.hull.ac.uk/pdf/LFHE_%20Morley_SP_v3.pdf. Accessed: February 1, 2017.
Morley, Louise. 2014a. Inside African Private Higher Education. In *Higher Education in the Global Age: Education Policy and Emerging Societies* London, ed. by Daniel Araya and Peter Marber, 140–159. New York: Routledge.
Morley, Louise. 2014b. Lost Leaders: Women in the Global Academy. *Higher Education Research and Development* 33 (1): 111–125.
Morley, Louise. 2015. Troubling Intra-actions: Gender, Neo-liberalism and Research in the Global Academy. *Journal of Education Policy* 31 (1): 28–45.
Morley, Louise, and Barbara Crossouard. 2016a. Gender in the Neoliberalised Global Academy: The Affective Economy of Women and Leadership in South Asia. *British Journal of Sociology of Education* 37 (1): 149–168.
Morley, Louise, and Barbara Crossouard. 2016b. Rejection, Refusal, Reluctance, Re-visioning: Women in Higher Education Leadership in South Asia. *Studies in Higher Education* 46 (5): 801–814.
Newman, Janet. 2013. Spaces of Power: Feminism, Neoliberalism and Gendered Labor. *Social Politics* 20 (2): 200–221.
Nikiforova, Irina. 2011. *The Paradox of Excellence: Merit and Occupational Attainments of Women in Computer Science.* Paper presented at *Gender Paradoxes of Changing Academic and Scientific Organisation(s)* Conference, Centre for Gender Excellence, Örebro University, Sweden, October 2011.
Ong, Aihwa 2006. *Neoliberalism as Exception*. Durham: Duke Press.
Ozga, Jenny. 2008. Governing Knowledge: Research Steering and Research Quality. *European Educational Research Journal* 7 (3): 261–272.
Parr, Chris. 2014. Imperial College Professor Stefan Grimm "Was Given Grant Income Target". https://www.timeshighereducation.com/news/imperial-college-professor-stefan-grimm-was-given-grant-income-target/2017369.article. Accessed: May 10, 2017.
Patrick, Fiona. 2013. Neoliberalism, the Knowledge Economy, and the Learner: Challenging the Inevitability of the Commodified Self as an Outcome of Education. *International Scholarly Research Notices* (2013). doi:http://dx.doi.org/10.1155/2013/108705. Accessed: July 25, 2016.
Peck, James, and Adam Tickell. 2007. Conceptualizing Neoliberalism, Thinking Thatcherism. In *Contesting Neoliberalism: Urban Frontier*, ed. by Helga Leitner, Jamie Peck and Eric S. Sheppard, 26–50. London: The Guilford Press.

Phipps, Alison, and Isabel Young. 2015. Neoliberalisation and "Lad Cultures" in Higher Education. *Sociology* 49 (2): 305–322.

Plehwe, Dieter, and Tom Mills. 2012. Defending Capitalism: The Rise Of The Neoliberal Thought Collective (Part 1). *New Left Project* 12 http://www.newleftproject.org/index.php/site/article_comments/defending_capitalism_the_rise_of_the_neoliberal_thought_collective_part_1. Accessed: July 25, 2016.

Popenici, Stefan. 2014. *MOOCs – A Tsunami of Promises* http://popenici.com/2014/04/22/moocs2014/. Accessed: January 5, 2017.

Radice, Hugo. 2013. How We Got Here: UK Higher Education under Neoliberalism. *ACME: An International E-Journal for Critical Geographies* 12 (3): 407–418.

Reay, Diane. 2000. "Dim Dross": Marginalised Women Both Inside and Outside the Academy. *Women's Studies International Forum* 23 (1): 13–22.

Rees, Teresa. 2011. The Gendered Construction of Scientific Excellence. *Interdisciplinary Science Reviews* 36 (2): 133–145.

Roberts, Peter, and Michael Peters. 2008. *Neoliberalism, Higher Education and Research.* Rotterdam: Sense Publishers.

Rottenberg, Catherine. 2014. The Rise of Neoliberal Feminism. *Cultural Studies* 28 (3): 418–437.

Sader, Emir. 2008. The Weakest Link? Neoliberalism in Latin America. *New Left Review* 52 (July – August): 5–31.

Sandberg, Sheryl. 2013. *Lean In: Women, Work, and the Will to Lead.* New York: Alfred A. Knopf.

Scharff, Christina. 2014. Gender and Neoliberalism: Exploring the Exclusions and Contours of Neoliberal Subjectivities. *Theory, Culture & Society Blog.* http://www.theorycultureso-ciety.org/christina-scharff-on-gender-and-neoliberalism/. Accessed: July 25, 2016.

Scharff, Christina. 2016. The Psychic Life of Neoliberalism: Mapping the Contours of Entrepreneurial Subjectivity. *Theory, Culture & Society* 33 (6): 107–122.

Schroeder, Julia, Hannah L. Dugdale, Reinder Radersma, Martin Hinsch, Deborah M. Buehler, Jennifer Saul, Lindsey Porter, András Liker, Isabelle De Cauwer, Paul J. Johnson, Anna W. Santure, Ashleigh S. Griffin, Elisabeth Bolund, Laura Ross, Thomas J. Webb, Philine G. D. Feulner, Isabel Winney, Marta Szulkin, Jan Komdeur, Maaike A. Versteegh, Charlotte K. Hemelrijk, Erik I. Svensson, Hannah Edwards, Maria Karlsson, Stuart A. West, Emma L. B. Barrett, David S. Richardson, Valentijn van den Brink, Joanna H. Wimpenny, Stephen A. Ellwood, Mark Rees, Kevin D. Matson, Anne Charmantier, Natalie dos Remedios, Nicole A. Schneider, Celine Teplitsky, William F. Laurance, Roger K. Butlin, Nicholas P. C. Horrocks. 2013. Fewer Invited Talks by Women in Evolutionary Biology Symposia. *Journal of Evolutionary Biology* 26 (9): 2063–2069. doi:10.1111/jeb.12198. Accessed: September 29, 2014.

Shore, Cris. 2010. Beyond the Multiversity: Neoliberalism and the Rise of the Schizophrenic University. *Social Anthropology/Anthropologie Sociale* 18 (1): 15–29.

Stiglitz, Joseph. 2008. The End of Neo-Liberalism. *Daily News Egypt*, July 7.

Thornton, Margaret. Ed. 2014. *Through a Glass Darkly: The Social Sciences Look at the Neoliberal University.* Canberra: ANU Press.

Tight, Malcolm. 2008. Higher Education Research as Tribe, Territory and/or Community: A Co-citation Analysis. *Higher Education* 55 (5): 593–605.

UNESCO. 2012. *World Atlas of Gender Equality in Education. United Nations Educational, Scientific and Cultural Organization.* http://www.uis.unesco.org/Education/Documents/unesco-world-atlas-gender-education-2012.pdf. Accessed: October 19, 2013.

Walby, Sylvia. 2011. Is the Knowledge Society Gendered? *Gender, Work and Organization* 18 (1): 1–29.
Walkerdine, Valerie. 1998. *Counting Girls Out: Girls and Mathematics*. Abingdon: Routledge Falmer.
Warner, Marina. 2015. Learning My Lesson. *London Review of Books* 37 (6): 8–14. http://www.lrb.co.uk/v37/n06/marina-warner/learning-my-lesson. Accessed: September 25, 2015.
Weller, Sally A., and Phillip M. O'Neill. 2014. An Argument with Neoliberalism: Australia's Place in a Global Imaginary. *Dialogues in Human Geography* 4 (2): 105–130.
Wennerås, Christine, and Agnes Wold. 1997. Nepotism and Sexism in Peer-review. *Nature* 387 (22 May): 341–343.
Wickramasinghe, Maithree. 2009. *Feminist Research Methodology: Making Meanings of Meaning-making*. London: Routledge.
Wilson, Robin. 2012. Scholarly Publishing's Gender Gap: Women Cluster in Certain Fields, According to a Study of Millions of Journal Articles, While Men Get More Credit. *The Chronicle of Higher Education*, October 22. http://chronicle.com/article/The-Hard-Numbers Behind/135236/?cid=wb&utm_source=wb&utm_medium=en. Accessed: October 26, 2013.
Winnubst, Shannon. 2012. The Queer Thing About Neoliberal Pleasure: A Foucauldian Warning. *Foucault Studies* 14 (September): 79–97.

Gender Studies at the Time of Neo-liberal Transformation in Estonian Academia

Kadri Aavik and Raili Marling

Abstract

This article discusses the impact of the neo-liberalisation of higher education on gender studies and feminist research in post-socialist settings. This is done using the example of Estonia, where the neo-liberal ideology (more broadly) and its implementation in universities is widely regarded as common sense and rarely challenged. In this article we consider how feminist scholars in Estonia both accommodate and challenge the corporatisation of universities. We argue that feminist scholars in Estonia are largely complicit in the neo-liberalisation of academia, playing by its rules rather than offering resistance. We contend that discursive interventions may not be sufficient in displacing neo-liberalisation in academic life and that it is crucial to also engage with material dimensions of academic precarity under neo-liberal conditions. Particularly in post-socialist settings, revitalising academic trade unions is an important task. Resistance to neo-liberalisation must be accomplished collectively. We suggest that advancing intersectional perspectives in feminist scholarship and forming intersectional coalitions to combat damaging neo-liberal processes in academia might be a way forward.

Keywords

Gender Studies, Feminist Research, Estonia, Academic Precarity, Neo-liberalism, Post-socialism, Critical University Studies, Resistance

1 Introduction

In recent years, a significant body of critical work has emerged documenting the corporatisation of higher education and the effects of this on academic life. Overwhelmingly, this literature has been produced in and about higher education and academic research in Western societies. However, while similar processes have increasingly started to take place in other geographical, social and cultural contexts, such as post-socialist Central and Eastern Europe (CEE), there is relatively little work critically engaging with the neo-liberalisation of academia in these particular settings and the implications of this for knowledge production.

As a crucial issue, the question of what impact the new academic governance has on the status and development of gender studies and feminist research in CEE remains largely unstudied. This article explores this matter using the example of Estonia. Estonia makes an interesting case for critically engaging with this question for a number of reasons: a) since it regained independence in 1991 after the collapse of the Soviet Union, the country has been ruled by governments that have largely implemented neo-liberal policies; b) the national strategic plan for research and teaching in higher education explicitly prioritises the hard sciences, especially information and communication technology, and de-emphasises social sciences;[1] c) recent structural reforms stemming from a neo-liberal logic completed or under way in major Estonian universities have met little or no resistance in the academic community. While none of these features are unique to Estonia, this combination has generated an intriguing setting for gender studies.

Gender studies in Estonia has yet to become an established discipline in its own right. However, gender research is being conducted within more traditional disciplines. While gender studies has survived in neo-liberal Estonian academia,[2] it has not succeeded and this presents a set of questions about whether and how gender studies can operate in a neo-liberal academic climate.

Thus far, no attention has been paid to ways in which Estonian gender studies and feminist researchers are affected by, respond to and are complicit in exacerbating the trends of the corporatisation of academia. Our aim in this article is to provide a critical account of this, with at least three aims. First, our article aims to

1 See Estonian Ministry of Education and Research (2016).

2 As gender studies is not an established discipline in Estonian academia, we use the phrase 'gender research' to denote academic research conducted within the humanities and the social sciences that deals with questions of gender. The majority, but not all of it, is done from a feminist perspective. Without the clear self-identification as feminist, the distinction is hard to make. We use 'feminist' for research and work that identify themselves as such.

complement other such research on the status and developments of gender studies elsewhere. At the time of the neo-liberal transformation in academia taking place in many national contexts, it is crucial to begin to identify some challenges that gender studies as an academic discipline faces globally, in order to begin to form international alliances and engage in solidarity politics. As such, we seek to contribute to the increasing international discussion on the status and developments of gender studies under neo-liberal conditions (cf. e.g. special issues like Nash and Owens 2015; Liinason and Grenz 2016). Second, the objective of our mapping here is to foster local solidarity and resistance by raising consciousness among Estonian gender researchers. This, we hope, will form a basis for concrete, collective action to question today's academic structures and practices. Third, we hope that our article will inspire others in gender studies and beyond to critically reflect on these recent developments in their academic work. Many academics today, including gender researchers, while certainly experiencing the negative effects of the increasing application of market principles in managing universities, have not necessarily incorporated these insights into their academic practice, including theorising. Among the reasons for this is the increasing individualisation and atomisation of academic life, fostered by individual and collective academic practices that blame individuals, not structural problems. Especially at the current time, we believe (following Smith) that it is crucial for feminist researchers to take into account, or even as the starting point of their theorising, their situatedness as knowers in the neo-liberal university (Smith 1987, 1990).

Drawing on our own experiences and recent observations as Estonian feminist scholars, as well as on international literature on neo-liberalisation in academia and contextualising it in post-socialist settings, we consider in this article how feminist scholars in Estonia accommodate and challenge the neo-liberal governance of research – how do neo-liberal academic subjectivities get (re)produced or resisted? Can gender studies and feminist research thrive under neo-liberal rationality? What avenues of protest remain open? Answers to these questions are crucial to begin conceptualising the future of gender studies and feminist research in Estonia and productive ways of collective resistance to the neo-liberalisation of academia.

2 Neo-liberalism as a Contested Concept

References to neo-liberalism abound in today's academic discussions in diverse fields, and overwhelmingly in the (critical) social sciences and the humanities. Yet, the term 'neo-liberalism' is anything but clear. Indeed, the term is applied to all sorts of problems in contemporary academic institutions (Whelan 2015). Hence the concept has been largely emptied of meaning, often merely signalling the critique of the practices described (see e.g. Venugopal 2015, p. 179; Whelan 2015), and as such "has diminished analytical value" (Venugopal 2015, p. 165).

Broadly, however, most existing conceptualisations of neo-liberalism/neo-liberalisation can be summarised as a critical "moral narrative in which recent history is understood in terms of a motivated shift away from public and collective values towards private and individualistic values [...] [with a] clear-cut divide between two sets of values – those of private, individualistic self-interest on the one hand, and those of public, collective interests on the other" (Barnett 2010, p. 271).

In the Estonian case neo-liberalism was adopted voluntarily by governments during post-socialist transition in the 1990s. Parties implementing neo-liberal policies have been in the governing coalitions ever since. It can be argued that neo-liberal policies, with their stress on the thin state and individualism, were perceived as the clearest alternative to the Soviet period that Estonia wanted to leave behind. Thus far, no significant grassroots protest has emerged to challenge this prevalent neo-liberal ideology. Indeed, neo-liberal policies, such as austerity measures and the thinning of the state are seen by the majority of Estonia's population as the cornerstone of Estonia's relative economic success after socialism, although the fruits of the success have been unequally distributed.[3] The Soviet period had made Estonians distrust socialism and political rhetoric related to it (equality, collective rights). This in turn plays a role in the erosion of trade unions as well as participation in civil society. Today, neo-liberalism is widely perceived as common sense in Estonia. This makes Estonia an intriguing case study as a sort of "laboratory society" (Talves 2016, p. 158).

Many existing academic accounts have a tendency to treat neo-liberalism as a rather abstract, ubiquitous and amorphous phenomenon (for a comprehensive critique of the usage of the concept of neo-liberalism, see Venugopal 2015) whose location is unspecific. The transmission of neo-liberal developments on different levels of society is usually left unexamined (Whelan 2015, p. 137). Academic institutions and people employed in these are primarily seen as passive victims or blind carriers of neo-liberal ideology and reforms (Whelan 2015, p. 142). This conceptualisation, however, not only divorces academic subjects from agency, but also leaves unexamined ways in which individuals are complicit in actively (re)producing neo-liberalism in various social contexts, such as in academia, in the course of their everyday (inter)actions. We think that in order to gain a more

3 The Estonian GINI index was 33.2 in 2012, compared with 27.3 for Sweden and 27.1 for Finland (The World Bank 2012).

comprehensive understanding of how neo-liberalism operates in academia, it is crucial to begin to better understand how neo-liberalism functions in micro-settings, including phenomena and practices involving contemporary academic subjects.

Critical analyses of processes of neo-liberalisation in various spheres of life have focused, among other issues, on ways in which neo-liberalism induces "changes in subjectivity by normalising individualistic self-interest, entrepreneurial values and consumerism" (Barnett 2010, p. 270). In higher education, it has been argued that the agency of contemporary "neoliberal academic subjects" (Morrissey 2015, p. 622) is conditioned via regimes of performance as they engage in practices of the normalised self (Morrissey 2015, p. 614), such as self-monitoring, flexibility and adopting new forms of auditing (Gill 2010). Ball (2000, p. 16) points out how we as academics are constantly "engaged in an indexing, a tabularising, of the self. Increasingly we represent and enact our academic selves in terms of productivities and tables of performance." In this system, we spend most of our time "doing the document" (Buikema and van der Tuin 2013). Academics are "represented and encouraged to think about themselves as individuals who calculate, 'add value' to themselves, and improve their productivity. They are to become 'enterprising subjects', who live their lives as 'an enterprise of the self' (Rose 1989)" (Ball 2000, p. 18). In this system, "terms like efficiency, accountability and transparency have been parasitized in order to maintain moral connotations" (Sifaki 2016, p. 111). Failure to perform and produce thus induces guilt, not protest.

3 Neo-liberalisation of Academia and Its Impacts on Gender Studies: Insights from Critical University Studies

Especially in the past few years, an increasing body of scholarship has emerged under the umbrella term 'critical university studies' in reaction to what has been seen by many academics as the increasing 'neo-liberalisation' of higher education. This often takes the form of self-reflexive and/or auto-ethnographic writing critically documenting and analysing this process in institutions of higher education. The work proceeds from the increasing collapsing of "the distinction between the social, the economic and the political" (Sifaki 2016, p. 112) and the growing pressure on universities to prove their "contribution to national economies" (Sifaki 2016, p. 112). This scholarship critically highlights ways in which universities have started to operate according to market principles (as an entrepreneurial or corporate university) (Clark 1998; Slaughter and Leslie 1997; Marginson 2013), as manifested in the emergence of performance indicators and ranking systems (including notably journal citation indexes – for critiques, see Lariviere et al. 2016; Adler and Harzing 2009) and 'quantified control' (Burrows 2012; Felt 2009), also known as 'audit culture' (Shore 2008), the troubling rise of the academic precariat (Ivancheva 2015; Whelan 2015) or "transnational 'scientific proletariat'" (Sifaki 2016, p. 113); the negative effects these processes have on the construction of knowledge (Ward 2012); on the physical and mental well-being of academics (Burrows 2012; Lynch 2010; Berg et al. 2014), especially in the context of an increasing number of tasks and time pressure (Gill and Donaghue 2015, p. 93), and the higher education system more broadly, as well as other related issues.

One of the central aims of neo-liberal reforms is to increase 'effectiveness' and reduce operating costs of academic institutions. However, the pervasive audit culture that has emerged from a neo-liberal logic in fact might not bring less bureaucracy, but more of it (Graeber 2015; Lorenz 2012). Graeber (2015, no pagination) aptly points to the paradox where in valorising the so-called free market, "government policies intending to reduce government interference in the economy actually end up producing more regulations, more bureaucrats". The same processes are evident in universities where recent years have seen the increase of positions designed to monitor research, student feedback and other measurable indicators. There is also a considerable human cost for scholars. As Buikema and van der Tuin (2013, p. 314) demonstrate, in a system where research grants are almost exclusively obtained on a competitive basis, the preparation of each grant application involves an exorbitant number of people-hours spent, including by those who were denied funding, the total of which when calculated into money might well exceed the entire funding of the grant scheme. Other scholars have also pointed out that a competitive grant-based funding system is not only inefficient, but also of a rather random nature (Graves et al. 2011).

Processes of neo-liberalisation in universities and academic subjects are not gender neutral. Lynch (2010) problematises the idealisation of an academic worker as a competitive individual, unburdened by care responsibilities and the gendered outcomes of this. Garforth and Cervinková (2009, p. 182) found that particularly women scientists are vulnerable to falling into precarious academic labour. Antecol et al. (2016) have recently shown that even policies designed to support women, such as parental leave, can end up being advantageous for men who use parental leave for publication, not childcare. Hierarchies in neo-liberal academia are not only based on the category of gender, but intersections involving other social divisions become significant as well. As Berg et al. (2014, p. 66) note, "the elite positions in the university are disproportionately reserved for white, heterosexual, middle-class, (en)abled masculine subjects". The burden of social as well as university reproduction is overwhelmingly on "feminine and racialised subjects" (Berg et al. 2014, p. 64).

Meyers (2013) has suggested that neo-liberal thinking is in harmony with the increasingly prevalent post-feminist ideas, as both are characterised by an individualist perspective that downplays external structural limitations. Women are expected to engage in self-management, while presenting these self-regulating practices as freely chosen. The term "choice feminism" has been used to describe this situation (Budgeon 2015, p. 312). Some scholars explicitly identify a neo-liberal feminism that celebrates upper-class women who have demonstrated their success both in the labour market and in the domestic sphere and whose rhetoric selectively borrows from feminism (Rottenberg 2013). As this is not so much a type of feminism as its appropriation, it would perhaps be more precise to call this process the neo-liberalisation of feminism (Prügl 2015, p. 615). Marling (2015, p. 43) argues that "the neoliberal feminist subject believes that she deserves success in the public sphere and that reaching the goal depends only on her own initiative. Such a subject does not believe she needs solidarity or social support."[4] Although the above-mentioned points were made about feminist subjects, they can be easily extended to academic ones, including academic feminist ones, who too may, through their everyday activities in neo-liberal academia, recreate and legitimise neo-liberal discourses.

4 The Neo-liberalisation of Estonian Academia

Estonian academia exists in a broader neo-liberal political context that has had a deep impact on how knowledge and knowledge production are defined and funded. In this section, we outline some relevant broader tendencies and developments characteristic of the current era of neo-liberalisation in and of Estonian academia, before examining these further in relation to gender studies and feminist research in Estonia. While some processes outlined below have already been found to be present in Western academia, others are specific to Estonia.

It is difficult to pinpoint when exactly the agenda of neo-liberalisation began to be implemented in Estonian academia. The restructuring of higher education has been very gradual, with no easily identifiable paradigm-changing event. Indeed, these shifts (e.g. adoption of the Bologna system, research rankings, changes in regulations governing research funding) have largely been seen as inevitable by

4 Translations from Estonian into English here and elsewhere in the article were done by the authors.

most academic stakeholders and, even when generating a short-term discussion or discontent, have soon been accepted as common sense. For instance, no heated debates within academia or in the mainstream media occurred over the implementation of the Bologna process, which was widely considered as a technical rather than a substantive change. Its negative effects became evident when the process was already irreversible.

Thus far, very little critical university studies scholarship has emerged in Estonia to examine the processes of the neo-liberalisation of academia. A few junior academics have voiced their concerns over this issue in the Estonian mainstream media. For example, Velmet (2015) has problematised the popular conceptualisation of higher education as a private good, not a public good, and has criticised the state's efforts to subdue it to market principles. Aidnik (2015) has critically noted the increasing prevalence of audit culture in academic institutions and universities being run by managers with no academic backgrounds.

A striking example of these trends in Estonian academia is a report commissioned by the Research and Development Council[5] at the Estonian State Chancellery and compiled by a team led by investment banker Gunnar Okk (2015). The report makes evident processes that had taken place in academia in the past few decades in the context of increasing neo-liberalisation. In offering recommendations to reform the Estonian higher education system, the report not only represents but also constitutes the neo-liberal reality. The report was designed to support the fulfilment of a national strategy on the development of knowledge-based Estonia in 2014–2020 (Okk 2015, p. 2). However, as Velmet (2015) has sarcastically noted, the text seems to be written from the perspective of the CEO of Estonian University, Ltd. That is, the report emphasises efficiency and marketing potentials (e.g. linking the admission to curricula to the number of graduates working in the speciality and market demand for graduates, increasing efficiency by reducing the number of degree programmes, merging universities and calling for the cooperation of researchers with enterprises), in addition to reinforcing the need for monitoring practices already in place (e.g. international review and accreditation) and even devising extra auditing measures (Okk 2015, p. 4–5). The language of the report stresses international competitiveness and economic sustainability as the core aims of education and research.

The idea to make admission entirely dependent on 'market needs' and drastically reducing admission to degree programmes for which there is "little or no market demand" (Okk 2015, p. 4) has obvious negative consequences for teaching and

5 Out of the six members of the council, four are representatives of the business community and only two are scholars.

research in certain areas of the humanities and the social sciences, including for gender studies, whose content cannot (and perhaps should not) be easily marketable.

Even before the report, Estonian universities and research funding bodies have prioritised not only knowledge that can be measured, but also marketed and sold (primarily in the STEM fields). Research grant competitions explicitly solicit research that has a specific practical value to enterprises (the wording has been borrowed from a recent case at Tallinn University). The development plan of the University of Tartu lists innovation and enterprise through which knowledge reaches the economy as being among its five aims. Academic degree programmes are increasingly being restructured to meet the needs of employers. For example, in restructuring its sociology Master of Arts programme, Tallinn University consulted representatives of employers, and in advertising the programme to potential students it is emphasised that the new curriculum "focuses more on practical skills with various types of data, thereby corresponding better to the wishes of graduates and the expectations of employers".[6] While cooperation with the private sector is increasingly valorised, the contribution of local enterprises to research funding remains negligible.

Mimicking similar developments in Western academia, Estonian universities also increasingly use different quantifiable indicators to measure all aspects of their work, such as numerically expressed student feedback,[7] graduation percentages within the standard study period, employed graduates per curriculum, etc. Curricula as well as individual scholars are constantly ranked and measured against each other not only in hiring but also in annual reviews and competitions for research grants and doctoral students. A central indicator is the number and rank of research publications.[8] Copying similar processes in Western universities, Estonian academia has increasingly begun fetishising bibliometric data (high-impact-factor journals and citations). Only publications in three categories count towards promotion and in research applications.[9] This, needless to say, has generated a publishing climate where choices are made not by the merit of a journal or publisher, but by their

---

6 Information email about the new sociology MA programme circulated in various Estonian academic and other mailing lists (Tallinn University 2016).

7 This despite evidence that female lecturers are consistently rated lower by students (cf. MacNell et al. 2014).

8 The ranking system in a public national database discriminates against the humanities and the social sciences as well as scholars writing in languages other than English.

9 The Estonian academic publishing system only recognises papers as 'excellent' if they are published in journals indexed by the Web of Science Citation Index Expanded, the Social Sciences Citation Index, the Arts & Humanities Citation Index and/or indexed by Scopus. For books, a list of 'recognised publishers' has been compiled. For critiques

ranking. As very few Estonian language academic journals are considered high ranking (in many fields of research none at all), academics are pushed to publish in English, neglecting the scholarship and dissemination of knowledge in Estonian.

The Estonian educational landscape as a whole is constructed around the notion of competition as a guarantee of progress. Research funding in Estonia, like elsewhere, is awarded on a competitive basis. This creates a situation where academics are set up to compete with each other for scarce funding and fosters a climate of competition, not of collaboration and mutual solidarity, leading to the rise of "atomistic individualism" (Berg et al. 2014, p. 11–12). The Estonian research community, like that in many other countries today, is dependent on short-term projects. There is pressure to secure at least a part of one's salary from research projects, which is a challenge in the context of limited funding. The limited funding, however, is accompanied by increasingly extensive paperwork, as is also evident in the West (cf. for example Buikema and van der Tuin 2013). Project-based thinking makes it hard to develop sustainable research teams. Securing large-scale and international funding is clearly more difficult for scholars working in the social sciences and particularly in the humanities.

In general, the Estonian academic world is characterised by a high degree of precarity. Until 2015, there were practically no permanent contracts in Estonian universities.[10] As a result of pressure from the EU, lifelong contracts have been granted from January 2015 onwards in Estonian academia, but this system still subjects all academics to regular review and even the contracts of full professors may be discontinued if they fail to meet performance standards. Many faculty members do not have steady positions and instead are hired as adjuncts with no job security or benefits.

Academic salaries, particularly in the humanities and social sciences, continue to be low, which is a wider problem faced by academics throughout the post-socialist space. For example, as of 2016 in Tallinn University, one of the largest public universities in Estonia specialising in the humanities and social sciences, a full-time lecturer with a PhD degree earns a minimum of EUR 1,100 per month (just about equal to the average salary in Estonia in 2016 and prior to the deduction of personal income tax), and a professor at least EUR 1,600 per month. Some lecturers and associate professors are employed part-time and must seek extra work (often

---

of academic ranking systems, including journal rankings, see Adler and Harzing (2009) and Lariviere et al. (2016).

10 Only a small number of full professors had tenure; other employees, including associate professors, had to re-compete for their positions every 3–5 years, depending on their academic rank.

outside academia) to make ends meet. This has implications for the commitments they are able to give to research. Yet in order to have a chance of getting promoted or to successfully compete for research funding, one must publish at the same rate as colleagues employed full time.

A direct consequence of the low salaries is an academic brain drain, with early career researchers, such as recent PhD graduates, seeking to continue their academic careers in Western universities, where research careers and similar workloads enable them to cover the basic costs of living and beyond. Thus, Estonia drastically differs from Western countries, where academics typically earn at least a middle-class income. In Estonia, in contrast, we might speak of the actual material poverty of at least some segments of the academic labour force. Thus, gender studies and activism needs to be viewed in this context.

The university system itself is characterised by constant reforms and restructuring (it is not rare for curricula to be reformed every year) that further deepens the precarity. Effective academic trade unions that could support academic as well as administrative and other staff are effectively missing in Estonian academia,[11] leaving academics to face universities as individuals without collective action against neo-liberal reforms and their consequences. The lack or weakness of trade unions is characteristic of much of post-socialist Europe.

Only very limited research has been conducted on Estonian academia and academic knowledge production from a gender perspective. Lõhkivi (2011, 2015) has documented the gendered nature of knowledge production and the negative effect of gender stereotypes on the careers of female academics. Talves (2016, p. 165) identifies three self-positioning strategies employed by Estonian female scientists – gender neutrality, trivialisation of their own achievements and displaying superiority over other women, all of which, she argues, "reinforce and reproduce gendered culture in academia".

The gendered impact of the developments described in this section is largely unknown, due to the lack of statistical information and empirical research. For example, in line with the predominant practice in Estonia even public institutions, such as universities, do not publish their wage statistics, and academics engage in individual salary negotiations, which are known to disadvantage women in particular. The non-disclosure of wage data and individual salary negotiations are believed to be among the reasons behind Estonia having the largest gender pay gap (30 per cent) in the EU (Eurostat 2012). For the first time in 2016, the Estonian

11 Formally, trade unions exist in Estonian academia but they tend to be Soviet relics that are ill-prepared for the neo-liberal challenges. Membership in a union is limited and passive.

Research Council compiled and published an analysis of wage data in Estonian universities. It was found that a considerable gender pay gap exists between academic salaries, with men earning on average 20 per cent more in major Estonian universities (Raudvere 2016, p. 3).

5 Gender Studies in Post-socialist Neo-liberal Estonian Academia: Status and Developments

Since its emergence in the first half of the 1990s, gender studies and feminist research has occupied an insecure position in the Estonian academic landscape, and this is exacerbated by the increasing prevalence of neo-liberal ideology and practices in Estonian universities as we will demonstrate in the following sections.

The uneasy positioning of Estonian gender studies and feminist research today can partly be explained by the historical circumstances and the particular genealogies of Estonian feminist and gender research, which differ from the development of gender studies in Western academia. According to the Soviet ideology, gender was irrelevant in the Soviet Union as the equality of men and women had supposedly been achieved. Publicly promulgated slogans suppressed the fact that the reality was anything but gender neutral or gender equal. Gender was not studied in Estonia under the Soviet regime; even sociology was considered a suspicious subject. Gender became visible and subsequently political only after Estonia regained independence in the early 1990s and this also led to gender's gradual appearance in Estonian academia. Individual scholars working in different disciplines started to use feminist and gender studies ideas in their teaching within their traditional fields, usually in elective courses (Marling 2011). The development of gender studies grew out of the enthusiasm of individual scholars, with no institutional support and with funding predominantly acquired from international rather than domestic sources.

The institutional development of gender studies has been less successful. It was advanced in the late 1990s by the work of an explicitly gender-oriented non-governmental organisation, the Estonian Women's Studies and Research Centre, which maintained a gender studies library and also initiated a gender studies minor at Tallinn University. The Estonian Women's Studies and Research Centre was also instrumental in establishing perhaps the most effective gender studies institution in Estonia, *Ariadne Lõng* (*Ariadne's Thread*), the peer-reviewed Estonian journal of gender studies, in 2000.

At the time of writing (spring 2017), gender studies is neither institutionalised nor recognised as an independent discipline, as there are no academic gender studies departments or professorships.[12] Rather, gender studies exists as a research perspective within a few disciplines and is largely developed through the work of individual scholars. Some feminist scholars have achieved senior positions in their traditional disciplines on the strength of their gender scholarship. A second generation of Estonian gender studies scholars has emerged.[13] By 2016, around a dozen PhDs have been defended in Estonian universities within different disciplines that have an explicit gender or feminist focus.[14]

Processes of neo-liberalisation have had a clear impact on the already-fragmented gender studies, both in terms of its material and symbolic presence in the Estonian academic landscape. Structural changes in universities implemented as part of neo-liberal reforms have made gender studies lose some of its hard-fought visibility in academia as curricula have been merged and research units scattered in cost-cutting efforts. For example, a gender studies minor offered at Tallinn University briefly in the early 2000s no longer found a place in the new curriculum. A gender studies unit founded in 1995 by the Department of Sociology at the University of Tartu has also vanished in institutional restructuring. The course *Sociology of Gender*, the only gender studies course at Tallinn University, was recently merged with the course *Sociology of Family*, thereby greatly reducing its analytical depth and the topics covered. Currently, no academic institution offers a major or minor in gender studies; however, a few sporadic courses exist on the BA and MA levels. These examples are an indication of the struggle that gender studies as a non-institutionalised discipline faces, increasingly finding itself in the margins of neo-liberal academia which devalues academic knowledge seen as lacking the capacity to generate profit. In this situation, institutionalising the discipline is an increasingly difficult task.

In parallel with these structural changes, the lack of institutionalisation and visibility of gender studies is enforced by processes on the discursive and symbolic levels. In Estonian academia, a gender-neutral image of science and a scientist prevails (Aavik 2016). These conceptualisations held by the majority of Estonian academics are reinforced by the neo-liberal conditions which further downplay the importance

12 In 2014, for the first time, the University of Tartu established two part-time positions with the words 'gender studies' in the job title. However, at the time of writing (spring 2017), these positions have been discontinued.

13 The authors of the present article are representatives of different academic generations.

14 Estonia has a small number of scholars who conduct feminist research (and name it as such), but not all scholars who work with gender are comfortable with the label. Hence it is important to make a distinction between the two kinds of scholarship.

of the category of gender in academic settings, instead encouraging the image of an academic as a genderless and otherwise unmarked individual entrepreneur.

In addition to neo-liberalism, scepticism towards engaging with questions of gender academically is also generated by nationalist and conservative public sentiments, which are in part related to the rise of populist far-right political groups. As in some other former socialist countries, most notably Hungary, these groups display anti-feminist attitudes, seeing feminism and gender studies as something imposed from outside (Félix 2015, p. 76) and posing a threat to the vitality of the nation. Leaders of far-right groups call for 'protection' and 'restoration' of 'traditional family values'. This discourse involves a resistance to 'gender ideology' and attempts to align itself with the idea of 'common sense' and nationalist sentiments. The idea of gender equality is also discredited as a socialist notion associated with the former Soviet regime (Félix 2015, p. 76). However, unlike in Hungary, far-right and populist ideologies are less dominant in neo-liberal Estonia, and notably the influence of religious forces is negligible. Although Estonian neo-liberalism has nationalist tendencies, neo-liberal arguments have prevailed in political decision-making affecting academia.

In order to survive in neo-liberal academia, Estonian feminist scholars have adopted a number of strategies, most of which however involve adaptation to rather than challenging the neo-liberal order. Hence there is a tendency to act as model neo-liberal subjects, even in the case of personal opposition to the neo-liberal ideology. We discuss the most prominent of these strategies and their implications below and have grouped our discussion into four broad themes.

5.1 Linguistic and Epistemic Practices

Gender scholars have resorted to learning and using the language of neo-liberal rationality. This has included justifying the utility of their research and doing so in the language of the markets. An example would be emphasising that gender equality is necessary to maximise the country's use of human resources and economic growth by giving more opportunities to women. This in turn has resulted in the prevalence of certain topics over others in Estonian gender research – for example, while there is rich academic literature on the work-life balance, the gender pay gap, women's political participation and media representations, gender in relation to poverty, class, sexuality and ethnic/racial differences continue to be understudied (cf. Koobak and Marling 2014). This is a prime example of how particular forms of knowledge and knowledge production become increasingly discouraged under neo-liberal conditions and how scholars censor themselves indirectly by choosing to study what is publishable.

5.2 Publishing Practices: 'Strategic Publishing'

As a major tactic, gender scholars are displaying complicity with research practices designed by neo-liberal rules, namely publishing in international top-ranked academic journals. International recognition is vital for the validation of otherwise marginalised gender studies research whose practitioners have to demonstrate their excellence to gain and maintain their positions. Hence, 'thanks to' the numerical data orientation of Estonian academia, publishing in international highly ranked journals has been a moderately successful strategy as no Estonian academic administrator quarrels with research that bears the signs of approval of a high-impact-factor journal, however politically radical the topic. In this publishing endeavour, gender researchers have become model self-disciplining neo-liberal subjects, harbouring feelings of guilt about their perceived lack of measurable results and impact factors.

This has crucial implications for the status of feminist research in the local settings and debates on gender issues in the Estonian public discourse. The need to publish or perish becomes an obstacle for writing in mass media or in activist feminist websites that bring no academic credit, yet where feminists need to be heard to shape public debate. In the current neo-liberal academic settings, the voices of Estonian gender researchers are not making as much of an impact in Estonian public debate as they could. The need to publish in English also means that not much gender studies work, especially critical work, becomes available for local readers, and crucially gender studies vocabulary in the Estonian language remains underdeveloped and underutilised.

5.3 Doing Applied Research and 'Equality Work'

Gender studies scholars, like other academics, are actively competing for research funding. For feminist researchers, particularly in the social sciences, this involves competing for (usually very meagre) funding to conduct applied gender research, often commissioned by state institutions (which, according to international commitments, are required to collect and analyse the status of gender equality in various spheres of life). Conducting applied research is in line with the neo-liberal academic system, which increasingly puts an emphasis on more applied and practical research in collaboration with the public and private sector, as well as encouraging academics to continuously seek external funding. Paradoxically this often extensive research, conducted in the Estonian language, does not count as high-impact academic output. These studies have, however, been vital in generating and disseminating gender-related knowledge that among other things potentially informs political decision-making (e.g. regular gender equality monitorings).

In a way, considering the academic merit system, doing research commissioned by the state constitutes a form of activism as it prioritises public knowledge and policy-making over the rewards granted by neo-liberal academia. It is through such applied research, the results of which are often introduced in the Estonian mainstream media, that gender scholars can make a contribution to local public debates, rather than through academic publications in English, which remain inaccessible for domestic audiences. However, the concern here is that in applied research, the category of gender is often used in a simplistic way, for example by unproblematically using the taken-for-granted categories of 'woman' and 'man', not questioning how these categories are constructed and fluid, but instead reifying them and thereby reproducing the gender binary. As applied studies are more accessible to the general public than academic and more theoretically oriented gender research, these studies might shape the idea of what feminist research looks like, not only for members of the general public, but also in the eyes of scholars in other academic disciplines not working on gender and feminist issues.

Gender researchers in Estonia often engage in "equality work" (Adsit et al. 2015, p. 25) in their own institutions, which is a form of academic activism that can render them vulnerable as this work is devalued by organisations (Ahmed 2012 quoted in Adsit et al. 2015, p. 25). In the Estonian case, public institutions, including universities, have shown a complete lack of interest and even resistance towards adopting measures to ensure gender equality and equal treatment within their organisation – a task they are legally obliged to undertake. Hence, equality work in this context is particularly ungratifying. Such equality work could be thought of as a mode of resistance to the trends of corporatisation in universities, yet thus far universities have been immune to this kind of resistance.

In addition to seeking to promote a more egalitarian organisational culture in their universities, Estonian gender scholars also undertake equality work and applied research for more practical reasons, as it constitutes a form of available funding, albeit on a competitive basis. This funding is sought to mitigate increasing precarity, and to supplement very low base salaries for academic workers. Several Estonian gender scholars also take part in civil society gender initiatives, mostly through one-off projects.

Engaging in applied research for state institutions and doing equality work within their own universities means that gender scholars – for example, sociologists

– involved in these initiatives are able to devote less time to developing advanced feminist scholarship (including theorising) in their own disciplines and areas of study.

5.4 Instrumentalising the Values of Neo-liberal Academia: The Case of 'Internationalisation'

Adaptation to neo-liberal principles of functioning includes using some aspects of neo-liberal academia for the benefit of one's own research and securing and improving one's position in the academic hierarchy. For example, the neo-liberal university's obsession with 'internationalisation' is being utilised by gender scholars. Because of the limitations of Estonian gender studies, local scholars have been relatively active in international scholarly networks and participate in international mobility. This however is a two-way process: such activities of Estonian gender scholars in turn improve the coveted internationalisation benchmarks of local universities. Thus, we are facing an ambiguous situation: while the Estonian research administration system does not value gender studies, they are willing to instrumentalise gender studies for the fulfilment of various neo-liberal aims.

In fact, international gender studies scholarship, with its institutionalisation and prestige, is what has given Estonian gender studies the legitimacy that it has. Thus, the Estonian situation echoes that described by Pereira (2014, p. 628, 649) in the case of Portugal. In international feminist literature the unequal position of gender studies in the West and its semi-periphery has usually been described through the critique of what is being suppressed. There is less awareness of what becomes speakable, writable and teachable in different local settings because of the prestige of (especially Anglo-American) academia. This acts as a means of downplaying local agencies and opportunities created. On the one hand, indeed, the local is silenced by hegemonic Western feminism, but on the other hand it is the prestige of the hegemonic centre that makes feminist thought and practice speakable and respectable in the local settings.

6 Conclusions

In this article, we have explored the status and developments of gender studies in Estonia at the time of the increasing neo-liberalisation of academia. We have outlined the broader processes of neo-liberalisation in the Estonian academic landscape and examined these in relation to gender studies and feminist research. We presented some major strategies that Estonian gender scholars have adopted in these settings and discussed their implications on the development of the discipline.

We have argued that despite its marginalisation (or perhaps because of it?) Estonian gender scholars have placed themselves strategically in the neo-liberal academic landscape largely by playing by its rules, rather than offering resistance. Those who have adopted the subjectivity of the scholar-entrepreneur are doing better than those who resist or are unable to fulfil this role for various reasons. Feminist researchers, including ourselves, are highly aware of the problematic relationship that we have to neo-liberal academia.

Despite Estonia's relatively recent socialist past, many trends of neo-liberalisation and their effects in Estonian higher education today are very similar to these processes in Western countries, where political landscapes are increasingly dominated by a neo-liberal logic. For example, similar to other non-English-speaking Western countries, academic publishing systems are intertwined with language politics – Estonian (gender) researchers face pressure to publish in English or perish. This is exacerbated by Estonia's small size and a virtual lack of academic publications in the local language. However, Estonia exhibits some specific elements, such as systematic precarity and lack of social security, including wages which barely sustain academic workers and an almost complete lack of politicisation of the academic labour force as testified by the extreme weakness of trade unions which can in part be traced to the socialist past.

The question of agency of gender scholars in this context needs to be addressed. Could we be considered and think of ourselves as model neo-liberal academic subjects (Morrissey 2015; Gill 2010), dutiful daughters of the neo-liberal academia, or actively designing our careers and lives in this setting? It is rather impossible to distinguish whether we have been co-opted by the system or are able to use the system to promote topics related to social justice. We would like to believe the latter, but we need to continue to be reflexive about the former.

In light of the coping strategies used by Estonian gender scholars that we discussed above, we have to ask how to challenge the processes of neo-liberalisation in academia beyond writing papers such as the present one. What kinds of options are available to Estonian gender scholars, and more broadly, other critical academics who want to challenge the general ethos?

It seems that in combatting the corporatisation of higher education, the discursive tools traditionally used by critical academics to foster social change do not function. Discursive interventions, as critical as they may be, are unlikely to prove effective in subverting the increasing neo-liberalisation of academic life, at least not on their own. Whelan (2016) points to the paradox that despite universities' devotion to knowledge production and dissemination and the increasingly thorough documentation of the problems of neo-liberal academia by academics, there is nevertheless a tendency towards the intensification of said problems in universities, despite evidence that processes of neo-liberalisation are damaging the whole institution of higher education. In Estonia, this damage has not been acknowledged as neo-liberal principles have been internalised as a public good and public university education is held accountable to the taxpayer via the application of market thinking. Discursive resistance also typically remains invisible to university managers (Lorenz 2012, p. 625–626).

Ironically, a large part of the critical university studies scholarship, while offering a profound critique of processes of neo-liberalisation in academia, may simultaneously uphold the very phenomena it is critiquing. For example, many academic papers (including this article!) problematising neo-liberal academic practices, such as the widespread metrics-based evaluation of research output, are published in academic publications ranked highest by this very system relying solely on numerical indicators to measure knowledge production. In publishing in the current system, the h-indexes[15] of their authors get boosted (an individual reward for them, but not a collective solution), and thereby their place in neo-liberal academia is strengthened. In other words, paradoxically, neo-liberal academia has the ability to successfully turn the critiques targeted at its operation into quantifiable scientific output, which in turn supports its continuing existence (cf. also Sifaki 2016, p. 116–117). Hence it appears that discursive tools are not sufficient on their own to destabilise the current system. As Whelan (2015, p. 19) puts it, "if critique is action, it is action of an indirect kind". We need to consider other ways in which we can resist neo-liberal academic subjectivity, in the form of material practices.

Several potentially productive practical interventions have been envisioned to challenge the demands on academics due to the neo-liberalisation of higher education. These include slow scholarship (Berg and Seeber 2016; Great Lakes Feminist Geography Collective 2015), work through trade unions, etc. Whether they prove to be useful in subverting current neo-liberal trends in academia remains to be seen. It seems, however, that to engage in these forms of academic activism, certain prerequisites are necessary. In order to practice slow scholarship, for example, one must have a secure job (preferably a tenured position) and a sufficient and stable income. These are, however, privileges which are available to fewer and fewer aca-

15 The h-index is a metric designed to measure the productivity of a scholar in terms of their number of publications and citations. However, the h-index does not necessarily give an accurate representation of what it is intended to measure (cf. Wendl 2007). It is used more in some disciplines than in others; for example, it is generally unknown among scholars in sociology.

demics in higher education today. Most Estonian gender scholars lack both of these. Thus, it seems that an important task in combatting neo-liberalisation would be to improve the material conditions for those performing academic labour.

Irrespective of the specific solution proposed, resistance to neo-liberalisation must be collective and undertaken in solidarity with all those engaged in academic labour. As Pereira (2014, p. 107) argues, "[W]e must spend more time developing collective strategies to resist the framing of productivity as the key goal in academia." As Berg et al. (2014, p. 66–67) point out, "acting individually allows scholars to disaffiliate themselves from the neoliberalism of the institution, all the while posing little (if any) threat to the academy, the masculinism it supports, or the neoliberal repression and violence reproduced within it. In fact, individuals are precisely what the neoliberal academy wants."

These calls to solidarising collective action may however be problematic in themselves. Whelan (2015) poignantly asks us to critically reflect on who the 'we' being constructed is and imagined as the victims in our critical narratives of neo-liberalism. He argues that this critique often functions as "solidarising social practice" (Whelan 2015, p. 13), yet with important implicitly presented limits to this solidarity (Whelan 2015, p. 14). Thus, we call for expanding the limits of the "solidarising *we*" (Whelan 2015, p. 17, original emphasis) to also include those whose labour, including manual labour, keeps universities running on a daily basis.

Here, intersectionality might prove to be helpful. It has often been used as a currently fashionable academic buzzword, but it can also be applied on a more practical level as a framework for guiding activism. The desire for positive social change and dismantling of power hierarchies is implicit in the intersectionality paradigm. As such, it offers a basis for building solidarity politics, for instance in the form of (temporary) intersectional coalitions between groups and individuals who might be positioned differently in the social hierarchy, yet might share some similar interests (Hancock 2011, p. 119).

In the context of academia, we could think of potential coalitions between academic and administrative workers as well as employees classified as 'support staff' of universities. In Estonia, the incomes of the latter group range well below the average to a typically minimum salary. Forming such coalitions has potential to "make alliances with depth beyond class shock" (Whelan 2015, p. 149). For example, the question of wages impacts all of these groups and could therefore constitute a common point of interest around which to organise. There is an urgent need to build such cross-cutting collaborations, to bridge these constructed divisions. In practice, forming intersectional coalitions is often a difficult task as it involves the need to consider differences, risks and contradictions (Reagon 1983). Yet such a task must be undertaken in a system that urges us to approach problems through individual solutions. Resistance could be accomplished through reviving university trade unions. In post-socialist contexts, such as Estonia, this remains a challenge.

Further, intersectional perspectives in Estonian gender studies and indeed in social science and humanities scholarship are still marginal. The adoption and development of this research paradigm in these disciplines would potentially contribute to a heightened awareness of intersecting oppressions and help build a sense of solidarity among those employed in universities. It seems that if we want to inhabit an academic space where advanced gender scholarship is recognised as providing a valuable perspective to understand the human experience (not just applied gender research and not only in immediately marketable formats), given the current processes of neo-liberalisation in academia and its troubling effects on feminist research, we must engage in some form of collective activism, with the aim to transform the settings we work in. This should involve critically reflecting on the kinds of academic subjectivities we are compelled to adopt under neo-liberal conditions. It seems that the current times necessitate us to increasingly take on the roles of academic-activists, and challenge those of academic-entrepreneurs if we are to make a meaningful impact on the status and developments of feminist academic research.

Acknowledgements

Raili Marling's work for this article was supported by the Estonian Research Council grant PUT1481 and by the European Union through the European Regional Development Fund (Centre of Excellence in Estonian Studies). Kadri Aavik's work for this article was supported by the Estonian Research Council grant PUT106.

References

Aavik, Kadri. Ed. 2016. *Developing a Research Career Model for Supporting Women's Academic Careers.* ENEKE Project research report (unpub.).

Adler, Nancy, and Anne-Wil Harzing. 2009. When Knowledge Wins: Transcending the Sense and Nonsense of Academic Rankings. *Academy of Management Learning & Education* 8 (1): 72–95.

Adsit, Janelle, Sue Doe, Marisa Allison, Paula Maggio and Maria Maisto. 2015. Affective Activism: Answering Institutional Productions of Precarity in the Corporate University. *Feminist Formations* 27 (3): 21–48.
Ahmed, Sara. 2012. *On Being Included*. Durham: Duke University Press.
Aidnik, Martin. 2015. Ülikoole koloniseerib manager'ide kultuur. *Sirp*, 4.12.2015.
Antecol, Heather, Kelly Bedard and Jenna Stearns. 2016. *Equal but Inequitable: Who Benefits from Gender-Neutral Tenure Clock-Stopping Policies?* Institute for the Study of Labor, Discussion Paper No. 9904.
Ball, Stephen J. 2000. Performativities and Fabrications in the Education Economy: Towards the Performative Society. *Australian Educational Researcher* 17 (3): 1–24.
Barnett, Clive. 2010. Publics and Markets: What's Wrong with Neoliberalism? In *The SAGE Handbook of Social Geographies*, ed. by Susan J. Smith, Rachel Pain, Sallie A. Marston and John Paul Jones III, 269–296. London: Sage.
Berg, Lawrence D., Levi Gahman and Neil Nunn. 2014. Neoliberalism, Masculinities and Academic Knowledge Production: Towards a Theory of Academic Masculinities. In *Masculinities and Place*, ed. by Andrew Gorman-Murray and Peter Hopkins, 57–74. Farnham, Burlington: Ashgate.
Berg, Maggie, and Barbara K. Seeber. 2016. *The Slow Professor: Challenging the Culture of Speed in the Academy*. Toronto: University of Toronto Press.
Budgeon, Shelley. 2015. Individualized Femininity and Feminist Politics of Choice. *European Journal of Women's Studies* 22 (3): 303–318.
Buikema, Rosemarie, and Iris van der Tuin. 2013. Doing the Document: Gender Studies in the Corporatized University in Europe. *European Journal of Women's Studies* 20 (3): 309–316.
Burrows, Roger. 2012. Living with the h-index? Metrics, Markets and Affect in the Contemporary Academy. *Sociological Review* 60 (2): 355–372.
Clark, Burton R. 1998. *Creating Entrepreneurial Universities: Organizational Pathways of Transformation*. Oxford: Pergamon-Elsevier Science.
Estonian Ministry of Education and Research. 2016. *Kõrgharidusprogramm 2016–2019*. https://www.hm.ee/sites/default/files/lisa_8_korghariduse_programm_2016-2019.pdf. Accessed: January 25, 2017.
Eurostat. 2012. *Gender Pay Gap Statistics*. http://epp.eurostat.ec.europa.eu/. Accessed: November 14, 2016.
Félix, Anikó. 2015. Hungary. In *Gender as Symbolic Glue. The Position and Role of Conservative and Far-Right Parties in the Anti-Gender Mobilizations in Europe*, ed. by Eszter Kováts and Maari Põim, 62–82. Brussels: Foundation for European Progressive Studies.
Felt, Ulrike. Ed. 2009. *Knowing and Living in Academic Research. Convergence and Heterogeneity in Research Cultures in the European Context*. Prague: Academy of Sciences of the Czech Republic.
Garforth, Lisa, and Alice Cervinková. 2009. Times and Trajectories in Academic Knowledge Production. In *Knowing and Living in Academic Research: Convergence and Heterogeneity in Research Cultures in the European Context*, ed. by Ulrike Felt, 169–240. Prague: Institute of Sociology of the Academy of Sciences of the Czech Republic.
Gill, Rosalind. 2010. Breaking the Silence. The Hidden Injuries of the Neoliberal University. In *Secrecy and Silence in the Research Process: Feminist Reflections*, ed. by Roisin Flood and Rosalind Gill, 228–244. London: Routledge.

Gill, Rosalind, and Ngaire Donaghue. 2015. Resilience, Apps and Reluctant Individualism: Technologies of Self in the Neoliberal Academy. *Women's Studies International Forum* 54: 91–99.

Graeber, David. 2015. *The Utopia of Rules*. Brooklyn, London: Melville House.

Graves, Nicholas, Adrian Barnett and Philip Clarke. 2011. Funding Grant Proposals for Scientific Research: Retrospective Analysis of Scores by Members of Grant Review Panel. *British Medical Journal* 343 (sep27): d4797.

Great Lakes Feminist Geography Collective (Alison Mountz, Anne Bonds, Becky Mansfield, Jenna Loyd, Jennifer Hyndman, Margaret Walton-Roberts, Ranu Basu, Rina Whitson, Roberta Hawkins, Trina Hamilton and Winifred Curran). 2015. "For Slow Scholarship: A Feminist Politics of Resistance through Collective Action in the Neoliberal University." *ACME* 14 (4): 1235–1259.

Hancock, Ange-Marie. 2011. *Solidarity Politics for Millennials. A Guide to Ending the Oppression Olympics*. New York: Palgrave Macmillan.

Ivancheva, Mariya. 2015. The Age of Precarity and the New Challenges to the Academic Profession. *Studia Europaea* LX (1): 39–47.

Koobak, Redi, and Raili Marling. 2014. Eesti akadeemiliste soouuringute lugu ajakirjas Ariadne Lõng, 2000–2013. *Ariadne Lõng* XV (1–2): 8–25.

Lariviere, Vincent, Veronique Kiermer, Catriona J. MacCallum, Marcia McNutt, Mark Patterson, Bernd Pulverer, Sowmya Swaminathan, Stuart Taylor and Stephen Curry. 2016. A Simple Proposal for the Publication of Journal Citation Distributions. *BioRxiv beta: The Preprint Server for Biology*, Posted July 5. http://biorxiv.org/content/early/2016/07/05/062109. Accessed: February 7, 2017.

Liinason, Mia, and Sabine Grenz. 2016. Women's/Gender Studies and Contemporary Changes in Academic Cultures: European Perspectives. *Women's Studies International Forum* 54: 79–83.

Lõhkivi, Endla. 2011. Soouurimus, teadusfilosoofia ja teaduse uuringud. In *Sissejuhatus soouuringutesse*, ed. by Raili Marling, 79–81. Tartu: Tartu Ülikooli Kirjastus.

Lõhkivi, Endla. 2015. Soostereotüübid ja episteemiline ebaõiglus. *Ariadne Lõng* XV (1–2): 7–21.

Lorenz, Chris. 2012. If You're So Smart, Why Are You under Surveillance? Universities, Neoliberalism, and New Public Management. *Critical Inquiry* 38 (3): 599–629.

Lynch, Kathleen. 2010. Carelessness: A Hidden Doxa of Higher Education. *Arts & Humanities in Higher Education* 9 (1): 54–67.

MacNell, Lillian, Adam Driscoll and Andrea N. Hunt. 2014. What's in a Name: Exposing Gender Bias in Student Ratings of Teachers. *Innovative Higher Education* 40 (4): 291–303.

Marginson, Simon. 2013. The Impossibility of Capitalist Markets in Higher Education. *Journal of Education Policy* 28 (3): 353–370.

Marling, Raili. 2011. Out of the Room of One's Own? Gender Studies in Estonia. *Aspasia: The International Yearbook of Central, Eastern and Southeastern European Women's and Gender History* 5: 157–165.

Marling, Raili. 2015. Feminismi ja neoliberalismi problemaatiline suhe. *Ariadne Lõng* XV (1–2): 37–49.

Meyers, Marian. 2013. The War on Academic Women: Reflections on Postfeminism in the Neoliberal Academy. *Journal of Communication Inquiry* 37 (4): 274–283.

Morrissey, John. 2015. Regimes of Performance: Practices of the Normalised Self in the Neoliberal University. *British Journal of Sociology of Education* 36 (4): 614–634.

Nash, Jennifer C., and Emily A. Owens. 2015. Introduction: Institutional Feelings. Practicing Women's Studies in the Corporate University. *Feminist Formations* 27 (3): vii–xi.

Okk, Gunnar. 2015. *Eesti ülikoolide, teadusasutuste ja rakenduskõrgkoolide võrgu ja tegevussuundade raport*. https://riigikantselei.ee/sites/default/files/riigikantselei/strateegiaburoo/eutarkvt_loppraport.pdf. Accessed: July 6, 2016.

Pereira, Maria do Mar. 2014. The Importance of Being "Modern" and Foreign: Feminist Scholarship and the Epistemic Status of Nations. *Signs: Journal of Women in Culture and Society* 39 (3): 627–657.

Prügl, Elisabeth. 2015. Neoliberalising Feminism. *New Political Economy* 20 (4): 614–631.

Raudvere, Kadri. 2016. *Eesti teadustöötajate keskmine brutokuupalk*. Tartu: Eesti Teadusagentuur.

Reagon, Bernice Johnson. 1983. Coalition Politics: Turning the Century. In *Homegirls: A Black Feminist Anthology*, ed. Barbara Smith, 343–355. New York: Kitchen Table/Women of Color Press.

Rose, Nikolas. 1989. *Governing the Soul: The Shaping of the Private Self*. London: Routledge.

Rottenberg, Catherine. 2013. The Rise of Neoliberal Feminism. *Cultural Studies* 28 (3): 418–437.

Shore, Cris. 2008. Audit Culture and Illiberal Governance: Universities and the Culture of Accountability. *Anthropological Theory* 8 (3): 278–298.

Sifaki, Aggeliki. 2016. Which Side Are We On? Feminist Studies in the Time of Neoliberalism or Neoliberalist Feminist Studies? *Women's Studies International Forum* 54: 111–118.

Slaughter, Sheila, and Larry L. Leslie. 1997. *Academic Capitalism: Politics, Policies and the Entrepreneurial University*. Baltimore, London: Johns Hopkins University Press.

Smith, Dorothy. 1987. *The Everyday World as Problematic: A Feminist Sociology*. Toronto: University of Toronto Press.

Smith, Dorothy. 1990. *The Conceptual Practices of Power: A Feminist Sociology of Knowledge*. Boston: Northeastern University Press.

Tallinn University. 2016. *Introducing the New Sociology MA Programme*. E-mail (unpub.).

Talves, Kairi. 2016. Discursive Self-Positioning Strategies of Estonian Female Scientists in Terms of Academic Career and Excellence. *Women's Studies International Forum* 54: 157–166.

The World Bank. 2012. *Gini index*. http://wdi.worldbank.org/table/2.9. Accessed: January 15, 2017.

Velmet, Aro. 2015. Aro Vermet: Alternatiiv Gunnar Oki haamrile. *Postimees*, 24.10.2015.

Venugopal, Rajesh. 2015. Neoliberalism as Concept. *Economy and Society* 44 (2): 165–187.

Ward, Steven. 2012. *Neoliberalism and the Global Restructuring of Knowledge and Education*. New York: Routledge.

Wendl, Michael. 2007. h-Index: However Ranked, Citations Need Context. *Nature* 449 (7161): 403.

Whelan, Andrew. 2015. Academic Critique of Neoliberal Academia. *Sites: New Series* 12 (1): 130–152.

Whelan, Andrew. 2016. Agnosis in the University Workplace. *Australian Universities' Review* 58 (2): 51–58.

Neo-liberalism and Feminism in the South African Academy

Desiree Lewis

Abstract

Internationally, neo-liberalism shapes universities' institutional cultures and research practices in similar ways. Neo-liberalism also augments and redeploys core-periphery relations, creating market-based and developmentalist knowledge-producing networks that pose distinctive challenges for feminists in different geopolitical spaces. By analysing the location of current feminist work in South African universities, this article considers how an analysis of globalisation's effects in specific contexts can help deepen transnational feminist critiques of the neo-liberal academy. The article is also concerned with how transnational feminism can challenge the entrenched power relations that global neo-liberal research and knowledge production reproduces.

Keywords

Centre, Globalisation, Knowledge Economy, Transnational Feminism, Periphery, South Africa, Neo-liberalism, Universities

1 Introduction

Neo-liberalism's effects on academic feminism have been remarkably similar in the global North and the South. At universities throughout the world, feminists confront the gutting of earlier feminist pedagogies, the 'mainstreaming' of feminist topics and registers, and the surreptitious institutionalisation of conformist research agendas. Feminist scholars such as Margaret Thornton (2009, 2014), writing about Australia, the Sangtin Writers Collective and Richa Nagar (2006) and their critique of trends in India, Shona Hunter (2015) and her analysis of neo-liberal whiteness in the United Kingdom, and Charmaine Pereira (2004) dealing with gender research and developmentalism in Nigeria have all honed in on the "overtly instrumental role" of universities and the ways in which sites of teaching and research on gender are "now deployed by the state specifically to serve the new knowledge economy" (Thornton 2014, p. 1).

As these scholars show, neo-liberalism's reach into universities has extended earlier affiliations between institutions of higher education, the state and corporate capitalism. Neo-liberalism has also harnessed specialist knowledge to the imperatives of the market, albeit in the guise of 'social responsiveness' in research and teaching. Traditionally, the mission of universities has been to undertake research and to teach, priorities that have easily laid them open to charges of elitism and ivory tower disengagement. With the emphasis on a 'third mission' in neo-liberal planning, university teaching and research have been yoked to the academy's direct engagement with economic growth activities that have been redefined as 'social engagement' (for a detailed discussion see Pinheiro et al. 2015). The call for engagement through a third mission consequently stems not from politically transformative agendas, but from a neo-liberal quest to mobilise knowledge commercially and for capitalist growth.

The current hegemony of the neo-liberal scenario has generated a chorus of lament among many radical commentators.[1] But while neo-liberalism's impact should be appraised sharply, urgently and consistently, it is also vital to ask what feminist possibilities exist or can be created to challenge its deadening effects.

In what follows, I am therefore concerned with two related aims. One is a careful unpacking of specific challenges for feminists in a specific neo-liberal context. In contributing to existing critiques, then, I offer a site-specific analysis of trends in South Africa as a distinctive periphery in a neo-liberal globalised circuit of cores and margins that both constitute and are constituted by global streams of capital

---

1 See, for example, John Higgins (2013) and Premesh Lalu (2012) writing about South Africa, and Stuart Hall (1990) and Terry Eagleton (2010) dealing with the UK.

and knowledge. By developing this context-specific analysis, I raise the broader significance of mapping the diverse forms that neo-liberal co-optation takes. A second, connected objective of this article is to reflect on the possibilities for radical feminist responses to the neo-liberalising of the academy. While the hegemony of neo-liberalism rests on how its logic of efficiency becomes entrenched in academic structures, institutions and the minds of managers, teachers and students, I argue that sites of dissent and opposition can continue to be driven by the spirit of feminism in the academy.

2 The Global Knowledge Economy Vortex and South African Feminism

As several radical critics (e.g. Duggan 2003) have shown, current global capitalism has become increasingly knowledge based, with the production, marketing and consolidation of commodities relying on specialised knowledge (and universities as key powerhouses for its production) in unprecedented ways. In *Universities in a Neoliberal World*, Alex Callinicos (2006) shows that it was mainly at the start of the twenty-first century that governments in the global North began to champion knowledge economies as engines of endless economic growth. University management, in synch with many governments' macroeconomic policies, began to ensure that the new knowledge economy would buttress neo-liberalism's concentration of productive expertise, political control and knowledge resources through what Callinicos (2006, p. 7) has described as "a particularly pure form of the logic of capital".

This vortex is not just regional or national; its global scope means that knowledge capital is instrumentalised around the world to serve the centres of global capitalism directly, or to support this system's levers. These levers include international policy, North-South research collaboration or research funding arrangements. Although rarely acknowledged, relations around academic research mirror those associated with the extraction and processing of material commodities such as food. In effect, knowledge and its production have therefore been thoroughly commoditised within the global capitalist chain: uneven flows of knowledge, funding and research expertise lead to concentrations of expertise and resources in the North that construct and feed off nodes of data and data gathering in the South.

This North-South dyad is often explained as a carry-over from neo-imperial and neo-colonial power relations. In other words, the definition of Southern research subjects by Northern researchers is seen to echo centuries of constructing subject matter and defining knowledge expertise according to colonial logic. As an identity-constituting process, colonialist knowledge production since the twentieth century othered objects of research in inventing the coherence of Western authority and superiority. Drawing on a tradition of postcolonial theorising in her analysis of Western feminism's colonialist logic, Chandra Mohanty (1984, p. 352–353) argued in the 1980s that the effect of Western-centric constructions of 'data' in the third-world South is to constitute 'Western' subjectivity.

> It is "only in so far as 'Woman/Women' and 'the East' are defined as Others, or as peripheral, that (Western) Man/Humanism can represent him/itself as the center. It is not the center that determines the periphery, but the periphery that, in its boundedness, determines the centre. [...] Universal images of 'the third world woman's (the veiled woman, chaste virgin, etc.), images constructed from adding the 'third world difference' to 'sexual difference' are predicated upon (and hence obviously bring into sharper focus) assumptions about Western women as secular, liberated and having control over their own lives. [...] I am referring to a discursive self-presentation, not necessarily to material reality."

Despite the ongoing relevance of identifying the discursive logic of colonial discourse, it has become more and more important to reconsider the material effects of core-periphery relations, since the economic logic of data-gathering in the South is becoming increasingly central to the neo-liberal knowledge economy. By reflecting on current gender and sexuality research in South Africa, I show that the colonial knowledge circuit has now become an instrument within broader economic imperatives that direct the production of knowledge towards consolidating a global market economy. As Lisa Duggan (2003) therefore stresses, neo-liberalism entrenches racialised and neo-colonial relations in efficiently mobilising cultural capital.

In *The Posthuman,* Rosi Braidotti (2013, p. 4) argues that theory has lost its pivotal status within feminist scholarship and is now often "dismissed as a form of fantasy or narcissistic self-indulgence". As she states, a philosophically eviscerating neo-empiricism – what she terms "data mining" (Braidotti 2013, p. 4) – has become the norm. Her critique echoes Margaret Thornton's identification (2009) of the way in which valued knowledge in the new knowledge economy has become data, rather than wisdom. It is data, Thornton (2009, p. 387) argues, rather than models and tools to explain and analyse structures and relationships, which constitutes an untapped source of wealth in terms of market logic.

Although Braidotti (2013) and Thornton (2009) confront an empiricising drift in the North, African feminist research, as Charmaine Pereira (2004) notes, has been even more data driven. Pereira describes the developmental agenda that determines how gender research sites operate and reproduce themselves in relation to the North, which retains epistemic and economic power. Since research on gender is often pivotal to the fields around which Northern policy and economic interventions into Africa revolve, applied research on gender plays a key role in a knowledge economy linked to fields such as epidemiology, public health, development or public participation.

Elsewhere I have explored the status and history of South African feminist research, showing that "South African universities, scholars and networks have featured prominently in collaborative networks with scholars in the United States, Britain and, more recently, Scandinavia" (Lewis 2007, p. 18). Compared with research in other post-colonial African countries, South Africa has not had a legacy of national sovereignty or cultural nationalism for driving African-centred research,[2] a situation that has been the focus of much of the student protest between 2015 and 2016. The Northern-centric focus of South Africa's global networks has also fed into the evolution of universities under rapid neo-liberal economic restructuring since the late 1990s. Humanities and social science work in the academy has therefore been informed both by a legacy of academic deference towards the North and by a more recent history of neo-liberal nation building.

Within work on gender, consolidated research testifying to these trajectories is evident in the steady and dramatic rise – since the start of the new millennium – of sexualities studies. As evidenced by the surge of interdisciplinary research in this area, funds that have been made available for research, and the industry of publications it has generated, 'sexualities' has become a prime locus for data mining and neo-empiricist study. The fact that sexuality has become an important subject in feminist research is of course not in itself noteworthy or alarming. Feminists have focused innovatively on sexualities by considering how heteronormative institutions and practices become hegemonic, and how gendered identities and ideology are sedimented under patriarchy and other authoritarian and exploitative systems.[3]

But much of the recent work on sexuality in South Africa demonstrates little of this theoretical and political insight into the entanglement of patriarchy, sexuality and power; instead, the focus has fallen largely on sexuality as a sectoral field amenable to being mapped, extensively described and brought within the purview of applied

---

2 This includes research trends, publishing houses focusing on the work of black African scholars and research capacity networks such as *Southern African Political Economic Series (SAPES)* in Zimbabwe and *Council for the Development of Social Science Research in Africa (CODESRIA)* in Dakar.

3 Such work includes Adrienne Rich's path-breaking essay in 1980, Lisa Duggan's more recent analysis of homonormativity and neo-liberalism (2003) and Patricia McFadden's attention to sexuality and feminist resistance (2003) defined with reference to Audre Lorde's notion of the erotic (1978).

research into developmental problems. What could be described as neo-empiricist humanities research therefore enlists aspects of post-positivist and theoretically grounded scholarship, yet ultimately falls back on the assumption that knowledge that matters is observable and quantifiable information, elicited through unmediated experience and/or comprehensive description. The neo-empiricist tradition therefore differs from the applied research comprehensively described in Pereira's discussion (2004) of donor-driven gender research that services the state. It has become a procedural approach, learned and passed down through formulae set in place by supervisors, mentors and established scholars (who often have the best of intentions) for producing 'rigorous' work sanctioned in the academy.

Within the wider global field of knowledge-making and interpretation, a large proportion of the sexualities research in South Africa is constituted by a multicultural gaze, a form of surveillance that only appears to make space for exploring difference in the globalised academy. Jigna Desai, Danielle Bouchara and Diane Detourney (2010, p. 59) remark astutely on this dynamic by stating:

> "The university's call for inclusion of 'global difference' is not simply benevolent and aimed at redressing past crimes of exclusion, but is necessary to the expansion of its global purview."

My intention in identifying how this is manifested in South Africa is not to condemn individual researchers, or to provide a detailed appraisal of their work on its own terms. Work on sexualities is frequently produced by writers with deep commitments to socially engaged education both in and beyond the academy. What does concern me, however, are the discursive effects of particular discursive and methodological emphases. As I go on to show, these reinforce the location of South African sexualities work in uneven knowledge-creation circuits.

The operation of these circuits is evident in the work anthologised in several publications[4] produced by the *Human Sciences Research Council (HSRC)*, the South African statutory organisation that conducts, coordinates and publishes research into aspects of human and social development. In 2009 alone, the *HSRC* published two volumes dealing with sexuality, *The Prize and the Price: Shaping Sexualities in South Africa* (Steyn and van Zyl 2009) and *From Social Silence to Social Science: Same-Sex Sexuality, HIV & AIDS and Gender in South Africa* (Reddy et al. 2009). The following neo-empiricist threads in these collections warrant attention.

---

4 Apart from books, see the archive of reports and articles on sexualities on the Human Sciences Research Council website at http://www.hsrc.ac.za/en.

A first is the explicit way in which the categorisation of sexual orientation and sexual practices entrenches health agendas that function, according to market logic, as mechanisms for reproducing economically viable bodies. As illustrated in writings collected in *From Social Silence to Social Science* (Reddy et al. 2009) the language for describing tabooed sexual identities often refers directly to bodily experiences and sexual activity. Thus, diagnostic terms such as MSM (men who have sex with men) or WSW (women who have sex with women) (see Reddy et al. 2009, p. xxix), focus on identifying and monitoring the sexual activity of high-risk groups. Such terms therefore become blunt tools for intervention-based surveillance research on HIV/AIDS.

Extensive work on youth and sexuality, in which gendered performances are explored in relation to sexual behaviour and practices, perpetuate the instrumentalist orientation of work on same-sex practices. The result, as Katarina Jungar and Elina Oinas (2011) have noted, is overdetermined data with direct-use value in epidemiology, public health policy and other interventions driven from the North.[5] Overall, therefore, conceptual and theoretical work, evident especially in the use of reductive terminology and concepts, is yoked to global discourses for locating and containing sexually transmitted diseases.

While research is often painstaking and detailed, it can indirectly feed into the moral panic evident in obviously 'biased' representations of diseased and unproductive bodies in South Africa. Websites, newspaper reports and non-academic accounts are fairly obvious in constructing spectacles of wasted South Africans and the region as a danger zone whose diseases threaten to spill over into the North. Although seemingly at odds with the alarmism and sensationalism of popularised information, much academic research on sexualities echoes the former's emphasis on the naming, surveillance and containment of sexualised and diseased bodies.

A second noteworthy pattern in sexuality research is its attention to meticulous research processes and 'methodological work'. For example, contributions on sexualities to two South African feminist journals, *Feminist Africa* and *Agenda* reveal a heavy emphasis on detailing the processes through which researchers extracted data about their research participants or subjects. The following extract from an article titled *Vela Bambhentsele: Intimacies and Complexities in Researching Within Black Lesbian Groups in Johannesburg* (Matebeni 2008, p. 90–92) illustrates this:

> "I embarked on a study to investigate the lives of black lesbian women in Gauteng. Throughout the study, I had to negotiate my own position as my identities and sexuality

5 The phrase here does not always literally involve interventions coming from the North, since those based in the South can echo and entrench Northern-oriented agendas.

> continue to be influenced by the people who inform my research. I am interested in what it means to be engaged in doing research in areas that have been considered taboo, unresearched or working with those who have been represented in ways that limit their agency. […] Prior to starting the research I was aware of some of the challenges I would face. While my identity as a lesbian was an asset in terms of gaining access, I had to be cautious of the implications this might have on my academic career as my study could be dismissed on the basis of writing 'for my own group' and my work 'tainted by personal concerns'."

As this writer's discussion reveals, a great deal of attention is paid to validating knowledge emanating from an "insider-outsider"[6] position, one that vindicates findings for a global academic gaze at 'difference'. The meticulous analysis of information about gender performance with reference to geopolitical space is a function of the writer's location between the academy and the non-academic world she has privileged access to. Her position therefore vindicates her role as a reliable data gatherer.

The theoretical, conceptual and methodological orientations traced above reveal the extent to which sexualities research can feed into the extractivist form of South African knowledge as meticulously obtained 'data' for its interpretation or resolution elsewhere. The valued knowledge produced is 'rational' in an instrumentalising sense, having 'use value' in the sense of serving the requirements of practical interventions or policy research grounded in others' primary interests. The significant amounts of donor funding that have gone into 'researching sexualities' reflect the servicing role of data and data gathers. 'Data' becomes the raw material within a global apparatus within which interpretive or responsive products and expertise are created elsewhere. In the same way that corporate capitalism plunders raw materials from the South for external processing, 'raw data', elicited from data gatherers as methodological experts, is extracted for expert processing in the North.

3 Governmentality, the Academy and Feminists

Shona Hunter's (2015) analysis of how neo-liberalism generates relations and responses of melancholia, loss, and revolutionary hope and renewal (Hunter 2016, p. 19) provides subtle insight into neo-liberalism's psychoanalytic and political

6 The author here explains her position as 'hybrid', seeming to question the neatness of "insider/outsider", yet adhering ultimately to the binaries that structure dominant ideas about 'expert' knowledge production (Matebeni 2008, p. 90–92).

paradoxes. Hunter demonstrates that, rather than these reactions being disparate, they often cohere in the messy entanglements that neo-liberal governance sets in place among subjects, institutions, morality and the state (Hunter 2015, p. 1–21). Drawing on Hunter's insights, this section maps out some of the key ways in which neo-liberal governance has affected feminists' agencies within the academy's institutional culture.

Growing critical commentary on neo-liberalism and governmentality stresses the extent to which governance in the interests of the state and capital are internalised by subjects who effectively rule themselves (see especially Callinicos 2006 and Thornton 2014). This self-rule is effected through discourses that stress, for example, individual responsibility, a deferential attentiveness to the 'social good', or the positivist myth of 'normless' academic research agendas. Analysing feminists' choices in the face of these discourses – as though individuals had the voluntarist option to conform or not – simplifies the complex ways in which neo-liberalism, especially within academic sites, recruits and positions willing participants in enterprises whose effects extend beyond the academy. In explaining the valence of sexuality research among many progressive South African scholars, it is therefore important to recognise that they are not simply 'duped by rewards'; instead, as Margaret Thornton (2009) and Hunter (2015) remind us, neo-liberalism recruits complicit subjects. Hunter describes this recruitment from a "feminist psychosocial" point of view, which sees "relational politics" as the "everyday actions, investments and practices of the multiple and shifting range of people [in relation to] other material and symbolic objects that make up the state" (Hunter 2015, p. 4). She consequently makes us aware of how governmentality persuades academics within the neo-liberal academy that their (politicised) relations with dominant bureaucratic structures, performance criteria and research processes are normative, irresistible and definitive measures of excellence.

The freighting of research agendas such as sexuality work among feminists occurs in the context of the comprehensive bureaucratising of the university in relation to the state. The relationships between universities and the state in South Africa have always been complex ones. Under apartheid, universities were often directly controlled by the government, although struggles by many staff, students and very often management meant that battles for academic freedom took the form of liberal struggles between those opposed to apartheid instrumentalisation and a profoundly authoritarian state. As John Higgins (2013) notes, however, the shift from the apartheid to post-apartheid university did not entail institutions' progressive extrication from state capture. Instead, higher educational policy and institutional management in various universities allowed "the system to be increasingly defined by a neoliberal agenda" (Higgins 2013, p. 50). State control became benign, masked by universities' seeming responsiveness to 'academic accountability' and 'social engagement'.

This situation demands thorough administration and oversight. And as the explosion of student protests between 2015 and 2016 for free public education and an end to the outsourcing of workers so clearly showed, it has also meant pernicious connections between university management and the state. From the start of the protests in October 2015, students quickly targeted both university managers and the neo-liberal post-apartheid state in condemning escalating fees, the exploitation of workers on their campus, and – from the perspective of many women and LGBTQ students – entrenched sexism and homophobia in institutions (see Bond 2017). Whether or not the South African government – like governments in the North – explicitly promotes an instrumental economic role for universities through managers, universities' purpose vis-à-vis the state is constantly stressed by the emphasis that the state-manager alliance places on universities' centrality to, for example, 'social cohesion', 'development', and rational and efficient 'growth'.

Regulation and reward systems associated with neo-liberal marketisation have been swiftly implemented at all levels. This rapid implementation is a sign of how deeply the "market has entered the soul of the university" (Thornton 2009, p. 3). Universities' regimes of auditing now emulate businesses' bureaucracies in regulating productivity and efficiency. Within the current regimes, academics, including feminist and progressive academics, are enlisted to police one another in terms of performance criteria that tend to prioritise quantifiable tasks and achievements rather than scholarly, intellectual and teaching ability. The main South African regulating mechanism, the National Research Foundation, rigidly grades research outputs and the standing of individual academics by locking academics into schemas that pay little attention to the merits of innovative and radical thought.

Related to the culture of regulation and reward has been a cutthroat ethos of individualism, one which pervades many levels of academic research. An aggressive ethic of survival of the fittest seems to have been naturalised as the only way to thrive in academies. Universities are always elite institutions that carefully regulate success, merit and ability, and have therefore historically encouraged exclusivity, individualism and competition. But the obsession with outputs, achievements and productivity under the present audit culture encourages unbridled and ruthless competitiveness.

Alan Burton-Jones (1999, p. 3) remarks on this by arguing:

> "Capitalism and emerging knowledge capitalism thrive on capital accumulation, open-market competition, free trade, the power of the individual and survival of the fittest."

Unlike the effects of racial, class and patriarchal injustices, then, the impact of neo-liberalism is extremely hard to identify and contest; it is often 'in here', rather than only, and of course, more manageably 'out there'. In other words, our universities' auditing technologies become generalised and often bring the aims, methods and passions of what individual feminist academics do in line with the institutional good.

The homogenising and monitoring of goals behind the aegis of collective good is especially evident in the new technocratic regulation of university teaching. South African feminist traditions have long pioneered innovative methods for encouraging critical literacy among students. In their introduction to a country-wide study of feminist popular education, Shirley Walters and Linzi Manicom (1996) explore the thriving body of feminist popular education in South Africa in the early 1980s. As they also demonstrate, this legacy sought to connect the intellect, the body, the spirit and the emotions, challenging separations that allow mainstream teaching and scholarship to marginalise certain knowledge-making and suppress certain areas of study (see Walters and Manicom 1996, p. 7–11). Feminists in South Africa have also experimented boldly with creativity, active learning, and the use of students' knowledges in challenging elite and masculinist forms of learning. In fact, feminist popular education in South Africa has a long history in the work of feminist activists working for non-governmental organisations and trade unions. Drawing on the philosophy of the Brazilian educator Paulo Freire, this work has enlisted traditions of popular education and specifically feminist pedagogies that establish the personal as political, and challenge hegemonic epistemologies and patriarchal claims to universality.

An example of this progressive teaching is the University of the Western Cape's *Centre for Continuing and Adult Education (CACE)*, which drove critical literacy programmes for adults whose social marginalisation had constrained their educational ambitions. Like other radical teaching sites, the *Centre for Continuing and Adult Education* not only sought to prepare students academically, but also sought to support students' critical engagement with their worlds, preparing them to challenge local, interpersonal and global forms of power and injustice, and the ways in which governments and market economies safeguard minority privileges (see Walters and Manicom 1996). The *Centre for Continuing and Adult Education*, like other popular educational sites in universities, therefore worked to make marginal voices heard within the confines of the academic centre.

In its pursuit for a market-oriented social engagement in 2014, the university's management recommended the Centre's closure[7] on the grounds of its no longer being relevant to the institution's educational priorities. At the same time, enormous financial and academic resources have gone into transforming teaching and learning into a new site for professionalism and regulation. Apart from the employment of a senior academic to oversee teaching and learning in all departments and faculties, the university appoints deputy deans in several faculties for this portfolio, and considerable energy and resources have been invested in managerial strategies for 'enhancing' teaching and learning. Long-established academics, with excellent track records of innovative teaching, are now required to submit elaborate teaching portfolios or attend training sessions to qualify for promotion.

This bureaucratic restructuring of teaching exemplifies not only the direction taken by one university, but also many others in South Africa. The new teaching and learning expertise offers far less than the rich, animated, organic and impassioned pedagogical explorations that feminists and popular educators have pursued in and beyond South Africa. Ultimately, the new technologies for teaching and learning operate within broader systems of managerialism and auditing.

4 Feminist Resistance in the Face of Neo-liberalism

What might it therefore mean to step outside of the academy as neo-liberalism's 'teaching machine'?[8] Given the overwhelming ways in which governmentality works not only to maintain the status quo, but also to assure all subjects that the status quo is rational and just, what does 'resistance' mean? It is worth stressing here that gendered forms of narcissism, competitiveness and manipulation quickly intensify among women located in institutions that exploit and encourage individualism and other socially learned behaviours. One important route for feminist resistance in the academy involves courageous, self-reflexive critiques not only of where we are currently situated, but also of our complex ties of co-dependence and complicity with the academy's various technologies of management and self-management. Such self-assessment would entail questioning collective stakes in security zones, the layered investments we make in affiliation, and the dangers of speaking out and

7 The *Centre for Continuing and Adult Education* has not closed; however, it has now merged with another centre, and its original focus on critical popular education has been significantly weakened.

8 I adapt the title of Gayatri Spivak's *Outside in the Teaching Machine* (1993) here.

stepping out of line. By drawing attention to the "psychosocial" and to the way that neo-liberal ethics and morality are manifested in our everyday actions, seemingly spontaneous responses and psyches, Shona Hunter (2015, p. 46) alerts us to the vigilance and humility that such self-interrogation must entail.

Yet in institutional contexts where the progressive effects of seemingly radical practices are easily compromised, 'self-reflexive' practices also warrant critical reconsideration. In her conceptual work on methodologies, Richa Nagar (2014) concludes that 'reflexivity' has become a mantra in much feminist work today. Invoked to mystify research that reproduces earlier blind spots, reflexivity often works to perpetuate moderate and even conservative ends. As her work with activists outside of the academy demonstrates, self-reflexivity in an age where neo-liberal logic clouds our every motivation requires risk, courage and humanity. It would mean, for example, that research into areas considered important or exciting must be subjected to a researcher's efforts to position herself at the very localised level of knowledge-making, and interrogate her motivations and efforts in relation to wider global contexts.

This would also entail questioning the implications of what work one does, and under which conditions within our particular sites as well as in wider domains of knowledge-making. One of the central arguments of this article is that the taken-for-granted tasks of researching and teaching in certain areas must be subjected to constant scrutiny by academics and students. Although South African feminists have fought hard and with great determination to introduce particular theoretical models, concepts and research areas into the academy,[9] it is, to say the least, cause for concern when industries of knowledge-making and funding accrue in some areas at certain moments. It is even more alarming when particular approaches to these research areas become institutionalised in the academy, forming a corpus of postgraduate study and writing by established researchers, and swiftly become a research industry with direct and indirect connections to national and international economic and foreign policy. Acknowledging how our work can sometimes feed into an economy that now relies on sectoral knowledge banks should therefore be central to our self-reflexive scrutiny.

Alongside this kind of self-reflexivity is the value of rebuilding research communities that have traditionally strengthened feminism. It is predictable that the neo-liberal emphasis on productivity has generated considerable interest in cross-country and cross-regional research collaboration, especially North-South

9 It is especially important to recognise the work on sexualities which particular feminists developed long before the growth of an industry around this work. Interventions by Mary Hames (2003) and Patricia McFadden (1992) are especially noteworthy here.

work where large amounts of donor funding go into, for example, researching sexualities or masculinities. In confronting the ongoing need for research and activist communities for feminists today, Chandra Mohanty (2013, p. 967–991) describes alternative forms of networking. By focusing on specific and general patterns in relation to sites including the US, Sweden, Mexico and Palestine, she unravels ways in which feminists located at centres and peripheries can activate critical alliances that actively trouble the exploitative North-South dyad associated with commodity extraction and processing.

Central to her conceptualising of radical networks is her distinction between global alliances (which function to consolidate North-South relations and the servicing role of universities), and substantively transnational connections[10] that seek to dismantle the discursive and material relations that create cores and peripheries in the first place. Among these relations, discourses of multiculturalism recruit peripheries into global circuits as 'respected' zones of difference, while ultimately mobilising these zones in larger global apparatuses for managing knowledge and information in the interests of the market, political stability, and the production of compliant and economically productive bodies.

5 Conclusion

It is not surprising that the knowledge economy underpinning university work in the present often leaves individual feminist academics and students extremely vulnerable, isolated, fragile and battered, even as it seems to offer certain individuals scope for quantitative growth and advancement within the academy. The testimonies of black South African feminists[11] especially indicate that they have endured tremendous physical, emotional and psychological distress. Their experiences of alienation in the academy raise the necessity for strengthening alliances and support networks.

Networking and research collaboration under neo-liberalism, however, continues to spawn larger, better-funded and increasingly aggressive global, rather than transnational, alliances. And global feminism, as is the case with global

10 Richa Nagar and Amanda Swarr distinguish between global and transnational alliances as editors of *Critical Transnational Feminist Praxis* (2010).

11 This became evident between 2015 and 2016 in the context of the *#Fees Must Fall* protests. Both radical black academics and students spoke out in print and social media about ongoing racism and patriarchy in the context of neo-liberal administration and bureaucracy.

orientations generally, effectively incorporates peripheries into the centres in line with the latter's strategic objectives. As students, academics and intellectual activists in the academy, feminists can continue to subvert or elude entrenched power relations under globalisation by strengthening transnational solidarity community-building. Neo-liberalism in the academy fosters the loss of perspective: losing sight of struggles, power relations and critical knowledge-making that satisfy our radical intellectual and political energies. In joining the race to produce outputs for outputs' sake, or to meet endless auditing and self-regulation criteria, we can quickly lose sight of the vital sources of our critical engagement in knowledge-making that thrives beyond the academy. Re-invigorating transnational alliances and regaining radical perspectives therefore require the (now) radical move of alliance-building with constituencies that first strengthened feminism,[12] but which academic feminists today seem to have little time for. Mohanty (2013, p. 991) articulates this cogently:

> "I believe we need to return to the radical feminist politics of the contextual as both local and structural and to the collectivity that is being defined out of existence by privatization projects. I think we need to recommit to insurgent knowledges and the complex politics of anti-racist, anti-imperialist feminisms."

References

Bond, Patrick. 2017. To Win Free Education, Fossilised Neoliberalism Must Fall. In *Fees Must Fall: Student Revolt, Decolonisation and Governance in South Africa*, ed. by Susan Booysen, 192–213. Johannesburg: Wits University Press.

Braidotti, Rosi. 2013. *The Posthuman*. Cambridge: Polity Press.

Burton-Jones, Alan. 1999. *Knowledge Capitalism, Business, Work and Learning in the New Economy*. Oxford: Oxford University Press.

Callinicos, Alex. 2006. *Universities in a Neoliberal World*. London: Bookmark Publications.

Desai, Jigna, Danielle Bouchard and Diane Detourney. 2010. Disavowed Legacies and Honourable Thievery: The Work of the 'Transnational' in LGBTQ Studies. In *Critical Transnational Feminist Praxis*, ed. by Amanda Swarr and Richa Nagar, 46–62. New York: SUNY Press.

Duggan, Lisa. 2003. *Twilight of Equality? Neoliberalism, Cultural Politics and the Attack on Democracy*. Boston: Beacon Press.

---

12 Academic feminists' connections to cultural activism, social movement activism and popular culture have become increasingly tenuous with the mainstreaming of feminist teaching and research in universities both in and outside of South Africa.

Eagleton, Terry. 2010. The Death of Universities. *The Guardian*, December 17.
Hall, Stuart. 1990. The Emergence of Cultural Studies and the Crisis of the Humanities. *October: The Humanities as Social Technology* 53, 11–23.
Hames, Mary. 2003. The Women's Movement and Lesbian and Gay Struggles in South Africa. *Feminist Africa* (2). http://agi.ac.za/sites/agi.ac.za/files/fa_2_standpoint_4.pdf. Accessed: August 24, 2017.
Higgins, John. 2013. *Academic Freedom in a Democratic South Africa*. Johannesburg: Wits University Press.
Hunter, Shona. 2015. *Power, Politics and the Emotions: Impossible Governance?* Oxford, New York: Routledge.
Jungar, Katarina, and Elina Oinas. 2011. Beyond Agency and Victimization: Rereading HIV and AIDS in African Contexts. *Social Dynamics* 37 (2): 248–262.
Lalu, Premesh. 2012. The Humanities After Apartheid. *Mail & Guardian*, May 4 May.
Lewis, Desiree. 2007. Feminism and the Radical Imagination. *Agenda* 21 (72): 18–31.
Lorde, Audre. 1978. *Uses of the Erotic: the Erotic as Power*. Brooklyn, N.Y.: Out & Out Books.
Matebeni, Zethu. 2008. *Vela Bambhentsele*: Intimacies and Complexities in Researching Within Black Lesbian Groups in Johannesburg. *Feminist Africa* (11): 89–96.
McFadden, Patricia. 1992. Nationalism and Gender Issues in South Africa. *Journal of Gender Studies* 1 (4): 510–520.
McFadden, Patricia. 2003. Sexual Pleasure as Feminist Choice. *Feminist Africa* (2). http://agi.ac.za/sites/agi.ac.za/files/fa_2_standpoint_1.pdf. Accessed: August 24, 2017.
Mohanty, Chandra Talpade. 1984. Under Western Eyes: Feminist Scholarship and Colonial Discourses. *boundary 2* 12 (3): 333–358.
Mohanty, Chandra Talpade. 2013. Transnational Feminist Crossings: On Neo-liberalism and Radical Critique. *Signs: Journal of Women in Culture and Society* 38 (4): 967–991.
Nagar, Richa. 2014. *Muddying the Waters: Co-Authoring Feminisms Across Scholarship and Activism*. Urbana: University of Illinois Press.
Pereira, Charmaine. 2004. Locating Gender and Women's Studies in Nigeria: What Trajectories for the Future? In *Gender Activism and Studies in Africa*. CODESRIA Gender Series Volume 3, ed. by Signe Arnfred and Babere Kerata Chacha, 1–26. Dakar: CODESRIA.
Pinheiro, Rómulo, Patricio Langa and Attila Pausits. 2015. The Institutionalization of Universities' Third Mission: Introduction to the Special Issue. In *Institutionalizing Universities' Third Mission*. European Journal of Higher Education, Special Issue 5 (3), ed. by Rómulo Pinheiro, Patricio Langa and Attila Pausits, 227–232. London: Taylor & Francis.
Reddy, Vasu, Theo Sandfort and Laetitia Rispel, 2009. *From Social Science to Social Silence: Same-sex Sexuality, HIV & AIDS and Gender in South Africa*. Cape Town: HSRC Press.
Rich, Adrienne. 1980. Compulsory Heterosexuality and Lesbian Existence. *Signs: Journal of Women in Culture and Society* 5 (4): 631–660.
Sangtin Writers Collective and Richa Nagar. 2006. *Playing with Fire: Feminist Thought and Activism through Seven Lives in India*. Minneapolis: University of Minnesota Press.
Spivak, Gayatri Chakravorty. 1993. *Outside in the Teaching Machine*. New York, London: Routledge.
Steyn, Melissa, and Mikki van Zyl. Eds. 2009. *The Prize and the Price: Shaping Sexualities in South Africa*. Cape Town: HSRC Press.
Swarr, Amanda, and Richa Nagar. 2010. Theorizing Transnational Feminist Praxis. In *Critical Transnational Feminist Praxis*, ed. by Richa Nagar and Amanda Swarr, 1–20. New York: SUNY Press.

Thornton, Margaret. 2009. *Universities Upside Down: The Impact of the New Knowledge Economy.* Australia National University College of Law Research Paper. No. 10–13.
Thornton, Margaret. 2014. Introduction: The Retreat from the Critical. In *Through a Glass Darkly: The Social Sciences Look at the Neoliberal University*, ed. by Thornton, Margaret, 1–15. Canberra: ACT ANU Press.
Walters, Shirley, and Linzi Manicom. 1996. Introduction. In *Gender in Popular Education: Methods for Empowerment*, ed. by Shirley Walters and Linzi Manicom, 1–22. Cape Town: Centre for Adult and Continuing Education.

II

Interactions: Gender Research, Academic Feminism and Society

The Relationship between Gender Research and Society in the Norwegian *Brainwash* Controversy of 2010–2011

Pia Vuolanto

Abstract

The author investigates the relationship between gender research and society in the current context of neo-liberal and managerial universities. In this context of the new governance of science, research is expected to actively interact with society and to be involved in transdisciplinary problem-solving in close collaboration with various social actors (Slaughter and Leslie 1997; Gibbons et al. 1994; Etzkowitz and Leydesdorff 1998). The article provides an in-depth empirical study of the relationship between gender research and society by analysing a recent public controversy in Norway that unveiled different social actors' definitions and expectations of gender research. The study focuses on the different views and perceptions that different actors had of the relationship between gender research and society during this unusually large public controversy. The analysis is conducted through a close reading of newspaper articles, articles in scholarly journals and blog posts. The article highlights the diverse understandings of the relationship between gender research and society, and hence strengthens claims that a transformation is taking place in universities from detached research systems to more interactive ones. The academic community as a whole, including gender researchers, can benefit from learning about the rhetorical strategies of the social world of gender research in this debate to maintain and change the public image of the interaction between science and society.

Keywords

Gender Research, Gender Research and Society, Science-society Relationship, Social Relevance, *Brainwash* Controversy, Social Sciences and Humanities, Controversies in Social Sciences

1 Introduction

This article analyses the relationship between gender research and society by scrutinising a recent public controversy in Norway. The controversy started in the spring of 2010, when *NRK*, the Norwegian broadcasting company, presented a popular science series called *Brainwash* (*Hjernevask* in Norwegian). The series started a heated and politicised nationwide debate about the place of science in society, which was especially dominated by a discussion about gender equality and gender research. The debate involved researchers from different disciplines, politicians, policymakers, the media and social movements. This controversy offers a rich and current context in which to study the relationship between gender research and society.

In higher education studies, it is often claimed that the relationship between research activities and society has changed, with a shift from discipline-based knowledge production and isolated research work to transdisciplinary collaborations and active interactions with society that aim to solve the serious problems of our time (Slaughter and Leslie 1997; Gibbons et al. 1994; Etzkowitz and Leydesdorff 1998; Hessels and van Lente 2008; Tuunainen 2013; Albert and McGuire 2014). This 'universities' transformation thesis' has been criticised for concentrating too heavily on the world of science, technology and medicine and not sufficiently including the humanities or social sciences (Albert 2003; Godin 1998). Moreover, it has been argued that the thesis is insufficiently empirically grounded and needs to be made more specific in order to capture the whole of the science-society relationship (Ylijoki 2003; Tuunainen 2005; Ylijoki et al. 2011; Albert and McGuire 2014; Miettinen et al. 2015). With this critique in mind, this article sets out to study the relationship between one social sciences and humanities domain – gender research – so as to provide a view into the variety of understandings of its relationship with society.

Gender research, engaged as it is in the political issues of welfare societies, has been shown to be particularly "vulnerable to distortion and to being framed in a negative, provocative manner" (Grauerholz and Baker-Sperry 2007, p. 274) by social movements such as anti-feminism. Previous studies on gender research as a discipline have considered its historical formation, academic status and relationship with other disciplines (Widerberg 2006; Skeggs 2008; Griffin 2009; Hemmings 2011; Pereira 2012). There is also research on feminism and anti-feminism as social movements (Blais and Dupuis-Déri 2012; Eriksson 2013; Johansson and Lilja 2013; Giebel and Röhrborn 2015; Derichs and Fennert 2015) and on gender researchers in the media (Scharff 2013). In this article, I unfold the perceptions of gender research among different actors from different social worlds in the context of Norway – a Nordic welfare state – during a large public debate about gender research. This will provide a view of the different aspirations and demands attached to gender research.

2 Theoretical Framework: Controversy Studies and the Science-society Relationship

Controversy studies on public debates involving science fall under the broad umbrella of science and technology studies. These controversy studies have focused on the interplay between science and society by analysing large, contentious topics such as climate change, ethical dilemmas in medical research and problems posed by technological development (Nelkin 1979; Engelhart and Caplan 1987; Brante et al. 1993; Hess et al. 2008; Kleinman et al. 2010). Some controversy studies have analysed the social sciences, both pure and applied (Fahnestock 1997; Salmon 2000; Ashmore et al. 2005; Vuolanto 2015); in particular, cases such as the so-called 'science wars' and the Sokal affair, which engage the field of science and technology studies itself in the debate, suggest that controversies are a fruitful entry point into the science-society relationship in the social sciences and humanities (Segerstråle 2000; Labinger and Collins 2001).

The central idea of controversy studies has been to analyse all sides of a debate and to symmetrically highlight the views of key participating actors, be they favourable or unfavourable to science as such (e.g. Bloor 1976; Martin et al. 1991; Cassidy 2007). This principle chimes with my intention to study the different views and perceptions of the science-society relationship by concentrating on one controversy in gender research: to study understandings of the science-society relationship among as many actors as possible, regardless of the fact that some of the actors' views stem from a hatred of feminism, gender equality and gender research. Indeed, this pinpointing of hatred of and opposition to science, and the understanding of science's opponents, its proponents and those who stand somewhere in between, is one of my study's contributions to the literature on the science-society relationship.

According to empirical research on the science-society relationship, it has been typical of the social sciences and humanities that their research is targeted at various audiences – including decision makers, public administrators, professionals, and ordinary people and citizens – who are not necessarily such important audiences for other disciplinary groups (Ylijoki et al. 2011). Likewise, it has been discovered that scholars in the social sciences and humanities use various forums to interact with society, including participating in discussions in daily newspapers, sitting on advisory committees, organising professional seminars, having unofficial discussions with policymakers and presenting their research on the Internet (Miettinen et al. 2015). In studies monitoring citizens' understandings of the value of science to society (e.g. Jacobi et al. 2009), the term 'science' is often used in a way that excludes the social sciences and humanities, and hence citizens' expectations of these domains remain largely unknown (Cassidy 2008). This article aims to complement these studies and to provide additional information about how the social sciences' and humanities' relationships with society are understood by a variety of actors – researchers, politicians and social movements – many of whom are neglected in studies that concentrate on researchers' or policymakers' views in less contentious situations, but who in controversial situations are actively engaged in defining the issue (e.g. Gieryn 1999; Cassidy 2007).

To empirically study the relationship between gender research and society, I will apply the idea of research markets developed by Ylijoki et al. (2011). They combined quantitative and qualitative data to distinguish five research markets: academic, corporate, policy, professional and public. The main reference group of the academic market is the scientific community, where the basic objective is to contribute to one's own field by publishing in top-rated journals and other established publication forums. In contrast, the reference group of the corporate market comprises companies, and the aim is to find commercial benefit through patents, unpublished reports and conference papers. In the policy market, public administrative bodies are the main reference group of the research, and policy relevance is highly emphasised as the basic objective through reports targeted at policymakers. The professional market aims to reach professionals and targets professional development. Its main outcomes are reports, guidelines and textbooks for the professional community. Ordinary people are the main reference group of the public market, the objective of which is empowerment. Outcomes for this market are published in popular forums such as newspapers, public events and increasingly the Internet. These markets vary greatly among disciplinary groups: all disciplinary groups are engaged in the academic and public markets; the corporate market is predominant in technological fields; the policy market is typical of the social sciences and medicine; and the professional market is important in disciplines closely related to professions such as medicine, nursing or the law. In this article, I specify the various markets of gender research and trace the demands, hopes and expectations that were addressed to gender research in the *Brainwash* controversy.

3 Research Materials and Methods

3.1 The *Brainwash* Controversy

The case through which I will study the science-society relationship in gender research is the '*Brainwash* debate', which took place in Norway in 2010–2011. In the spring of 2010, *NRK*, the Norwegian broadcasting company, presented a popular science series called *Brainwash* (*Hjernevask* in Norwegian). The series comprised seven programmes: *The Gender Equality Paradox, Parental Effects, Gay/Straight, Violence, Sex, Race*, and *Nature or Nurture*. The first 40-minute programme, *The Gender Equality Paradox*, discussed gender equality in Norwegian workplaces. Its starting point was that gender equality, despite having been on the policy agenda for decades, had not been achieved in the workplace because women continue to choose to become nurses and men to become engineers. In search of the causes of this so-called gender equality paradox, the programme interviewed researchers who favoured biological explanations. They stated that girls choose 'naturally', because of their different brain functions and genes, to care for human beings, whereas boys, for the same reason, take an interest in technical tools and mechanical toys. In addition, the programme also interviewed gender researchers, using sound bites and cutting long interviews short to present these researchers as stating that the explanation of occupation choices in terms of genetics and biology was ridiculous and old-fashioned and stemmed from poor research. In the programme, gender researchers represented actors who understood the selection of occupations as a culturally learned issue rather than as stemming from biology. They stated that cultural milieus coded choices of occupation, and that children were given relatively limited opportunities to choose an occupation. According to them, there were different cultural expectations of boys and girls, and as a result these choices were not made freely and independently, but instead were determined by norms, upbringing and environment.

The programme did not present these researchers' views neutrally. It took the position that the social sciences and humanities, represented by gender researchers, had forgotten about human biology and genetics, and that they explained behaviour only in terms of cultural norms, upbringing and environment (for an overview, see

Lie 2011 and Helland 2014). In other words, the programme neglected the fact that gender research has widely problematised the nature-nurture debate (e.g. Keller 2010; Åsberg and Birke 2010). Gender research has contested the dualisms of 'sex and gender' and 'nature and nurture', and has called for the integration of perspectives and an interpretation of the concept of gender as having both biological and social dimensions (Fausto-Sterling 2000). However, these gender research perspectives were not taken into account in the programme. Additionally, some actors connected the programme with the ending of targeted funding for gender research at the Norwegian Research Council and the closing down of the *Nordic Gender Institute*, both of which coincided with the debate. This gave certain actors a justification for presenting the view that gender research had been terminated in Norway, a 'promised land of gender equality', and for distributing this message to different countries through the Internet. The programme started a lively public debate that continued as more programmes in the series were released. This debate comprises about 3,700 separate published articles (opinion pieces, columns and reportage), several discussion programmes on television and a broad social media discussion.

3.2 Research Material

My research material consists of the *Brainwash* programme series (the versions available on the Internet with English subtitles; see *Hjernevask* 2017), articles in Norwegian newspapers, articles in scholarly journals and blog posts. The programme series was analysed to identify the views and understandings of the different social worlds in the debate. The newspaper material was obtained from *Retriever*, the Norwegian media archive which covers most Norwegian newspapers, both local and national. The data was first sought with the search terms *hjernevask and kjønn* to find the broadest possible data set to analyse (*hjernevask* is the name of the *Brainwash* programme in Norwegian; *kjønn* is gender in Norwegian, encompassing both the English words sex and gender). After the overlapping articles were eliminated, the results of this search totalled 2,012 separate newspaper articles. The articles were mostly from 2010 (1,325), but also extended to subsequent years (in 2011, 171 articles; in 2012, 122; in 2013, 110; in 2014, 90; in 2015, 72). Within this main article corpus, I searched for articles that included the word *kjønnsforskning* (meaning gender research) to find the discussion centring on gender research. This search was conducted with the Adobe Acrobat Reader search tool in the PDF files obtained from *Retriever*. This method revealed 301 articles, forming a core set of research material.

To cover the broader discussion in the social world of researchers in particular, it was also necessary to search for articles in scholarly journals. These were retrieved from *Idunn*, the library database that is the main source for Norwegian scholarly journals, which includes around 26,000 articles. I used the search term *hjernevask* and found 30 articles (the time frame was not limited; those before the programme were not relevant to this study). Blog posts were obtained from 13 separate blogs. These were found through Google searches for *hjernevask* and Harald Eia (the name of the journalist who was the main presenter in the *Brainwash* programme series), and by picking up references to other blogs in the blogs found through the Google search. I also conducted nine interviews with gender researchers during a four-month research visit to the *Centre for Gender Research* at the University of Oslo in the spring and summer of 2015, five years after the *Brainwash* programme had aired. I started by approaching some people from the centre and asking them to point out individuals who would know about the *Brainwash* debate. The interviewees I recruited had been working at a Norwegian gender research centre during the time of the debate and knew about the debate. For anonymity reasons, I will not give more details about the roles of the interviewees with respect to the *Brainwash* debate. The interviews were used as background information for understanding the entire *Brainwash* debate, not as research material.

3.3 Analysis

The analysis focused on the different views expressed in the research material about the relationship between gender research and society. I applied the social worlds framework (Clarke and Star 2008) from science and technology studies, which meant that I centred my analysis on the different meanings that people from different social worlds (Star and Griesemer 1989) attached to the relationship between gender research and society in the arena of the *Brainwash* controversy. The starting point of this framework is that there are "multiplicities of perspective" (Clarke and Montini 1993, p. 45) in any controversy situation. My main research question was: how did participants from different social worlds understand the relationship between gender research and society in the *Brainwash* controversy?

I proceeded with close textual analysis (see e. g. Fahnestock 2009) of the research material. First, I classified the core research material (301 articles) and articles in scholarly journals, treating the writers of the texts as representatives of social worlds. The blog posts all represented the social world of anti-feminists. Second, I eliminated all the texts where the writer could not be identified or was clearly a journalist. This was done in order to concentrate on writings by the actors themselves, rather than on commentary or interpretation by journalists. This process excluded about one-third of the core research material. Third, I read all the material that represented one social world, e. g. all the texts by social scientists and humanities practitioners, or those by anti-feminists. Finally, I analysed the views and perceptions inside each social world by trying to find general patterns and similarities within them. Through this analysis, I started to see the most dominant rhetorical strategies in each social world, that is, the means by which the social world expressed the relationship between gender research and society. I understood these views and perceptions as representing a certain social world, not as an individual's opinion of the issue. The quotations from the texts below are to be read as illustrative examples from the research material, not as the only accounts of one rhetorical strategy. All translations from original texts in Norwegian were done by me.

3.4 Limitations

I recognise that the research material has limitations. My analysis is predominantly focused on textual material from newspapers, scholarly journals and blogs. I spent substantial time among Norwegian gender researchers during the collection of the research material, which no doubt had an effect on my interpretations. This was necessary, however, because I intended to write about a field that was not my own (even though I share a lot of the basic ideas of gender research and am a feminist). I am a Finn who was educated in nursing science, and I did my PhD in sociology, and science and technology studies. I have been involved in research on women in science, but the period at the University of Oslo was my first longer attachment to a gender research community. Without the interviews, I would not have been able to capture the entire debate.

In this article I open up the discussion about the relationship between gender research and society that was interpretable through the research material. However, I do not aim to offer an interpretation of the position of Norwegian gender research as a whole. The *Brainwash* controversy makes possible a science-and-technology-studies-oriented study of the relationship between gender research and society, and my primary intention is to try to interpret, as an outsider to Norwegian gender research and as a science and technology studies scholar, the different ways in which this relationship was understood by the actors in the different social worlds.

I found five social worlds in which the relationship between gender research and society became explicit: gender research, social sciences and humanities, natural sciences, policymaking, and anti-feminism. The social world of journalism was much larger in the debate than those worlds that I was able to analyse in this study.

Journalists wrote articles in which they interviewed various social actors who made statements about the relationship between gender research and society, but it would require an entire separate analysis to study the actors involved in these interviews and their views of gender research.

I was not able to discover the perceptions of the general public (other than in the world of anti-feminism) of the relationship, because there were very few people commenting on it in the research material. There were teachers, experts and artists who did discuss the issue, but they did so without using the word *kjønnsforskning*, which I had used as a search term. The different social worlds of research – those of gender research, social sciences and humanities, and natural sciences – are dominant in the analysis for perhaps the same reason: they made explicit claims about gender research, whereas some other social actors might have participated in the debate but used different terms and forums. For a study of the relationship between gender research and society, this might be a sufficient first step forwards, but for a study of all the actors and their interests in the *Brainwash* debate it presents the tip of the iceberg in that it is limited to the analysis of five social worlds.

I present my analysis of the perceptions of the relationship between gender research and society in five social worlds by answering the following questions. How did the actors in this social world come to the controversy, and what was their position in it? What concerns and fears were expressed regarding the place of gender research in society? What was gender research expected to do in society? I discuss the relationship between gender research and society in the light of different research markets, as proposed in Ylijoki et al. (2011).

4 The Multiple Perceptions of the Relationship between Gender Research and Society in Different Social Worlds

4.1 Gender Research

Actors in the social world of gender research could be identified as gender researchers who were active participants in the debate. They were interviewed in the *Brainwash* programme series, in the newspapers and in multiple public seminars during the debate; they also actively wrote in different forums, such as newspapers, scholarly journals, blogs and books. It must be borne in mind that there were also many gender researchers who publicly remained silent. However, it is telling of the comprehensiveness and breadth of the debate in the media that there were probably no Norwegian gender researchers who were unaffected by its claims, the public attention it brought to gender issues, or the pressure it created to state something about the role of gender research in society. For some gender researchers, the debate might have caused traumas or shifts in their career. One of the major concerns in the social world of gender research was that gender issues would be understood solely within a biological frame, and that the social and cultural frame would be continuously misinterpreted. It was also feared that the role of gender research would be misunderstood and interpreted in the way presented in the *Brainwash* programme: as a field unable to make any improvements to the situation of gender equality in Norway.

As a first rhetorical strategy for explicating the relationship between gender research and society, the social world of gender research emphasised that gender research was an academic domain which through research aimed to understand and make sense of both the biological and cultural aspects of gender, sexuality, inequality and related issues, and that it had also pioneered the explanation and understanding of these issues in different fields of academia, including the social sciences, humanities, technological fields and natural sciences. In this respect, gender research was perceived as a field that had crossed boundaries between academic disciplines and changed the course of research across academic borders: "Gender research today is a collaboration project that contains society, culture and biology." (Gullvåg Holter 2010, p. 5) It was essential in this rhetorical strategy to give the impression that gender research was deeply concerned with these debates and aimed to make an academic contribution through basic research to intensify scholarly understanding of gender issues, in the gender research domain and beyond. Hence in the *Brainwash* debate the social world of gender research was grounded in traditional academic ethos and ideals, aiming to make a contribution to the *academic market*, the reference group of which is the broad scientific community (Ylijoki et al. 2011, p. 733).

There also appeared to be a second strategy for demonstrating the relationship between gender research and society in this social world – namely, to stress that gender research was an ally of society that was helping change society for the better: "These disciplines carry out a truly necessary task for the self-reflection, self-critique and self-correcting of society." (Bjerrum Nielsen 2010, p. 5) Hence gender research was also seen to act as a servant of a gender-equal society and the Nordic welfare state, especially with regard to social problems such as inequalities, vulnerable groups and racism. This type of rhetorical strategy is close to what Ylijoki et al. (2011, p. 734) call the *policy market* of research, which aims to give the impression that gender research produces knowledge that is relevant for policymaking by various decision makers and public administrative bodies. According to my analysis, the academic and policy markets were the main factors in the understanding of the relationship between gender research and society in the social world of gender research.

I could not find traces of corporate, professional or public markets in the social world of gender research. In the case of corporate and professional markets this was not surprising, since gender research was understood as predominantly a social science and humanities domain. Ylijoki et al. (2011) state that the corporate market is most common in technological fields that target the commercial benefits of research, and that professional markets are most common in disciplines that operate in close relationship with professions such as medicine, nursing or social work. However, the absence of the public market is somewhat surprising. In other words, the social world of gender research did not target its message at the general public and did not engage in empowering ordinary people in their lives. This might be interpreted in two ways. First, gender research was in a defensive position in the *Brainwash* controversy, and to some extent gender researchers were forced to present their discipline as academically and socially credible. Second, it would have been typical of this kind of rhetoric that gender researchers would personally engage in explaining the role of gender research through rather informal discussions about sex, gender, inequality or similar themes.

4.2 Social Sciences and Humanities

Besides the social world of gender research, similar understandings of the relationship between gender research and society were expressed inside the social world of other social sciences and humanities fields, representatives of which were also active in the *Brainwash* debate. I was able to identify sociologists, philosophers, literary and cultural scholars, historians, political scientists, anthropologists, philologists, media researchers, and educationalists. It was actually very difficult to distinguish scholars in the social sciences and humanities from those in gender research, and indeed to do so would not do justice to the penetration of gender perspectives into these disciplines. However, the slight differences from the rhetoric of gender research through which the relationship between gender research and society was presented deserve attention.

The academic and policy markets were emphasised as relevant in depictions of the relationship between gender research and society in this social world. However, the academic market was explicated through a rhetoric that emphasised collaboration between disciplinary groups rather than stressing the role of gender research as a strong academic domain in its own right that could act as a change maker (as was stressed in the social world of gender research). In this rhetoric, collaboration across disciplines would bring academic strength and enhance the relevance of research:

> "Natural-science-oriented gender research gives good results, but to be able to illuminate all sides of the gender situation it needs approaches from the social sciences and humanities. The two fields seem to fertilise rather than exclude each other." (Pötzsch 2010, p. 5)

Likewise, the rhetoric of the social world of gender research with regard to the policy market appeared to have a slightly different undertone. Rather than being regarded as an ally of society, gender research was seen as a critical change agent in society with a special ability to highlight – especially for policymakers – the political strategies through which different social actors sought to legitimate their views and actions and to neutralise social power positions and relations. The final similarity between the social world of gender research and that of the social sciences and humanities was that the other research markets – corporate, professional and public – could not be found.

4.3 Natural Sciences

Actors in the social world of natural sciences represented biology, medicine and evolutionary psychology, among other fields. They entered the debate by being interviewed on the *Brainwash* programme, in newspapers or at public seminars. They also wrote opinion pieces in newspapers and scholarly journals. One way of participating in defining the relationship between gender research and society in this social world was for a natural scientist to read a text (article or book) by a gender researcher and then comment on it in a newspaper in the manner of a book review, concentrating on defining what science is and what it is not. A major concern in this social world was that the basic principles of good science would be forgotten in the academic community, and that this in turn would harm the reputation of research. The *Brainwash* programme emphasised the benefits of the natural sciences for the understanding of society, and actors in this social world aligned themselves with the view that gender research must not emphasise the sociocultural environment too much and instead must take into account the findings of the natural sciences.

As a first strategy to explicate the relationship between gender research and society, the social world of the natural sciences stressed the impressiveness of research based on facts, empirical findings and logic. In this strategy, this social world seemed to have the impression that gender researchers had not updated their knowledge about the natural sciences, behavioural genetics, evolutionary psychology, biological and evolutionary sciences, and other related disciplines, and that this had led to a neglect of the basic facts of the natural sciences and the foundation of gender research exclusively on theories rather than empirical research (Mysterud 2011). In this social world, the social and scientific impact of all research, including gender research, should rest on the scientific nature of research, and not on ideological or political wishes or abstract individual feelings:

> "There is hope that the Norwegian researchers that have been criticised in both the [*Brainwash*] programme and book have become more motivated to rid themselves of certain fundamental academic 'duds' that have gone out of date." (Mysterud 2011, p. 237)

The actors in this social world emphasised the traditional academic ethos and ideals of the natural sciences, or "the correct presentation of facts, claims based on empirical data and usual logic" (Gundersen 2010, p. 57), and argued that scientific knowledge must therefore be fundamental to gender research too. This type of understanding of the relationship between gender research and society speaks to what Ylijoki et al. (2011, p. 735) call the *academic market*. However, this particular academic market differs greatly from that presented in the social world of gender research (or the social sciences and humanities). Here it is understood within the frame of natural sciences, emphasising the benefits of deploying the scientific method (or even its world view) rather than having an impact by bringing up gender issues across the academic community as in the social world of gender research.

In this social world, research, including gender research, hardly had relevance to the *policy market* (Ylijoki et al. 2011, p. 734). One way to explicate this was to say that science was not and should not be political if it was to have credibility as a knowledge mediator. In this social world, science aimed to provide knowledge, and its goal was not to set up ethical or political norms in society. It seems that in this social world, policymaking, social planning and decision-making were messy domains to be kept separate from knowledge-making in the scientific domain. The requirement for the credibility and purity of gender research was to keep it politically neutral and not to mingle too much with government bodies, politicians or other decision makers. This finding is not surprising in light of Ylijoki et al.'s (2011, p. 732) claim that in the natural sciences the academic market seems to be especially vital and relations with international academics to be especially fundamental. However, it is interesting that in making claims about gender research, the social world of natural sciences did not acknowledge the variety of demands and hopes pinned on other disciplinary groups, but instead represented the view that the academic market of the natural sciences ought to be generalised to the whole of the academic community. This may be interpreted as a certain unwillingness to see that the relationship between research and society takes in different fields, and a reluctance to admit the various links that different disciplines have in society.

4.4 Policymaking

The *Brainwash* debate extended to various policy issues, especially in science, education, gender equality, health and immigration. The actors in the social world of policymaking were politicians from the different parliamentary parties in Norway. Actors could be identified on the right, centre and left of the political spectrum. They took part in the *Brainwash* debate in interviews on the original programme and in newspapers, in discussions in public and in parliament, and by writing articles and blogs. One of the main concerns within this social world was that the *Brainwash* debate would provide reasons for an opposing party to change Norwegian policies in the wrong direction. This concern stemmed from the fear that the policies that one's own party was fighting or had fought for would be forgotten, neglected or nullified to society's detriment, causing harm to one's supporters. As a consequence, politicians were actively involved in the debate and presented their views about how Norwegian society should be run, what the main concerns and targets of domestic policymaking ought to be, how the policies previously implemented in Norwegian society could be defended, and what Norwegian society should be like in the future.

Two main rhetorical strategies of the social world of policymaking could be identified with regard to the relationship between gender research and society. The first strategy, found especially in the accounts of the representatives of left-wing and centrist parties, was to demonstrate the benefits of gender research to society in terms of increasing educational opportunities for women and other minorities and decreasing different forms of social inequality, and to present the parties that did not see the benefits of gender research as "opposed to knowledge" (Lødrup 2010, p. 4, left-wing party). In this strategy, gender research had helped make society more democratic and open to different people. According to this logic, gender research was valuable to society's policymaking and social planning – in other words, it produced policy-relevant knowledge for the use of diverse public administrative bodies. This is a typical way of understanding what Ylijoki et al. (2011, p. 734) call the *policy market* of research. In this market, knowledge produced by research is valuable for national, regional and local policymaking and for solving social problems. This is a usual way to understand the relationship between research and society in the social sciences and medicine, and it is no surprise that it came up in the social world of policymaking when the actors were discussing gender research, the quintessence of a social science field in this respect.

The second rhetorical strategy in the social world of policymaking was to present the ideological nature of gender research and its character as a politically programmatic discipline:

> "The left wing has kidnapped women's issues, dipped them in its own equality ideology, wrapped them in sacrificial ideas, and now presents the results as a scientific fact. Based on the socialist movement's goal that we should all be equal, the women's movement does not accept either fundamental biological or cultural differences between women and men." (Listhaug 2010, p. 5, populist right-wing party)

These views were typically expressed in the accounts of the right-wing populist party. This strategy stressed that biological differences had been obscured by policies that were driven by current gender research and that strove to reduce inequality, and it claimed that these policies had led to an unrealistic and unfeasible wish for a gender-free society. By contrast with the first strategy, this appeared to be a counter-policy market discourse, as the rhetoric suggested that research should be politically neutral. There seemed to be some aspects of this rhetoric that could also be related to the *corporate market* of research (Ylijoki et al. 2011, p. 733): this rhetorical strategy discussed the credibility of research in monetary terms in that it stated that society should expect value for taxpayers' money from research, and if research was irrelevant or outdated its government funding should be removed. In terms of actual political actions in the *Brainwash* debate, the right-wing populist party did make a case about the funding of Norwegian gender research on the basis of this rhetoric: the Norwegian Minister of Education and Research was approached on the matter. After some months, the news broke that the Norwegian Research Council had ended its funding directed to gender research, and the logical continuation of this rhetoric was to spread the story that Norwegian gender research had been debunked.

The different rhetorical strategies reveal the two different ways of understanding the value of research for society in this social world, and reflect the opposing political parties' views about gender research in particular. Yet both strategies show that the policy market of research is important for this social world, and that the academic and professional markets are less relevant here. What about the public market: why does it not appear here? The reference group of the public market consists of ordinary people and citizens, the very audience to which politicians seek to appeal. It could be interpreted that the social world of policymaking targeted its message at researchers and other policymakers rather than at the general public because it was trying to make sense of the role of gender research in a situation where policies based on it had been questioned. Had the audience been the general public, the message would not have been the same, and the public market might have been more dominant. This might also have to do with the vulnerability of the public market, or an expectation among politicians that the general public would not be very interested in gender research – even though the *Brainwash* debate had proved the opposite.

4.5 Anti-feminism

The actors in the social world of anti-feminism were activists in men's rights and various anti-feminist or anti-democratic social movements. They took part in the *Brainwash* debate especially by writing and commenting in blogs and opinion columns. One of the major concerns of this social world was that science would strengthen views that did not fit or that opposed its own social goals and views. The fear was that science would strengthen the position of the enemies of this social world instead of the position of anti-feminism. Hence the social world of anti-feminism took actions to nullify and debunk gender research, which it saw as a threat to its values concerning men's rights, traditional family values and sexual relations based on male dominance.

One rhetorical strategy used by this social world was to underline the harmfulness of gender research to society, especially its destructive nature in terms of traditional family values and men's rights. Another strategy was to present gender research as unscientific and contrast it with real science by using such terms as 'pseudoscience':

> "Norway's bogus science provoked amusement and incredulity among the international scientific community – especially because it was not supported by any empirical research, was based on mere theory and had no scientific credentials… when confronted with empirical science, the 'Gender Researchers' were speechless, and completely unable to defend their theories against the reality check." (WMSAW 2013, no pagination)

This latter strategy included the portrayal of gender research as based on feelings and theories. The expectation in these strategies was that science would be seen to validate the authority of certain – especially anti-feminist – social groups and would strengthen their social position through that validation. If gender research were to be valuable for society, it would empower the ordinary people who belonged to these social movements. The message of this social world was that gender research had failed to do that empowerment work, and in this way was not answering its expected reference group, the general public.

This understanding of the relationship between gender research and society represents what Ylijoki et al. (2011, p. 735) call the *public market* of research. To put it differently, in the social world of anti-feminism it was hoped and demanded that the relationship between gender research and society would participate in strengthening positions in the struggle between different social groups. The public market seemed to be dominant in the social world of anti-feminism, with no other understandings of the relationship. This was not surprising, because Ylijoki et al. (2011) see the public market as distinguishable from all but the technological fields. What was apparent was that the strong division between the two worlds – the natural sciences on the one hand and the social sciences and humanities on the other – was decisive in the public market. This division was strongly present in the *Brainwash* programme, and was adopted and transferred by different social actors to strengthen their own views – and not only among Norwegian anti-feminist groups: the same rhetoric involving the public market of research also travelled to such countries as Poland, Germany and France to serve the purposes of anti-feminist, anti-democratic and racist groups.

5 Discussion and Conclusion

This article contributes to our understanding of the transformation of universities in the context of one domain, gender research. The analysis highlights the various expectations and hopes pinned on gender research, and hence it strengthens claims that a transformation is indeed taking place in universities, from a detached research system to a more interactive one. The analysis of the research markets in the different social worlds is a helpful tool for tracing this variety. Inside the academic community, views about the relationship between gender research and society largely draw on the impact of knowledge production as such, but even there the relationship with policymaking is emphasised. The closer the actor is to the general public, the more references there are to views that research is meant for ordinary people, to empower their ways and views of living in society. My analysis of the relationship between gender research and society may indicate that the different research markets will also appear in similar ways in other social science and humanities controversy situations. Hopefully, this study opens up ideas for further research, and especially develops ways to analyse contemporary controversies in science and technology studies.

Based on the finding that the professional market seemed to be absent, it could be argued that gender research's linkage to the professional market might be looser than for fields with strong links to professional domains such as medicine, law or nursing. However, Ylijoki et al. (2011, p. 735) argue that "all disciplinary groups have some sort of linkage with some professional fields, but the strength of the relationship varies across them". In line with this argument, it is also possible that the professional research market was not sufficiently strong in gender research to emerge in the *Brainwash* controversy, or at least not as strong as in nursing science, for example, which I have analysed elsewhere (Vuolanto 2017). Therefore it is also likely that in the social world of the general public there might have been teachers or other professionals, for instance, who could have highlighted the professional market in education in schools. This is to be investigated more closely in future studies of *Brainwash* and other debates in gender research.

One contribution of this article has been to show that a controversy situation invokes different interpretations of the science-society relationship with regard to gender research, and also exposes different understandings of the boundaries between scientific knowledge and unscientific knowledge in the public market. It is striking – and telling of the hierarchies of knowledge production – that in the social world of the general public, understandings of the science-society relationship can be targeted *against* some areas of knowledge production while giving weight to other fields of knowledge production. The strong division between the two worlds – the natural sciences on the one hand and the social sciences and humanities on the other – is a powerful tool for devaluing areas of knowledge production, which researchers in all fields need to take into account when they talk about research and science in public. The *Brainwash* debate indicates that the public understanding of research collaborations and interdisciplinary efforts needs to be clarified. This means explaining the relevance of many disciplinary perspectives in knowledge production and respect for the variety of disciplinary traditions to the public. To place this pressure on only one domain (such as gender research) is not fair – it is a responsibility all researchers should take.

For the social world of gender research, the *Brainwash* debate was an occasion when multiple demands and expectations concerning its duties in society became visible. It was a time when there was an attempt to make this domain vulnerable. Referring to such controversies, Grauerholz and Baker-Sperry (2007, p. 287) put it bluntly: "Assume that your words and work will be misinterpreted [in the public domain]." Nonetheless, the rhetorical strategies deployed in the *Brainwash* controversy powerfully illustrate the strength of this domain, and could be applied to other situations and academic disciplines as well. There is a need to continuously demonstrate the power of crossing the boundaries of academic disciplines in a united effort by all disciplines to attract and maintain the academic market, which is becoming more and more important in the face of the pressures (evidenced by this article) arising from the current transformation of the science-society relationship. It is equally important to explicate the mission of the university as a change maker and ally of society, a rhetorical strategy powerfully deployed in the debate by the social world of gender research. The academic community as a whole, including gender researchers, can benefit from learning about these rhetorical strategies.

References

Albert, Mathieu. 2003. Universities and the Market Economy: The Differential Impact on Knowledge Production in Sociology and Economics. *Higher Education* 45 (2): 147–182.

Albert, Mathieu, and Wendy McGuire. 2014. Understanding Change in Academic Knowledge Production in a Neoliberal Era. In *Fields of Knowledge: Science, Politics and Publics in the Neoliberal Age*, ed. by Scott Frickel and David J. Hess, 33–57. Bingley: Emerald Group Publishing Limited.

Ashmore, Malcolm, Steven D. Brown and Katie Macmillan. 2005. Lost in the Mall with Mesmer and Wundt: Demarcations and Demonstrations in the Psychologies. *Science, Technology & Human Values* 30 (1): 76–110.

Blais, Melissa, and Francis Dupuis-Déri. 2012. Masculinism and the Antifeminist Countermovement. *Social Movement Studies: Journal of Social, Cultural and Political Protest* 11 (1): 21–39.

Bjerrum Nielsen, Harriet. 2010. Kriterier i forskning. [Criteria in Research]. *Aftenposten*, 26.3.2010: 5.

Bloor, David. 1976. *Knowledge and Social Imagery*. London: Routledge Direct Editions.

Brante, Thomas, Steven Fuller and William Lynch. Eds. 1993. *Controversial Science. From Content to Contention*. Albany: State University of New York Press.

Cassidy, Angela. 2007. The (Sexual) Politics of Evolution. Popular Controversy in the Late 20th-Century United Kingdom. *History of Psychology* 10 (2): 199–226.

Cassidy, Angela. 2008. Communicating the Social Sciences. In *Handbook of Public Communication of Science and Technology*, ed. by Massimiano Bucchi and Brian Trench, 225–236. London, New York: Routledge.

Clarke, Adele, and Teresa Montini. 1993. The Many Faces of RU486: Tales of Situated Knowledges and Technological Contestations. *Science, Technology & Human Values* 18 (1): 42–78.

Clarke, Adele, and Susan Leigh Star. 2008. The Social Worlds Framework: A Theory/Methods Package. In *Handbook of Science and Technology Studies*, ed. by Edward J. Hackett, Olga Amsterdamska, Michael Lynch and Judy Wajcman, 113–137. Cambridge: The MIT Press.

Derichs, Claudia, and Dana Fennert. 2015. *Women's Movements and Countermovements. The Quest for Gender Equality in Southeast Asia and the Middle East*. Newcastle: Cambridge Scholars Publishing.

Engelhart, H. Tristram, and Arthur L. Caplan. 1987. *Scientific Controversies. Case Studies in the Resolution and Closure of Disputes in Science and Technology*. Cambridge: Cambridge University Press.

Eriksson, Mia. 2013. "Wronged White Men": The Performativity of Hate in Feminist Narratives about Anti-Feminism in Sweden. *NORA: Nordic Journal of Feminist and Gender Research* 21 (4): 249–263.

Etzkowitz, Henry, and Loet Leydesdorff. 1998. The Endless Transition: A "Triple Helix" of University-Industry-Government Relations. *Minerva* 36 (3): 203–208.
Fahnestock, Jeanne. 1997. Arguing in Different Forums: The Bering Crossover Controversy. In *Landmark Essays on Rhetoric of Science: Case Studies*, ed. by Randy Allen Harris, 53–67. Mahwah: Hermagoras Press.
Fahnestock, Jeanne. 2009. The Rhetoric of the Natural Sciences. In *The SAGE Handbook of Rhetorical Studies*, ed. by Andrea A. Lunsford, Kirt H. Wilson and Rosa A. Eberly, 175–195. Los Angeles: Sage.
Fausto-Sterling, Anne. 2000. *Gender Politics and the Construction of Sexuality.* New York: Basic Books.
Gibbons, Michael, Camilla Limoges, Helga Nowotny, Simon Schwartzman, Peter Scott and Martin Trow. 1994. *The New Production of Knowledge: The Dynamics of Science and Research in Contemporary Societies.* London: Sage.
Giebel, Katja, and Gert Röhrborn. 2015. *Anti-Gender Movements on the Rise? Strategising for Gender Equality in Central and Eastern Europe.* Berlin: Heinrich Böll Foundation.
Gieryn, Thomas F. 1999. *Cultural Boundaries of Science: Credibility on the Line.* Chicago, London: University of Chicago Press.
Godin, Benoit. 1998. Writing Performative History: The New "New Atlantis"? *Social Studies of Science* 28 (3): 465–483.
Grauerholz, Liz, and Lori Baker-Sperry. 2007. Feminist Research in the Public Domain. Risks and Recommendations. *Gender and Society* 21 (2): 272–294.
Griffin, Gabriele. 2009. The "Ins" and "Outs" of Women's/Gender Studies: A Response to Reports of Its Demise in 2008. *Women's History Review* 18 (3): 485–496.
Gullvåg Holter, Øystein. 2010. Mellom forskjell og makt. [Between Difference and Power]. *Aftenposten*, 6.4.2010: 5.
Gundersen, Kristian. 2010. Kjønnsforskning tatt på alvor. [Gender Research Taken Seriously]. *Dagbladet*, 23.3.2010: 57.
Helland, Frode. 2014. Rasisme Uten Rasister i Norge. *Agora: Journal for metafysisk Spekulasjon 32* (3–4): 108–143.
Hemmings, Clare. 2011. *Why Stories Matter. The Political Grammar of Feminist Theory.* Durham, London: Duke University Press.
Hess, David, Steve Breyman, Nancy Campbell and Brian Martin. 2008. *Science, Technology, and Social Movements.* In *The Handbook of Science and Technology Studies*, ed. by Edward D. Hackett, Olga Amsterdamska, Michael Lynch and Judy Wajcman, 473–498. Cambridge: The MIT Press.
Hessels, Laurens K., and Harro van Lente. 2008. Re-thinking New Knowledge Production: A Literature Review and a Research Agenda. *Research Policy* 37 (4): 740–760.
Hjernevask. 2017. *"Hjernevask" – English subtitles. Brainwashing in Norway.* Dailymotion. http://www.dailymotion.com/playlist/x1xv47_BrainwashingInNorway_hjernevask-english/1#video=xp0tg8. Accessed: May 10, 2017.
Idunn. Online database. Accessed via University of Oslo Library, June–July 2015.
Jacobi, Anders, Lars Klüver and Mikko Rask. 2009. *Relevant Research in a Knowledge Democracy: Citizens Participation in Defining Research Agendas for Europe.* Paper for the International Conference *Towards Knowledge Democracy, Consequences for Science, Politics and Media*, Leiden, Netherlands, 25–27 August 2009.

Johansson, Evelina, and Mona Lilja. 2013. Understanding Power and Performing Resistance: Swedish Feminists, Civil Society Voices, Biopolitics and "Angry" Men. *NORA: Nordic Journal of Feminist and Gender Research* 21 (4): 264–279.

Keller, Evelyn Fox. 2010. *The Mirage of Space between Nature and Nurture*. Durham: Duke University Press.

Kleinman, Daniel L., Jason Delborne, Karen A. Cloud-Hansen and Jo Handelsman. 2010. *Controversies in Science and Technology Volume 3: From Evolution to Energy*. New Rochelle: Mary Ann Liebert Inc. Publishers.

Labinger, Jay A., and Harry Collins. 2001. *The One Culture? A Conversation about Science*. Chicago, London: University of Chicago Press.

Lie, Merete. 2011. Brainwashing: Taking Another Turn with Biology. *NORA: Nordic Journal of Feminist and Gender Research* 19 (1): 53–58.

Listhaug, Sylvi. 2010. Ikke i mitt navn! [Not in My Name!]. *Dagsavisen*, 8.3.2010: 5.

Lødrup, Julie. 2010. Vi skylder kvinnekampen alt. [We Owe the Women's Movement Everything]. *Dagsavisen*, 10.3.2010: 4.

Martin, Brian, Evelleen Richards and Peter Scott. 1991. Who's a Captive? Who's a Victim? Response to Collins's Method Talk. *Science, Technology and Human Values* 16 (2): 252–255.

Miettinen, Reijo, Juha Tuunainen and Terhi Esko. 2015. Epistemological, Artefactual and Interactional-Institutional Foundations of Social Impact of Academic Research. *Minerva* 53 (3): 257-277.

Mysterud, Iver. 2011. Ekko fra en nyttig Hjernevask. [Echoes from an Advantageous Brainwash]. *Naturen* 135 (5): 235–240.

Nelkin, Dorothy. 1979. *Controversy. Politics of Technical Decisions*. Beverly Hills, London: Sage.

Pereira, Maria do Mar. 2012. "Feminist Theory Is Proper Knowledge, But?...": The Status of Feminist Scholarship in the Academy. *Feminist Theory* 13 (3): 283–303.

Pötzsch, Holger. 2010. Kunstige konflikter [Artificial Conflicts]. *Klassekampen*, 8.3.2010: 16.

Retriever. Online database. Accessed via University of Oslo Library, June–July 2015.

Salmon, Merrilee H. 2000. Anthropology: Art or Science? A Controversy about the Evidence for Cannibalism. In *Scientific Controversies. Philosophical and Historical Perspectives*, ed. by Peter Machamer, Marcello Pera and Aristides Baltas, 199–212. New York, Oxford: Oxford University Press.

Scharff, Christina. 2013. Schröder versus Schwarzer? Analysing the Discursive Terrain of Media Debates about Feminism. *Feminist Media Studies* 14 (5): 837–852.

Segerstråle, Ullica. 2000. *Beyond the Science Wars. The Missing Discourse about Science and Society*. Albany: State University of New York Press.

Skeggs, Beverley. 2008. The Dirty History of Feminism and Sociology: Or the War of Conceptual Attrition. *Sociological Review* 56 (4): 670–690.

Slaughter, Sheila, and Larry L. Leslie. 1997. *Academic Capitalism: Politics, Policies and the Entrepreneurial University*. Baltimore, London: Johns Hopkins University Press.

Star, Susan Leigh, and James R. Griesemer. 1989. Institutional Ecology, "Translations" and Boundary Objects: Amateurs and Professionals in Berkeley's Museum of Vertebrate Zoology, 1907–39. *Social Studies of Science* 19 (3): 387–420.

Tuunainen, Juha. 2005. Contesting a Hybrid Firm at a Traditional University. *Social Studies of Science* 35 (2): 173–210.

Tuunainen, Juha. 2013. Science Transformed? Reflections on Professed Changes in Knowledge Production. In *Organisations, People and Strategies in Astronomy (OPSA 2)*, ed. by André Heck, 43–71. Duttelheim: Venngeist.

Vuolanto, Pia. 2015. Boundary Work and Power in the Controversy over Therapeutic Touch in Finnish Nursing Science. *Minerva* 53 (4): 359–380.
Vuolanto, Pia. 2017. The Universities' Transformation Thesis Revisited: A Case Study of the Relationship between Nursing Science and Society. *Science and Technology Studies* 30 (2): 34–52.
Widerberg, Karin. 2006. Disciplinization of Gender Studies. Old Questions, New Answers? Nordic Strategies in the European Context. *Nordic Journal of Women's Studies* 14 (2): 131–140.
WMASAW. 2013. *What Men Are Saying about Women. Hooray!!! Nordic Countries Defund Gender Ideology.* http://whatmenthinkofwomen.blogspot.fi/2013/04/hooray-nordic-countries-defund-gender.html. Accessed: February 3, 2017.
Ylijoki, Oili-Helena. 2003. Entangled in Academic Capitalism? A Case-Study on Changing Ideals and Practices of University Research. *Higher Education* 45 (3): 307–335.
Ylijoki, Oili-Helena, Anu Lyytinen and Liisa Marttila. 2011. Different Research Markets: A Disciplinary Perspective. *Higher Education* 62 (6): 721–740.
Åsberg, Cecilia, and Lynda Birke. 2010. Biology Is a Feminist Issue: Interview with Lynda Birke. *European Journal of Women's Studies* 17 (4): 413–423.

The Place for Gender Research in Contemporary Portuguese Science and Higher Education Policies within the Context of Neo-liberalism

Amélia Augusto, Catarina Sales Oliveira, Emília Araújo and Carla Cerqueira

Abstract

This article will discuss the place of gender research and gender studies in universities under the current neo-liberal modes of governance. Although gender studies has a considerable history within academia and science, gender studies' contributions in several fields were either kept invisible or just voided. The current neo-liberal rationale has promoted commodification in higher education, individualisation, excessive workloads and performativity in academia. How can these new issues associated with the neo-liberal university be articulated with 'old' issues related to gender inequality and to the affirmation of gender studies? Critically analysing the trajectory of science policymaking and the evolution of gender studies in Portugal as well as gender mainstreaming policies implemented in recent years, we argue that it is possible to promote a gender science policy that is able to resist and ultimately make a transformative difference in the neo-liberal university.

Keywords

Gender, Science Policy, Neo-liberalism, Gender Studies, University, Gender Mainstreaming, Gender Equality Plans

1 Introduction

In recent decades, as a result of transnational influences, the science policies and consequently the higher education policies of European countries (including Portugal), have undergone profound transformations. These have been taking place against a backdrop of neo-liberalisation and the growing precariousness of work and commoditisation, characterised as academic and scientific capitalism. According to Hark (2016), the triangle formed by the state, the market and the university has become completely dominated by neo-liberalism, with the university being increasingly pushed towards the market. The university has become more like a business, increasingly geared towards producing responses to emerging needs dictated by the market's rationales and seeking to position itself in terms of global competitiveness. However, the state, instead of intervening as a regulator, has been creating conditions for market competition, while the market forces the appropriation of state assets (Naidoo 2008 in Naidoo 2016, p. 220). Gill and Donaghue (2016) also believe that the combination of the withdrawal of the state coupled with an increasing individualisation and the introduction of market logic are part of neo-liberalism as a political and economic rationale.[1]

Under these principles, which underpin the capitalist mode of governance, the issues which are targeted for research and the methodologies applied in scientific work as well as in research and educational activities are largely conditioned by the logic of rationalisation, specialisation, accumulation and standardisation (Martins 2015). According to this logic, the impact of science is overshadowed by the principles of internationalisation, indexed publications and patenting. This is a process that puts humanities and social sciences in general under great pressure to align with the ideals and modes of the production of science. This pressure, along with cuts in spending, also threatens some disciplines and creates competition between them, which puts interdisciplinary collaboration, and thus gender studies, in a difficult position (Fahlgren et al. 2016). In fact, gender studies tends to be still seen in the scientific arena as a minority field targeted at women and sexual minorities. At the same time, as noted by Pereira (2016), universities have been the institutions on which the results of such studies have had the least impact. This has happened through structural mechanisms by which the organisations themselves

1 We use here the concept of individualisation to account for the process that results from a growing neo-liberal focus on personal performativity, responsibility and accountability, in which both failures and success are understood as results of personal characteristics (such as autonomy, commitment, self-improvement and work capacity) and not as results of structural constraints (Bal et al. 2014; Waring 2013; Gill and Donaghue 2016; Fahlgren et al. 2016).

and knowledge are idealised which in general terms are based on the idea of the inevitability of the adoption of the model of academic capitalism.

Gender is also marginalised at the level of academic management and strategic orientation, despite all the European Commission efforts to strengthen gender equality awareness. The *She Figures* report (European Commission 2016) shows the low number of European universities with plans for gender equality, and Portugal is not an exception. Taking into account the fundamental presupposition that gender studies has produced a wealth of essential information for the understanding and discussion of multiple levels of inequality that are observed in the worlds of science and education, it is clear that these conclusions have not been the subject of sufficient consideration in the formulation of public policy for science and higher education.

In this article, we will reflect upon and discuss this process, arguing that gender studies is central to the objectives, direction and social purpose of both education and science, as both a driver for the future and for the transformation of societies. The main questions we will discuss in this text include the following: what is the impact, in terms of gender, of the neo-liberal university, increasing individualisation, excessive workload and performativity? How can these new issues associated with a neo-liberal rationale be articulated with 'old' issues related to gender inequality and to the affirmation of gender studies? What is the present situation of gender studies and gender research in Portugal, and what is their future? How can gender equality policies learn from gender research in order to contribute to the construction of a project for a sustainable, fair and affirmative university?

Using the European reality as a guideline, as well as some Portuguese specificities, we will discuss the impacts of neo-liberal policies of science and higher education on the prioritisation of scientific fields and scientific outputs, on the privilege of some modes of production of science, on the depolitisation of gender issues in the university, and ultimately on the possibilities and constraints for the affirmation and consolidation of gender studies. We will also provide a brief outline of the place and the status of gender studies in Portugal, bearing in mind the social context of its emergence and development and also discussing its future possibilities. Finally, we will analyse the recent experiences of gender equality mainstreaming in higher education and research institutions in Portugal from a critical perspective, based on the authors' experience in the implementation, monitoring and evaluation of gender equality plans in Portugal.

2 Pillars of the Contemporary Governance Models of Science and Their Impacts on Academia and Scholars

Gutiérrez-Rodrigues (2016) traces the context of transformations of the university in recent decades. The adoption of the Bologna Process in the early 2000s introduced the necessary conditions for the existence of comparable quality standards in higher education at the European level. More recently the adoption of austerity policies resulting from the post-2008 financial crisis led to cuts in public spending, particularly in education, that are still producing effects, namely in Portugal (Martins 2015). In addition to these aspects, public education has been increasingly subject to commoditisation, which has fostered new formats driven by market logic. A series of transnational and national processes have also transformed the modes of governance of higher education institutions. Many of the transnational changes in governance and in science policy resulted from the will to reconceptualise and reposition universities as institutions subordinate to the needs of the economy and market requirements, promoting a particular understanding of education which favours, above all, the development of a professional and technical profile adequate for the employment market (Pereira 2016).

In this scenario of corporatisation and global competitiveness, there is a proliferation of rating, measurement and quantification systems comparing individuals and universities, whether in research, education or the transfer of knowledge, and these systems score academics in various rankings. Pereira (2016) speaks of performativity schemes designed to monitor individual and institutional performance which according to Burrows (2012) are based on metrics and ranking structures that enable and legitimise a "quantified control" (Burrows 2012 in Pereira 2016, p. 100) of the different types of academic work, throwing many research activities, including publication, into contexts of new proletarianisations. There is a pursuit of excellence and efficiency of a measurable quality, and growing levels of accountability are being implemented. A culture of extensive and penetrating auditing is thus being fostered, aligned with new ideals and new methods for the production of science. It is necessary to publish more, quicker and in top journals and at the same time attract funding, transfer knowledge to both businesses and society, react to an ever-increasing bureaucratic and administrative load, and above all compete. Naidoo (2016, p. 1) says that "universities worldwide are trapped in a competition fetish". This trend has increasingly perverse effects "on the quality of what is researched, on what is published, as well as on the fate of scientific journals" (Rego

2014, p. 330).[2] All this contributes to the promotion of a scenario of decreasing job security and cuts in higher education and in scientific research which is not only typical in Europe or Portugal, but also observable in several other contexts. Gill and Donaghue (2016) believe that the crisis affecting universities, besides being a matter of structural and institutional transformations on a large scale, is also a psychosocial and somatic crisis which is responsible for chronic stress, anxiety, insecurity and exhaustion, accompanied by growing rates of physical and mental illness. This is a set of consequences that Gill (2010, p. 228) called "hidden injuries of the academy". Pereira (2016) also refers to academics who, in contemporary higher education, struggle to manage their workloads, to fulfil unrelenting institutional requirements, to balance family life with their professional life and their personal interests, and to preserve their physical and mental health and their well-being.

As previously mentioned, one of the features of neo-liberalism is an increase in individualisation.

> "In neo-liberalism, people are exhorted to become autonomous, choosing, self-managing and self-improving subjects who are reliable, responsible and accountable – modalities of subjectivity that, we suggest, are highly visible within the contemporary academy." (Gill and Donaghue 2016, p. 92)

As a result of these logics and rationales which place an emphasis on quantified performance and on individual responsibility, academics tend to perceive their difficulty in corresponding to dominant ideals as a personal failure, seeing this not as a result of structural problems, but rather as a result of personal shortcomings. Changes are therefore effected at the individual level, with academics assuming they need to increase their self-discipline and to undergo improvement, apparently choosing to alter their lifestyles in light of growing professional requirements, whilst work increasingly colonises more and more aspects of their lives.

Morley and Crossouard (2016) believe the strong competitiveness which underlies market rationale and logic is fomenting a cognitive capitalism which generates arbitrary inequalities, and that the neo-liberal project for a global academy is producing a set of exclusions and differences, considering that a fundamental difference exists between the leaders and the led. Paradoxically, there is a strong belief that universities are meritocratic and gender neutral, and that achievements or failures should be seen as the result of personal characteristics, since opportunities are available to everyone and are equally distributed. The meritocracy discourse places the emphasis on individualisation and obscures the unequal structures of

2 All translations into English from original texts in Portuguese were done by the authors of this article.

opportunity available to men and women. Husu's work (2004 in Talves 2016, p. 157) about researchers demonstrated how the structural factors determined by gender are hard to recognise, as it seems that women voluntarily accept the spaces institutions granted them, perceiving these positions as their own achievement. As a result, the unequal positions occupied by women seem to be of their own choice, despite being the result of the male structures in which they act. Often, putting family first or assuming the existence of tensions between work and family life are seen as matters of personal choice and not the result of gender-related constraints. Given this, women researchers tend to be considered less involved with professional goals than their male counterparts (Palermo et al. 2008). Talves (2016, p. 160–161) suggests that a strategy of gender neutrality can be used by women as a coping strategy in an environment dominated by men. According to the author, women try to deny gender issues in order to conform to the male order, which allows them to resist the idea of subordination and discrimination, granting them self-esteem.

In her study, the author found a strategy of gender neutrality expressed by the interviewees; they said that there is no difference between men and women and stated that success is not dependent on gender. The individualisation discourse, a trait of neo-liberalism, assumes in the case of gender particular contours, since it contributes to the denial of discrimination resulting from structural and institutional barriers, transforming the results of unequal relations of power into personal problems and the product of individual characteristics.

According to Morley (2006), many women saw in higher education a way to mitigate gender oppression through, for example, social mobility, financial independence, professional identity and academic authority. However, as the author stresses, this experience is accompanied by tensions and contradictions, since women experience a number of discriminatory practices, genderised processes and exclusions within the higher education institutions themselves. In all EU countries, women represent only 15 per cent of full professors, and their underrepresentation is even stronger in grant-awarding bodies, editorial boards and other important forums (Gill and Donaghue 2016).

Several studies show that gender inequalities in science are persistent, particularly among top academic positions, with a scarcity of women in executive positions and in decision-making bodies (Talves 2016).

At the same time the information available about the progress in higher education, with an emphasis on access to and on obtaining a master's degree or higher, suggests an increase in the number of women at these levels of education, in all areas (European Commission 2016). These trends are also observable in Portugal. Increasing numbers of women have had access to education after the 1970s, propelled by political and cultural changes. For example, in 1998 only 7 per cent of women held a higher education degree, but in 2014 it was 19.6 per cent (PORDATA 2016c).[3] The access to higher education after the 1980s was therefore the main factor of women's social mobility, as they could now compete with men in intellectual and administrative professions. For illustration purposes, data available in PORDATA (2016b)[4] indicates that the percentage of women with a diploma (bachelor's degree, master's degree and PhD) was 59.3 per cent in 2014. This was slightly higher than the EU-28 average (57.9 per cent). Also, in Portugal, only 6.7 of the total number of PhDs were held by women in 1970. In 2013, this percentage was 54.8 per cent (PORDATA 2016a).[5] Nonetheless, this has been a long journey, as the road of women with credentials in the labour market is greatly barred by many discriminatory and segregationist processes and mechanisms that are still linked to male domination. This happens across all sectors, with higher incidence in those fields that are more traditionally male dominated, such as science and higher education, and STEM (science, technology, engineering and mathematics) areas. In fact, studies indicate that despite women being more and more present in higher education, their access to decision-making positions is permanently hampered. Amongst other cultural and social barriers within the work contexts, they are still strongly pushed into taking care of household and other tasks related to family well-being. If we look at higher education and science professions, data gives us an account of the permanence of that gender bias. In Portuguese public universities in the 2015–16 academic year, women represented 42 per cent of university teachers but only 33 per cent of associate professors and just 23 per cent of full professors (DGEEC/Med-MCTES 2016). The numbers are very similar in public polytechnics, in private universities and in private polytechnics.

The multiple requirements and tensions between different social roles are clearly more evident for women, especially when there are young children or other family obligations that make it difficult to balance work and family life, largely due to persistent assumptions that domestic and family tasks are women's responsibilities.

---

3 This data refers to the population aged 15 or older. This is published by PORDATA, on the basis of information also published by national government bodies/INE. We would like to add that in 1970, in Portugal, 25.7 per cent of the population/19.7 per cent of the men and 31 per cent of the women/had no advanced educational degree. This number dropped to 5.2 per cent/3.5 per cent of men and 6.8 per cent women in 2011, the last year available (PORDATA 2016d).

4 This data is published by PORDATA, based on information also published by Eurostat, UNESCO-UIS and OCDE. These numbers refer to the percentage of women in the total number of graduates (ISCED 5-8).

5 This data is published by PORDATA, based on information also published by national government bodies/DGEEC/Med-MCTES A.

Time perception and management play important roles here, and time research is important to highlight these questions (Araújo 2015). It is also important to keep in mind that although statistics are important, they do not reveal the full spectrum of inequality. According to Gill and Donaghue (2016), gender inequality has to be analysed in finer detail, particularly in what relates to the differences felt between men and women regarding emotional work in the workplace, the perception that administrative work is unevenly distributed, the particular challenges that women can feel due to working in an environment dominated by men, and the way in which the requirement for self-promotion can promote genderised conflicts. Alongside official reports, it is worth mentioning the discussions and debates that have been held in various settings, including in social networks and other media, such as blogs, about the prevalence of the discrimination and segregation of women in science. The process of review and approval of scientific papers continues to be mentioned as an axis of discrimination against female authors. The same applies to the methods of assessment of projects for funding, including grants. With regard to this, there are discussions concerning the correctness of the criteria used, including what is considered to be an excessive concern with individual curricula in comparison with the quality of the projects themselves, resulting in the favouring of careers that are more linear and accumulative. Another topic which has been more recently discussed refers to the perpetuated stereotyped patterns of relationship with tutors (Boring 2017). Cañibano et al. (2008) highlighted the excessive importance given to international mobility in academic careers, considered a 'rite of passage', which discriminates against women. Morley (2006) also argues that, in addition to the structural barriers of discrimination, the discrimination experienced by informal agents of power should also be taken into account. The author states that many women reported ways in which they were subtly treated as different in gendered corporate cultures, despite their professional status, including the use of sarcasm, jokes, comments or exclusions (Morley 2006). Priola (2007) considers that the changes that are happening in academia coexist with the persistence of a traditional culture based on bureaucratic systems and hierarchies that are associated with the particular configurations of gender relations, highlighting the persistence of a male culture in the institutions of higher education.

To analyse and discuss gender bias in the university can be a difficult task. The theme is hardly seen as a serious matter and the university tends to be seen as the last place where this discussion makes sense, due to its meritocratic connotation. Ahmed (2012, p. 179) uses the concept of "overing" to criticise the idea that gender questions have already been overcome. Gender studies has the potential to identify old and new forms of gender inequality associated with old and new structural barriers of discrimination in universities, demonstrating that gender issues are far from being overcome, stating the need to include a gender dimension in higher education and science policies, which are usually presented as gender neutral. Gender studies can also contribute to the deconstruction of the idea that the lesser participation of women in the leadership of education and research institutions is due to either their lesser interest in assuming the role or being less competent to do so. Knowing that women are, by and large, excluded from leadership roles, they are the biggest losers in this highly competitive, performative and patriarchal environment. From this perspective, deconstructing the prejudices related to the ideal behavioural pattern of leadership, the nature of governance models in question, as well as the mechanisms of selection of the women themselves, gender studies can trigger the implementation of measures that promote women to positions of management, differentiating them and encouraging changes in the time schemes some institutions use that are incompatible with other activities, such as those relating to family or community roles.

In a setting where the governance of higher education institutions is strongly geared towards market logic, global competitiveness, performativity and the quantified assessment of the various aspects of the academic career, there are emerging risks that promise to affect nearly everyone, but which constitute particular risks for women. Morley (2006) considers that the implications of reconciling an academic career with family life can lead to women being seen as a risk for the departments in terms of their contribution to the indexes and productivity rankings, perpetuating and strengthening the discrimination against women in academia. Gill and Donaghue (2016) also claim that the hidden injuries of academia to which they allude affect everyone, but are marked by broader patterns of inequality and injustice with regard to gender, age, class and other social divisions. The authors defend the importance of analysing the gendered impacts of the performativity and surveillance cultures, a field that is still unexplored, and stress that the solution is not merely to increase the number of women. In their view, it is necessary to make a more comprehensive critique of the neo-liberal university.

According to McRobbie (2009 in Morley and Crossouard 2016, p. 155), contemporary neo-liberal cultures tend to produce a re-traditionalisation of gender and a reinstatement of gender hierarchies by means of subtle new forms of patriarchal power. Among these is the privilege of an individualisation logic, which obscures the structural relations of power and undermines the collective political struggle against the structural and institutional barriers that women face in academia. Fahlgren et al. (2016) claim that this process of individualisation can also undermine the possibility of legitimising feminist theory.

We will now discuss the impacts of neo-liberal governance models of science on gender studies as well as the challenges and risks facing its affirmation and consolidation in the current scientific and academic context. We will also describe the Portuguese context of gender studies, providing an analysis of its emergence, trajectories and future prospects.

3 The Impacts of Neo-liberal Governance Models in Science and in the Consolidation of Gender Studies

We have long learned that science development is neither naive nor taken for granted. On the contrary, it is propelled by several interests, inclusively those of scientists themselves moved by the need for recognition, symbolic power and prestige. We argue following Bourdieu (2004) that science is a field of several forces struggling with each other and following the rules of the games as well as the rules of the markets. In other words, and also in line with Bourdieu's theory, science and academia are dynamic realities largely based on power relations and defined, established and cultivated by the different actors alongside their daily practices. Scientific field nominations, as well as topics to be researched and approached within the fields, are products of power relations therefore supporting their own hierarchy and stratification between themselves. In what concerns gender studies and research, its difficult path is immediately visible in the dilemmatic nomination of this field of study which has been intensely debated in recent decades by those working within and outside it. Hemmings (2006) states that choices about the field's name are contested and play out differently across national contexts (Hemmings 2006 in Pereira 2016, p. 108).[6]

The historical development and metamorphoses of academic institutions are therefore not dependent only on the changes in management and administration of this type of organisation. It has to do greatly, though in an invisible and implicit way, with the power relations between scientific areas whose nominations are also a political product of decisions made on the basis of the same presuppositions about

6 It can be argued that women's studies focuses particularly on women's issues and is critically necessary both for intellectual and political reasons. A shift to gender studies that includes a broader interest on how gender affects people and explores both men's and women's experiences can be seen as an attempt to depoliticise feminist scholarship, obscuring women as an oppressed group. However, this is not the case if we think of gender not as a classificatory category but as a relational social structure generating power differentials and thus inequality between men and women. Following Pereira (2012) and Torres et al. (2015), we discuss this field of studies encompassing women's, gender and feminist studies.

what makes a scientific field important, worthy of prestige, funds and incentive to expand. In fact, we should assume that the nominations used to classify scientific areas, despite being possibly grounded on manuals and other official documents (some of them provided by international organisations, such as the *Frascati Manual*[7], and others defined by funding institutions and ministers of science), are mainly conventional; they are social constructions embedded in assumed ideas about how a national system of science and education should look.

Nevertheless, this intertwining of science and higher education is rather tortoise in practice, as models of modes of knowledge management insistently focus on rationalisation modes of operating and quick results. The overemphasis on productivity indicators, specialisation and, above all, the fixation on a science/higher education for a market-driven innovation are being strongly justified in the light of the management models which characterise the new public management of universities and research institutions in Portugal. This tendency is leading to the reconfiguration of scientific fields which struggle for their place and for their legitimacy as areas of knowledge (Martins 2015).

The impact of science is surpassed by the principles of internationalisation, indexed publication and patenting. Humanities and social sciences feel pressured to converge with the dominant and widely adopted models of the production of science. This pressure, along with cuts in spending, places some disciplines under threat and creates competition between them which situates interdisciplinary collaboration, and thus gender studies, in a difficult position (Fahlgren et al. 2016). In this scenario gender research is struggling to gain recognition, but it has long been seen as not proper knowledge (Pereira 2008).

Interestingly, gender studies has the capacity to deconstruct the foundations of these science hierarchies that sometimes are presented as being self-explanatory. To teach and to research gender in an academic context dominated by a male culture that is oriented by neo-liberal goals of performativity is a challenge to all feminist

---

7 In June 1963, the OECD met with national experts on research and experimental development (R&D) statistics at the Villa Falcioneri in Frascati, Italy. The result was the first official version of the Proposed Standard Practice for Surveys of Research and Development, which has come to be better known as the *Frascati Manual*. The *Frascati Manual* is the internationally recognised methodology for collecting and using R&D statistics. The term R&D covers three activities: basic research, applied research and experimental development. It provides an internationally accepted definition of R&D and a classification of its component activities. The manual also organises the field of science into main categories and subcategories. The definitions provided by the *Frascati Manual* have been adopted by many governments and serve as a common language for discussions of science and technology policy. In 2015 the 7th edition was published.

scholars. But this challenge is not without risk, both to scholars and to the field of gender studies. As Hark (2016) points out, how feminist knowledge is permeated by academic structures and conventions and by higher education policies has barely been addressed. Yet, she states, we urgently need to ask what kind of research in gender will survive the transformation of universities into entrepreneurial entities. And, we add, what kind of risks are academic women in general and feminist scholars in particular facing due to this neo-liberal mode of science production?

Kašić (2016) says that more and more feminist scholars in Croatia and elsewhere, in order to efficiently respond to imposed professional demands, tend to integrate some neo-liberal norms such as self-surveillance monitoring and self-discipline in their own academic routines. The need to address the increasing levels of performativity leads to a focus on individual careers. Therefore, feminism has become a way of advancing individual careers, rather than a call for collective activism or transformation.

So we must ask to what extent gender studies in academia has boosted the questioning and the transformation of the existing frameworks and modes of knowledge production, which cannot be separated from the analysis of the place and the status of gender studies in academia. As we have discussed, in a scenario of corporatisation and global competitiveness fostered by a neo-liberal rationality and where some scientific fields are judged to be more efficient and proficient than others, gender studies faces a difficult position, since it seems to be more vulnerable to all these changes. In addition to being an academically young subject, and still with little recognition (Hark 2016), operating in a male-culture-dominated environment and having to confront the depolitisation of gender issues brought by neo-liberal discourses, gender studies is mainly conducted by women who, as we have discussed, are particularly affected by the risks raised by these new ideals and models of science production.

The logic of the neo-liberal rationale leaves little or no room for the allocation of resources (financial, but not only) to scientific fields that are not seen as generators of competitiveness. As Grove suggests, gender equality is not an indicator on any table of the top league of universities. Success in these rankings does not seem to require that attention be paid to gender (Grove 2013 in Morley and Crossouard 2016, p. 153).

In what concerns the place and status of gender studies, the Portuguese case presents some particular features. While other countries have assisted in a proliferation of gender research projects and the creation of numerous courses and research centres in this area from the 1960s and 1970s onward, Portugal began this journey later on, starting in the late 1980s and with a major expansion in the past decades (Amâncio 2003; Silveirinha 2004; Nogueira 2001).

> "Only from that time on, it [gender studies] starts to consciously formulate itself as gender studies and from an innovative perspective of rediscovery or new readings of the reality." (Silva 1999, p. 17)

Amâncio (2003) highlights several factors that contributed to this specificity of the Portuguese context: women's rights organisations arose only in the 1970s but were still invisible after a long dictatorial period in which the historical memory of feminism seemed to be absent; additionally, the Portuguese population had a low educational level (another result of the *Estado Novo* regime that further penalised women) and the financial situation of higher education institutions continued to have investment difficulties until the 1990s. Joaquim (2007) mentions that this field of study is related to the institutionalisation of feminism, particularly through the creation of the Commission of Women in 1977. This institution began with studies on women, first focusing on women who have distinguished themselves in various areas, and then from the 1980s onward focusing on anonymous women (Vaquinhas 2002). It is also about this time that women started entering academia, having more visibility as a group from the 1990s onward and representing in recent years "a notorious outbreak in universities" (Vaquinhas 2002, p. 207).

Amâncio (2003) also mentions several initiatives that contributed to the creation of what is gender studies in Portugal nowadays, always stressing the dispersion of projects and activities within the social sciences and humanities. As stated by Torres et al. (2015), despite the proliferation of books and articles resulting from research in the field, institutionalisation in the academy has been slow, marked by many difficulties and encountering some resistance. According to Pereira (2016), it was common to hear Portuguese academics state that gender studies had no value or relevance which created significant obstacles to the emergence and development of gender education and research in Portugal. In recent years gender studies focusing on gender equality has encountered more space to evolve, mainly due to the growing social visibility of the theme, particularly the issue of domestic violence. At the same time other areas continue to face resistance and even are at risk of being absorbed. In this respect Joaquim (2007) claims that it is important to legitimise women's studies as the result of the historical fight for women's rights and citizenship.

The existence of working groups on gender in major scientific associations of research has contributed towards enlarging the debate and ultimately the reinforcement of the field. Among the scientific areas that have promoted more gender studies in Portugal is, remarkably, sociology. The sociology of gender, although relatively new (as is Portuguese sociology itself, since it was born only in the 1970s due to the social historical condition of the dictatorial regime), is responsible for much of the studies on gender in the past decades as we can easily see in the proceedings of the National Sociology Association's congresses (Rodrigues 2009). Many gender researchers are sociologists. On the one hand, and until the 1990s, the study of gender in sociology tended to be strongly associated with the field of sociology of the family, and subjects such as, for example, masculinities were completely absent (Rodrigues 2009) which indicates a certain conservatism. On the other hand, the emergence in 1999 of the Portuguese Association of Studies on Women and more recently some graduate courses and projects funded in this area have strengthened the importance of gender studies in the academy. We are currently witnessing the emergence of a renewed interest in this area, which is not unrelated to recent (mainly European) research funding incentives in this field.

Fahlgren et al. (2016, p. 121) say that the specific training and research in gender studies is carried out in many universities in "a room of their own" such as a centre or a department of gender studies in the university. This has not been the case of gender studies in Portugal, since gender training and research, as we have shown above, has been carried out by researchers located in various disciplinary fields of social sciences, as is the case with sociology, and as part of personal research agendas. Therefore, gender studies in Portugal is still a relatively dispersed field. Its importance, configuration and institutionalisation vary by institutions, as well as by scientific areas. Only as recently as 2012 was the first interdisciplinary centre for gender studies – the *Centro Interdisciplinar de Estudos de Género* – created in Portugal, a centre that is entirely dedicated to this subject and currently recognised by *Fundação para a Ciência e a Tecnologia*, which is the main science and research public funding institution in Portugal. *Centro Interdisciplinar de Estudos de Género* researchers mainly have a social and human sciences background but the basis for an environment of interdisciplinary cooperation is set, and it is assumed as one of the purposes of the centre (Torres et al. 2015). This was an important step to foster the development of gender research from an interdisciplinary perspective and to claim a scientifically recognisable and recognised space for gender research. In fact, the aim of creating this centre and the concern of researchers involved in it was to establish a basis to overcome the fragmentation and lack of recognition that gender studies has long faced in the Portuguese academy. It is, however, interesting to note that to achieve that recognition the (possibly inevitably) chosen path was to lead gender studies to achieve excellent results in the main performance indicators of the neo-liberal university. The recognition that gender studies could have financial and institutional value made it more valuable in a context of changing scientific policies and extremely large education cutbacks.

There is, in contemporary Portuguese academia, an increasing public recognition of the epistemic status and relevance of gender research (Pereira 2016). Nevertheless, according to the author, the institutional positioning of this area in Portugal is still relatively marginal and precarious, and its epistemic status is not fully recognised which makes feminist scholars susceptible of being dismissed. "Thus, negotiations of the epistemic status of women, gender and feminist studies are ongoing, unrelenting and extremely arduous." (Pereira 2016, p. 102)

Gender studies in Portugal – but mainly gender studies focusing on gender equality – has been representing an important background of gender mainstreaming, mostly in areas of work and social policy in general. In recent years all over Europe as a result of the impetus of gender mainstreaming several universities and research centres have developed their own gender equality plans (EIGE 2016b). There was a new initiative in Portugal as recently as 2011, so it is timely and important to reflect upon its impacts and to discuss to what extent gender mainstreaming in the academy incorporates the main questions and positioning brought by gender studies and effectively contributes to a transformative difference in the neo-liberal university. In the next section we will analyse the relation between gender mainstreaming and gender studies with a focus on the Portuguese experience of implementing a university gender equality plan.

Still it is important to highlight that gender studies also produces impacts when addressing cutting-edge research without any immediate application. Therefore, despite trends being directed towards accountability and continuous enhancement, gender studies is called on to develop innovative epistemological and theoretical ideas able to provide answers to complex and sometimes unforeseen questions.

4 The Gender Mainstreaming Perspective: Part of the Solution or Part of the Problem?

Due to the recognition of the existence of gender biases and of a frankly unfavourable context to the entry and progression of women in the labour market in general and in scientific careers in particular, in the past years many European countries have implemented work legislation that promotes equality and other specific measures and strategies that promote gender equality. The Council of Europe has assumed a very strong position recommending gender mainstreaming as a strategy to achieve gender equality (EIGE 2016b, 2016c; Lipinsky 2014) highlighting that performance assessment models shall be revised and the need for institutions to develop a cultural change. In framing the definition and implementation of these measures, the Council of Europe has encouraged the implementation of gender equality plans in a wide array of work organisations, including universities and higher education and research institutions. A gender equality plan is an instrument of organisational management that seeks to streamline institutional change from a gender-mainstreaming angle. In this sense, it is expected that the success of the plan corresponds to a real change in organisational culture in terms of parity (Sales Oliveira and Villas-Boas 2012).

In 2009, when the University of Beira Interior started working towards the development of a gender equality plan whose design and implementation some of us were responsible for, it represented a pioneering initiative at the national level. Up until then, no other Portuguese university had any organisational intervention in this area, unlike their European counterparts, namely in neighbouring Spain (Sales Oliveira and Villas-Boas 2012). However, it is important to say that in Portugal, differently from the majority of the countries that implemented this measure, implementing gender equality plans at universities and research centres is not mandatory by law which is to say that University of Beira Interior's initiative was completely voluntary.

Gender mainstreaming in Portugal is still considered to be in the stage of preliminary measures. Under the National Equality Plans, until very recently universities were not contemplated, in great part due to generally being considered gender-neutral institutions. On the subject of the implementation of gender mainstreaming in Portugal, Ferreira (2011, p. 51) points out:

> "The degree of implementation of these policies at the national level is low, and the explanation for this discontinuity is rooted, at least in part, in the fact that the governing elites and state bureaucracies see the issue as a foreign imposition with few internal benefits."

University of Beira Interior is currently an institution that has a gender equality plan in place which is not the same as saying that it is already an egalitarian institution. The limitations of a gender equality plan in a university setting became progressively clear throughout the project. From the onset, there were initiatives that were not provided for in the funding typology, but which are essential in the university context such as publication and dissemination through scientific events. Additionally, there was a need to involve all groups, namely the students who are the soul of the organisation, and not just the people who work there such as academics and other workers. There were also the specificities of the university as an institution to take into consideration, with the differences between the management and the hierarchical academic logic; on top of that there were the idiosyncrasies of the various academic career paths.

All these specificities are starting to be taken into account through several networks and developed projects and tools such as, for example, the recent launch of

GEAR[8] (EIGE 2016a) in which we were involved. Thus, currently the decision to set up a gender equality plan in a university is better supported by the counterparts' experiences and research on this subject. Still, from our point of view, the core of the issue is deeper. While gender mainstreaming is still pointed out by many as a promising pathway to gender equality, for its potential transversal applicability to the governance of institutions (Hoard 2015), it is also questioned (Daly 2005; Rees 2005; Walby 2005) as something vague and lacking in achievement. Having analysed its results, some authors, including feminists, see the gender mainstreaming strategy as having limitations (Walby 2004). Daly (2005) points out that, despite the various measures that have been implemented, gender mainstreaming has not managed to produce social change, and institutions carry on being guided by policies and by a culture that oscillates between traditional values and the emerging neo-liberalism. The implementation of gender mainstreaming has been conducted by technocrats and not by the civil society movements which have always identified themselves with the cause of women's rights. Another critical claim argues that gender mainstreaming sits comfortably within a neo-liberal logic of flexibility (Bacchi and Eveline 2010). From our point of view another limitation of gender mainstreaming is the main focus on a binary (women/men) vision of gender and not including the diversity and richness of the field.

Walby (2004) refers to a sustained resistance when addressing the introduction of gender equality policies in organisations, particularly in organisations where the dominant culture is a patriarchal one, as is the case with universities. This sustained resistance was encountered at University of Beira Interior, both at an institutional level and at the individual level. Despite some gender concerns having been integrated into part of the existing structures, we are still far from actually transforming those structures in the sense of influencing the policies and agenda-setting of the university.

---

8 *GEAR*, meaning *Gender Equality in Academia and Research*, is a web platform designed for the support of European academic and research institutions aiming to implement gender mainstreaming, namely a gender equality plan. For more information, see http://eige.europa.eu/gender-mainstreaming/toolkits/gear.

5 Concluding Remarks

Remembering our initial questions and addressing the impact in terms of gender at the neo-liberal university, it becomes clear that transformations in higher education and in science policies that are occurring in a scenario of neo-liberalisation, individualisation, precarisation of labour and commodification of education not only have impacts on scholars, as teachers and researchers, but are also threatening the expected development and consolidation of gender studies in academia. This neo-liberal scenario in part neglects gender studies and/or demands their adequacy to the prevalent academic orientation towards results and achievements measurements, depriving them of their heuristic and transformative potential.

In what concerns the present and future for gender studies in Portugal, we saw that despite the growth of work and publications in this area and the recent creation of an interdisciplinary centre exclusively dedicated to gender research, we can say that the field still suffers from scientific underestimation although important changes are being made. This is clear at the level of policymaking, considering the small amounts of national funds given to research within this field. Inside higher education institutions, mostly administered by men, gender studies still needs further recognition which is somehow concomitant with what happens with social sciences and humanities in general. This underestimation is not only anchored in the cultural values and the strong resistance of gender stereotypes that largely pervade the academy (Sales Oliveira and Villas-Boas 2012), but is also linked with the structure of the field, its strong feminisation and the subjects of research (private life, family, sexualities, care issues), still perceived as women's or minority matters, which strongly contributes to the mainstream vision of this scientific field as less valuable, less competitive and less important. Additionally, the path gender studies was making in order to achieve recognition became more difficult with the emergence of the capitalist university, so gender research also has to struggle with the dilemma of whether to contest neo-liberal values and risk becoming even more marginal or to accept the rules and try to position itself in the dominant setting. So we can conclude that new issues associated with a neo-liberal rationale are articulated with 'old' issues related to gender inequalities such as the unequal participation of men and women or the work and family balance.

This state of affairs is contradictory to the growing importance given to gender equality by the European Council and the proliferation of projects promoting gender mainstreaming in higher education and research institutions. To profit from these opportunities meant that gender researchers need to sympathise and accept the gender mainstreaming concept and philosophy which is not always the case. In fact, several authors consider that gender mainstreaming is not part of the solution but part of the problem, since it tends to align with the status quo instead of effectively discussing it (Walby 2004; Daly 2005). In order to develop a gender mainstreaming effectively informed by the contributions of gender studies, it is important to enlarge the perspective through which gender studies are addressed by gender mainstreaming and therefore assuring its critical and transformative standpoint, and not only the integration of gender equality issues in organisations, without questioning and deconstructing structural and institutional orders of power and discrimination.

Today, as before, gender studies aims to identify and make visible the structural and institutional orders of power, to deconstruct the dominant assumptions, and to identify inequality and discrimination. Its contribution has the potential to not only understand but also to resist and ultimately make a transformative difference in the neo-liberal university. However, can this be done from a peripheral standpoint? Probably not.

Until now, gender studies has managed to balance the commitment to the aim of the field with the production of the demanded outputs of contemporary academia. An example of that is the activist work developed by scholars and researchers simultaneously with the increase in publications. Nevertheless, we cannot say that the impacts of gender studies in the contemporary academy are such that they managed to change the actual scenario and circumstances from within, questioning and overall transforming the existing frameworks and modes of science production. It is a difficult balance, since the dominant logic of individualisation tends to absorb and destroy diversity and inclusiveness features, so the subjugation to the neo-liberal mode of governance will eventually undermine the aim and character of the field.

In this scenario, it is important to promote an open debate and analyse the undergoing changes in European universities, because their transformations are closely linked with the actual and future status of gender studies and with the possibilities of resistance and transformation brought by gender research.

References

Ahmed, Sarah. 2012. *On Being Included: Racism and Diversity in Institutional Life*. Durham: Duke University Press.

Amâncio, Lígia. 2003. O género no discurso das ciências sociais. *Análise Social* 38 (168): 687–714.

Araújo, Emília R. 2015. O tempo dos (para) os docentes e pesquisadores numa perspetiva do gênero. *Revista Ártemis* XX (ago–dez): 39–56.

Bacchi, Carol, and Joan Eveline. 2010. *Mainstreaming Politics: Gendering Practices and Feminist Theory*. Adelaide: University of Adelaide Press.
Bal, Ellen, Erella Grassiani and Kate Kirk. 2014. Neoliberal Individualism in Dutch Universities: Teaching and Learning Anthropology in an Insecure Environment. *Learning and Teaching* 7 (3): 46–72.
Boring, Anne. 2017. Gender Biases in Student Evaluations of Teaching. *Journal of Public Economics* 145 (Issue C): 27–41.
Bourdieu, Pierre. 2004. *Science of Science and Reflexivity*. Cambridge: Polity Press.
Cañibano, Javier Otamendi and Inés Andujar. 2008. Measuring and Assessing Researcher Mobility from CV Analysis: The Case of the Ramón y Cajal Programme in Spain. *Research Evaluation* 17 (1): 17–3.
Daly, Mary. 2005. Gender Mainstreaming in Theory and Practice. *Social Politics: International Studies in Gender, State & Society* 12 (3): 433–450.
DGEEC/MEd-MCTES 2016. *Perfil do Docente*, 2015. http://www.dgeec.mec.pt/np4/np4/np4/EstatDocentes/%7B$clientServletPath%7D/?newsId=138&fileName=DGEEC_DSEE_DEEBS_DEES_2016_PerfilDocente.pdf. Accessed: August 12, 2016.
EIGE. 2016a. *Gender Equality in Academia and Research: GEAR Tool*. Vilnius: EIGE.
EIGE. 2016b. *Integrating Gender Mainstreaming in Academia and Research Institutions: Analytical Paper*. Vilnius: EIGE.
EIGE. 2016c. *Positive Impact of Gender Mainstreaming in Academia and Research Institutions: Opinion Paper*. Vilnius: EIGE.
European Commission. 2016. *She Figures 2015*. https://ec.europa.eu/research/swafs/pdf/pub_gender_equality/she_figures_2015-leaflet-web.pdf. Accessed: August 14, 2016.
Fahlgren, Siv, Katarina Giritli-Nygren and Angelica Sjöstedt Landén. 2016. Resisting "Overing": Teaching and Researching Gender Studies in Sweden. *Women's Studies International Forum* 54: 119–128.
Ferreira, Virgínia. 2011. Os planos para a Igualdade nas organizações e a estratégia de mainstreaming. In *Atas do seminário: Igualdade de Género – Responsabilidade Social e Cidadania*, ed. by Catarina Sales Oliveira and Susana Villas-Boas, 49–53. Covilhã: Universidade da Beira Interior.
Gill, Rosalind. 2010. Breaking the Silence: The Hidden Injuries of the Neoliberal University. In *Secrecy and Silence in the Research Process: Feminist Reflections*, ed. by Róisín Ryan-Flood and Rosalind Gill, 228–244. New York, London: Routledge.
Gill, Rosalind, and Ngaire Donaghue. 2016. Resilience, Apps and Reluctant Individualism: Technologies of Self in the Neoliberal Academy. *Women's Studies International Forum* 54: 91–99.
Gutierrez-Rodriguez, Encarnación. 2016. Sensing Dispossession: Women and Gender Studies between Institutional Racism and Migration Control Policies in the Neo-liberal University. *Women's Studies International Forum* 54: 167–177.
Hark, Sabine. 2016. Contending Directions. Gender Studies in the Entrepreneurial University. *Women's Studies International Forum* 54: 84–90.
Hoard, Season. 2015. *Gender Expertise in Public Policy: Towards a Theory of Policy Success*. Basingstoke: Palgrave Macmillan.
Joaquim, Teresa. 2007. Feminismos, Estudos sobre as Mulheres ou "para onde vai este barco?". In *O longo caminho das mulheres: feminismos 80 anos depois*, ed. by Lígia Amâncio, Manuela Tavares, Teresa Joaquim and Teresa Almeida, 203–216. Lisboa: Dom Quixote.

Kašić, Biljana. 2016. "Unsettling" Women's Studies, Settling Neoliberal Threats in the Academia: A Feminist Gaze from Croatia. *Women's Studies International Forum* 54: 129–137.
Lipinsky, Anke. 2014. *Gender Equality Policies in Public Research*. Brussels: European Union Publications.
Martins, Moisés. 2015. Repensar a política científica em Portugal – sugestões a partir da área de Ciências da Comunicação Carta ao ministro da Ciência e Tecnologia. *Revista Lusófona de Estudos Culturais* 3 (2): 361–365.
Morley, Louise. 2006. Hidden Transcripts: The Micropolitics of Gender in Commonwealth Universities. *Women's International Forum* 29: 543–551.
Morley, Louise, and Barbara Crossouard. 2016. Gender in the Neoliberalised Academy: The Affective Economy of Women and Leadership in South Asia. *British Journal of Sociology of Education* 37 (1): 149–168.
Naidoo, Rajani. 2016. The Competition Fetish in Higher Education: Varieties, Animators and Consequences. *British Journal of Sociology of Education* 37 (1): 1–10.
Nogueira, Conceição. 2001. *Um novo olhar sobre as relações sociais de género: Feminismo e perspectiva crítica na psicologia social.* Lisboa: Fundação Gulbenkian.
Palermo, Simona, Elisabetta Giuffra, Valeria Arzenton and Massimiano Bucchi. 2008. *EMBO reports* 9 (6): 494–495.
Pereira, Maria do Mar. 2008. The Epistemic Status of Women's, Gender, Feminist Studies: Notes for Analysis. In *The Making of European Women's Studies: Volume VIII. A Work in Progress Report on Curriculum Development and Related Issues in Gender Education and Research*, ed. by Berteke Waaldijk, Else van der Tuin and Mischa Peters, 145–156. Utrecht: Athena.
Pereira, Maria do Mar. 2012. "Feminist Theory Is Proper Knowledge, But…" The Status of Feminist Scholarship in the Academy. *Feminist Theory* 13 (3): 283–303.
Pereira, Maria do Mar. 2016. Struggling Within and Beyond the Performativity University: Articulating Activism and Work in "Academia Without Walls". *Women's Studies International Forum* 54: 100–110.
PORDATA. 2016a. *Mulheres doutoradas em Portugal*. http://www.pordata.pt/Portugal/Mulheres+no+total+de+doutoramentos+(percentagem)-682. Accessed: August 8, 2016.
PORDATA. 2016b. *Mulheres graduadas em Portugal*. http://www.pordata.pt/Europa/Mulheres+no+total+de+diplomados+no+ensino+superior+(ISCED+5+8)+(percentagem)-1664. Accessed: December 5, 2016.
PORDATA. 2016c. *População residente do sexo feminino com 15 e mais anos por nível de escolaridade completo*. http://www.pordata.pt/Portugal/Popula%c3%a7%c3%a3o+residente+do+sexo+feminino+com+15+e+mais+anos+por+n%c3%advel+de+escolaridade+-completo+mais+elevado+(percentagem)-885. Accessed: December 5, 2016.
PORDATA. 2016d. *Taxa de analfabetismo total e por sexo*. http://www.pordata.pt/Portugal/Taxa+de+analfabetismo+segundo+os+Censos+total+e+por+sexo-2517. Accessed: December 5, 2016.
Priola, Vicenza. 2007. Being Female Doing Gender. Narratives of Women in Education Management. *Gender and Education* 19 (1): 21–40.
Rees, Teresa. 2005. Reflections on the Uneven Development of Gender Mainstreaming in Europe. *International Feminist Journal of Politics* 7 (4): 555–574.
Rego, Teresa C. 2014. Produtivismo, pesquisa e comunicação científica: entre o veneno e o remédio. *Educação e Pesquisa* 40 (2): 325–346.

Rodrigues, Elisabete. 2009. *O lugar do gênero, dos homens e das mulheres na sociologia portuguesa: uma análise a partir da Associação Portuguesa de Sociologia*. CIES e-Working Paper No. 64 (unpub.). http://cies.iscte-iul.pt/destaques/documents/CIES-WP64_Rodrigues.pdf. Accessed: July 14, 2016.
Sales Oliveira, Catarina, and Susana Villas-Boas. 2012. Igualdade de Género na Universidade da Beira Interior. *Ex aequo* 25: 119–136.
Silva, Manuela. 1999. *A Igualdade de Género, Caminhos e Atalhos para uma Sociedade Inclusiva*. Lisboa: Comissão para a Igualdade e para os Direitos das Mulheres.
Silveirinha, Maria João. 2004. Os media e as mulheres: horizontes de representação, de construção e de práticas significantes. In *As mulheres e os media*, ed. by Maria João Silveirinha, 5–12. Lisboa: Livros Horizonte.
Talves, Kari. 2016. Discursive Self-Positioning Strategies of Estonian Female Scientists in Terms of Academic Career and Excellence. *Women's Studies International Forum* 54: 157–166.
Torres, Anália, Diana Maciel and Helena Sant'Ana. 2015. *Estudos de Género numa perspetiva interdisciplinar*. Lisboa: Mundos Sociais.
Vaquinhas, Irene. 2002. Linhas de investigação para a história das mulheres nos séculos XIX e XX. Breve esboço. *Revista da Faculdade de Letras. História* III (3): 201–221.
Walby, Sylvia. 2004. The European Union and Gender Equality: Emergent Varieties of Gender Regime. *Social Politics: International Studies in Gender, State & Society* 11 (1): 4–29.
Walby, Sylvia. 2005. Gender Mainstreaming: Productive Tensions in Theory and Practice. *Social Politics: International Studies in Gender, State & Society* 12 (3): 321–343.
Waring, Matthew. 2013. All in This Together? HRM and the Individualisation of the Academic Worker. *Higher Education Policy* 26 (3): 397–419.

On the Use of Innovation Arguments for Getting Gender Research into STEM[1]

Sigrid Schmitz

Abstract

Recent international top-down initiatives invoke the integration of sex and gender into the governance of all fields of science and technology, from funding to research and development to publication policies, and to the assessment of the impact of scientific knowledge and technical products in society. But how can these initiatives be assessed relative to the call for a new governance of science and technology by inter-disciplinary research? The *Gendered Innovations* project is a main resource for these governmental actions. This article elaborates on contents and concepts of 'gendered innovations' in relation to the findings and scope of knowledge available from feminist science and technology studies. It contrasts the separation of sex and gender in this project with current changes in dialogue between feminist science and technology studies, and science, technology, engineering and mathematics fields that can guide transdisciplinary exchange and the acknowledgement of research for sex/gender interactions and intersectional categories. Finally, the strategic invocation of innovation is questioned and the article offers approaches to include feminist epistemologies and postcolonial perspectives in science, technology, engineering and mathematics.

1 STEM stands for Science (including Biomedicine), Technology, Engineering, and Mathematics.

Keywords

Feminist Science and Technology Studies, Gendered Innovations Project, Sex/Gender, Governance of STEM, Innovation, Intersectionality, Postcolonial Perspectives, Feminist Epistemologies

1 Sex and Gender in STEM: A Window of Opportunities for Governing Science?

In September 2015, the *League of European Research Universities (LERU)*,[2] published an advice paper titled *Gender Research and Innovation: Integrating Sex and Gender Analysis into Research Processes* (Buitendijk and Maes 2015). Likewise, the *European Research Area Roadmap (ERA)* (European Union 2015)[3] and the guidelines from the US *National Institutes of Health (NIH)* (NIH 2016)[4] have put the inclusion of sex and gender on the agenda for funding and publication policies. These recent top-down initiatives from leading academic and funding institutions consider sex and gender research as innovative for science and technology; the results, in turn, should inform the governance of these fields at several levels. Firstly, the inclusion of gender research can promote cultural change within science, technology, engineering and mathematics fields, which is a necessary prerequisite for the better inclusion of female scientists, the latter being a motor for achieving excellent research in international competition (European Union 2015; Buitendijk and Maes 2015). Secondly, the integration of sex and gender aspects into health research and therapy could

2 The *LERU*, a consortium of 21 research universities established in 2002, aims at "furthering the understanding and knowledge of politicians, policymakers and opinion leaders about the role and activities of research-intensive universities" (League of European Research Universities n.d.).

3 Part of the European research funding programme, the *ERA Roadmap's* "purpose is to identify a limited number of key implementation priorities which are likely to have the biggest impact on Europe's science, research and innovation systems" (European Union 2015, p. 13–14). "Gender equality and gender mainstreaming in research" is positioned as priority 4 (amongst 6) for funding applications in *Horizon 2020*.

4 Part of the United States Department of Health and Human Services, the *National Institutes of Health* is the US major funding agency for medical research. It calls for the integration of sex and gender into the governance of health-related issues (National Institutes of Health 2016).

reduce costs in the health sector caused by inadequate diagnoses and treatments (Buitendijk and Maes 2015; NIH 2016). Thirdly, gender research improves the social inclusion of all members of society into developments of technical innovations and gives them access to the latest scientific findings (Buitendijk and Maes 2015; European Union 2015; NIH 2016). In this article, I will discuss these initiatives under the framing of a new governance of science and technology that stresses the need for more integrated research and policies to solve global problems, and consequently calls for interdisciplinary approaches from different disciplines (Lyall 2005). Gender research can be seen as an innovative approach to these problems because of its genuine inter- and transdisciplinary perspective for targeting these objectives. The question, however, is to what extent sex and gender is taken up by science and technology, which actors take sex and gender into the governance of science and technology, and which concepts have been integrated so far.

The European and international initiatives can be read as based on a definition of 'social innovation' that

> "refers broadly to innovation in meeting social needs of, or delivering social benefits to, communities – in creation of new products, services, organizational structures or activities that are 'better' or 'more effective' than traditional public sector, philanthropic or market-reliant approaches in responding to social exclusion" (Moulaert et al. 2013, p. 1).

Recent gender initiatives such as the *Gender-Net ERA-Net* programme[5] similarly use the notion of social innovation to position the 'value of gender research' for achieving scientific excellence "through structural change by developing and implementing gender-equality plans [...] and consequently improving the recruitment and career paths of female scientists" and through the "integration of sex and gender analysis into all phases of basic and applied research" (Gender-Net 2013).

Last but not least, besides the improvement of numbers and knowledge, critical reflectivity and positioning is at the core of social innovation because "debate, controversy and imagination will be the key to methodological improvement" and "the final reason is probably the most important and also the most challenging for researchers: it is about how to position themselves in the 'social arena' and how to contribute to its transformation" (Moulaert et al. 2013, p. 3).

Sabine Hark (1998) and Gudrun-Axeli Knapp (1998) show how the first phase of academic institutionalisation of women and gender studies in Germany during the 1990s was partly successful because it was linked to the branding of universities

5 *Gender-Net*, funded by the *7th European Union's Framework Programme*, particularly targets transnational networking (Gender-Net 2013).

when it came to promoting their innovative standing in interdisciplinary encounters. Nevertheless, Hark and Knapp point to the limits of this institutionalisation. Gender research should be more than a mere interdisciplinary complement to disciplinary research which leaves borders intact. Instead, at its core there should be a transdisciplinary traversing of concepts, methods and terms (Knapp 1998, p. 43). Transdisciplinarity always includes critical reflection on the social and cultural impacts on the mechanisms of scientific knowledge production. Both Hark and Knapp ask how far transdisciplinarity as a deconstructive practice of gender research (Hark 1998, p. 16) has been lost on its long march through the institutions – and how its reflective impetus is inevitably silenced when institutionalisation is labelled *innovation* (Knapp 1998, p. 51).

Therefore, the particular question I take up in this article is about the benefits and the disadvantages of the recent initiatives for the integration of sex and gender, particularly into science, technology, engineering and mathematics, which are again driven and legitimized from both governmental and gender actors in advertising the *innovative potential of gender research*. This analysis will lead to the question of the (strategic) use of the innovation argument per se: is it a help or a hindrance for feminist concerns, and at what cost?

The recent advice for a new governance of science *with* sex and gender, i. e. the *League of European Research Universities'* paper in particular, and also the *European Research Area Roadmap*, the *National Institues of Health's* guidelines and even the *Gender-Net ERA-Net*[6] refer to the *Gendered Innovations* project (Schiebinger et al. 2016a) as their main source of information and guidance. Taking this project as a case study, I will first outline the setup of the *Gendered Innovations* website, elaborate how it addresses the term *innovation*, and point to the demands arising from a perspective of science and technology studies to consider mechanisms of knowledge production (section 2). I will then analyse some challenges that result from relating the knowledge presented by *Gendered Innovations* to the concepts and findings of feminist science and technology studies: its definitions of sex and gender as well as its concepts of female versus male needs and the question of how far intersectional and epistemological approaches could be implemented and disseminated into the initiatives of academic governance (section 3). In section 4, I will consider the aims and decisions of the *Gendered Innovations* developers concerning the strategic use of innovation arguments. Section 5 will deal with the argument of utilisation and usability of a new governance of science and technology which is advertised to develop to its fullest under the rules of a free market (Rothbard 2015), i. e. decisions

6 The *Gender-Net Era-Net* is the only initiative which also refers to another resource: the *Gender Toolkit* (European Commission 2009) to which I will return in section 6.

for funding a particular type of research should be based on the expectation of its economic benefit. Should the integration of gender research follow this call to be an innovative supporter for economic benefit, and could it reach gender equity with this strategic movement? Based on these analyses, I will finally (in section 6) take up the question of the potential and the limits of the strategical use of the innovation argument to open up a window of opportunities for the integration of sex/gender studies, particularly into science, technology, engineering and mathematics, and will call for a pluralism of strategies instead of one 'master's tool'.

2 *Gendered Innovations* – Innovative for What?

The *Gendered Innovations* project, fully titled *Gendered Innovations in Science, Health and Medicine, Engineering, and Environment,* was initiated in 2009 by Londa Schiebinger from Stanford University and has been co-opted by the European Union in 2012, based on her collaboration with Ineke Klinge and Martina Schraudner. The project's website presents case studies to inform science, technology, engineering and mathematics disciplines on how they could benefit from considering the categories of sex and gender in research and development. Definitions of "terms" and "methods" (Schiebinger et al. 2016a) are provided in subsites and are linked to the case studies. Further rubrics address "design thinking" (including advertising tips for 'gendered products'), "policy recommendations" and ideas for "institutional transformation" (Schiebinger et al. 2016a).

Schiebinger is a historian whose papers and books on the inscription of gender in the emergence of science as an academic discipline from the 17th to the 19th centuries (Schiebinger 1989) inspired feminist science studies. Recently, she edited a four-volume handbook with relevant papers in this field of research (Schiebinger 2014). Klinge, a biologist by training, is professor of Gender Medicine at Maastricht University. She has a long-standing engagement in the EU governance of biomedicine and works on the multiplicity of differences concerning sex, gender, ethnic origin, age, sexual orientation and (dis)ability (Klinge and Bosch 2005; Klinge and Wiesemann 2010). Schraudner, an expert in biology and biotechnology, heads the *Centre for Responsible Research and Innovation* at the Fraunhofer Institute and is professor for Gender und Diversity Aspects in Organisations at the Technical University of Berlin.[7]

---

7 I outline the research backgrounds of the developers of *Gendered Innovations* here because of their self-positioning within a critical feminist agenda.

Already in 2006, Schraudner disseminated an approach to include gender for technological developments under the slogan of the "innovative potential of gender" (Bührer and Schraudner 2006, p. 3). When Schiebinger started the *Gendered Innovations* project, she also invoked the notion of innovation to affirm the qualitative improvement of scientific research through the introduction of a reflective standpoint from a gender perspective.[8] Such a strategic usage of the innovation argument could turn Hannah Arendt's philosophical-political question whether the

> "activity of thinking as such, the habit of examining whatever happens to come to pass or to attract attention, regardless of results and specific content, could this activity be among the conditions that make men abstain from evil-doing or even actually 'condition' them against it?" (Arendt 1978, p. 5)

into a scientific-political statement, i. e. that the ability to think, debate and obtain critical reflexivity should be introduced as a necessary requisite for any emancipatory scientific work, or in short: think gender, and you begin to think critically about your own practices and their outcomes.[9]

As a consequence, this invocation of innovation could call (again) for epistemological reflections, particularly within the science, technology, engineering and mathematics scientific programme. Thomas Kuhn's influential work (1962) on the mechanisms of knowledge production unmasked the long-held Enlightenment paradigm of a step-by-step discovery of more and more objective knowledge. Instead, he identified knowledge production as a process of historically and socially embedded negotiations. Ian Hacking (1983) explained how every kind of scientific research is an *intervention* as much as it claims to be a *representation*, because all experimental procedures are part of laboratory negotiations that produce results. According to Sandra Harding (1991), every experiment derives from a preceding theory (the theory-ladenness of observation), and the same scientific results can be used to support contradicting theories (the indeterminacy of theory). Since then, science and technology studies have produced an abundancy of analyses (Hackett et al. 2007) to show *how* scientific knowledge production is influenced by political, economic and social power relations, as well as by the researcher's objectives – both consciously and unconsciously.[10]

---

8 Personal communication at a *Gendered Innovations* expert workshop in Brussels, 2012.

9 Sabine Hark already described a similar argument (1998, p. 15) for the first phase of gender institutionalisation.

10 That does not mean that scientific knowledge production is not applicable, but that it is constructed and socially situated.

For more than 30 years feminist science and technology studies, a transdisciplinary discipline, has differentiated these approaches by uncovering the gender-ladenness of Western scientific knowledge production. Scholars of feminist science and technology studies pointed out the gendered social impact and the cultural norms transported into science and technology and, conversely, the impact of scientific knowledge on gendered beliefs and social power relations, with both trends resulting in in- and exclusions of individuals according to their categorisation in particular gender groups; in short, as Evelyn Fox Keller defined it, "gender in science" (Keller 1995, p. 86) is – as well as in society – a structuring component of knowledge production. After that, standpoint approaches called for the inclusion of various intersecting categories of difference such as gender, ethnicity, class, age or dis/ability into scientific research. Where now can these facets of feminist science and technology studies – its definitions of sex/gender, its intersections with other categories and its epistemological perspectives – be found in the *Gendered Innovations* project?

3 Contrasting *Gendered Innovations* with Feminist Science and Technology Studies

The introductory webpage of *Gendered Innovations, Why Gendered Innovations?* begins by saying, "'*Gendered Innovations* employs methods of sex and gender analysis to create new knowledge" (Schiebinger et al. 2016a, author's emphasis), establishing a link to the benefit of gender research for new knowledge in science and technology and to the term *innovation*. For my analyses of the innovative value of gender research for a new governance of science and technology, particularly concerning its demands for inter- and transdisciplinary research to solve global problems (see section 1), the obvious question is: what kind of innovation is targeted by *Gendered Innovations* and what newness of knowledge is created by it? In the following, I will discuss the arguments and concepts of the *Gendered Innovations'* website in relation to the scope of knowledge already available from feminist science and technology studies. My analysis addresses three mutually interconnected challenges: (1) the sex and gender concepts and how they are assigned to women and men, respectively, (2) the inclusion or neglect of sex/gender interactions, and (3) the integration of intersectional perspectives and feminist epistemologies. Throughout this analysis, I consider how the *Gendered Innovations* project impacts on the recent European and US initiatives to the new governance of science due to its dominance as a reference.

3.1 Challenge 1: The Two-Sex Model and Its Assignments to Women and Men

Feminist science and technology studies have uncovered reductionist sexisms in scientific research and technological development (Schiebinger 2014). They unveiled the primary scientific focus on sex difference research and, simultaneously, the neglect of contrary or null results (i. e. the lack of mentioning differences between or the variations within the two sex groups). The referencing practice of that scientific knowledge, i. e. the so-called publication bias, established a binary two-sex model and the notion of behaviour, attitudes, preferences and desires as determined by biological sex. Feminist science scholars in primatology, behavioural studies, evolutionary and sociobiological research, developmental biology, immunology, endocrinology, and the fields of neurosciences analysed biases and distortions in the selection of the research objects, the research methodologies, the inclusion or exclusion of data in analyses, and the interpretations of results. They discovered inaccurate generalisations from animals to humans, from small participant groups to the general sex categories, and the maintenance of the two-sex model with its inherent homogeny and proposed differences of women versus men (Schmitz 2016).

So far, feminist science and technology studies have not only provided a theoretical and methodological framework for critical reflection of knowledge production in the science, technology, engineering and mathematics disciplines, but have also uncovered its social entanglements. During the 1980s, feminist scientists revealed that the assumptions that women have less intellectual capacities for scientific work reach as far back as classical antiquity. The interwoven mechanisms of gender discrimination served systematically to exclude women from particular disciplines throughout the history of science. The separation of public and private spheres in 19th-century bourgeois society, the masculinisation of the public sphere and the feminisation of the private sphere relegated women to simply their roles as housewives and mothers, and the naturalisation of social gender relations was manifested by linking femininity to nature and objecthood (Keller 1985; Merchant 1980).

The contributions of feminist science scholars in exchange with feminist sociologists increasingly challenged the legitimisation of gender roles, gender norms and gendered societal structures by naturalisations. The separation of biological sex categories from psychosocial gender categories beginning in the 1970s helped explain how differences between female and male groups result from 'doing gender' within gendered social power relations. As such, gender differences are constructed but nevertheless become real. However, this was not only an emancipatory step for women's empowerment and for promoting gender equity. It was perhaps even more important in terms of *social innovations*, because it pointed out the variability within the gender groups; the intersections of discriminations by sexism, rassism and classism; and the possibility of crossing gender borders. All of these perspectives require much more differentiated research than a binary concept in order to solve intersected demands of discriminated groups, to reach beyond a simple ascription of different needs of women and men, or to utilize their capacities as human resources for economic benefit.

The criticisable binary assignments to women and men that resulted from the two-sex model, however, are still present in most of the case studies in the *Gendered Innovations* project, and the embeddedness of gender relations in powerful societal structures are only mentioned very rarely in some of them. The same critique holds for the *Discover Gender* project, launched by the Fraunhofer Institute (Bührer and Schraudner 2006) which derives its guidelines for research and technical developments from the same binary two-sex model with its assignments to distinct two-gender needs and its ignorance of all research on inherent variabilities and entanglements of gender within powerful social structures (Bath 2007).

The European Commission described the message of *Gendered Innovations* as follows:

> "The case studies presented in this report demonstrate that differences between the needs, behaviours and attitudes of women compared to men really matter, and accounting for them in research makes it relevant to the whole of society." (European Commission 2013, p. 5)

A closer look into the *League of European Research Universities'* advice paper (Buitendijk and Maes 2015) – which calls for the inclusion of sex and gender at all levels of research and development, from funding to research design to methods to data analyses and interpretation and up to the assessment of their impacts on all individuals and on social levels – reveals the following: the paper mostly takes up the binary assignments to different needs of women and men from the case studies of *Gendered Innovations*. However, it also briefly hints at some possible discriminatory outcomes by stating that "the risk of exaggerating existing small differences, or of wrongly claiming differences […], can result in perpetuating stereotypical views and/or in unjustifiably treating men and women differently" (Buitendijk and Maes 2015, p. 12). What becomes obvious here is the notion that possibly discriminatory consequences are due to social beliefs and norms, and are not anchored in the scientific knowledge itself.

Already in the 1980s, feminist scientists scrutinized the biologically determined two-sex model, calling for the de-pathologisation of intersex variety and of other than female/male sex categories (Fausto-Sterling 2000). A recently published paper (Ainsworth 2015) stresses the variety of sex in the genome, counts the many variations in chromosomal settings other than xx and xy as 'normal', and denies their definitions as pathological. This paper could be called innovative as it was published in the leading science journal *Nature*. Keeping the focus on sex-based individual development, however, it follows a sex-line for biomedical research which was already determined by the US *National Institutes of Health* around the turn of the millennium (Wizeman and Pardue 2001). Following the recent appeal to research, "Sex in Every Cell" (Clayton and Collins 2014), most analyses continue to research sex (only) but not gender, and mostly stick to the traditional two-sex model (e.g. McCarthy et al. 2012).

3.2 Challenge 2: Sex/Gender or Sex and Gender?

The separation of the categories of sex and gender has led to its own problems as the sex-gender dualism follows the notion of a nature-culture dichotomy with far-reaching consequences. Alongside the assignments of sex analyses to the biomedical disciplines for decades, sex retained its status as an ontological category prior to culture and, in consequence, was deemed not a fitting research category for gender research. Vice versa, gender research, which was primarily based in the social and cultural disciplines, neglected analyses of sex until the 1990s, precisely to avoid the essentialism and naturalisation of sex research.

In recent decades, however, two major changes in conceptual and methodological approaches have turned the sex *or* gender debates into sex/gender debates. Firstly, since the 1990s the appropriateness of the separation of the categories of sex and gender has come into question within scholarly feminist debates. Poststructuralist notions stressed the constructed nature of sex as well as that of gender (Butler 1993) and feminist science and technology studies, by showing how gender influences become embodied, explained 'sex/gender' as always indivisible (Fausto-Sterling 2000). Using the term of *embodying*, concepts and research of the bio-socio-cultural interactions in sex/gender development aimed at bridging the nature-culture divide. Today, corporal sociology analyses bodies both as products as well as producers of society: social experiences form bodily materialities and functions; bodily dynamics influence individual and social praxis; bodies carry social values and cultural norms (Cregan 2006); gendered and sexed bodies only become intelligible through performative interpellations (Butler 1993). Such perspectives inevitably lead to the notion of diversity instead of sticking to a binary division of women versus men. Moreover, analyses of the dynamics of embodying establish methodological frameworks for researching the dynamic incorporations of the social and the socialisation of corporal materiality beyond pure construction or determinism (Schmitz and Degele 2010). Not least, the upcoming feminist materialisms conceptualise the intra-actions of material dynamics, agencies, discourses, meaning-making processes and norms as constitutive for the becoming of any worldly phenomena (Dolphijn and van der Tuin 2012).

Secondly, the scientific and technological disciplines also increasingly struggle with the nature-culture divide. Today a variety of biomedical and technological fields work at the intersection of nature, technology and culture. They address aspects of diversity, of social and cultural forming of the biological and technical matter, and of categorical intersections as crucial targets of their research. For example, the neurosciences try to explore the mutual interchanges of brain development with social experience through brain plasticity; embodied cognition more and more focusses on the intersection of corporeal, affective and rational processing; nature-culture transgressions reach far into the body down to gene regulation in current debates of epigenetics (Schmitz 2016). Gender medicine not only increasingly acknowledges sex/gender interactions in the development, diagnosis and therapy of diseases, but also starts to account for the mutual and intersected social impacts of ethnicity, class and gender in health research, as Nancy Krieger (2012) shows in her eco-social embodiment approach.

In consequence, at least some of the science, technology, engineering and mathematics fields today seek dialogues with the humanities and the social and cultural sciences when interdisciplinary programmes target global challenges, as for example was recently advocated in *Nature* (2015). They meet the call of a new governance of science for innovative interdisciplinary intersections as, for example, with the *Gender-Net ERA-Net* initiative which points to the necessity of networking transnationally to find solutions to fight global gender discrimination. Even the *League of European Research Universities'* advice paper argues for transdisciplinary exchange for "creating new knowledge and to finding solutions to global challenges" (Buitendijk and Maes 2015, p. 3). Therefore, it has to be questioned whether such advocating of inter- and transdisciplinary approaches conjoin with sex/gender perspectives to assess whether they can lead to an anti-discriminatory governance of science.

The *Gendered Innovations* website refers separately to the categories of sex and gender in its sections titled *Methods* (Schiebinger et al. 2016a, author's emphasis) and *Terms* and always positions sex ahead of gender and analyses of sex ahead of analyses of gender (Schiebinger et al. 2016a, author's emphasis). The section *Sex and Gender Are Distinct Terms* is the first subsite in *Terms*, although at the end of this subsite, it states that "[i]n reality, sex and gender interact (mutually shape one another) to form individual bodies, cognitive abilities, and disease patterns, for example" (Schiebinger et al. 2016a). Another subsite states that "'[s]ex' and 'gender' are analytically distinct but not independent terms" (Schiebinger et al. 2016a). Thus, the *Gendered Innovations* project, while referring to sex/gender interactions, insists first and foremost on the analytical separation of the categories of sex and gender when it comes to pointing out the innovative potential of the project.

This separation and order is adopted by the European position that starts with sex definitions followed by gender definitions (European Commission 2013, p. 43–47). The *National Institutes of Health* take up exactly the same separation in their online newsletter of May 2016: "Many people use the words sex and gender interchangeably, but they're distinct concepts to scientists" (NIH 2016).

The *League of European Research Universities*' advice paper, however, besides referring to the sex and gender separation, includes the following sentence:

> "Biological sex differences and behavioural gender differences – and the interaction between the two – can produce very different [...] outcomes [...] Interaction often occurs between sex- and gender-relevant factors and it can be hard to distinguish between the two." (Buitendijk and Maes 2015, p. 6)

This short hint at sex/gender interactions can – in my view – be singled out as the most innovative part of the *League of European Research Universities*' paper. It could guide transdisciplinary research between gender research, science and biomedicine to explore exactly these interactions.

However, most recently intra-science publication policies seem to follow the invocation of separation and, even more strikingly, recall sex analysis as *the* domain of the sciences, legitimized by the governance of science through the advice from the *National Institutes of Health*. In November 2016 the pre-published version of a special issue of the *Journal of Neuroscience Research (JNR)* was launched online with the title *An Issue Whose Time Has Come: Sex/Gender Influences on Nervous System Function*. But despite sex and gender or even sex/gender interactions, guest editor Larry Cahill presents a sample of 73 (!) papers which exclusively refer to sex differences in the brain. In his editorial he points to the journal's new policy aligned with the guidelines of the *National Institutes of Health*:

> "Coinciding with this issue (which will be permanently open access), *JNR* is announcing editorial policy changes whereby all new submissions to the journal must carefully attend to potential sex influences (see *Editorial Comment* by Prager 2017). These new policies dovetail nicely with the new *NIH* requirements regarding the

consideration of sex as a biological variable (see Clayton and Collins, 2014)." (Cahill 2017, p. 13, author's emphasis)[11]

This launch of a special issue, however, also has another herstory. In the past 10 years the international *NeuroGenderings* expert network (NeuroGenderings 2014) has implemented constructive concepts and research methodologies for sex/gender research (Schmitz and Höppner 2014). Coming from critical analyses of neuro-sexisms in brain research, the network developed approaches for a more adequate empirical neuroscience that could account for the mutual interactions of biological, psychological, social and cultural aspects of sex/gender. Appropriate analyses (e.g. Joel et al. 2015) and guidelines have been published in prestigious neuroscience journals (e.g. Rippon et al. 2014), and *NeuroGenderings* can be considered as having gained more acknowledgement within the brain research community. However, every recommended publication from the *NeuroGenderings* experts almost always triggers anti-genderisms from within the neurosciences, the foremost being from Larry Cahill (e.g. the debate between Cahill 2014 and Fine et al. 2014).

One could argue that the publication policies for sex difference research in line with the *National Institutes of Health* recommendations set back the sex/gender discourse by 30 years (see above in section 3.1) and distort the upcoming dialogue between feminist science and technology studies and science, technology, engineering and mathematics on the inseparability of nature/culture, which I previously elaborated on. This form of a new governance of science to sex-only research hinders the inclusion of the innovative potential of such an integrative dialogue. At the same time, however, the sex-only policies turn out to have a logic in themselves. As long as *Gendered Innovations* advocates researching sex *and* gender separately (as recently proposed in the high-impacted biomedical journal *The Lancet*, Schiebinger et al. 2016b), it is a legitimate position to say: OK, then we (*Journal of Neuroscientific Research*) research sex and you (feminists) may research gender. Anne Fausto-Sterling (2003) precisely points out that the allocation of sex research to the science disciplines and of gender research to the social and cultural

11 The *Journal of Neuroscientific Research (JNR)* explicates its sex-difference-related publication policy: "We recognize that sex fundamentally influences the brain and have now established a policy requiring all authors to ensure proper consideration of sex as a biological variable." (Prager 2017, p. 11) Along with serious advice to include male and female subjects into every analyses (down to cells), it states further: "*JNR* understands the real risk of false-positive errors associated with subgroup analysis, but that risk is balanced by the equal or greater risk of false-negative errors resulting from a failure to consider possible sex influences." (Prager 2017, p. 11, author's emphasis)

disciplines will persist as a problem as long as feminist discourse does not overcome its own sex-gender separations.

3.3 Challenge 3: Lack of Intersectionality and Epistemology

Sex and gender research has been challenged for leaving discriminatory policies against other categories out of focus. Intersectional approaches have shown that sex, gender, ethnicity, cultural background, class, age, education, dis/ability, preferences of desire and gender identifications have to be accounted for to assess impacts through privileging and discriminating categories. Gendered and intersected categories (and ascriptions of who is able to do and think what) within social relations (which are hierarchical and powerful inclusive and exclusive practices) are impacted by scientific knowledge production and technological developments. Cultural norms, beliefs and social structures, conversely, impact science and technology. In consequence, intersectional 'gender' research, even in science, technology, engineering and mathematics, has to be more than that on men and/or women. Moreover, intersectional approaches could be taken up to call for the inclusion of diversity instead of binaries.

Intersectional debates have been introduced recently on the *Gendered Innovations* website with a particular subsite under *Methods* (Schiebinger et al. 2016a) and a subsite on *Race and Ethnicity* under *Terms* (Schiebinger et al. 2016a). They offer some discussion and reference related literature. Interestingly, there are links to case studies on the subsite for intersected aspects, but no case studies are included for questions concerning racism.

The neglect of connected impacts of sexism and racism in mostly all of the new initiatives for the governance of science I mentioned can be interpreted as being part of a long-held Western epistemic power, i. e. the negligence of colonial-based hierarchies inherent to the notion of what counts as intelligible knowledge and, following that, the disregard for non-Western knowledge production. Particularly from the perspective of postcolonial[12] feminist science and technology studies (Harding 2011), the following question can be posed: what kind of knowledge should

12 Postcolonial discourse does not designate a historical 'after' but is rather a politically motivated category for analyses of the historical, political, cultural and discursive aspects of the enduring colonial discourse. The concept of *othering* functions to assert white Western subjectivity and collective identity of civilisational superiority against a non-Western non-white perception of the uncivilized.

be acknowledged in science, technology, engineering and mathematics and how can this acknowledgement be reached?

One of the most genuine and important influences of feminist science and technology studies at the epistemological level have been the debates and concepts on how to develop some form of anti-discriminatory knowledge production which can be used more adequately for world problems. Feminist epistemologies in the late 1980s, such as Helen Longino's 'contextualized empiricism' (Longino 1990), Sandra Harding's 'strong objectivity' (Harding 1991) and Donna Haraway's 'situated knowledges' (Haraway 1988) did not reject the applicability of knowledge, but stressed its always constructed 'nature'. Not aiming at following a metaphysics of the Enlightenment and not claiming to make progress in gathering objective truth, they developed concepts for the integration of a variety of actors and their standpoints in negotiating knowledge. Feminist epistemologies urge making these processes of meaning-making visible and transparent (among academics as well as to the general public). One important step was to uncover scientific practices and research as being indivisibly enacted in producing knowledge through the "apparatus of bodily production" (Haraway 1988, p. 591) which includes experimental procedures and techniques as well as the bodily prerequisites of the researchers. In consequence, these perspectives deconstruct the myth of knowledge as being a transcendent truth. To say it in the words of recent feminist materialisms: knowledge is always a phenomenon that constitutes itself through matter *and* meaning (Barad 2007). The framework of feminist materialisms from the mid-1990s onwards highlights the pluralisms of its perspectives, applicable to different research objectives (Schmitz 2017).

Epistemological reflection should be a central part of scientific research. On the *Gendered Innovations* website, I could not find any epistemological reflections related to knowledge production or to the questioning of the scientific paradigm of objectivity. Only a subsite under *Methods* on *Rethink Concepts and Theories* explains:

> "The point of rethinking central concepts and theories in relation to sex and gender is to ensure:
> 1. that any assumptions made or issues addressed are based on the best available evidence and information,
> 2. and that the concepts and theories adopted do not blind researchers to important aspects of sex and gender that could be a fertile source for innovation." (Schiebinger et al. 2016a)

These epistemological shortenings are remarkable as Schiebinger, a historian, has provided long-standing and prominent input into feminist science and technology studies. For her part, Klinge recently related the project precisely to the feminist epistemologies of strong objectivity and of situated knowledges (Singh and Klinge 2015).

4 *Gendered Innovations* (Only) as an Eye-opener?

Why did the developers of *Gendered Innovations* choose a strategy of addressing sex and gender and female versus male needs? Not wanting to speculate, I take some hints from an interview with Schiebinger (Zemp et al. 2015), where she explained the reason for the neglect of grounding the *Gendered Innovations* project in feminist epistemologies as follows. Her aim, she said, was to fight against reductionist biological determinism and to get people to understand "how knowledge is gendered" (Zemp et al. 2015, p. 119), but "the public is not *captured* by political debates" (Zemp et al. 2015, p. 121, author's emphasis). In order to reach "policy makers, government funders, and the general public we [gender theorists] need elevator speech" (Zemp et al. 2015, p. 120). In order to catch the attention of these target groups as well as that of researchers, senior and junior scholars, and students, she used "Google analytics to learn how people use our website. Some people stay for 10 seconds only. Even if they are there only for 10 seconds, I want them to learn something!" (Zemp et al. 2015, p. 123) Therefore, the titles and case studies of *Gendered Innovations* are designed as "eye-catching examples" (Zemp et al. 2015, p. 120). Asked about the still-reifying distinction of sex and gender in the selected case studies, Schiebinger justified this with their use as "*teaching moments*" (Zemp et al. 2015, p. 124, original emphasis) and "yes, we [first] distinguish sex and gender, and then we discuss how they interact" (Zemp et al. 2015, p. 124).

However, several questions still remain. Firstly, what exactly is the something (see above) that 'people' can learn in 10 seconds? Is it that men and women are different, bound in their opposite sexes, habits and needs; is it that sex and gender are distinct categories? Schiebinger herself admits that "I don't think that I communicate well, or what people don't get, is that gender analysis goes through the whole research process" (Zemp et al. 2015, p. 124).

Secondly, are policymakers, government funders, researchers, scholars and students, and the general public really naïve and gender blind to that extent? My experience from science, technology, engineering and mathematics dialogues and governmental engagement (e.g. ZAG 2016), and from public lectures on sex/gender aspects suggests that this is more a naïve view of the developers of the *Gendered Innovations* website than is true for their target groups. But insisting on a superficial entrance via the sex and gender separation again bears the danger that common knowledge and gender awareness remain on exactly that level: women and men are different and have to be treated differently.

Thirdly, who are the people who are specified as the target groups, and can a strategy really be developed and applied to catch them all in the same way? *Gendered Innovations*' strategy may be successful in making policymakers and funding agencies aware of the need to include sex and gender analysis in the governing, funding and research of science, technology, engineering and mathematics. However, the inclusion of sex/gender-adequate and intersected concepts and methods into research practices, as well as the development of inter- and transdisciplinary communication, need a more differentiated approach to guide the governing actors of science and technology to anti-discriminatory research. For example, the guidelines from the *NeuroGenderings* expert network were developed from an abundant scope of previous analyses and based on intensive transdisciplinary discussions within the network (Rippon et al. 2014). Therefore, the argument of naïveté as a guide for the *Gendered Innovations'* strategy and website setup either seems a bit naïve itself, or we have to look for other reasons.

5 *Gendered Innovations* Pays Off

A search on the *Gendered Innovations* website reveals the following: "[t]he goal of the *Gendered Innovations* project is to provide scientists and engineers with practical methods for sex and gender analysis." (Schiebinger et al. 2016a, author's emphasis) The invocation of innovation is the highlighted term for advertising:

> "*Why Gendered Innovations?* [red coloured]
> 'Doing research wrong costs lives and money. [...] Doing research right can save lives and money. [...]
> *Gendered Innovations* [red coloured]
> - *Add value to research and engineering* by ensuring excellence and quality in outcomes and enhancing sustainability.
> - *Add value to society* by making research more responsive to social needs.
> - *Add value to business* by developing new ideas, patents, and technology'." (Schiebinger et al. 2016a, italic emphases are bold in the original)

Gendered Innovations captures an economic challenge of the healthcare system. The bullet points establish a link between excellence as a criterion for valuable research and knowledge and the prospect of economic benefit (patents and technologies), both connected by the ability of research to address social needs.

Thus, the branding of the *Gendered Innovations* project can be read in several ways: it targets the responsibility of science and technology for society (social innovation) as well as it fits to the economisation and commodification of research for entrepreneurial universities and their outsourcings. One particular sub-site under the header *Design Thinking* offers advice for companies on how to develop and advertise their products to their best benefit, e.g. "[a]ccounting for gender differences can increase your market share" (Schiebinger et al. 2016a).

This combination of possible readings under both marketability and social innovation aspects seems to be a central strategy of the *Gendered Innovations* project. It has to be analysed in more detail how this establishing of a connection to economic valuing could open or close reflexive consideration of the innovation argument. At the very least, it has to be debated to which kind of innovation – if any – feminist discourse aims to connect, and what would be the costs of the pressure to permanently produce 'innovative' outputs.

6 How to Deal with *Gendered Innovations*: A Call for Pluralism?

Science and technology studies have characterised academic disciplines as powerful *systems of knowledge production* (and that holds for biology, medicine, chemistry, physics, engineering and technology as well as for the social and cultural sciences and for the humanities). They all are embedded in and impacted by social, political and economic systems, and so are the scientists (the experts, the young scholars and the students) with their aims, beliefs, targets, financial needs or career objectives – even with their aims to make the world a better place. Not to criticise scientific disciplines, research and development, but to recall Hannah Arendt from the beginning of this article, I wish to stress the need for a reflective and also critical standpoint that scientists should develop with regard to their own system.

From my analysis of the *Gendered Innovations* project and its impact on recent initiatives of the governance of science, I conclude that the attempts to integrate 'gender' research (in its intersected understandings) into science, technology, engineering and mathematics still face similar constraints to those that Sabine Hark (1998) and Gudrun-Axeli Knapp (1998) recognized for the first phase of gender institutionalisation: it ends at the latest at the barrier of epistemic concepts that question the paradigms of objectivity and neutrality in science, technology, engineering and mathematics.

The crucial question then is: should we trade off *situated knowledges* (Haraway 1988) for a minimum of consensus in order to include sex and gender in science and technology? And conversely: how far can critical approaches of postcolonial feminist science and technology studies be introduced into science, technology, engineering and mathematics – more precisely, how can we break through the wall of the still-existing metaphysics of Enlightenment to allow for the immigration of other epistemologies on knowledge production otherwise?

The oscillation between the objectives and the limits of the inclusion of transdisciplinary gender research into science, technology, engineering and mathematics mirrors these two positions. The *Gendered Innovations* project focusses on acting as an eye-opener: to integrate knowledge on sex and gender as distinct categories first, while ignoring epistemological considerations for the time being. This strategy aims at raising awareness and perhaps the acknowledgement of gender research in science, technology, engineering and mathematics. The other side of the argument is illustrated by Audre Lorde's famous words, "[t]he master's tools will never dismantle the master's house" (Lorde 1984, p. 110). She argued that powerful and discriminatory systems can only be changed from the outside.

The recent changes within feminist debates and within science, technology, engineering and mathematics, when it comes to research *naturecultures* in intersection, and the increasing dialogue between both academic fields to integrate transdisciplinary approaches to face local and global challenges (as outlined in section 3.2), show that reflective approaches of 'gender' research are neither unknown nor incomprehensible. Therefore, I advocate for approaching the problem otherwise: to combine the benefits of feminist science and technology studies with a critical postcolonial perspective. Postcolonial feminist science and technology studies (Harding 2011) can help explain the co-construction and mutual influence of scientific knowledge production, gendered and intersected beliefs and norms, enacted in social, economic and political structures upon each other.[13] It can uncover the mechanisms of power which establish a ranking of better over worse knowledge. It questions not only the colonial heritage of epistemic violence but also the putting of scientific knowledge (seemingly objective) above feminist knowledge (seemingly ideological). How now can such an approach with its far-reaching objectives fill the gap between the two positions outlined above?

Gayatri Spivak (2012, p. 4) calls for strategies of "affirmative sabotage" to subvert the powerful science systems using their own tools and policies, but only those "with which we are in sympathy, enough to subvert!". Based on her detailed analysis of the various standpoints in Enlightenment discourse over the past 200 years, Nikita Dhawan follows Spivak in arguing that "the Enlightenment ideals are eminently indispensable, and we 'cannot not want them', even as their coer-

13 The postcolonial feminist science and technology studies' approach has been gaining more influence recently, e.g. in a noticeable section of panels and talks on the joint conference of the *Society for Social Studies of Science (4S)* and the *European Association for the Study of Science and Technology (EASST)* in Barcelona 2016.

cive mobilisation in service of the continued justification of imperialism must be contested" (Dhawan 2014, p. 71).

Coming back to the positioning of the *Gendered Innovations* project to include sex and gender strategically step by step, its dissemination, referencing and publicity confirms it as an entrance to a new governance of science, technology, engineering and mathematics. The *Gendered Innovations* project has been used to justify the promotion of women in higher academic positions in science and technology (Buitendijk and Maes 2015), and it was a first step in making actors aware of sex and gendered aspects, particularly within those disciplines which are still far away from gender knowledge (Buitendijk and Maes 2015). The fact that debates are beginning about how to integrate gender studies broadly into the studies of the sciences and technologies is also worth mentioning (Buitendijk and Maes 2015; NIH 2016; European Union 2015).

In my view, the problem, however, is that the *Gendered Innovations* project turns out to be the *only* resource when advocating for the inclusion of sex/gender into science, technology, engineering and mathematics. Its branding as the only reference point for innovative, intelligible gender research silences other approaches and standpoints – and has led recently to the legitimisation of counteractions as illustrated by the case of the sex-line of the *Journal of Neuroscience Research* (*An Issue Whose Time Has Come*).

Critical reflexivity – a core of gender research – should also be a target of the new governance of science and technology. "Government, control of science, government planning of science, is bound to result in the politization of science" (Rothbard 2015, p. 12). Reflective approaches of transdisciplinarity as a deconstructive practice (Hark 1998, p. 16) are deeply grounded in the recognition of multiple standpoints, of the communication between multiple perspectives and of dissenting voices. This is not to generally criticise the *Gendered Innovations* project per se, but to caution against its being considered and advertising itself as the one and only 'master's tool'. Instead, and following the line of current debates of feminist materialisms (see section 3.3), this is a call for strategies of plurality. At least two strategies could be combined here. Firstly, other resources could and should be communicated more actively in national, European and other contexts to actors of the governance of science. The already-mentioned *Gender Toolkit* (European Commission 2009), for example, contains differentiated gender-relevant and even epistemologically based literature. It has developed further specifications for particular fields, e. g. the *CARE Gender Toolkit* with a particular focus on "reflections on analysis of gender and power" in intercultural exchange (Picard and Gillingham 2012, no pagination). Secondly, the *Gendered Innovations* website is changing dynamically. Having gained acknowledgment so far in current top-down initiatives of the governance of science, technology, engineering and mathematics, the authors of the website could and should now integrate more reflective components, e. g. addressing the interaction between sex and gender more pronouncedly and right from the beginning, pointing to the intersections with other categories of discrimination such as racism, classism and dis/ablism with case studies, highlighting their embeddedness in the social order and cultural norms, and referencing epistemological frameworks of postcolonial feminist science and technology studies.

As a first step, feminist actors in this field could enter into a discussion about using the innovation argument, and begin a debate on how *not to silence critical reflexivity*, but how to develop *constructive perspectives based on criticism.*

Acknowledgement

I would like to thank Ruth Schmitz for fruitful discussions and for her English-language editorial support.

References

Ainsworth, Claire. 2015. Sex Redefined. *Nature* 518 (7539): 288–291.

Arendt, Hannah. 1978. *The Life of the Mind. Part I Thinking.* New York: Harcourt.

Barad, Karen. 2007. *Meeting the Universe Halfway.* Durham, London: Duke University Press.

Bath, Corinna. 2007. "Discover Gender" in Forschung und Technologieentwicklung? *Soziale Technik* 17 (4): 3–5.

Bührer, Susanne, and Martina Schraudner. 2006. *Wie können Gender-Aspekte in Forschungsvorhaben erkannt und bewertet werden?* Karlsruhe: Fraunhofer ISI.

Buitendijk, Simone, and Katrien Maes. 2015. *Gendered Research and Innovation: Integrating Sex and Gender Analysis into the Research Process.* Leuven: LERU. http://www.leru.org/index.php/public/publications/category/advice-papers/. Accessed: September 17, 2016.

Butler, Judith. 1993. *Bodies That Matter.* New York: Routledge.

Cahill, Larry. 2014. Equal ≠ The Same: Sex Differences in the Human Brain. *Cerebrum,* 1 April 2014. eCollection. http://www.dana.org/Cerebrum/2014/Equal_%E2%89%A0_The_Same__Sex_Differences_in_the_Human_Brain/. Accessed: December 12, 2016.

Cahill, Larry. Ed. 2017. An Issue Whose Time Has Come: Sex/Gender Influences on Nervous System Function. Special Issue. *Journal of Neuroscience Research* 95 (1–2): 1–791. doi: 10.1002/jnr.23934. Accessed: December 12, 2016.

Clayton, Janine A., and Francis S. Collins. 2014. NIH to Balance Sex in Cell and Animal Studies. *Nature* 509 (7500): 282–282.

Cregan, Kate. 2006. *The Sociology of the Body*. London: Sage.
Dhawan, Nikita. 2014. Affirmative Sabotage of the Master's Tools: The Paradox of Postcolonial Enlightenment. In *Decolonizing Enlightenment*, ed. by Nikita Dhawan, 19–78. Opladen: Barbara Budrich.
Dolphijn, Rick, and Iris van der Tuin. 2012. *New Materialism: Interviews & Cartographies*. Ann Arbor: Open Humanities Press.
European Commission. 2009. *Toolkit. Gender in EU-funded Research*. Brussels: European Commission. http://bookshop.europa.eu/en/toolkit-gender-in-eu-funded-research-pbKINA24840/. Accessed: December 12, 2016.
European Commission. 2013. *Gendered Innovations. How Gender Analysis Contributes to Research*. Brussels: European Commission. http://www.stanford.edu/dept/HPS/2012.4808_Gendered%20Innovations_web2.pdf. Accessed: September 17, 2016.
European Union. 2015. *European Research Area (ERA) Roadmap 2015–2020*. Brussels: European Union/European Research Area and Innovation Committee. https://era.gv.at/object/document/1845. Accessed: September 17, 2016.
Fausto-Sterling, Anne. 2000. *Sexing the Body. Gender Politics and the Construction of Sexuality*. New York: Basic Books.
Fausto-Sterling, Anne. 2003. The Problem with Sex/Gender and Nature/Nurture. In *Debating Biology: Sociological Reflections on Health, Medicine and Society*, ed. by Simon J. Williams, Lynda Birke and Gillian A. Bendelow, 123–132. London: Routledge.
Fine, Cordelia, Daphna Joel, Rebecca Jordan-Young, Anelis Kaiser and Gina Rippon. 2014. Why Males ≠ Corvettes, Females ≠ Volvos, and Scientific Criticism ≠ Ideology: A Response to "Equal ≠ The Same: Sex Differences in the Human Brain". *Cerebrum*, 15 December 2014. eCollection. http://dana.org/Cerebrum/2014/Reaction_to_%E2%80%9CEqual_%E2%89%A0_The_Same__Sex_Differences_in_the_Human_Brain%E2%80%9D/#. Accessed: December 12, 2016.
Gender-Net. 2013. *Promoting Gender Equality in Research Institutions and Integration of the Gender Dimension in Research Contents*. http://www.gender-net.eu. Accessed: December 12, 2016.
Hackett, Edward J., Olga Amsterdamska, Michael E. Lynch and Judy Wajcman. 2007. *The Handbook of Science Technology Studies*. 3rd Edition. Cambridge: MIT Press.
Hacking, Ian. 1983. *Representing and Intervening: Introductory Topics in the Philosophy of Natural Science*. Cambridge: Cambridge University Press.
Haraway, Donna. 1988. Situated Knowledges: The Science Question in Feminism and the Privilege of Partial Perspective. *Feminist Studies* 14 (3): 575–599.
Harding, Sandra. 1991. *Whose Science? Whose Knowledge? Thinking from Women's Lives*. Cornell: Cornell University Press.
Harding, Sandra. Ed. 2011. *The Postcolonial Science and Technology Studies Reader*. Durham: Duke University Press.
Hark, Sabine. 1998. Disziplinäre Quergänge. (Un)Möglichkeiten transdisziplinärer Frauen- und Geschlechterforschung. *Potsdamer Studien zur Frauen- und Geschlechterforschung* 2 (2): 7–22.
Joel, Daphna, Zohar Berman, Ido Tavoc, Nadav Wexle, Olga Gabe, Yaniv Stein, Nisan Shefi, Jared Poole, Sebastian Urchse, Daniel S. Margulies, Franziskus Lieme, Jürgen Hänggi, Lutz Jäncke and Yaniv Assa. 2015. Sex Beyond the Genitalia: The Human Brain Mosaic. *Proceedings of the National Academy of Sciences* 112 (50): doi: 10.1073/pnas.1509654112.
Keller, Evelyn Fox. 1985. *Reflections on Gender and Science*. New Haven: Yale University Press.

Keller, Evelyn Fox. 1995. Origin, History, and Politics of the Subject Called "Gender and Science" – A First Person Account. In *Handbook of Science and Technology Studies*, ed. by Sheila Jasanoff, Gerald E. Markle, James C. Petersen and Trevor Pinch, 80–94. Thousand Oaks: Sage.

Klinge, Ineke, and Mineke Bosch. 2005. Transforming Research Methodologies in EU Life Sciences and Biomedicine. Gender-Sensitive Ways of Doing Research. State of the Art. *European Journal of Women's Studies* 12 (3): 377–395.

Klinge, Ineke, and Claudia Wiesemann. Eds. 2010. *Sex and Gender in Biomedicine: Theories, Methodologies, Results*. Göttingen: University Press Göttingen.

Knapp, Gudrun-Axeli. 1998. Beziehungssinn und Unterscheidungsvermögen. *Potsdamer Studien zur Frauen- und Geschlechterforschung* 2 (2): 42–53.

Krieger, Nancy. 2012. Methods for the Scientific Study of Discrimination and Health: From Societal Injustice to Embodied Inequality – An Ecosocial Approach. *American Journal of Public Health* 102 (5): 936–945.

Kuhn, Thomas S. 1962. *The Structure of Scientific Revolutions*. Chicago: University of Chicago Press.

League of European Research Universities (n.d.). http://www.leru.org/index.php/public/about-leru. Accessed: December 08, 2016.

Longino, Helen. 1990. *Science as Social Knowledge*. Princeton: Princeton University Press.

Lorde, Audre. 1984. The Master's Tools Will Never Dismantle the Master's House. In *Sister Outsider: Essays and Speeches*, by Audre Lorde, 110–113. New York: Crossing Press.

Lyall, Catherine. 2005. *New Modes of Governance*. New York: Routledge.

McCarthy, Margaret M., Arthur P. Arnold, Gregory F. Ball, Jeffrey D. Blaustein and Geert J. De Vries. 2012. Sex Differences in the Brain: The Not So Inconvenient Truth. *Journal of Neuroscience* 32 (7): 2241–2247.

Merchant, Carolyn. 1980. *The Death of Nature. Women, Ecology and the Scientific Revolution*. New York: Harper.

Moulaert, Frank, Diana MacCullum, Abid Mehmood and Abdelillah Hamdouch. Eds. 2013. *The International Handbook on Social Innovation. Collective Action, Social Learning and Transdisciplinary Research*. Cheltenham/Northampton: Edward Elgar.

Nature. 2015. *Why Interdisciplinary Research Matters. Scientists Must Work Together to Save the World*. Special Issue. Nature 525 (7569): 289–418. http://www.nature.com/news/why-interdisciplinary-research-matters-1.18370. Accessed: September 17, 2016.

NeuroGenderings. 2014. *The NeuroGenderings Network*. https://neurogenderings.wordpress.com/. Accessed: September 17, 2016.

National Institutes of Health (NIH). 2016. Sex and Gender. How Being Male or Female Can Affect Your Health. *NIH News in Health*. Online May 2016. https://newsinhealth.nih.gov/issue/may2016/feature1. Accessed: September 17, 2016.

Picard, Mary, and Sarah Gillingham. 2012. *WEIMI. Women's Empowerment Impact Measurement Initiative Guidance*. http://gendertoolkit.care.org/weimi/introduction.aspx. Accessed: December 12, 2016.

Prager, Eric M. 2017. Addressing Sex as a Biological Variable. *Journal of Neuroscience Research* 95 (1): 11.

Rippon, Gina, Rebecca Jordan-Young, Anelis Kaiser and Cordelia Fine. 2014. Recommendations for Sex/Gender Neuroimaging Research: Key Principles and Implications for Research Design, Analysis, and Interpretation. *Frontiers in Human Neuroscience* 8. doi: 10.3389/fnhum.2014.00650.

Rothbard, Murray N. 2015 [1959]. *Science, Technology, and Government.* Auburn/Alabama: Mises Institute.
Schiebinger, Londa. 1989. *The Mind Has No Sex? Women in the Origins of Modern Science.* Cambridge: Harvard University Press.
Schiebinger, Londa. Ed. 2014. *Women and Gender in Science and Technology.* Vol. I–IV. New York: Routledge.
Schiebinger, Londa, Ineke Klinge, Hye-Young Paik, Ines Sánchez de Madariaga, Martina Schraudner and Marcia Stefanick. Eds. 2016a. *Gendered Innovations in Science, Health & Medicine, Engineering, and Environment.* https://genderedinnovations.stanford.edu. Accessed: September 17, 2016.
Schiebinger, Londa, Seth S. Leopold and Virginia M. Miller. 2016b. Editorial Policies for Sex and Gender Analysis. *The Lancet* 388 (10062): 2841–2842.
Schmitz, Sigrid. 2016. Science. In *Gender: Sources, Perspectives, and Methodologies*, ed. by Renée C. Hoogland, 347–362. Farmington Hills: Macmillan.
Schmitz, Sigrid. 2017. Die Un/Verfügbarkeit von BrainBodies-in-TechnoCultures: Feministisch materialistische Auseinandersetzungen mit Brain-Computer-Interfaces. In *Verantwortung und Un/Verfügbarkeit. Impulse und Zugänge eines (neo)materialistischen Feminismus*, ed. by Corinna Bath, Hanna Meißner, Stephan Trinkaus and Susanne Völker, 207–223. Münster: Verlag Westfälisches Dampfboot.
Schmitz, Sigrid, and Nina Degele. 2010. Embodying – ein dynamischer Ansatz für Körper und Geschlecht in Bewegung. In *Gendered Bodies in Motion*, ed. by Nina Degele, Sigrid Schmitz, Marion Mangelsdorf and Elke Gramespacher, 13–36. Leverkusen: Budrich UniPress.
Schmitz, Sigrid, and Grit Höppner. 2014. Feminist Neuroscience: A Critical Review of Contemporary Brain Research. *Frontiers in Human Neuroscience* 8, doi: 10.3389/fnhum.2014.00546.
Singh, Sarah, and Ineke Klinge. 2015. Mining for Method. A Critical Review of the Theoretical and Methodological Contributions of Feminist Science Scholars for Biomedicine and Public Health Research. *Freiburger Zeitschrift für GeschlechterStudien* 21 (2): 15–31.
Spivak, Gayatri Chakraworty. 2012. *An Aesthetic Education in the Era of Globalization.* Cambridge: Harvard University Press.
Wizemann, Thereza M., and Mary-Lou Pardue. Eds. 2001. *Exploring the Biological Contributions to Human Health: Does Sex Matter?* Committee on Understanding the Biology of Sex and Gender Differences. Washington/DC: National Academies Press.
Zemp, Elisabeth, Elke Gramespacher and Londa Schiebinger. 2015. Harnessing the Creative Power of Sex and Gender Analysis for Discovery and Innovation. Londa Schiebinger Meets Elisabeth Zemp and Elke Gramespacher. *Freiburger Zeitschrift für Geschlechter-Studien* 21 (2): 115–125.
Zentrum für Anthropologie und Gender Studies (ZAG). 2016. *Vernetzung von Gender-Perspektiven in den Natur- und Technikwissenschaften.* http://www.genderingmint.uni-freiburg.de/index.php. Accessed: September 17, 2016.

Academic Feminism and Exclusion in Brazil: Bringing Back Some of the Missing Voices

Cristiano Rodrigues and Mariana Prandini Assis

Abstract

By investigating the constitution of gender and feminist studies in Brazil as part of the larger 'feminist discursive field of action' (Alvarez 2014), we claim that throughout its development and particularly in its struggle with mainstream academia and science governance to contest its scientific marginalisation, this portion of the feminist field ended up producing some other exclusions of its own. Thus, and unintentionally, it contributed to perpetuating part of the marginalisation that is characteristic of hegemonic modes of thinking and knowledge production. More specifically, besides attaching itself to rather reductive notions of what its political subject is (femaleness/womanhood), it also did not create the conditions and the space within which voices articulated from the far margins, such as that of Black women, could flourish. Along these lines, we claim that in the Brazilian context, one of the ways for gender studies and research to continue to be asserted as scientifically and socially useful and relevant is to continuously confront the exclusions that it itself produces. Therefore, a commitment to radical inclusion, which in our article appears through the acknowledgment of Black feminist knowledge production in Brazil, appears as an important and effective means to reassert gender studies' social usefulness.

Keywords

Academic Feminism, Brazil, Inclusion, Exclusion, Black Feminist Voices

1 Introduction

Academic feminism has become an established field and critical assessments of it are now commonplace everywhere. From teachers who resent the fact that their students are introduced to feminism through academic texts rather than politics to activists who understand feminism's entrance into universities as a kind of betrayal of its radical transformative political project (Wigeman 2002), multiple voices have risen to question the decision of challenging women's exclusion from the academy by becoming part of this very same structure.

While in Brazil many of these questions resonate, our article focuses on a different challenge posed by the institutionalisation of feminism. We are concerned with the process through which academic feminists challenge educational institutions and ultimately hegemonic forms of knowledge production and dissemination for their exclusionary tendencies towards women. It is our contention that, in confronting these patterns, Brazilian academic feminists took a contradictory path that reproduced exclusionary forms of interaction already present within broadly conceived feminism. Such a course, as we demonstrate by taking up Black feminist contributions, generated forms of feminist knowledge that did not respond fully to the needs of women occupying very different and even unequal social positions. In other words, Brazilian academic feminism unintentionally built itself upon exclusions, as most of its debates were constructed in the absence of Black women's voices, amongst other groups. Black feminists, in intervening in these debates, not only challenged the consequences of such exclusions for feminist knowledge production, but also pointed to their relation to larger structures of oppression prevalent in Brazilian society. In doing so, they affirmed the societal usefulness of feminist studies which consists, in our view, in providing a critique of exclusionary social arrangements from the perspectives of race, gender and class.

To show how the process described above unfolded in recent Brazilian history, we start by highlighting the first steps taken by feminist academics towards the establishment of academic feminism in the country, within what Alvarez (2014) has called 'the feminist discursive field of action'[1]. Next, we not only identify the Black feminists' critique of the restrictive character of the research agenda then proposed by those who entered the academy, but also discuss what we see as their four major points of contention, namely patriarchy, paid domestic work, sexual and reproductive rights, and the implicit subject of feminism itself. In the third section of the article, after establishing that only very recently has race been incorporated

1 All the sources in Portuguese used and cited in this article have been translated into English by the authors.

into the women's and gender studies' agenda in Brazil, we examine the three large and interrelated factors responsible for this ongoing shift: first, the democratisation of access to higher education; second, the positive reception of intersectionality as a scholarly concept and third, the profound transformation in the discourses about oppression.

In summary, it is our contention that in order not only to enter academia, but also to be recognised as equals within this specialised space, feminist academics adopted a "tightrope strategy" (Costa 1994, p. 402). Such a strategy, which was deemed successful, consisted in finding a point of equilibrium between the advantages and disadvantages of institutionalisation through a minimal formalisation that would serve as a shield against criticism from more established fields. We argue, however, that an unintended effect of this plan of action was the reproduction of fissures and exclusions that not only already characterised feminism at large, but also became more accentuated in the academic intervention. Particularly, issues of race were neglected, if not dismissed altogether, by feminists who successfully established themselves as recognised researchers.

In conclusion, we claim that one of the ways for feminist studies and research to continue to be asserted as scientifically and socially useful and relevant in the Brazilian context is to steadily acknowledge and confront the exclusions that it itself produces. This means a commitment to radical inclusion that is a necessary consequence of such a critique, which we embrace in our article through the recognition of Black feminist knowledge production.

2 Academic Feminism in Brazil: Axes of Conflict, Exclusion and Solidarity

Various feminist scholars, such as Teresa de Lauretis (1986), Joan Scott (2008), Sonia Alvarez (2014) and Cecilia Sardenberg (2007), to mention but a few, have shown that the institutionalisation of feminism in academia is a process full of contradictions and marked by a permanent crisis of identity. Since the establishment of the first women's studies programmes in the United States in the 1960s, there has been a constant attempt to establish the connections between feminist activism, political consciousness and the production of knowledge that is academically validated. And despite its continuous institutionalisation, academic feminism still faces strong criticisms about its validity.

On the one hand, there are critiques from those who see academic feminism as excessively politicised and of this very reason has little scientific value. On the other hand, there are feminists who consider the institutionalisation of feminism as one of the factors that contributed to distancing academics and activists. In addition, the latter also believe that institutionalisation diminished feminism's emancipatory potential, as the traditional academic model of production and validation of knowledge gradually tamed the former (Messer-Davidow 2002). Derrida (1987, p. 190) pointed to the fact that, by institutionalising themselves, women's studies programmes would risk becoming "just another cell in the university beehive".

Even though originally directed at the North American and European contexts, Derrida's critique also resonated in Latin America, as Costa and Sardenberg (1994) have shown, prompting a diverse range of debates about the successes and limits of women's studies as an academic-political project. Amidst disputes, it is faithful to claim that Latin American feminists regard academic feminism as a political-analytical space, with a twofold dimension. First, the establishment of academic feminism is for them a response to the vindication, vocalised by historically marginalised social groups, that there should be more representation in science and research. Second, academic feminism is also a space to produce knowledge and political reasoning with relevant impact on the university curriculum (Miranda 2003), opening it up for gender and intersectional politics and policies.

The publication of Heleieth Saffioti's PhD dissertation in 1967, titled *A Mulher na Sociedade de Classes: Mito e Realidade (Women in Class Society: Myth and Reality),* is often seen as a landmark of the institutionalisation of academic feminism in Brazil. Saffioti's work, which was strongly influenced by a Marxist perspective and with a focus on women's work, domestic violence and patriarchy, has become highly influential among feminists, setting the tone for much of the research carried out in the awakening of academic feminism in the country.

The institutionalisation of feminism in Brazil, led mostly by white middle-class women, embodies some of the dilemmas and contradictions highlighted by Derrida (1987). In the struggle to establish themselves in the universities and have their epistemic and scientific relevance acknowledged by their peers, many feminists started occupying the position of "guardians of the law" (Derrida 1987, p. 190). Such a position contributed to their reluctance in including other voices, which, in and of itself, generated other forms of exclusion and marginalisation as we attempt to demonstrate in this article.

At the end of the 1960s and the beginning of the 1970s, Brazil went through a period of profound social and political transformations that not only both directly and indirectly affected the social status of women but also significantly altered the university structure. A reform of the higher education system took place in

1968. Despite being led by the dictatorial government,[2] this reform created the conditions that enabled some higher education institutions, particularly the public ones, to connect teaching and research activities.[3] Lifetime chairs became extinct, departmental structures were created and academic careers were institutionalised, determining that entry and progression in professorship positions would be based on the criteria of academic titles rather than personal relationships with state bureaucrats. The government also instituted a graduate national policy, strengthening the role of federal and state development agencies and the organisation of the first master's and PhD programmes in the country.

In the social realm, there was an expansion of the migratory flux to large urban centres in the southeast, an increase in urbanisation, higher levels of schooling, diffusion of the means of communication, greater participation of women in the workforce and a reduction in the reproduction rates. These transformations altogether profoundly altered traditional gender relations and created new demands from different social groups, particularly women (Costa 1994).

The expansion of higher education meant not only that the number of female students increased almost to the same levels of male students, but also that this new contingent of women in the universities could qualify themselves for insertion in the academic field, particularly the social sciences (Costa 1994). For Costa (1994, p. 403), before the 1970s, women's studies were in a kind of a limbo in Brazil, with very few relevant contributions, mostly concentrated on topics with more legitimacy within the social sciences, such as work, development and population.

The emergence in the 1970s of more systematic studies about women is a direct consequence of the changes taking place, on the one hand, in the realm of social life and the structure of the universities, as described above, and on the other hand, the expansion of feminist political mobilisation. Feminist activism played a fundamental role at this moment in the direction of the types of research conducted, which concentrated their efforts in "giving visibility to women, recovering their presence in history, and, within social life, in unveiling androcentrism as a vice for scientific knowledge, therefore conferring legitimacy to the new field of studies" (Costa 1994, p. 404).

---

2 After a military coup against democratically elected President João Goulart in 1964, Brazil lived under a civil-military dictatorship until 1985. For more on the dictatorial rule in Brazil, see Skidmore (1988).

3 Ironically, the civil-military dictatorship was also responsible for implementing some legal reforms, such as laws allowing for divorce and for married women to own property, which contributed not only to the improvement of women's legal status in Brazilian society, but also to their entrance into the workforce. For more on this issue, see Htun (2003).

We understand the process of institutionalisation of academic feminism in Brazil as a part of the larger development of 'the feminist discursive field of action', as Alvarez (2014) argues. To ground this claim, we first need to clarify that Alvarez's analytical category, 'the feminist discursive field of action', emerged within her project of contesting the adequacy of the social movement in its classical sense[4] for describing Latin American feminism. Alvarez's research agenda is committed to mapping a feminist field she sees as "large, heterogeneous, polycentric, multifaceted and polyphonic, [...] extending well beyond the organisations or groups that belonged to the movement *strictu sensu*" (Alvarez 1998, p. 265, original emphasis). For describing such a thing that cannot be understood as a social movement, Alvarez (2014, p. 16) coined the term "discursive field of action", a permanent formation of late/decolonial modernity.

As such, the discursive fields of action describe much more than mere collections of organisations focused on a specific issue; they in fact congregate "a vast array of individual and collective actors as well as social, cultural and political places" (Alvarez 2014, p. 18). These dynamic discursive fields of action are historically configured and reconfigured, which means that "both their more politically and culturally visible sectors, as well as the nodal points articulated within them, vary throughout time" (Alvarez 2014, p. 18). As Alvarez describes them, the development of the feminist discursive fields of action can be captured in three different moments:

> "1) a first moment of 'centering' and the configuration of 'feminism in the singular'; 2) a second moment of 'decentering' and pluralization of feminisms and gender mainstreaming (flux or vertical transversality); and 3) a third moment, the current one, in which we see what I call '*sidestreaming*', the horizontal flux of discourses and practices of plural feminisms to various parallel sectors in civil society, and the resulting multiplication of feminist fields." (Alvarez 2014, p. 16–17, original emphasis)

We propose to understand the first decade of institutionalisation of academic feminism in Brazil as a period of 'centering', characterised by an attempt to delimitate the boundaries of what both the object and the subject of such a feminism would be. According to Bandeira (2000, p. 17), the feminist movement of the 1970s, formed in its majority by white middle-class women, became a prisoner of the temptation

4 In the classical sense of the term, a social movement is "derived from the social struggles that have been developing since the nineteenth century and that afterward is reformulated with the paradigm of the 'new social movements' in the 1980s, but in the two instances denotes massive protests on the street, visible, palpable and constant mobilizations, etc." (Alvarez 1998, p. 265).

of equality: a certain way of being a woman (Western, white, heterosexual and middle class) prevailed. From this woman defined in the singular, an intra-gender solidarity, based exclusively on biological identity, was envisioned and defended. Differences and inequalities among women coming from diverse social places, religious experiences, racial backgrounds and sexual orientation, to mention only a few, were dismissed altogether. It was against this temptation of equality that Brazilian Black women insurrected within, and counter to, hegemonic feminism. They claimed that the struggle for democratising social relations had to go beyond the search for equality between men and women, because such a demand alone would not guarantee a sorority among the latter.

For this reason, the relationship between Black and white feminists, in academic and activist spaces alike was, from the very beginning, characterised by several controversies and disputes around a political grammar not attentive enough to the intersections of gender, race and class. A close reading of the works of important Brazilian Black feminists, such as Lélia Gonzalez, Luiza Bairros, Matilde Ribeiro, Sueli Carneiro and Jurema Werneck, among many others, reveals a shared perception that prevalent feminist demands did not touch upon issues deemed crucial to Black women at the time. Moreover, they also identified that white feminists did not recognise the centrality of race and racism in Black women's lives. Indeed, as acknowledged by Corrêa (2001), there was an explicit lack of reflection on the relationship between race and gender. If feminism enabled women to constitute a political subject that gave voice to their struggle and allowed them to enter the academic space, this unified and universal identity was quickly destabilised by Black feminist voices.

Nonetheless, we argue that this destabilisation only very recently started to affect feminist interventions in the Brazilian academy. It is our contention that this late response to the marginalisation of Black feminist voices is a result of the "tightrope strategy" (Costa 1994, p. 402) adopted by feminists who first occupied academic spaces. While they were fearless in denouncing the marginalisation of women by hegemonic forms of knowledge production, they were also blind to other structures of oppression, such as racism, and their influence on academic structures and careers. By not paying attention to the critiques developed by Black feminists outside the walls of universities and research centres, academic feminists turned out to reproduce the same kind of exclusions that characterise Brazilian society at large and hegemonic academic spaces particularly. Addressing such a shortcoming is, in our view, crucial for reasserting the social usefulness of feminist studies, which is certainly linked to a steady critique of various exclusions produced by entrenched systems of oppression, such as patriarchy and racism. One of the ways of tackling this issue, in the Brazilian case, is to take seriously some of the most salient controversies developed by Black feminist scholars, as we do below.

2.1 Black Women with and against Patriarchy

The concept of patriarchy, which was very influential for the political mobilisation of women in the 1960s and 1970s, continually extrapolated the limits of activism in the next few decades with its incorporation of different studies about women. According to Costa (1998), radical feminists defined patriarchy as a sexual system of power that perpetuates itself through marriage, family and the sexual division of labour. Some authors, such as Piscitelli (2002), point out that feminism sought in patriarchy an explanation for the origins of women's oppression. However, academic reflections about this concept left behind some of its central components, making it almost empty of meaning, a mere signifier of masculine domination.

For Black feminists, the concept of patriarchy, albeit useful, is ahistorical, generalist and essentialist, and therefore incapable of accounting for the experience of Black women in multiracial societies structurally marked by racism, such as Brazil. The testimony of Luiza Bairros, an important Brazilian Black feminist, sheds light on some of these divergences:[5]

> "When we began to dialogue with the white feminist movement, there was, on the part of white feminists, a great misunderstanding of the questions facing black women. In retrospect I see that, for example, the feminist discussion of patriarchy as a system that promotes the superiority of men over women was a very important thing. But black women never absorbed this analysis of patriarchy as being '*the* analysis'. For black women discussing the issues of women, the starting point was always racism. And as racism is a system of oppression that seems, in my opinion, to affect a much larger sphere than patriarchy itself, I mean to say this: it wasn't enough for us, in that time, to just analyze the question of how oppression expressed itself as man over woman, because we understood that the black man was also disempowered within society. So actually, this thing of the black men's machismo was not exactly equal to the machismo of white men, in that the black men's machismo was subordinate, undervalued by the racism of the white man." (Bairros cited by Rodrigues 2006, p. 159, original emphasis)

In this context, while for white feminists the focus of the struggle should be the value accorded by the systems of explanation for existing social inequalities between

---

5 The quotation originates from an interview with Luiza Bairros conducted by Cristiano Rodrigues (2006) for his master's thesis.

men and women, and thus maintaining the centrality of patriarchy as the main source of women's oppression, Black feminists understood things differently. For them, racism was a more comprehensive category to explain the subaltern position they occupied and, in fact, still occupy, in Brazilian society.

Albeit still marginalised in relation to mainstream feminist scholarly production, Black feminist critiques on the concept of patriarchy ended up contributing to its reformulation within the debate taking place among a few other Brazilian feminists. Such a conclusion can be drawn, for example, from a reading of Saffioti's – a white feminist – definition of patriarchy,

> "as one of the schemes of domination-exploitation that make up a symbiosis in which the capitalist mode of production and racism also participate. [...] It can, therefore, be used to designate another conception of gender relations (symbiosis patriarchy-racism-capitalism), which is distinct from approaches that borrow dualistic positions such as of Weber (1964) and Rubin (1975)." (Saffioti 1992, p. 194)

The idea of a patriarchal racism, which can be found in the works of Gonzalez (1979, 1988), plays an important role in explaining how, in Brazilian society, the interconnections between the whitening ideology and the myth of racial democracy generated a sophisticated form of racism. By sustaining the harmonious coexistence amongst whites, Blacks and indigenous peoples, this sophisticated form of racism obliterates the power asymmetries that mark social interactions between these distinct racial groups, thus naturalising various forms of oppressions. For Gonzalez (1984, p. 228), the myth of racial democracy is particularly cruel for Black women because its patriarchal-racist ideological system of domination (Gonzalez 1988) highlights the specific forms in which gender inequalities intersect racial inequalities in ways that position Black women at the very bottom of the Brazilian social pyramid. Nonetheless, and despite its explanatory capacity, the notion of patriarchal racism continues to be an overlooked category in feminist analyses of the forms of oppression and domination that characterise social relations in Brazil.

2.2 Black Women and Paid Domestic Work

One of the effects of patriarchal racism, frequently alluded to by Black feminists in different moments during the past four decades, are the intra-gender asymmetries characterising the entrance and participation of Black women in the formal workforce.

In 1985, the year when the UN Women's Decade ended, Sueli Carneiro and Thereza Santos published the book *Mulher Negra (Black Woman)*, which continues to be to this day one of the most complete works on the social condition of Black women in Brazil. The authors argue that despite the many studies on the condition of Brazilian women published during the Women's Decade, "the variable race was not considered in a systematic manner in such theoretical engagement, particularly in a way that Black women could benefit from the studies in question" (Carneiro and Santos 1985, p. 39).

Relying on the statistical data collected by the census from the 1950s until the 1980s, Carneiro and Santos (1985) show the underprivileged socioeconomic position occupied by Black women in comparison with that of white men and women. The authors also provide a basis to understand the conflicts and tensions that exist between Black and white women within feminism. For them, white women were the only ones who benefited from the professional and educational diversification that happened between the 1960s and 1980s in Brazil, thus obtaining advantages in terms of access to education, integration in the job market and higher salaries. Therefore, "the mentioned inequalities between Black and white women anticipate the political and ideological tensions that derive from them, putting whites and Blacks in a political contradiction most of the time, despite their shared female condition" (Carneiro and Santos 1985, p. 40).

In 2016, a study conducted by the Brazilian Ministry of Labour and the Institute of Economic Applied Research reinforced the claims put forth by Carneiro and Santos more than 30 years earlier. According to this study, paid domestic work in Brazil is an almost exclusively female job (92 per cent of domestic workers are women). Paid domestic work is the occupation of 5,939,240 Brazilian women, making up to 14 per cent of the female employed workforce in the country. There is a caveat, though: Black women are the majority of the workers in this sector; more specifically, they are 61 per cent versus 39 per cent of white women. The reason for this overrepresentation is the precariousness of the activity. Black women have lower levels of education – a medium of 7.6 years of schooling, in comparison with 9 years of schooling for white women – and until 2014, when a constitutional amendment was passed, 70 per cent of the domestic workers did not have their labour rights secured (Instituto de Pesquisas Econômicas Aplicadas 2016, p. 28).

These data and information, long highlighted by Black feminist scholars and activists, point not only to a crucial source of inequality amongst women, but also perhaps to something even more politically relevant. White women active in the workforce, including academics, benefit from the low-paid domestic work of Black women. In very simple terms, in order to break through the glass ceiling in various careers in the job market, white women lean on other women, particularly Black women (Fraser and Gutting 2015). In such conditions, in which Black women can identify their white counterparts as their immediate exploiters, it is hardly an easy task to envision an agenda of solidarity and shared goals. Contradictions of this kind are the ones that Black feminist voices highlight when exposing the veiled dimensions of paid domestic work in Brazil.

2.3 Black Women and the Contestation about Health, Sexual and Reproductive Rights

The public debate about reproductive health, race and gender in Brazil is not only very complex but also extremely contentious. However, it is a fundamental debate to consider if one aims at understanding the particularities of what many Black feminists have named patriarchal racism in the country.

The Brazilian government adopted, in the 1970s and 1980s, the surgical sterilisation of women both as a means of demographic control and as a contraceptive method. Due to the indiscriminate use of sterilisation in the mid-1980s, 27 per cent of the women who made use of some kind of contraceptive method had been surgically sterilised (Instituto Brasileiro de Geografia e Estatística 1986). The rates for the same procedure were flagrantly lower in European countries during the same time frame: 6 per cent in France, 7 per cent in the United Kingdom and 4 per cent in Italy, which points to its being abused in Brazil. In this scenario, anti-racist activists urged Black women not to subject themselves to birth control, because they understood that the state was engaged in a bio-political strategy aimed at exterminating the Black population. White feminists, on the other hand, advocated the complete deregulation of any practices of birth control.

In 1993, *Geledés*, a leading Black women's non-governmental organisation in the country, organised the *National Seminar on the Reproductive Policies and Rights of Black Women* as part of the preparatory events for the UN *International Conference on Population and Development* to be held in Cairo the following year. Fifty-five participants, all of them connected to women's organisations, Black organisations, universities and public health services, attended the seminar. The seminar released, as its closing document, the *Itapecerica da Serra Declaration (National Seminar on the Reproductive Policies and Rights of Black Women* 1993), which faulted the Brazilian government for treating reproduction as a public issue and the means of sustaining life as a private matter (Ribeiro 1995; Roland 1995, 2000). The final document asserted:

> "The state has basically come to treat reproduction as a public issue, and the means of sustaining life – housing, health, education, food and work – as a private matter. Understanding this role reversal is crucial at this juncture in preparation for the *International Population and Development Conference* III [...]. *Reproductive freedom*

> *is essential for those ethnicities that are discriminated against.* Therefore, we must fight so that reproductive decisions are made in the private realm, with the state guaranteeing reproductive rights and ensuring healthy conditions for sustaining life." (*National Seminar on the Reproductive Policies and Rights of Black Women* 1993, p. 3, authors' emphasis)

The debate initiated during this seminar surpassed the frontiers of activism and became a theme for academic investigation as well as institutional political scrutiny, with the establishment of parliamentary inquiry commissions on the racial character of sterilisation in the country. In addition, since the seminar, most non-governmental organisations and Black women's collectives have enhanced their health programmes for Black women, receiving funding from an array of agencies as diverse as the Brazilian Ministry of Health, the International Women's Health Coalition, the MacArthur Foundation, the Ford Foundation and the United Nations, among others, to develop their projects (Roland 2000).

In 1996, the Ministry of Health sponsored a roundtable on the health of the Black population. However, no consensus was reached on the need to create programmes focused specifically on Black people's health. The only exception was the *Sickle Cell Anaemia Programme*, a disease with proven greater impact on the Black population, which presented sufficiently compelling statistics to justify it as a public health priority (Roland 2001; Maio and Monteiro 2005; Rodrigues 2010). In 1997, the federal government established the *Programme for the Health of the Black Population* that nonetheless turned out to be a failure from the very beginning because it received neither an allocation of resources nor a defined set of guidelines (Roland 2001).

In 2004, under the first Worker's Party administration, the Ministry of Health and the Special Secretariat for the Promotion of Racial Equality signed a commitment with the intent of implementing a national health policy for the Black population. As part of this agreement, the Technical Committee on the Health of Black People was created with the task of systematising proposals for the promotion of racial equity in healthcare access.

The First Seminar on the Health of Black People, which produced the document *National Health Policy for the Black Population: A Question of Equity*, followed the creation of the Technical Committee. The document emphasised the need to expand Black people's access to the public health system, the importance of including race/colour on birth and death certificates, and the need to develop policies that could meet the particular health needs of specific ethnic and racial groups (Maio and Monteiro 2005).

In 2006, the National Health Council approved the *National Health Policy for the Black Population*. Amongst the programme's guidelines, there were distinguishing intrinsic factors of certain diseases prevalent among the Black population from factors resulting from social exclusion, such as poverty and lack of education. Further, the programme asserted that there is institutional racism within the public health system in Brazil that negatively affects the care provided to the Black population (Rodrigues 2010).

This other layer of inequality amongst Black and white women, despite being highlighted in both Black feminists' texts and more recently in specific public policies, has also not received the necessary attention from mainstream feminist intervention in the academy. Sexual and reproductive rights are an extremely relevant topic for feminists in Brazil, a country that still criminalises abortion in most situations. However, until race is fully integrated into an intersectional approach to sexuality and reproduction, we will continue to provide a partial and exclusionary account of what the needs and issues confronted by women are.

2.4 Feminist Theoretical Production, the Politics of Translation and the Production of 'Implicit Subjects'

The core of Black women's critiques of feminism in the 1970s and 1980s is the marginalisation and ultimately the neglect of Black women's political actions. According to Ribeiro (2006), both in feminist discourses and theoretical production, Black women appear as neglected subjects because:

> "Historically, society has absorbed in a more efficacious manner the demands of white women as part of a 'natural process'. Race is still a taboo; the struggle against racism, for racism's subtlety and masking, has not succeeded as a relevant social theme." (Ribeiro 2006, p. 803–804)

Azeredo (1994), when discussing the reception and diffusion of feminist theories coming from the global north amongst us, reaches similar conclusions. She attempts to understand the reasons why, in such an unequal and multiracial society that has been deeply marked by the experience of slavery, race and racism remain largely ignored by feminist theoretical production and practice. While comparing the American and Brazilian feminist scholarships, Azeredo argues that in Brazil the debate on race has been almost entirely left for Black women to do, as if only they have been marked by race.

The first groups (and a nucleus for women's studies) which were established in the country in the 1980s were inspired by the American model of women's studies programmes (Azeredo 1994). However, this inspiration was only partial. A critique of racism within the feminist movements and academic circuits as it had taken place in the United States and was expressed in various books[6] was not present here. Following Azeredo's critiques (1994), we argue that the reception and diffusion of the theories developed by Black, Latina and African feminists as well as women of colour has happened late and only partially in Brazil. The focus on translations is important, because we understand feminism as a multi-located practice, and the politics of translation as essential to engender "epistemologies and feminist, anti-racist and postcolonial political alliances" (Alvarez 2009, p. 744).

While imported white feminists stormed academia, greatly influencing the scholarship theorising women's role in Brazilian society, the impact of the intersections of gender, race and class along with the specific forms in which racism and sexism affect Black women had, for a long time, been practically forgotten by Brazilian academia, and only recently have gained some attention (Rodrigues 2006). This is reflected by the fact that on the one hand there are thousands of academic publications on women, gender relations and feminist movements, but on the other hand there are very few works on Black women within the feminist debate.

The lateness characterising the translations of non-white feminists in Brazil may be explained by the disparity in terms of participation in the academy: there are very few Black women occupying positions in the universities. In a study about gender and racial inequalities in the access to academic positions, Silva (2010, p. 27) reveals that from a total of 58,618 university professors with a PhD until 2005, as Table 1 shows, only 251 were Black women:

Table 1 Professors by Sex and Colour/Race

Colour/Race	Female	Male	No Information	Total
Asian Brazilian	345	503	0	848
White	15,854	21,662	1	37,517
Native Brazilian	52	92	0	144
Black	251	374	0	625
Brown	1,312	2,114	0	3,426
No Information	5,830	9,457	771	16,058
Total	23,644	34,202	772	58,618

Source: Original compilation by the authors based on Silva's work (2010, p. 28)

6 Such as bell hooks' *Ain't I a Woman? Black Women and Feminism* (1981), Angela Davis's *Women, Race & Class* (1981), and Cherrie Moraga's and Gloria Anzaldúa's *This Bridge Called My Back: Writings by Radical Women of Color* (1981).

The organisation of the Brazilian educational system is in itself one of the factors responsible for this absence of Blacks, men and women alike, in colleges and universities: primary and secondary schooling as well as higher education can be public and tuition-free, or private and paid. However, private primary and secondary schools tend to be of a better quality than public ones, even though the latter have more enrolment capacity than the former. In higher education, there is an inversion. On the one hand, public institutions federally funded or financed by state governments are very prestigious and conduct most of the research in the country; however, access to them is extremely competitive. On the other hand, private institutions are responsible for the majority of the enrolment, dedicating very little funding or personnel for research. The strong interconnection between race and class meant, until very recently, that very few Blacks could access a university. As they could not afford private primary and secondary schooling, ending up in low-quality and poorly funded public schools, they could not effectively compete for a place in public universities. Such an unequal and unjust scheme has only recently started to change, with the adoption of affirmative action in the higher education system, as we show in the next section.

It is thus not by chance that seminal texts, such as Angela Davis's (1981) book mentioned earlier in footnote 6, have only recently been translated and started to circulate amongst a larger audience. Until the mid-2000s, very few articles dealt specifically with the interrelation between gender and race both in *Revista Estudos Femnistas (REF)* and *Cadernos Pagu,* the two major Brazilian feminist journals. One exception was a special issue of *REF*, published in 1995. The *Dossier Black Women* was organised by Matilde Ribeiro, and featured articles written by Lourdes Siqueira, Matilde Ribeiro, Luiza Bairros, bell hooks, Maria Aparecida Silva Bento, Márcia Lima, Rebecca Reichmann, Edna Roland, Maria Aparecida da Silva, Ângela Gilliam, Onik'a Gilliam and Sueli Carneiro.

In the dossier's introduction, Matilde Ribeiro claims that her initial proposal intended to encourage the propagation of empirical research or theoretical arguments about the interconnection between gender, race, racism and political participation. However, after a year of conversations with Brazilian researchers, she realised such a project was doomed to fail because there was not enough research being carried out at that time on such topics. As a result, she ended up inviting a group of Black and white activists and scholars to contribute to the dossier. For her, there was a necessity to intensify the studies about gender and race and, most important, to break away from the taboo that only Black women are responsible for disseminating works on these issues (Ribeiro 1995). The dossier was an important step in this direction.

Alongside the scarcity of empirical and theoretical studies on the intersectionality between gender and race, there is also little systematisation of the ones available. The works produced by authors situated in different disciplinary fields, covering issues that many times juxtapose one another, often do not follow up on previous research or further and critically engage with themes already debated. There is also, perhaps due to the restricted circulation of translations and the lack of deeper engagement with certain themes, a deficiency in terms of theoretical strength (Rodrigues and Prado 2013).

The aforementioned lack of systematisation and continuity of the studies can be explained by various factors. Among them, we highlight the following. First, the limited presence of Black women and representatives of other social minorities in the Brazilian universities. Second, the seemingly unbridgeable gap between the reflections that continuously happen within social movements and the academic analyses about those very social movements. Third, the almost complete absence of Portuguese versions of African-American, European and Latin American Black feminist writings. The lack of a collective effort for translating these works is a symptom of the partial influence American women's studies had on their Brazilian counterparts.[7] And finally, the very absence of discussion among feminists about the impact of racism on women's lives that contributed to the marginalisation of the life experiences of Black women in the Brazilian academy.

3 Bringing Back the Missing Voices? Towards a Multivocal Feminism in Academia

There are no doubts that feminism has had a profound impact on the Brazilian academy, propelling important studies about women and gender relations in the country, while also stimulating the adoption of legislation and public policies with a gender perspective. In addition, the proliferation of outreach and online specialisation

7 It is important to clarify that here we are not romanticising American women's and gender studies programmes as fully inclusionary spaces. However, as we look at their Brazilian counterparts, it is hard to dismiss how deeper exclusions mark the latter. In our view, this can be explained by a socio-political fact. American feminism started dealing with its problems of exclusion a long time before the establishment of its academic arm. Therefore, when it entered the universities, American feminism brought with it the racial tensions and contentions that existed within the movements. In Brazil, the issue of exclusion, despite being constitutive of our society, was raised in a vocal way much later on, when feminists had already occupied spaces within the academy.

programmes on gender studies offered by various universities in different regions of the country, as well as the establishment of the first graduate programme on *Interdisciplinary Studies on Women, Gender and Feminism* at the Federal University of Bahia and, more recently, the first department and undergraduate programme in the same university, are evidence of the scope of that impact.

Nonetheless, until recently race had not been adequately incorporated into the studies on women, gender, and feminism in Brazil. Such a scenario has been slowly changing since the beginning of the 2000s. It is our contention that the confluence of three larger factors contributed not only to the inclusion of race as a category of analysis in recent feminist studies, but also to an expanded dialogue with Black feminist thought. They are, first, the democratisation of access to higher education, second, the positive reception of intersectionality as a concept and third, the profound transformation in the discourses about oppression.

The first government of the Worker's Party, starting in 2003, significantly increased the number of state measures for promoting gender and racial equality. In this context, the debates about the adoption of affirmative action in the public higher education system, which had started during the preparation for the third United Nations *World Conference against Racism, Racial Discrimination, Xenophobia and Related Intolerance* (the so-called Durban Conference), acquired a new footing under Lula's presidency.

Various universities started implementing different formats of affirmative action programmes in their selection processes. The quota system for students coming from the public educational system was the most-adopted model, followed by the one that established the ethnic-racial criteria with the reservation of vacancies for Black and indigenous students. In 2012, the universities maintained by the federal government had their affirmative action policies unified by the *Federal Act* n. 12.711, which established the reservation of vacancies for students coming from the public education system as well as Black, Brown, and indigenous students coming from low-income families.

The policies of affirmative action in the higher education system along with other measures of inclusion in its private counterpart dramatically changed the face of the Brazilian universities. One of the impacts of the greater participation of Black students can be observed in the emergent research and activism issues. New research centres on gender and race have been created in different universities, courses on Black feminist thought have been offered in undergraduate and graduate programmes, and special issues on topics such as 'intersectionality', 'intersectional feminism', and 'racism and sexism' among others have been published in important scientific journals. Finally, even if in a dispersed and informal manner, the works of relevant Latin American, American and African Black feminists have been translated and discussed in study groups and feminist collectives throughout the country.

The quite positive reception of the concept of intersectionality among us has also contributed to a larger incorporation of race as an important category of analysis by feminist studies. In the Anglo-Saxon context, intersectionality has a long history that goes back to Sojourner Truth's famous speech *Ain't I a Woman?* (Truth, 1989 [1851]), continues with the Combahee River Collective's statement (Combahee River Collective 1986), and finally reaches Crenshaw's famous formulation originally published in 1989 (Crenshaw 1989). In Brazil the research agenda on the relationship between race and class is relatively old, starting long before the seminal studies of Gilberto Freyre (1933). The 1950s, when a field of inquiry known as the *Sociology of Race Relations* began to develop more systematically, were particularly prolific at producing studies with such an approach. Works on the interweaving of race, gender and class, however, were rare and peripheral until the 1980s. Ruth Landes' book, *The City of Women* (1947), which concentrated on the woman-centred dimension of Bahia's *candomblé*, along with Virginia Bicudo's master's thesis, defended in 1945, which concentrated on the racial attitudes of Blacks and Browns in São Paulo, are great examples of research with a perspective that later would be considered intersectional but which were completely neglected at the time of their appearance.

In the 1980s, Lélia Gonzalez (1988) and Sueli Carneiro (2003), important Black intellectuals and activists, tried to articulate in a more systematic way race, class and gender in their theorisation, at the same time when the term 'intersectionality' was coined in the United States. Carneiro (2003, p. 119) stated, for instance, that Black women had to "blacken" the agenda of the feminist movement and "sexualize" that of the Black movement, all at once. In so doing, they would promote a diversity of ideas and political practices within both movements while also claiming themselves as new political subjects and producers of knowledge.

Lélia Gonzalez (1988), however, critiqued the dominant paradigms in the social sciences and academic feminism for their failure to acknowledge and reflect upon the trajectories of resistance of Black and indigenous women in Latin America. Her writings can also be seen as 'decolonial' insofar as Gonzalez sought to subvert both stylistically and linguistically textual forms considered canonical in the humanities. She adopted a hybrid language, representative of a mestizo identity or, as Patricia Hill Collins (1986, p. 514) would put it, made a creative use of her "outsider within" status. Gonzalez (1988, p. 76) herself calls this hybridism "pretoguês", that is, an assemblage that marks the Africanisation of the Portuguese spoken in Brazil. She also coined the concept of "*amefricanity*" to refer to the shared experience of

Black people in the diaspora and the indigenous people's struggle against colonial domination (Gonzalez 1988, p. 76, original emphasis).

The writings of Carneiro and Gonzalez, although original and forerunners of the intersectional paradigm that would become very influential in the 2000s, had little impact in academia in the 1980s and 1990s. It is our contention that four factors contributed to this. First, the marginal position that both intellectuals occupied within the Brazilian academy at the time. Lélia Gonzalez only became a university professor shortly before her death while Sueli Carneiro has dedicated herself more to activism and to strengthening *Geledés*, the most important Black women's non-governmental organisation in the country, which she co-founded in the 1980s. Second, academics in more hegemonic fields of the social sciences and humanities often see Gonzalez and Carneiro's writings as excessively activist. Third, the geopolitical division of labour in the system of knowledge production creates a situation in which concepts coined in the global north have greater recognition than those developed in the global south. In the case we examine, this means that the pioneering ideas of Gonzalez and Carneiro would never achieve the same visibility and legitimacy that intersectionality enjoys now in Brazil, which does not mean the latter concept undoubtedly has a strong explanatory quality. Finally, as we mentioned earlier, the greater participation of Black students in the universities (considering that they would be more interested in carrying out research on the intersectionality of race, class and gender) is a relatively recent phenomenon.

One last aspect that we highlight in order to examine this growing inclusion of race in feminist studies is the transformation of a certain political grammar of hierarchies and forms of oppression. In the 1970s and 1980s, the hegemonic debate within Brazilian feminism had as its central axes class and sex/gender. Other issues, race included, were considered secondary in a political agenda aimed at achieving equality between men and women, restoring democracy in Brazil, and engendering public policies that would reduce socioeconomic inequalities.

The impact of post-structuralism in the Brazilian academy in the 1990s and of queer theories more recently, combined with a number of other social processes, contributed to dislocating the analytical axis from class-gender to the triad racism-sexism-homo/lesbo/transphobia. While this triad of oppressions still demands a better operationalisation, it is often deployed in different spaces of political intervention and as such has prompted an academic debate that attempts to establish connections and intersections among these different axes of social hierarchisation.

The juxtaposition of the three factors we have just analysed allows us to claim, along with Alvarez (2014), that a process of side-streaming is now taking place within Brazilian academic feminism, which for us has the capacity of expanding the political and social usefulness of feminist studies. That is to say, the fact that gender is migrating or sometimes infiltrating various academic fields and political mobilisations means that it can prompt intersectional politics and policies which in turn contribute to building a more just world. Nonetheless, it is still too early to answer whether such developments will take place, and whether the pluralisation and analytical-theoretical dislocations created by Black feminists will succeed in bringing subjects and themes historically neglected within feminism to centre stage.

4 Conclusion

Inclusion and exclusion has haunted feminism since its inception, and it is no different when we look at its development in Brazil. In this article, we attempted to show that in its establishment within the academy, Brazilian feminism, while contending the exclusion of women, produced and reproduced some other exclusions of its own. This is highlighted by an extensive review of Black feminist intervention, which calls attention to a number of ways that an intersectional approach to race and gender uncover deeper forms of inequalities running through Brazilian society.

While we acknowledge the advances made by feminist scholars in their struggle with mainstream academia, we also identify the shortcomings of a strategy that builds upon a unified and non-existent subject of knowledge. Therefore, it is our contention that in the Brazilian context one of the ways for women's and gender studies and research to assert its scientific and social usefulness and relevance is to continuously confront the exclusions that it itself produces. A commitment to radical inclusion, which in our article appears through the acknowledgment of Black feminist knowledge production in Brazil, is shown to be an important and effective way to reassert feminist studies' social usefulness.

References

Alvarez, Sonia E. 1998. Feminismos latinoamericanos. *Revista Estudos Feministas* 6 (2): 265–285.

Alvarez, Sonia E. 2009. Construindo uma política feminista translocal de tradução. *Revista Estudos Feministas* 17 (3): 743–753.

Alvarez, Sonia E. 2014. Para Além da Sociedade Civil: Reflexões sobre os Campos Feministas. *Cadernos PAGU* 12 (43): 13–56.

Azeredo, Sandra. 1994. Teorizando sobre gênero e relações raciais. In *Colóquio Internacional Brasil, França e Quebec*. Revista Estudos Feministas, Special Issue 2 (2), ed. by Lena Lavinas, 203–216. Rio de Janeiro: UFRJ.

Bandeira, Lourdes. 2000. Feminismo: memória e história. In *Feminismo: memória e história*, ed. by Celecina de Maria Veras Sales, Célia Chaves Gurgel do Amaral and Gema Galgani Silveira Leite Esmeraldo, 15–41. Fortaleza: Imprensa Universitária.

Bicudo, Virgínia Leone. 1945. *Estudo de Atitudes raciais de pretos e mulatos em São Paulo*. Master's Thesis. São Paulo: Escola Livre de Sociologia e Política.

Carneiro, Sueli. 2003. Mulheres em movimento. *Estudos Avançados* 17 (49): 117–132.

Carneiro, Sueli, and Theresa Santos. 1985. *Mulher negra*. São Paulo: Nobel/Conselho Estadual da Condição Feminina.

Collins, Patricia Hill. 1986. Learning from the Outsider Within: The Sociological Significance of Black Feminist Thought. *Social Problems* 33 (6): 514–532.

Combahee River Collective. 1986. *The Combahee River Collective Statement: Black Feminist Organizing in the Seventies and Eighties*. Boston: Kitchen Table/Women of Color.

Corrêa, Mariza. 2001. Do feminismo aos estudos de gênero no Brasil: Um exemplo pessoal. *Cadernos Pagu* (16): 13–30.

Costa, Albertina. 1994. Os estudos da mulher no Brasil ou a estratégia da corda bamba. In *Colóquio Internacional Brasil, França e Quebec*. Revista Estudos Feministas, Special Issue 2 (2), ed. by Lena Lavinas, 401–409. Rio de Janeiro: UFRJ.

Costa, Ana Alice. 1998. *As donas do poder: mulher e política na Bahia*. Salvador: NEIM/UFBa, Assembleia Legislativa da Bahia.

Costa, Ana Alice, and Cecilia Sardenberg. 1994. Teoria e práxis feminista na academia: os núcleos de estudos sobre a mulher nas universidades brasileiras. In *Colóquio Internacional Brasil, França e Quebec*. Revista Estudos Feministas, Special Issue 2 (2), ed. by Lena Lavinas, 387–400. Rio de Janeiro: UFRJ.

Crenshaw, Kimberle. 1989. Demarginalizing the Intersection of Race and Sex: A Black Feminist Critique of Antidiscrimination Doctrine, Feminist Theory and Antiracist Politics. *The University of Chicago Legal Forum* 1989 (1, Art. 8): 139–167.

Derrida, Jacques. 1987. Women in the Beehive: A Seminar with Jacques Derrida. In *Men in Feminism*, ed. by Alice Jardine and Paul Smith, 189–203. New York, London: Routledge.

Fraser, Nancy, and Gary Gutting. 2015. A Feminism Where "Lean In" Means Leaning on Others. *New York Times*, October 15th.

Freyre, Gilberto. 1933. *Casa-grande e senzala*. Rio de Janeiro: Maia & Schmidt.

Gonzalez, Lélia. 1979. Cultura, Etnicidade e Trabalho: Efeitos Linguísticos e Políticos da Exploração da Mulher. 8° *Encontro Nacional da Latin American Studies Association*. Pittsburgh: Encontro Nacional da Latin American Studies Association.

Gonzalez, Lélia. 1984. Racismo e Sexismo na Cultura Brasileira. *Ciências Sociais Hoje* 2 (1): 223–244.

Gonzalez, Lélia. 1988. A categoria político-cultural de amefricanidade. *Tempo Brasileiro* (92–93): 69–82.

Htun, Mala. 2003. *Sex and the State: Abortion, Divorce, and the Family under Latin American Dictatorships and Democracies*. Cambridge: Cambridge University Press.

Instituto Brasileiro de Geografia e Estatística (IBGE). 1986. *Síntese de Indicadores Sociais*. Rio de Janeiro: IBGE.

Instituto de Pesquisas Econômicas Aplicadas (IPEA). 2016. *Retrato das Desigualdades de Gênero e Raça*. Brasília: Ipea.
Landes, Ruth. 1947. *The City of Women*. New York: Macmillan Company.
Lauretis, Teresa de. Ed. 1986. *Feminist Studies, Critical Studies*. Bloomington: Indiana University Press.
Maio, Marcos Chor, and Simone Monteiro. 2005. Tempos de racialização: o caso da "saúde da população negra" no Brasil. *História, Ciências, Saúde - Manguinhos* 12 (2): 419–446.
Messer-Davidow, Ellen. 2002. *Disciplining Feminism: From Social Activism to Academic Discourse*. Durham, London: Duke University Press.
Miranda, Maria Soledad Martinez. 2003. Algunos debates contemporâneos em torno a la categoría género y sus implicaciones para el contexto universitário. *Identidades* 1 (1): 33–38.
National Seminar on the Reproductive Policies and Rights of Black Women. 1993. *Itapecirica da Serra Declaration of Brazilian Black Women*. São Paulo: Geledés.
Piscitelli, Adriana. 2002. Recriando a (categoria) mulher? In A prática feminista e o conceito de gênero. Textos Didáticos, ed. by Leila Algranti, 7–42. Campinas: IFCH-Unicamp.
Ribeiro, Matilde. 1995. Mulheres negras brasileiras: de Bertioga e Beijing. *Revista Estudos Feministas* 3 (2): 446–457.
Ribeiro, Matilde. 2006. O feminismo em novas rotas e visões. *Revista Estudos Feministas* 14 (3): 801–811.
Rodrigues, Carolina Cantarino. 2010. Produção de substâncias, revelação e outras armadilhas no combate ao racismo no Brasil contemporâneo. *Sociedade e Cultura* 13 (1): 125–136.
Rodrigues, Cristiano. 2006. *As Fronteiras entre Raça e Gênero na Cena Pública Brasileira: um estudo da construção da identidade coletiva do Movimento de Mulheres Negras*. Masters's thesis. Belo Horizonte: Universidade Federal de Minas Gerais.
Rodrigues, Cristiano, and Marco Aurélio Prado. 2013. A History of the Black Women's Movement in Brazil: Mobilization, Political Trajectory and Articulations with the State. *Social Movement Studies* 12 (2): 158–177.
Roland, Edna. 1995. Direitos Reprodutivos e Racismo no Brasil. *Revista Estudos Feministas* 3 (2): 506–514.
Roland, Edna. 2000. O movimento de mulheres negras brasileiras: desafios e perspectivas. In *Tirando a máscara: ensaios sobre o racismo no Brasil*, ed. by Antonio Sergio Guimarães and Lynn Huntley, 237–256. São Paulo: Paz e Terra.
Roland, Edna. 2001. Saúde reprodutiva da população negra no Brasil: um campo em construção. *Perspectivas em saúde e direitos reprodutivos* 2 (4): 17–23.
Saffioti, Heleieth I.B. 1978 [1967]. *A mulher na sociedade de classes. Mito e Realidade*. Petrópolis: Vozes.
Saffioti, Heleieth I.B. 1992. Rearticulando gênero e classe social. In *Uma questão de gênero*, ed. by Albertina Costa and Cristina Bruschini, 183–215. Rio de Janeiro: Editora Rosa dos Tempos.
Sardenberg, Cecília. 2007. Da crítica feminista à ciência a uma ciência feminista? *Labrys. Estudos Feministas*11 (1): 45–62.
Scott, Joan. Ed. 2008. *Women's Studies on the Edge*. Durham, London: Duke University Press.
Silva, Joselina da. 2010. Doutoras professoras negras: o que nos dizem os indicadores oficiais. *Perspectiva* 1 (28): 19–36.
Skidmore, Thomas E. 1988. *The Politics of Military Rule in Brazil: 1964–85*. New York, Oxford: Oxford University Press.

Truth, Sojourner. 1989 [1851]. Speech at The Women's Rights Convention Akron, Ohio, 1851. In *Man Cannot Speak for Her: Key Texts of the Early Feminists*, Vol. 2, ed. by Karlyn Kohrs Campbell, 99–102. Westport: Greenwood.

Wigeman, Robin. 2002. Academic Feminism Against Itself. *The National Women's Studies Association Journal* 14 (2): 18–37.

III

Institutionalisations: Gender Studies' Epistemic and Organisational Statuses in the Academy

The Institutionalisation of Gender Studies and the New Academic Governance: Longstanding Patterns and Emerging Paradoxes

Maria do Mar Pereira

Abstract

For several decades, feminist scholars have been producing detailed macro- and micro-level studies of processes of institutionalisation of women's, gender and feminist studies (WGFS). Through that research, they have generated valuable knowledge about the patterns and profiles of WGFS' institutionalisation, and the actors and factors that shape it. In this article, I review that literature and systematise some of its key findings. I then draw on an ethnography of academia to argue that, in some contexts, established patterns in the institutionalisation of WGFS are being transformed by the emergence of new models of academic governance. I identify some of those transformations and highlight the paradoxes that they generate for the institutionalisation of WGFS. I conclude by arguing that an analysis of gender studies in times of new academic governance must consider both the 'new' aspects of that governance and the 'old' inequalities that it covertly reproduces.

Keywords

Gender Studies, Gender Research, Women's Studies, Feminist Research, Institutionalisation, New Academic Governance, Higher Education, Universities, Neo-liberalism

1 Gender Studies in Contemporary Universities

The fact that you are currently holding this book in your hands, or maybe reading it on a screen, is telling. It says something very significant not just about your own (evidently excellent!) taste, but also about contemporary academia more broadly. The impetus to produce this book emerged from a large research project, supported by research council funding and undertaken by a team of gender experts. I received the call for submissions for this book through the mailing list of an international network of academics in women's, gender and feminist studies (WGFS),[1] where I represent my own institution's WGFS research centre and have met colleagues working in WGFS departments around the world. Some of the articles contained here were first presented at WGFS conferences, and the book is being published by an academic publisher with an established gender catalogue. It will no doubt be reviewed (hopefully favourably) in WGFS journals, and it will be shelved in many university libraries alongside other WGFS books, maybe in a section devoted exclusively to WGFS. At some point in the future, sections from the book might be set as recommended reading for undergraduate and postgraduate students taking WGFS courses in other disciplines or enrolled in WGFS degree programmes. You might be one of those students yourself.

Reflecting on the life of this particular book, and the concrete conditions of its production, highlights how institutionalised WGFS currently is as an academic field of teaching, learning and research. WGFS has grown immensely in recent decades; it now has space in buildings and on library shelves, and is represented by professorships and scholarships, specialist degrees and courses, dedicated conferences and publications, physical and online networks, and professional associations. Therefore, WGFS can be described as becoming in the past decades gradually, though not linearly, institutionalised in two distinct but related senses. Firstly, a more or less large and stable space for it has been, and is being, created or extended within many existing institutions, such as the traditional disciplines and the organisations – universities and research centres – where academic work is carried out. Secondly, WGFS has also become an academic institution in itself, one which is more or less (inter)disciplinary (Lykke 2004) and autonomous, and which has its own structures of creation and validation of knowledge and its canonical but

1 Choices about the naming of the field are diverse, complex and contested; play out differently across national contexts; and are shaped by a range of (theoretical, institutional and political) considerations (Hemmings 2006a; Pereira 2017). While I want to acknowledge the importance of these debates, I cannot engage in depth with issues of naming here, and thus use this umbrella term to refer to the field.

contested narratives about what its objects, boundaries, aims and histories are, or should be (Hemmings 2006a, 2011; Pereira 2013b). In other words, we might say that WGFS has gradually become formalised (at many levels: epistemic, organisational, professional, etc.) *as part of* academic structures, and *as an* academic structure, of production, certification and circulation of knowledge.[2]

And yet, this institutionalisation is extremely uneven and context-specific (Braidotti 2000; Griffin 2005a). WGFS is most certainly not institutionalised everywhere; the spaces and resources I identify above are not available at present to WGFS scholars in many countries and contexts. Personally, I can only take advantage of some of those resources myself because I left my country of origin and moved abroad, much like hundreds of other 'educational migrants' who every year travel elsewhere in search of WGFS degrees or jobs (Juhász et al. 2005), though many are increasingly finding their opportunities curtailed by racist migration-control policies and institutional cultures (Gutiérrez-Rodríguez 2016). Processes of institutionalisation of WGFS are not just uneven; they are also complex, unpredictable, shifting and rarely linear. This means that to fully understand the state and status of gender research in times of new academic governance, we must consider the dynamics of the institutionalisation of the field and the ways in which these have changed over time.

But making sense of the dynamics of the institutionalisation of WGFS is not easy. WGFS' institutionalisation, with its diverse local configurations, paces and effects, has been described and debated extensively and in an overwhelming number of publications; it is a body of "literature [which] has [...] expanded beyond one individual's capacity to encompass" (Boxer 1998, p. xvii). This is partly because of the sheer number of publications on the topic and the range of languages in which they are written; it is also because this is an especially complex and heterogeneous body of literature. The tone varies significantly: some texts are more conventionally scholarly research pieces published in peer-reviewed journals or books, many are written in a format more similar to a policy or briefing paper, and others are published outside or "between the lines" (Fernandes 2008, p. 89)[3] of habitual academic outlets, as polemics, interchanges or manifestos.

2 The definition of *institutionalisation* that I use here – and which is inspired by Chen (2004, p. 5) – is not consensual within WGFS. Some authors prefer a narrower definition, where 'institutionalisation' refers specifically to the incorporation of WGFS in academic institutions and is distinguished from 'disciplinisation', understood as the constitution of WGFS as a discipline (Widerberg 2006).

3 All translations into English are made by the author.

This article uses that established and diverse literature about the origins and history of the institutionalisation of WGFS as a starting point to reflect on the situation of WGFS in contemporary times of a new academic governance. I hope to contribute to laying the groundwork for this book's discussion of the relationship between gender research and the new academic governance by discussing how that new governance has affected the longstanding patterns of institutionalisation of WGFS described in the literature. I begin the article by reviewing the literature on the institutionalisation of WGFS, and briefly systematising some of its key findings about the patterns of that institutionalisation. I will then use findings from an ethnographic study of academia in Portugal (Pereira 2012, 2014, 2015, 2016, 2017) to show that recent changes in academic governance have in some instances transformed those patterns of institutionalisation. I will demonstrate that those transformations have, in several ways, been paradoxical and thus argue that, when thinking about WGFS, we must understand the transition to the new academic governance as a process characterised both by change and by continuity.

2 The Institutionalisation of Gender Studies: Macro- and Micro-Level Patterns

Since the emergence of WGFS, many authors have produced detailed, located accounts of processes of institutionalisation. Their aim is usually to identify how those processes have been shaped by different actors and factors. Many of these studies also have a second aim: they seek to compare and contrast the institutionalisation of WGFS in different contexts. Studies of institutionalisation are usually based on prolonged and in-depth empirical research, with collection of quantitative and qualitative data through surveys, interviews, archival research, and analysis of personal and organisational documents.

Some of this work is *macro-level* research which takes large regions or countries as its unit of analysis and focuses on broad political, economic, or educational structures and trends. It shows that the forms and pace of the institutionalisation of WGFS in a given location are shaped by a complex combination of several macro-level factors. This research has demonstrated, for example, that the structure of higher education in a given region has a significant impact on the possibilities for institutionalisation: creation of WGFS courses and degrees has generally been faster and more extensive in countries where there is a high degree of university autonomy in developing curricula, flexible and modular degree structures, and state support for the creation of lectureships or chairs in WGFS (Barazzetti and Leone

2003; Bird 2001; Braidotti et al. 1995, 1998; Griffin 2005a; Silius 2002; Zimmermann 2007). The configuration of academic communities also affects the opportunities of, and preferred strategies for, institutionalisation: in contexts where academia is more rigidly disciplinary, there is usually less support for WGFS and the field tends to be formalised as part of existing disciplines rather than as an autonomous field/department (Barazzetti and Leone 2003; Griffin 2002; Hirsch and Widerberg 2005; Magalhães 2001; Üşür 2006).

Another important factor is availability of funding. Access to financial support from governments, private funders, non-governmental organisations or intergovernmental bodies (such as the European Commission[4] or the United Nations) may facilitate the founding of WGFS degrees, centres, journals or international networks (Barazzetti and Leone 2003; Desai et al. 2002; Ferreira 2000; Góngora 2002; Jain and Rajput 2002; Pinto 2008; Silius 2002; Stratigaki 2001; Tavares da Silva 1999; Zimmermann 2007). Pavlidou (2006, p. 179) explains that after several years of ministerial rejections of applications to create new postgraduate degrees in WGFS, "the Greek state had to change its tune. This was neither accidental nor an act of enlightenment, but a direct consequence of the EU directive that 10 % of the education budget [...] had to be spent on measures promoting 'Gender and Equality'".

An additional factor encouraging or hindering the institutionalisation of WGFS is student demand for courses and degrees in WGFS, which is in turn shaped by a range of factors, such as the relationship between universities and the job market, the degree to which students with different profiles (including mature, part-time students) have access to higher education, and popular representations about the extent to which gender equality has been achieved and is still a relevant issue (Bird 2001; Duchen and Zmroczek 2001; Griffin and Hanmer 2002; Silius 2005; Skeggs 1995).

Political context has also been described as playing a decisive role. Research shows that institutionalisation tends to be stronger and more supported where and when the state considers the promotion of gender equality a key area of intervention (Griffin 2002, 2005b; Holm 2001; Le Feuvre 2000). Conservative and authoritarian regimes are particularly unsupportive of, and sometimes hostile to, research and education in WGFS, and therefore the fall of such regimes can pave the way for the expansion of the field (Amâncio 2003; Borderias 2002; Braidotti et al. 1995; Chen 2004; Góngora 2002; Griffin 2005a; Joaquim 2001; Nikolchina 2006; Petö 2000; Santos 2009). Another element of the political context which has had a significant

4 For discussions of the impacts of European Commission support on the establishment and strengthening of a specifically *European* WGFS community, see Braidotti (2000), Hanmer (2000), Hemmings (2008) and Lykke (2005).

impact on the institutionalisation of WGFS is the strength and structure of feminist movements and the degree to which they were/are supportive of the development of feminist education and research in academia (Amâncio 2003; Barazzetti and Leone 2003; Chen 2004; Gerhard 2002; Griffin 2005a; Lafuente 2002; Silius 2002; Šribar 2002; Tavares 2011; Zmroczek and Duchen 1991).

Other studies focus on the *micro-level* dimensions of the institutionalisation of WGFS. Rather than describe general trends in a country or region, they consider specific WGFS centres, degrees, journals or associations, charting their creation, expansion or closure. This research makes a crucial contribution by highlighting how processes of institutionalisation have demanded intense individual and organisational struggle. It also provides important insight into the ways in which the structural factors described above are negotiated at the micro levels of organisational change and daily practices of teaching and research. These studies demonstrate that institutionalisation initiatives are more effective when spearheaded by academics who have access to valued academic resources and spaces (i. e. hold tenured positions, are members of academic committees, are seen as authorities in their fields, or have powerful allies and supportive national/international networks) and can deploy those resources to bolster the credibility of their attempts to institutionalise WGFS (Armitage and Pedwell 2005; Duhaček 2004; Gumport 2002; Jain and Rajput 2002; Magalhães 2001; McMartin 1993; Pereira 2017; Westkott 2003). These texts also show that academics use a range of strategies to produce space for WGFS in unreceptive or hostile institutional contexts, such as teaching feminist content in courses with neutral or inconspicuous titles (Barazzetti et al. 2002; Chen 2004; Coate 1999, 2000; Vieira 2007).

Attempts have been made to use the findings of these macro- and micro-level studies to identify general patterns in the effects of different (f)actors in the institutionalisation of WGFS, and then draw on those trends to define typologies of institutionalisation profiles which might allow for institutional, geographical and historical comparison (Barazzetti and Michel 2000; Griffin 2002, 2005a; Michel 2001; Silius 2002). The ability to compare degrees and forms of institutionalisation has been described as instrumental, not just as an analytical tool to enrich understanding of these processes, but also as a political tool which can be used to justify and strengthen demands for increased national and supranational support to WGFS (Braidotti 2000; Gerhard 2002). Indeed, the explicit aim of several of the first and biggest studies of institutionalisation – especially the large-scale comparative European studies like *SIGMA* (Braidotti et al. 1995), *GRACE* (Zmroczek and Duchen 1991), the *Employment and Women's Studies* project (Griffin 2005b; Silius 2002) or the 'work-in-progress reports' published in the series *The Making of European Women's Studies*, edited by ATHENA (Braidotti and Vonk 2000) – was to demonstrate the global disparities in the field's development and to assert the need for international support mechanisms that would counteract the particular obstacles found locally and nationally (Braidotti 2000; Hanmer 2000). This points to what I would argue is an important feature of the literature on institutionalisation: the aim of many of these texts is not just to describe or analyse processes of institutionalisation, but also to more or less directly intervene in and advance those processes. Many of these texts are agents of that institutionalisation, and in that sense this literature can be seen as partly *constitutive* of the phenomena it is examining.

Researchers have, however, reported facing many challenges when conducting comparative studies (Barazzetti and Michel 2000; Bird 1996; Griffin 2005a; Hanmer 2005, 2006; Lykke 2000; Lykke et al. 2001; Michel 2001). This has led Donatella Barazzetti and Mariagrazia Leone (2003) to describe comparison as one of the biggest theoretical and methodological problems in the study of the institutionalisation of WGFS. Comparing cases is difficult because processes of institutionalisation are influenced by many factors, which interact with each other in diverse, context-specific and often unpredictable ways: it has been noted that similar conditions and strategies of institutionalisation sometimes lead to different results in distinct contexts (Barazzetti and Leone 2003; Bird 1996; Griffin 2005a). Moreover, even within the same country, there is usually some unevenness across institutions, levels of education or disciplines. In the UK, for instance, demand for undergraduate WGFS degree programmes dropped during the 2000s (Griffin 2009; Marchbank and Letherby 2006; Oxford 2008). At the same time, however, many postgraduate degree programmes reported stable or increasing intakes (Griffin and Hanmer 2002; Hemmings 2006a, 2006b, 2008), namely due to the inflow of 'educational migrants'[5] mentioned earlier in this article.

Comparing levels and models of institutionalisation of WGFS is challenging also because there is no agreement in WGFS about what constitutes an ideal or successful institutionalisation. This means that a particular institutionalisation profile may be assessed very differently, "according to which threads one traces and who is speaking" (Hemmings 2010, p. 1). An exchange published in the *European Journal of Women's Studies* provides a compelling illustration of this. It was triggered by an article by Veronica Pravadelli (2010b) in which she discusses contemporary WGFS in Italy and describes the field as not yet institutionalised. In a scathing response, Chiara Saraceno (2010, p. 269) argues that Italian WGFS is not characterised by a "lack of institutionalization" but rather a "different kind of institutionalization"

---

5 This provides a valuable illustration of the fact that national trends can often only be adequately understood if one considers how they are positioned vis-à-vis other national contexts and transnational flows of people and knowledge.

and accuses Pravadelli of having an (Anglo-American-inspired) conception of institutionalisation which does not allow her to "'see' and assess the different forms of institutionalization which have been developed" in Italy (2010, p. 270). Saraceno then lists examples of those "different forms" (including the existence of a PhD programme in WGFS). However, in her own response Pravadelli (2010a) disputes the claim that those examples constitute evidence of institutionalisation, and argues that they can be interpreted as indicating precisely the opposite: that WGFS is marginal. (For example, the WGFS PhD programme does exist, but none of its graduates have yet been able to secure an academic job.) Pravadelli ends by noting that her own and Saraceno's views on the institutionalisation of Italian WGFS are shaped by their different generational locations, academic trajectories and positions within professional hierarchies. Indeed, I would argue that because our perception of institutionalisation is, to some extent, necessarily situated and personal, accounts of institutionalisation are always disparate[6] and potentially contested.

As I demonstrate elsewhere in much more detail (Pereira 2017), a key dimension of the institutionalisation of WGFS is what I have called the field's *epistemic status*, i.e. the *degree to which, and terms in which, WGFS scholarship is recognised as fulfilling the requisite criteria to be considered credible and relevant knowledge, however those criteria are defined in specific spaces, communities and moments.* References to the epistemic status of WGFS appear very frequently in the literature on institutionalisation, although not in those terms. Be it under the labels of the "value of feminist knowledge" (Coate 1999, p. 142), its "prestige" (Lykke 2000, p. 79), "scientific status" (Varikas 2006, p. 160), "intellectual credibility" (Messer-Davidow 2002, p. 157), "academic significan[ce] or acceptab[ility]" (Evans 1997, p. 59), "scientific legitimacy" (Mayorga 2002, p. 28) or "academic respectability" (Brunt et al. 1983, p. 285), numerous texts written at very different points in time and about distinct contexts allude to whether WGFS' ability to produce proper academic knowledge is recognised in that particular context. These allusions show that in many sites WGFS is sometimes or often described and dismissed as scholarship that is inferior, less relevant and/or not entirely credible.[7] Claims about the epistemic inferiority or inadequacy of WGFS are made in many formal and informal settings, and in some contexts this dismissal has been so virulent (Suleri 1992), frequent and intense that it constitutes a form of intellectual harassment, as Kolodny (1996) designates it. As a result, the field is sometimes positioned "toward the bottom of the hierarchy of regard and status of academic disciplines" (Price and Owen

---

6 I am using the term both in the sense of "different; dissimilar" and of difficult "or impossible to compare" (Oxford English Dictionary 2016, no pagination).

7 For a detailed review of this aspect of the literature, see Pereira (2017).

1998, p. 185), and WGFS scholars may be more or less openly dismissed as "not academically qualified" (Chen 2004, p. 245). This can have a detrimental impact on WGFS scholars' and students' self-confidence, grades or career progression, and their access to funding and publishing opportunities (Corrin 1997; Griffin 2005a; Griffin and Hanmer 2005; Marchbank and Letherby 2006; Morley 1998; Packer 1995; Seller 1997; Silius 2005; Worell 1994).

However, the epistemic status of the field is not static and may change as institutionalisation unfolds, with several academic and non-academic actors and institutions playing a more or less direct and decisive role (Chen 2004; Messer-Davidow 2002; Pereira 2017). Due to all of the above, considerations about epistemic status take centre stage when WGFS scholars make located decisions about strategies of institutionalisation or formulate more general arguments about which strategies may be best. WGFS scholars often do not agree on this and have ongoing debates about the extent to which profiles of institutionalisation of WGFS allow for the production of proper WGFS knowledge (Hemmings 2006a). Therefore, negotiations of epistemic status should be seen not only as struggles that WGFS scholars engage in as they try to create spaces for WGFS in sometimes inhospitable academic landscapes, but also as internal contestations that are a central and generative dimension of the constitution and institutionalisation of the field itself (Pereira 2017; Stanley 1997).

3 The New Academic Governance and the Changing Status of Gender Research

The literature which I have reviewed above provides important insight into the macro- and micro-level patterns of institutionalisation of WGFS, and how they are affected by a range of different actors and factors – academic, political, institutional and personal, among others. However, the established patterns described in that literature are, to some extent, being transformed by the broader changes that have occurred in academic governance in many Western countries in the past two decades.

In many contexts, new models of governance of science have changed assessments of what constitutes 'proper' and 'valuable' scholarship (Burrows 2012; Butterwick and Dawson 2005; Gibbons et al. 1994; Mirowski and Sent 2008; Morley 2003; Santos Pereira 2004). In these models of scientific governance, academic activity is reconceptualised as work which must aim to achieve the highest possible levels of productivity and profitability, and whose quality can be assessed on the basis of the number of products produced (whether these be articles, patents or successful

– or satisfied – students) and income generated (Burrows 2012; Leathwood and Read 2013; Lund 2012; Morley 2003; Shore 2010; Sifaki 2016; Strathern 2000). This orientation towards the maximisation, monetisation and internationalisation of outputs is buttressed by regular auditing and monitoring of individual and collective productivity, using complex technologies of metricisation and ranking. This auditing then serves as the basis for the allocation of (in many contexts, decreasing) public funding for research and higher education (Ball 2000; Buikema and van der Tuin 2013; Burrows 2012; Leathwood and Read 2013; Pereira 2016, 2017; Shore 2010; Sifaki 2016).

In this environment, specific factors – particularly the level of productivity and profitability of WGFS scholarship – are playing an increasingly central role in determining the space and status granted to WGFS (Buikema and van der Tuin 2013; Hark 2016; Sifaki 2016; Skeggs 2008). This means that new models of academic governance are reshaping the longstanding patterns of institutionalisation of WGFS which I described above.

In my own research, I have been studying precisely those changes and their effects. I have explored them in an ethnography which examines how the status of WGFS is negotiated in everyday work, decision-making and sociability in academia. In other words, it analyses how scholars demarcate the boundaries of what counts as 'proper' knowledge, how WGFS scholars and scholarship get positioned in relation to those boundaries, and how all this has been transformed as new models of academic governance become institutionalised. To conduct this study, I articulated feminist epistemology (particularly the work of Lorraine Code 1991, 1995), feminist analyses of academic work (such as Amâncio 2005; Bellacasa 2001; Butterwick and Dawson 2005; Evans 2004; Gill 2010; Messer-Davidow 2002; Morley 1995, 1998; Strathern 2000), research in science and technology studies (Amsler 2007; Gieryn 1999), and Michel Foucault's discussions of *epistemes* (2003). The ethnography focused on Portuguese academia as a case study, drawing on full-time fieldwork over one year in 2008–2009. This included 36 interviews with academics, students and representatives of funding bodies; visits to institutions and archival research; and participant observation in over 50 academic events, including conferences, undergraduate and postgraduate teaching, meetings of associations and conference organising committees, PhD vivas, and book/journal launches. That primary fieldwork was supported by a second round of interviews with 12 of the original interviewees in 2015–2016. This has been supplemented by *ad hoc* observation of daily academic practice in UK (2006–2016), Sweden (2011) and Portugal (2006–2016).[8]

Through this ethnographic study, I found that the epistemic status of WGFS in Portugal is being significantly transformed by the institutionalisation of the new models of academic governance described above. Elsewhere, I analyse in detail how these changes play out in Portugal (Pereira 2012, 2015, 2016, 2017), so here I will provide only a brief summary of those findings and identify some of the questions that those specific findings raise for our broader debates about the relationship between gender research and the new academic governance.

According to the WGFS scholars I interviewed, until the early 2000s the dismissal and repudiation of gender studies and gender research in Portuguese academia was pervasive, public, intense, and sometimes verbally or institutionally violent. In the interviews, many senior WGFS scholars described their early work as leading to 'traumatic' PhD vivas, stalled careers and 'silent treatments' or denigration from colleagues. The situation changed in the 21st century. From 2000 onwards, successive centre-right and centre-left governments in Portugal reduced funding for higher education institutions and pressured universities to expand and diversify their sources of income, namely by creating new postgraduate degrees as part of the restructurings associated with the Bologna Process (Cabrito 2004; Graça 2009). The increased orientation within Portuguese universities towards profitability as a central criterion in the planning and assessment of scientific and higher education initiatives (Santos Pereira 2004) both animated and constrained the development of WGFS, as has also been observed in other countries and periods (Hemmings 2006a; Holm 2001; Skeggs 1995). It led to heightened competition between WGFS scholars and eroded their working conditions, placing them under increased pressure to maintain high productivity. At the same time, however, it brought more space, opportunities and recognition for WGFS in many institutions. Because many Portuguese WGFS staff are high-performing, internationally well-networked scholars with a good track record of securing funding, and WGFS courses and degrees attracted some student interest, university administrations that had long been hostile to WGFS became – gradually (or sometimes suddenly) – more accepting of WGFS work and more supportive of feminist scholars. This recognition that WGFS had *financial* and *institutional* value (i. e. that it could yield profit at a time when institutions sorely needed it) seemed to dissuade many scholars from publicly questioning WGFS' *epistemic* value. Thus, there is in contemporary Portuguese

8 For more information about the fieldwork, and a discussion of the challenges of conducting ethnographies of academia, see Pereira (2013a, 2017).

academia an increasing public recognition of the epistemic status and relevance of research on gender.

This climate of public recognition coexists, nevertheless, with a regular unofficial dismissal of WGFS scholarship and scholars (Pereira 2012, 2015). Claims that research about gender cannot count as 'proper' knowledge are frequently made informally and in a humorous way, creating what one interviewee called a "culture of teasing" around WGFS. In other words, affirmations that WGFS is less, or not at all, scientific are rarely heard in official discourse, but are still very present as a form of corridor talk, in Downey et al.'s (1997, p. 245) sense: they are "the unsaid, but frequently said anyway (though not to everyone)". Moreover, although gender research is considered potentially valuable, it tends to be framed in mainstream academic talk as valuable only in part, or only in certain circumstances or for very specific ends. This means that its broader contributions to the development of academic knowledge are not acknowledged, its influence is circumscribed and domesticated, and the distinctive expertise of WGFS scholars is not recognised (Pereira 2012, 2017). This unofficial culture of teasing and limited recognition of WGFS has significant and problematic effects. It means that even when WGFS is formally institutionalised as an equal field, WGFS scholars and scholarship may be perceived to lack scientificity and credibility, and hence be treated as inferior 'others' vis-à-vis supposedly more 'serious' scholars and more 'scientific' scholarship.

This means that the transformation of the institutionalisation of WGFS triggered by international changes in academic governance have not been straightforward. As Morley (1995, p. 180) argues, "The academy, like any other organization, is full of contradictions – structures are both fixed and volatile, enabling and constraining". This has certainly also been the case in relation to the situation of gender studies and gender research within the new academic governance. That situation is *paradoxical*, in at least two senses:

a. it is possible to identify trends both of continuity and of change; and
b. within the new academic governance, WGFS has in many contexts become undoubtedly more recognised at the institutional level and in official discourse. However, this institutional recognition often co-exists with the dismissing of the field at the epistemic level and in everyday corridor talk and unofficial discourse.

These paradoxes place the WGFS scholars I interviewed in a challenging and conflicted position. Recognition of the relevance of their work may be growing but it is conditional, because it is dependent on (over-)compliance with a productivist model of organisation and evaluation of academic work which clashes with key principles of WGFS and demands levels of competitive productivity that are detrimental for WGFS. They are detrimental because they compromise scholars' health and well-being, undermine their knowledge production (because they are forced to produce work at a speed and in formats that are not always those they consider the most fruitful), and erode collegiality within the field (because scholars have less time to read others' work and attend events, and because they have to more fiercely compete with each other for the students and opportunities available) (Gill 2010; Pereira 2016, 2017). As Hark (2016, p. 84) writes in her discussion of the place of WGFS in what she calls the "entrepreneurial university", "the paradoxical precondition for [feminist] dissent is participation" in "the academic 'game'" of productivity and audit. If WGFS scholars are "ideal functionaries" (Evans 2004, p. 73) – i. e. highly productive scholars frequently bringing in funding and regularly generating outputs, preferably in highly ranked international journals – they have a chance to create and sustain space for their critical scholarship in contemporary universities. However, in doing so they reproduce a system of academic governance which damages working conditions and makes it extremely difficult for WGFS scholars to care for themselves and others (Gill 2010; Gill and Donaghue 2016; Lynch 2010; Wånggren et al. 2017) and to maintain the time-intensive intra- and extra-academic social and political engagement often seen as a hallmark of WGFS (Pereira 2016, 2017).

4 Conclusion: 'New' Governance, 'Old' Hierarchies?

Recent transformations in academia are changing the state and status of WGFS, and it is crucial that we analyse and debate these new, or emerging, effects of the new academic governance. And yet, I would argue that we must be very careful in how we conceptualise and write about these new forms of governance. Yes, they are undoubtedly new… but what makes these trends of change especially challenging for gender studies and gender research is the fact that they are partly buttressed by elements of continuity. To adapt Evans' (1995, p. 83) words, "many tattered remnants remain" of the 'old' "monolithic patriarchy" within the 'new' governance of universities. In many Western countries, academic governance is currently driven by relatively new principles and managed in relatively new ways, but longstanding sexist hierarchies (as well as racist hierarchies and other forms of inequality) still affect scholars' official and unofficial assessments of others' work (Ahmed 2012; Husu 2011; Mählck 2013; Moss-Racusin et al. 2012; van den Brink 2010), and are regularly invoked in 'corridor talk'. As Kašić (2016, p. 130) argues, "the neoliberal trend [is] impregnated with the old-fashioned order of academic design that counts on (neo)conservatism". The spectral – but unmistakeable – presence of these supposedly 'old' attitudes creates a constant threat of potential epistemic disqualification for scholars from traditionally marginalised fields, or scholars who are not male, white, middle-class or cisgender, for example. This means that being an "ideal functionary" (Evans 2004, p. 73) and complying with 'new' modes of governance becomes especially important, or even a *sine qua non* condition for the institutional survival of WGFS and its scholars.

This coexistence of change and continuity, of recognition and marginalisation of WGFS, is more than just a sign that academic communities are heterogeneous, or that some dimensions of university life change faster than others. That coexistence is a key mechanism of contemporary academic governance. It allows academic institutions to access some of the benefits that WGFS may yield – namely funds or research ratings, or the fact that it can work as an 'alibi' symbolising an institution's modernity and commitment to equality (Ahmed 2012; *ex aequo* Editorial Board 1999; Pereira 2014, 2017) – without always fully recognising the epistemic status of WGFS. Therefore, important as it may be (and I believe it is crucial!) to highlight the many fruitful openings that new models of the academic governance have created for WGFS, we must also recognise the ongoing closures that those new models reproduce, sometimes more covertly, and thus more challengingly. Important as it may be to recognise the very distinctive *new* elements of contemporary academic governance, we must not focus so fully on that 'newness' that we neglect the *continuing* structural inequalities (namely of gender, race, class, [dis]ability, or geopolitics) which produce systematic inequalities in academia and which create obstacles to the recognition, institutionalisation and development of gender research.

References

Ahmed, Sara. 2012. *On Being Included: Racism and Diversity in Institutional Life*. Durham: Duke University Press.

Amâncio, Lígia. 2003. Gender and Science in Portugal. *Portuguese Journal of Social Science* 1 (3): 185–198.

Amâncio, Lígia. 2005. Reflections on Science as a Gendered Endeavour: Changes and Continuities. *Social Science Information* 44 (1): 65–83.

Amsler, Sarah. 2007. *The Politics of Knowledge in Central Asia: Science between Marx and the Market*. London: Routledge.

Armitage, Faith, and Carolyn Pedwell. 2005. *Putting Gender on the Map: The LSE Gender Institute's First Fifteen Years*. London: Gender Institute (LSE).

Ball, Stephen J. 2000. Performativities and Fabrications in the Education Economy: Towards the Performative Society? *The Australian Educational Researcher* 27 (2): 1–23.
Barazzetti, Donatella, and Mariagrazia Leone. 2003. *The Institutionalisation of Women's Studies Training in Europe*. Hull: University of Hull.
Barazzetti, Donatella, and Christine Michel. 2000. Reflections on Criteria for Comparisons of Degrees of Institutionalization and on Relevant Typologies. *The Making of European Women's Studies* I: 74–76.
Barazzetti, Donatella, Carmen Leccardi, Mariagrazia Leone and Sveva Magaraggia. 2002. Italy. In *Women's Employment, Women's Studies, and Equal Opportunities (1945-2001): Reports from Nine European Countries*, ed. by Gabriele Griffin, 177–230. Hull: University of Hull.
Bellacasa, María Puig de la. 2001. Beyond Nostalgia and Celebration: Contexts for Academic Women's Studies in Contemporary Universities. In *Women's Studies: From Institutional Innovations to New Job Qualifications*, ed. by Nina Lykke, Christine Michel and María Puig de la Bellacasa, 25–45. Utrecht: ATHENA.
Bird, Elizabeth. 1996. Women's Studies in European Higher Education: SIGMA and Coimbra. *European Journal of Women's Studies* 3 (2): 151–166.
Bird, Elizabeth. 2001. SIGMA Report: Women's Studies in the UK. *The Making of European Women's Studies* III: 196–216.
Borderias, Cristina. 2002. Feminist Studies and Research in Spain, 1989. *The Making of European Women's Studies* IV: 204–209.
Boxer, Marilyn J. 1998. *When Women Ask the Questions: Creating Women's Studies in America*. Baltimore: Johns Hopkins University Press.
Braidotti, Rosi. 2000. Key Terms and Issues in the Making of European Women's Studies. *The Making of European Women's Studies* I: 23–36.
Braidotti, Rosi, and Esther Vonk. 2000. Introduction. *The Making of European Women's Studies* I: 9–11.
Braidotti, Rosi, Ellen de Dreu and Christine Rammrath. Eds. 1995. *National Reports for the SIGMA European Subject Area Evaluation of Women's Studies*. Brussels: European Commission.
Braidotti, Rosi, Evelien Delhez and Christine Rammrath. 1998. *Institutionalisation of Gender Studies/Women's Studies in Europe*. Berne: Swiss Science Council.
Brunt, Rosalind, Eileen Green, Karen Jones and Diana Woodward. 1983. Sell-Out or Challenge? The Contradiction of a Masters in Women's Studies. *Women's Studies International Forum* 6 (3): 283–290.
Buikema, Rosemarie, and Iris van der Tuin. 2013. Doing the Document: Gender Studies at the Corporatized University in Europe. *European Journal of Women's Studies* 20 (3): 309–316.
Burrows, Roger. 2012. Living with the H-Index? Metric Assemblages in the Contemporary Academy. *The Sociological Review* 60 (2): 355–372.
Butterwick, Shauna, and Jane Dawson. 2005. Undone Business: Examining the Production of Academic Labour. *Women's Studies International Forum* 28 (1): 51–65.
Cabrito, Belmiro Gil. 2004. O Financiamento do Ensino Superior em Portugal: Entre o Estado e o Mercado. *Educação & Sociedade* 25 (88): 977–996.
Chen, Peiying. 2004. *Acting "Otherwise": The Institutionalization of Women's/Gender Studies in Taiwan Universities*. London: RoutledgeFalmer.
Coate, Kelly. 1999. Feminist Knowledge and the Ivory Tower: A Case Study. *Gender and Education* 11 (2): 141–159.

Coate, Kelly. 2000. *The History of Women's Studies as an Academic Subject Area in Higher Education in the UK: 1970–1990*. Dissertation. London: Institute of Education.

Code, Lorraine. 1991. *What Can She Know? Feminist Theory and the Construction of Knowledge*. Ithaca: Cornell University Press.

Code, Lorraine. 1995. *Rhetorical Spaces: Essays on Gendered Locations*. New York: Routledge.

Corrin, Chris. 1997. Bordering on Change. In *Knowing Feminisms: On Academic Borders, Territories and Tribes*, ed. by Liz Stanley, 85–96. London: Sage.

Desai, Neera, Vina Mazumdar and Kamalini Bhansali. 2002. From Women's Education to Women's Studies: The Long Struggle for Legitimacy. In *Narratives from the Women's Studies Family: Recreating Knowledge*, ed. by Devaki Jain and Pam Rajput, 44–77. Thousand Oaks: Sage.

Downey, Gary Lee, Joseph Dumit and Sharon Traweek. 1997. Corridor Talk. In *Cyborgs & Citadels: Anthropological Interventions in Emerging Sciences and Technologies*, ed. by Joseph Dumit and Gary Lee Downey, 245–264. Santa Fe: School of American Research Press.

Duchen, Claire, and Christine Zmroczek. 2001. Survey of Women's Studies and Feminist Research in the UK (1989). *The Making of European Women's Studies* III: 188–195.

Duhaček, Daša. 2004. The Belgrade Women's Studies Centre: The Next Stage? *The Making of European Women's Studies* V: 41–45.

Evans, Mary. 1995. Ivory Towers: Life in the Mind. In *Feminist Academics: Creative Agents for Change*, ed. by Louise Morley and Val Walsh, 73–85. London: Taylor & Francis.

Evans, Mary. 1997. *Introducing Contemporary Feminist Thought*. Cambridge: Polity.

Evans, Mary. 2004. *Killing Thinking: The Death of the Universities*. London: Continuum.

ex aequo Editorial Board. 1999. Editorial. *ex aequo* 1: 5–10.

Fernandes, Emília. 2008. Elas por Elas: Corpos Ruidosos, Corpos Silenciados em Contexto Organizacional. *Diacrítica* 22 (3): 87–102.

Ferreira, Virgínia. 2000. A Associação Portuguesa de Estudos sobre as Mulheres. *Faces de Eva* 4: 125–128.

Foucault, Michel. 2003. *Society Must Be Defended: Lectures at the Collège de France, 1975–76*. New York: Picador.

Gerhard, Ute. 2002. Introduction: Women's Movements and Feminist Research. In *Thinking Differently: A Reader in European Women's Studies*, ed. by Gabriele Griffin and Rosi Braidotti, 321–331. London: Zed.

Gibbons, Michael, Camille Limoges, Helga Nowotny, Simon Schwartzman, Peter Scott and Martin Trow. 1994. *The New Production of Knowledge: the Dynamics of Science and Research in Contemporary Societies*. London: Sage.

Gieryn, Thomas. 1999. *Cultural Boundaries of Science: Credibility on the Line*. Chicago: University of Chicago Press.

Gill, Rosalind. 2010. Breaking the Silence: The Hidden Injuries of the Neoliberal University. In *Secrecy and Silence in the Research Process: Feminist Reflections*, ed. by Róisín Ryan-Flood and Rosalind Gill, 228–244. Abingdon: Routledge.

Gill, Rosalind, and Ngaire Donaghue. 2016. Resilience, Apps and Reluctant Individualism: Technologies of Self in the Neoliberal Academy. *Women's Studies International Forum* 54: 91–99.

Góngora, Jimena Gallardo. 2002. Contradictions in the Institutionalisation Process of Women's and Gender Studies in Chile. *The Making of European Women's Studies* IV: 47–60.

Graça, Vasco. 2009. Sobre o Financiamento da Educação: Condicionantes Globais e Realidades Nacionais. *Revista Lusófona de Educação* 13: 49–80.

Griffin, Gabriele. 2005a. The Institutionalization of Women's Studies in Europe. In *Doing Women's Studies: Employment Opportunities, Personal Impacts and Social Consequences*, ed. by Gabriele Griffin, 89–110. London: Zed.
Griffin, Gabriele. 2009. The "Ins" and "Outs" of Women's/Gender Studies: A Response to the Reports of Its Demise in 2008. *Women's History Review* 18 (3): 485–496.
Griffin, Gabriele. Ed. 2002. *Women's Employment, Women's Studies, and Equal Opportunities (1945–2001): Reports from Nine European Countries*. Hull: University of Hull.
Griffin, Gabriele Ed. 2005b. *Doing Women's Studies: Employment Opportunities, Personal Impacts and Social Consequences*. London: Zed.
Griffin, Gabriele, and Jalna Hanmer. 2002. The UK. In *Women's Employment, Women's Studies, and Equal Opportunities (1945–2001): Reports from Nine European Countries*, ed. by Gabriele Griffin, 1–68. Hull: University of Hull.
Griffin, Gabriele, and Jalna Hanmer. 2005. The Impact of Women's Studies on Its Students' Relationships and Everyday Practices. In *Doing Women's Studies: Employment Opportunities, Personal Impacts and Social Consequences*, ed. by Gabriele Griffin, 141–167. London: Zed.
Gumport, Patricia. 2002. *Academic Pathfinders: Knowledge Creation and Feminist Scholarship*. Westport: Greenwood Press.
Gutiérrez-Rodríguez, Encarnación. 2016. Sensing Dispossession: Women and Gender Studies Between Institutional Racism and Migration Control Policies in the Neoliberal University. *Women's Studies International Forum* 54: 167–177.
Hanmer, Jalna. 2000. Towards a Life-line of European Women's Studies. *The Making of European Women's Studies* I: 12–22.
Hanmer, Jalna. 2005. Comparative Research in Europe. In *Doing Women's Studies: Employment Opportunities, Personal Impacts and Social Consequences*, ed. by Gabriele Griffin, 213–235. London: Zed.
Hanmer, Jalna. 2006. What Is the Relevance of Women's and Gender Studies? In *Gender Studies: Trends/Tensions in Greece and Other European Countries*, ed. by Theodossia-Soula Pavlidou, 141–150. Thessaloniki: ΕΚΔΟΣΕΙΣ ΖΗΤΗ.
Hark, Sabine. 2016. Contending Directions: Gender Studies in the Entrepreneurial University. *Women's Studies International Forum* 54: 84–90.
Hemmings, Clare. 2006a. The Life and Times of Academic Feminism. In *Handbook of Gender and Women's Studies*, ed. by Kathy Davis, Mary Evans and Judith Lorber, 13–34. London: Sage.
Hemmings, Clare. 2006b. Ready for Bologna? The Impact of the Declaration on Women's and Gender Studies in the UK. *European Journal of Women's Studies* 13 (4): 315–323.
Hemmings, Clare. 2008. Tuning Problems? Notes on Women's and Gender Studies and the Bologna Process. *European Journal of Women's Studies* 15 (2): 117–127.
Hemmings, Clare. 2010. Editorial: Transforming Academies, Global Genealogies. *Feminist Review* 95: 1–4.
Hemmings, Clare. 2011. *Why Stories Matter: The Political Grammar of Feminist Theory*. Durham: Duke University Press.
Hirsch, Silje, and Karin Widerberg. 2005. *Change in Disciplinization: Two Case Studies*. http://www.york.ac.uk/res/researchintegration. Accessed: April 2, 2017.
Holm, Ulla. 2001. Paradoxical Conditions for Women's Studies Centres in Sweden. In *Women's Studies: From Institutional Innovations to New Job Qualifications*, ed. by Nina Lykke, Christine Michel and María Puig de la Bellacasa, 172–201. Utrecht: ATHENA.

Husu, Liisa. 2011. *Sexism, Support and Survival in Academia*. Helsinki: University of Helsinki Press.

Jain, Devaki, and Pam Rajput. 2002. *Narratives from the Women's Studies Family: Recreating Knowledge*. Thousand Oaks: Sage.

Joaquim, Teresa. 2001. Os Estudos sobre as Mulheres em Filosofia. *ex aequo* 5: 69–83.

Juhász, Borbála, Andrea Petö, Jeannette Van der Sanden and Berteke Waaldijk. 2005. Educational Migration and Gender: Women's Studies Students' Educational Mobility in Europe. In *Doing Women's Studies: Employment Opportunities, Personal Impacts and Social Consequences*, ed. by Gabriele Griffin, 168–194. London: Zed.

Kašić, Biljana. 2016. "Unsettling" Women's Studies, Settling Neoliberal Threats in the Academia: A Feminist Gaze from Croatia. *Women's Studies International Forum* 54: 129–137.

Kolodny, Annette. 1996. Paying the Price of Antifeminist Intellectual Harassment. In *Antifeminism in the Academy*, ed. by Vèvè A. Clark, Shirley Nelson Garner, Margaret Higonnet and Ketu H. Katrak, 3–34. New York: Routledge.

Lafuente, María Suarez. 2002. Women's Associations and Education in Spain. In *Thinking Differently: A Reader in European Women's Studies*, ed. by Gabriele Griffin and Rosi Braidotti, 378–385. London: Zed.

Le Feuvre, Nicky. 2000. Women's Studies in France: Update 2000. *The Making of European Women's Studies* II: 178–208.

Leathwood, Carole, and Barbara Read. 2013. Research Policy and Academic Performativity: Compliance, Contestation and Complicity. *Studies in Higher Education* 38 (8): 1162–1174.

Lund, Rebecca. 2012. Publishing to Become an "Ideal Academic": An Institutional Ethnography and a Feminist Critique. *Scandinavian Journal of Management* 28 (3): 218–228.

Lykke, Nina. 2000. Towards an Evaluation of Women's Studies in Relation to the Job Prospects of Its Graduates. *The Making of European Women's Studies* I: 77–79.

Lykke, Nina. 2004. Women's/Gender/Feminist Studies: A Post-disciplinary Discipline? *The Making of European Women's Studies* V: 91–101.

Lykke, Nina. 2005. Towards a New Professional Organisation for Women's/Gender/Feminist Studies in Europe? *The Making of European Women's Studies* VI: 147–157.

Lykke, Nina, Christine Michel and María Puig de la Bellacasa. 2001. Women's Studies: From Institutional Innovations to New Job Qualifications. *The Making of European Women's Studies* III: 123–133.

Lynch, Kathleen. 2010. Carelessness: A Hidden Doxa of Higher Education. *Arts and Humanities in Higher Education* 9 (1): 54–67.

Magalhães, Maria José. 2001. Dez Anos da APEM: Percorrer as Vozes, Significar os Percursos. *ex aequo* 5: 27–68.

Mählck, Paula. 2013. Academic Women with Migrant Background in the Global Knowledge Economy: Bodies, Hierarchies and Resistance. *Women's Studies International Forum* 36: 65–74.

Marchbank, Jen, and Gayle Letherby. 2006. Views and Perspectives of Women's Studies: A Survey of Women and Men Students. *Gender and Education* 18 (2): 157–182.

Mayorga, Cláudia. 2002. Gender, Race and Women's Studies in Brazil. *The Making of European Women's Studies* IV: 25–36.

McMartin, Flora. 1993. *The Institutionalization of Women's Centers and Women's Studies Programs at Three Research Universities*. Dissertation. Berkeley: University of California.

Messer-Davidow, Ellen. 2002. *Disciplining Feminism: From Social Activism to Academic Discourse*. Durham: Duke University Press.

Michel, Christine. 2001. Reflections about the Comparability of Women's Studies in Europe. In *Women's Studies: From Institutional Innovations to New Job Qualifications*, ed. by Nina Lykke, Christine Michel, and María Puig de la Bellacasa, 14–17. Utrecht: ATHENA.

Mirowski, Philip, and Esther-Mirjam Sent. 2008. The Commercialization of Science and the Response of STS. In *The Handbook of Science and Technology Studies*, ed. by Edward J. Hackett, Olga Amsterdamska, Judy Wajcman and Michael Lynch (3rd ed.), 635–689. Cambridge: The MIT Press.

Morley, Louise. 1995. The Micropolitics of Women's Studies: Feminism and Organizational Change in the Academy. In *(Hetero)sexual Politics*, ed. by June Purvis and Mary Maynard, 171–185. Washington: Taylor & Francis.

Morley, Louise. 1998. *Organising Feminisms: The Micropolitics of the Academy*. New York: St. Martin's Press.

Morley, Louise. 2003. *Quality and Power in Higher Education*. Buckingham: Open University Press.

Moss-Racusina, Corinne, John F. Dovidio, Victoria L. Brescoll, Mark J. Graham and Jo Handelsman. 2012. Science Faculty's Subtle Gender Biases Favour Male Students. *Proceedings of the National Academy of Sciences* 109 (41): 16474–16479.

Nikolchina, Miglena. 2006. Gender Studies and the University: The Bulgarian Case. In *Gender Studies: Trends/Tensions in Greece and Other European Countries*, ed. by Theodossia-Soula Pavlidou, 117–128. Thessaloniki: ΕΚΔΟΣΕΙΣ ΖΗΤΗ.

Oxford English Dictionary. 2016. *Oxford English Dictionary Online*. Internet Edition (www.oed.com). Oxford: : Oxford University Press.

Oxford, Esther. 2008. *Last Women Standing*. https://www.timeshighereducation.com/features/last-women-standing/400363.article. Accessed: April 2, 2017.

Packer, Barbara Brown. 1995. Irrigating the Sacred Grove: Stages of Gender Equity Development. In *Feminist Academics: Creative Agents for Change*, ed. by Louise Morley and Val Walsh, 42–55. London: Taylor & Francis.

Pavlidou, Theodossia-Soula. 2006. Women's Studies in Greece: An Update (2006). *The Making of European Women's Studies* VII: 178–185.

Pereira, Maria do Mar. 2012. "Feminist Theory Is Proper Knowledge, But…": The Status of Feminist Scholarship in the Academy. *Feminist Theory* 13 (3): 283–303.

Pereira, Maria do Mar. 2013a. On Being Invisible and Dangerous: The Challenges of Conducting Ethnographies in/of Academia. In *Gender Paradoxes in Changing Academic and Scientific Organisation(s)*. GEXcel Reports, Vol. XVII, ed. by Sofia Strid and Liisa Husu, 191–212. Örebro: University of Örebro.

Pereira, Maria do Mar. 2013b. Women's and Gender Studies. In *Gender: The Key Concepts*, ed. by Mary Evans and Carolyn Williams, 215–223. London: Routledge.

Pereira, Maria do Mar. 2014. The Importance of Being "Modern" and Foreign: Feminist Scholarship and the Epistemic Status of Nations. *Signs: Journal of Women in Culture and Society* 39 (3): 627–657.

Pereira, Maria do Mar. 2015. Higher Education Cutbacks and the Reshaping of Epistemic Hierarchies: An Ethnographic Study of the Case of Feminist Scholarship. *Sociology* 49 (2): 287–304.

Pereira, Maria do Mar. 2016. Struggling Within and Beyond the Performative University: Articulating Activism and Work in an "Academia Without Walls". *Women's Studies International Forum* 54: 100–110.

Pereira, Maria do Mar. 2017. *Power, Knowledge and Feminist Scholarship: An Ethnography of Academia*. London: Routledge.
Petö, Andrea. 2000. The Process of Institutionalising Gender Studies in Hungary. *The Making of European Women's Studies* I: 49–53.
Pinto, Teresa. 2008. *A Formação Profissional das Mulheres no Ensino Industrial Público (1884-1910): Realidades e Representações*. PhD Dissertation. Lisbon: Universidade Aberta.
Pravadelli, Veronica. 2010a. Legitimacy/Change/Power: Is a New Course in Italian Gender Studies Possible? A Response to Chiara Saraceno. *European Journal of Women's Studies* 17 (3): 275–269.
Pravadelli, Veronica. 2010b. Women and Gender Studies, Italian Style. *European Journal of Women's Studies* 17 (1): 61–67.
Price, Marion, and Mairead Owen. 1998. Who Studies Women's Studies? *Gender and Education* 10 (2): 185–198.
Santos, Maria Irene Ramalho de Sousa. 2009. SIGMA National Report: Portugal (1995). *The Making of European Women's Studies* IX: 119–136.
Santos Pereira, Tiago. 2004. Processos de Governação da Ciência: O Debate em Torno do Modelo de Financiamento das Unidades de Investigação em Portugal. *Revista Crítica de Ciências Sociais* 70: 5–32.
Saraceno, Chiara. 2010. Women and Gender Studies in Italy: Lack of Institutionalization or a Different Kind of Institutionalization? *European Journal of Women's Studies* 17 (3): 269–274.
Seller, Anne. 1997. Whose Women's Studies? Whose Philosophy? Whose Borderland? In *Knowing Feminisms: On Academic Borders, Territories and Tribes*, ed. by Liz Stanley, 18–31. London: Sage.
Shore, Cris. 2010. Beyond the Multiversity: Neoliberalism and the Rise of the Schizophrenic University. *Social Anthropology/Anthropologie Sociale* 18 (1): 15–29.
Sifaki, Aggeliki. 2016. Which Side Are We On? Feminist Studies in the Time of Neoliberalism or Neoliberal Feminist Studies? *Women's Studies International Forum* 54: 111–118.
Silius, Harriet. 2002. Comparative Summary. In *Women's Employment, Women's Studies, and Equal Opportunities (1945-2001): Reports from Nine European Countries*, ed. by Gabriele Griffin, 470–514. Hull: University of Hull.
Silius, Harriet. 2005. The Professionalization of Women's Studies Students in Europe: Expectations and Experiences. In *Doing Women's Studies: Employment Opportunities, Personal Impacts and Social Consequences*, ed. by Gabriele Griffin, 111–140. London: Zed.
Skeggs, Beverley. 1995. Women's Studies in Britain in the 1990s: Entitlement Cultures and Institutional Constraints. *Women's Studies International Forum* 18 (4): 475–485.
Skeggs, Beverley. 2008. The Dirty History of Feminism and Sociology: Or the War of Conceptual Attrition. *The Sociological Review* 56 (4): 670–690.
Šribar, Renata. 2002. Lacking Integration: The Relationship between the Women's Movement and Gender/Women's Studies in Transitional Slovenia. In *Thinking Differently: A Reader in European Women's Studies*, ed. by Gabriele Griffin and Rosi Braidotti, 372–377. London: Zed.
Stanley, Liz. 1997. Introduction: On Academic Borders, Territories, Tribes and Knowledges. In *Knowing Feminisms: On Academic Borders, Territories and Tribes*, ed. by Liz Stanley, 1–17. London: Sage.
Strathern, Marilyn. 2000. Introduction: New Accountabilities. In *Audit Cultures: Anthropological Studies in Accountability, Ethics and the Academy*, ed. by Marilyn Strathern, 1–18. London: Routledge.

Stratigaki, Maria. 2001. EU Policies' Impact in Promoting Gender Equality Expertise. A General Assessment with a Focus on Greece. In *Women's Studies: From Institutional Innovations to New Job Qualifications*, ed. by Nina Lykke, Christine Michel and María Puig de la Bellacasa, 46–55. Utrecht: ATHENA.
Suleri, Sara. 1992. Woman Skin Deep: Feminism and the Postcolonial Condition. *Critical Inquiry* 18 (4): 756–769.
Tavares da Silva, Regina. 1999. Estudos sobre as Mulheres em Portugal: um Olhar sobre o Passado. *ex aequo* 1: 17–28.
Tavares, Manuela. 2011. *Feminismos em Portugal: Percursos e Desafios*. Lisboa: Texto Editora.
Üşür, Serpil Sancar. 2006. Women's Studies in Turkish Academic Life. In *Gender Studies: Trends/Tensions in Greece and Other European Countries*, ed. by Theodossia-Soula Pavlidou, 129–138. Thessaloniki: ΕΚΔΟΣΕΙΣ ΖΗΤΗ.
Van den Brink, Marieke. 2010. *Behind the Scenes of Science: Gender Practices in the Recruitment and Selection of Professors in the Netherlands*. Amsterdam: Amsterdam University Press.
Varikas, Eleni. 2006. GRACE Report: Women's Studies in Greece 1988. *The Making of European Women's Studies* VII: 159–163.
Vieira, Cristina. 2007. A Dimensão do Género nos Curricula do Ensino Superior: Factos e Reflexões a Partir de uma Entrevista Focalizada de Grupo a Especialistas Portuguesas no Domínio. *ex aequo* 16: 151–160.
Wånggren, Lena, Órla Murray and Muireann Crowley. 2017. Feminist Work in Academia and Beyond. In *Being an Early Career Feminist Academic: Global Perspectives, Experiences and Challenges*, ed. by Rachel Thwaites and Amy Pressland, 215–236, Basingstoke: Palgrave Macmillan.
Westkott, Marcia. 2003. Institutional Success and Political Vulnerability: A Lesson in the Importance of Allies. In *Women's Studies on Its Own*, ed. by Robyn Wiegman, 293–311. Durham: Duke University Press.
Widerberg, Karin. 2006. Disciplinization of Gender Studies. Old Questions, New Answers? Nordic Strategies in the European Context. *NORA: Nordic Journal of Feminist and Gender Research* 14 (2): 131–140.
Worell, Judith. 1994. Feminist Publication: Academic Empowerment or Professional Liability? In *Gender and Academe: Feminist Pedagogy and Politics*, ed. by Sara Munson Deats and Lagretta Tallent Lenker, 207–216. Lanham: Rowman & Littlefield.
Zimmermann, Susan. 2007. The Institutionalization of Women and Gender Studies in Higher Education in Central and Eastern Europe and the Former Soviet Union: Asymmetric Politics and the Regional-Transnational Configuration. *East Central Europe* 34 (1): 131–160.
Zmroczek, Christine, and Claire Duchen. 1991. What Are Those Women Up To? Women's Studies and Feminist Research in the European Community. In *Out of the Margins: Women's Studies in the Nineties*, ed. by Jane Aaron and Sylvia Walby, 11–29. London: Falmer Press.

Gender Studies: A 'Cheeky Knowledge' Renormalised?

Farinaz Fassa and Sabine Kradolfer

Abstract

Our contribution investigates the institutionalisation process of gender studies in a Swiss French-speaking university, with a particular focus on its articulation with local social demands. The new academic governance has transformed the debates around such studies in a way that might have been expected to benefit gender studies, whose interdisciplinarity was initially seen as an undeniable advantage. Nevertheless, comparison with the changes that have occurred over the past 25 years in another interdisciplinary field of knowledge, area studies, suggests that the social resistances and new scientific objects offered by women's/gender studies or area studies tend to be diluted under the joint influence of new social demands, fragmentation and globalisation, paving the way for new (?) academic disciplinary definitions that bring back to normal the 'cheeky knowledge' built by these studies.

Keywords

Gender Studies, Area Studies, Social Demand, Tertiary Education, Disciplines, Accountability, Switzerland, Knowledge, Institutionalisation

1 Introduction

Debates on the effects of the institutionalisation of studies specifically taking into account the question of women have gone on since the 1970s, when feminists brought women's studies into American and British universities. In the French-speaking world they emerged much later, not least because of a division of disciplines "that puts a brake on innovation" (Chaperon 2002, p. 54), and the low academic recognition of works on gender and/or sexualities. On the latter point, Revenin (2007, no pagination) speculates that it springs from a fear of "studies seen as too specific or too 'political' (such as feminist, queer or post-colonial studies)" owing to the links between feminist/gay or lesbian activism and research in these areas. These links, noted by all authors who have worked on the emergence of what we call a 'cheeky knowledge', have led to suspicions of weak scientificity and a lack of objectivity being associated with these works by the advocates of a 'normal science', thus reducing social demand to being no more than the demand of the dominant. Now, as Castel shows, "if there is bias, it only counterbalances another bias, that of the 'neutral' discourse of objectivism which takes de facto situations for granted and so ratifies them" (2002, p. 73). Pursuing Castel's point, one may ask to what extent 'normal science' and its modes of constitution have taken as their implicit reference white, middle- or upper-class heterosexual men.

The new academic governance, which goes hand in hand with marketisation, the introduction of managerialist tools into scientific organisations and the demand for scientific excellence, has transformed these debates in a way that might have been expected to benefit gender studies, whose interdisciplinarity was initially seen as an undeniable advantage. But as Joseph (2010) observes with reference to another field of interdisciplinary research (cultural studies), women's/gender studies is now faced with three dimensions of accountability, which are in tension with one another: the professional, the political and the institutional/managerial dimensions. These tensions were present from the moment when the question of the construction of knowledge on women and social gender relations first arose more than 40 years ago. They are now exacerbated by the growing recourse to accountability in new public management, especially at the intersection of its professional and its institutional/managerial dimensions. Since the criteria of scientific excellence have remained mainly rooted in a quite traditional disciplinary approach, researchers have to prove their adequacy to academia in a very definite field if they wish to pursue an academic career. This also means that they have to endorse the ways of doing 'normal science' in their epistemological and methodological choices. This happens even though the place of universities and their mode of governance have changed, together with the clientele of higher education, opening the doors of elitist institutions to a higher proportion of the population – and although gender equality has, at least at the level of rhetoric, achieved a legitimacy that is no longer contested.

As a consequence, analysis of the history of the birth and institutionalisation of gender studies at the University of Lausanne, the first French-speaking Swiss university to have explicitly made an official place for this 'unruly knowledge' by appointing a professor of gender studies in 2000, may shed light on the logics and tensions that come into play when the knowledge that enters universities is knowledge driven by demands stemming from civil society and calling into question some power relations, such as gender, heterosexuality and coloniality. It was in this light that we considered that this history could constitute a case study as Burawoy (2003) defines it, since it seems to us to make it possible to extract the general from the particular, to be situated between the micro and the macro, and to relate the present to the past. Our aim is to define the issues around and the limits of institutionalisation of what we have chosen to describe as a knowledge that is 'cheeky' or 'insolent' with regard to other knowledges and their monopoly of legitimacy.

Comparison with the changes that have occurred over the past 25 years in another disciplinary area, area studies, suggests that the social resistances and new scientific objects offered by disciplines such as women's/gender studies or area studies tend to be diluted under the joint influence of social demands, fragmentation and globalisation, paving the way for a new (?) definition of academic disciplines, which brings the 'cheeky knowledge' constructed by women's/gender studies back into normality and subsumes the local knowledge of area studies under the term 'global studies'.

After briefly clarifying what is at stake when one takes epistemological and/or methodological choices linked either to disciplinarity or to inter-/transdisciplinarity, we first present the history of gender studies at the University of Lausanne, then review the recent situation of area studies in Switzerland, and finally examine the difficulties encountered by interdisciplinary knowledges such as gender studies or area studies, so long as the understanding of utility is exclusively economic and very short term.

We have based our contribution on analysis of the archives of the Centre for Gender Studies at the University of Lausanne and on our experience of having participated in that Centre from its creation. The documentary analysis we have made shows that they tell a rich and complex story explaining the setup and the transformations that mark this unusual academic field of knowledge. The comparison with area studies is based on the work and conclusions of an ad hoc working group on accountability and its problematic links with area studies (Künzler et al. 2016).

2 Inter-/Trans-, and Postdisciplinarity: What Does the Knowledge Built in Gender Studies Refer To?

We will borrow most of our definitions from the work of Darbellay's team[1] on inter- and transdisciplinarity (2014) as its research was carried out in Switzerland; it therefore analyses the same context as we do and thus is significant for our purpose. According to its results, academics belonging to interdisciplinary units but coming from different fields of knowledge and various Swiss universities insist on the necessity of opening dialogs with other fields of science, but they also report on the difficulties of practicing interdisciplinarity. The most common definition they give implies the adoption of a positioning that "brings into play two or more established disciplines so that they interact dynamically to allow the complexity of a given object of study to be described, analysed and understood" (Darbellay 2014, p. 165).[2] However, such an epistemology and methodology can be understood in two different ways. The first one, aiming to cross the "disciplinary boundaries, [...] entails a major reconfiguring of disciplinary divisions within a systemic, global and integrated perspective" (Darbellay 2014, p. 166). While this understanding of inter-/transdisciplinarity produces new 'thought styles', the second definition given to inter-/transdisciplinarity tries mainly to bridge the gap between fundamental and applied sciences. It is "more pragmatic, participative and applied and [it] can be thought of as a method of research that brings political, social and economic actors, as well as ordinary citizens, into the research process itself, in a 'problem-solving' perspective". In this view, "actors from outside the scientific field could contribute to the construction of knowledge and solution of social problems that fall outside disciplinary boundaries" (Darbellay 2014, p. 166). This was clearly the situation of gender studies at its beginning.

---

1 Sixty-six academics involved in interdisciplinary research were interviewed and surveyed through the research project *Analysing Interdisciplinary Research: From Theory to Practice. Case Studies in the Swiss University Context*, funded in 2013–2014 by the Swiss National Science Foundation by a committee specialised in interdisciplinary research. The project leaders were Frédéric Darbellay (main applicant), Pasqualina Perrig-Chiello, Anne-Claude Berthoud and François Höpflinger (co-applicants). The members of the research staff were Ayuko Sedooka, Theres Paulsen and Gabriela Steffen.

2 Thus, inter-/transdisciplinarity contrasts with pluri-/multidisciplinarity, as these approaches respect the "idea of the institutionalised and standardised nature of teaching and research practices, both socially and historically, which are governed by compartmentalised scientific paradigms" and offer only a mere addition of "disciplinary viewpoints, in succession and in isolation without any real interaction between them" (Darbellay 2014, p. 165).

The development of gender studies and other areas of teaching and research classified under the heading of 'studies' and their relative institutionalisation during the past 40 years change the place given to these outsiders, especially when these hybrid bodies of knowledge cannot show their immediate utility. To compensate for their difficulty in responding to such a demand, they have to look for other justifications than efficiency (managerial and political accountabilities) to justify their existence. They tend to emphasise professional accountability, which is even more than previously guided by the criteria of normal disciplinary science, as the quest for so-called 'scientific excellence' has been amplified by commodification and competition in an academia ruled by neo-liberal policies.

Therefore, the paradox that surrounds interdisciplinarity, as noted by one of Darbellay's interviewees, is particularly relevant to gender studies; it is officially praised as it may increase the body of knowledge and respond to new thematic problems, but it also makes careers difficult for young researchers who are fighting to have their areas of knowledge recognised as ordinary fields of teaching and searching in academia:

> "Officially there is an open discourse on interdisciplinarity but it is not serious about interdisciplinarity. It is makeshift. And when a professor is appointed, he cannot be appointed on the basis of his interdisciplinary qualities because that comes later. There you have it. If we recruit someone who is young, he must be highly specialised, highly disciplinary." (Darbellay 2014, p. 168)

The tension between the individual goal of making a career and the collective and emancipatory aims of developing hybrid knowledge that answers social demands linked to feminist/gay or lesbian activism and research in these areas is especially important. Gender studies, which rooted itself in social contestations of an unfair gender order and included a very unruly epistemology (e.g. 'situated knowledge' – Haraway 1991; Harding and Norberg 2005) that paid attention to social demands emanating from activists, is nowadays being pushed to withdraw into academia. Thus, it is under pressure to accept the dominant order that it fought at its beginning and to break off the dialogues it was prone to have with civil society.

The same analysis can be made for any studies whose main research theme is constituted by a social group that is dominated, e.g. gay and lesbian studies, postcolonial studies, or cultural studies, when related to areas that do not count for much within the new competitive (knowledge) economy. But it certainly does not apply as such to tourism studies, Darbellay's field, so his plea for a postdisciplinarity "that can both capitalise on the contributions of disciplines while transforming them into new theoretical, methodological and practical frameworks" (2016, p. 371) cannot be directly transposed to gender studies. For all the reasons given above and because this area of knowledge is suspected of being too political, in gender studies one may have doubts about whether the "emergence and development of these new profiles of researchers, who release disciplinary anchors and who are able to transform disciplines in a dialogical perspective in order to analyse and understand the complexity of tourism practices, are perhaps now possible" (Darbellay 2016, p. 370).

3 Social Demands, Indiscipline and Discipline: *LIEGE* and Gender Studies at Lausanne

The institutional place assigned in Switzerland to knowledge on women and social gender relations cannot be understood unless it is integrated into a context marked by intellectual influences and career management. However, geographical proximity (to Germany or France) does not always mean intellectual proximity, because the ideas and knowledge at the heart of disciplines circulate and are retranslated locally.

3.1 A Complex Social Demand

It should be added that the articulation of Swiss policies on gender equality in education and training with the international or national agenda is far from accidental. Switzerland's signature of a number of international treaties (the 1990 UN *International Convention on the Protection of the Rights of All Migrant Workers and Members of Their Families*, the 1979 UN *Convention on the Elimination of All Forms of Discrimination against Women*, etc.) which bear on women's rights, and the development of structures to promote gender equality in the cantons and higher education institutions (Fassa 2016b), should also not be neglected; likewise the reorganisation of Swiss higher education and the development of the *Hautes Écoles Spécialisées* (Universities of Applied Sciences, i. e. higher education establishments whose teaching and training are more immediately vocationally oriented) since 1995.

As regards higher education, the first Federal Equal Opportunities Programme, *Gender Equality in Universities (Federal Equal Opportunities Programme 2000–2004)*, came shortly after Switzerland signed the Bologna Declaration and was integrated into what is now referred to as the European Research Area. The exhortations of the European Parliament in 1988 urging states to create professorial chairs and set up specialised courses on women (ANEF 2014), followed by those of the European Commission, which has funded several studies on the situation of women in universities and research, in which Switzerland has sometimes participated (e. g.

in the framework of the *Helsinki Group* [Rehmann 2004]), catalysed the process of institutionalisation of gender studies in the academic world. Like gender equality, it also benefited considerably from the reorganisation of the universities at the turn of the century. The 1999 law on the universities (*Federal Law of 8 October, 1999 on Financial Aid to Universities*) redefined the objectives and means of Swiss science policy, one of the most significant features of this reform being the delegation of more power to university executives through the *Swiss University Conference*,[3] which served as "a common strategic organ of the confederation and the cantons, empowered to take binding decisions for the sector" (Joye-Cagnard 2008, p. 39).

In this framework, the birth of the Swiss University Conference contributed both to the development of gender studies and to the permanent incorporation of gender equality in the governance of universities. Under its aegis, three nation-wide programmes were set up, two of which very directly concern our subject: the *Federal Equal Opportunities Programmes* and the *Cooperation and Innovation Programmes*[4] (the third programme was for the setup of a 'virtual campus') which aimed to restructure the organisation and teaching activities of the universities and reduce their fragmentation. It was with the aid of this instrument that the *Network Gender Studies Switzerland* was set up and teaching posts on gender could be financed in some universities.

---

3 The management of this specific programme was initially in the hands of the *Swiss Conference of Universities' Rectorates* (2000–2004). The *Swiss University Conference* then took over until the implementation of the *Law on the Encouragement and Coordination of the Swiss Higher Education Sector* on 1 January 2015. At that time, the *Swiss University Conference* was replaced by *Swissuniversities*, a conference which brings together all higher education institutions, both universities and vocational institutions.

4 The *Cooperation and Innovation Programmes* favour "project-based, competitive funding. This instrument is limited in time (but renewable), and oriented towards the provision of particular services, conditional on matching funding. It is fundamentally conceived as an impulse-giving measure: the projects selected must respond to a specific interest – at a given time – relating to the policy of Swiss higher education institutions" (Joye-Cagnard 2008, p. 41). The *Network Gender Studies Switzerland* figures among the projects selected, which since 2004 have associated all Swiss universities (with the exception of the University of Italian Switzerland) to develop a network of complementary and distinctive courses and degree programmes (BA and MA). This specific programme became one of the sub-projects of the *Swiss University Conference-Programme P-4 Equal Opportunities for Women and Men at Universities/Gender Studies 2013–2016*. In this respect, and others, this last programme can be seen as a period of transition between a top-down mode of governance and a bottom-up mode of governance, the mainstreaming and institutionalising of gender equality and gender teaching being more clearly affirmed as from this fourth *Federal Equal Opportunities Programme* (cf. Fassa 2016a).

The activities of the *Network Gender Studies Switzerland* were initially aimed at promoting teaching and programmes in gender studies at the national level. They developed in two areas: designing courses and coordinating them among the various universities, and setting up study programmes in the universities concerned. This project very directly responded to the recommendations of the *Swiss University Conference*, since it involved the networking of partial projects already running in the universities themselves, and required – as in Lausanne – posts to be specifically dedicated to gender teaching and/or its coordination.

Alongside these elements it should be added – as shown by the research project led by one of the present authors on compulsory education and equality (Fassa et al. 2014) – that the few advances observed in the legal texts on compulsory schooling are, by contrast, earlier and should mainly be attributed to events linked to women's statuses in Swiss society and/or major feminist mobilisations. It was not until women won the right to vote in 1971 that the question of equality in education was raised; it was only after the introduction of an article on equality in the *Federal Constitution* (Article 8) in 1981 that the attitude of the cantons began to be questioned, and it was not until the women's strike of 1991 – more than half a million women went on strike to demand that the 1981 article be applied – that the differential socialisation performed by the school system was challenged (Fassa et al. 2014).

3.2 Campaigning and Mobilisation to Demand the Creation of an Interfaculty and Interdisciplinary Structure

Rather than exhaustively retracing the trajectory followed by the "specialised knowledge with a hybrid character" (Perrig-Chiello and Darbellay 2004, p. 35) that is at the heart of gender studies, the aspects that we shall discuss will make it possible to observe that interdisciplinarity has been at the heart of the Lausanne project from its inception and that has been bound up with the need for a strong institutionalisation "that corresponds to the necessity of structuring the scientific field of gender issues" (LIEGE 1998, p. 2). The same concern, according to Pannatier and Roux (2006), marked the creation of the Chair in Gender Studies at the University of Basel (2001), but in that German-speaking region it was more directly set in a form of interdisciplinarity already implemented in other interdisciplinary gender research centres.[5] This was most probably due to the vigour of the German

5 The *Kompetenzzentrum Gender Studies* was founded in Zurich in 1998; a professorial chair in gender studies was not created until 2009 – half time, since its holder also worked half time in Islamology.

academic feminist movement and its involvement with issues related to diversity or post-feminism. Mostly for cultural reasons, the French-speaking part of Switzerland was much more under the influence of the debates that were prominent in the French universities, these being mostly organised around topics emerging from materialist feminism. Another difference between these two regions has mainly to do with the academic and cultural world they broadly share; the proximity to Germany, and the radicality of the reforms its academic world had to go through, organised contestation in a different way than in the French part of Switzerland, in which it was closer to the anti-liberal stances promoted by numerous researchers, among whom Dardot and Laval (2009) constitute a prominent example.

For lack of space, only a few markers will be laid down to give an understanding of how gender studies was established at the University of Lausanne and the strategic options it has taken between 1998 and 2016. December 1998, as the starting point, was the date of the request made to the Rectorate by a group of people mainly from the various echelons of the Faculty of Social and Political Sciences[6] for the creation of an *Interfaculty Laboratory for Gender Studies (Laboratoire Interfacultaire en Études Genre*,[7] in French, with the acronym *LIEGE*; see LIEGE 1998).

The events we have highlighted make it clear that two of the three dimensions (professional, political and institutional/managerial) that Joseph (2010) distinguishes with regard to accountability were central to the *LIEGE* project from its inception, with the professional dimension mainly emerging after the institutionalisation and disciplinisation of gender studies with the creation of the *Centre for Gender Studies [Centre en Études Genre]-LIEGE* in 2008 (cf. section 3.4). For Dardot and Laval (2009), this 'accounting' is one of the key elements of new public management and it gives rise to the alignment of public institutions with those of the private sector, with the benefits and costs of every decision becoming amenable to a managerial approach that takes little account of advances in terms of the common good. They also show clearly that gender studies at the University of Lausanne has been able to draw on very different references in order to construct itself in a context marked by a major transformation of the academic arena and its modes of governance and by social movements that condemn these same political choices as those of neo-liberal policies exclusively driven by the interests of the market and/or of greater efficiency

6 Seven of the eight signatories (one of them a man) belonged to the Faculty of Social and Political Sciences; only one had the title of professor, and two of the women also declared their membership of a student organisation (the *CLOU – Collectif de Lutte contre Orchidée* à l'Université de Lausanne) campaigning against the austerity measures and public spending cuts imposed by the canton administration.

7 After its creation *LIEGE* became an inter-university centre and its official name in French was *Laboratoire Interuniversitaire en Études Genre* with the same acronym: *LIEGE*.

in the public sector. The special feature of the Lausanne project is that it can be understood both as a result of changes in science policy – and its implementation from a 'managerial' perspective – and as a result of the response given locally to a social demand inspired by the struggle against the austerity policies applied in the public administration of the canton of Vaud. This dual parentage has marked the history of gender studies in Lausanne and has the interesting feature that it invites one to try to understand how the 'cheeky knowledge' that underlays women's/gender studies in the English-speaking world had to 'behave itself' in order to survive and develop in the Swiss university environment.

The project presented in December 1998 stressed the need to "create an interfaculty institutional cluster for teaching and research" (LIEGE 1998, p. 1). This positioning was justified by the nature of gender studies, which "requires an integrated, cross-cutting approach which constructs relationships between different domains and disciplines, [since it cannot] be confined within a single discipline. On the contrary, the knowledge has so far made it possible to accumulate leads one to question the pertinence of the current division of disciplines, which are at least partly based on gender differences or similarities." (LIEGE 1998, p. 2)

In this context, *LIEGE* set out a 'twofold strategy' that would make it possible to sensitise the university community to the question of social gender relations "both through interdisciplinary teaching and research centred on gender and through the integration of these inquiries in all faculties and disciplines" (Pannatier and Roux 2006, p. 116). The first strategy aimed to develop gender studies itself through the creation of professorial chairs in this area, and the second aimed to promote teaching by networking researchers active in the field. In more practical terms it was proposed:

- to offer a number of courses to form the core of a programme integrating social gender relations – the other courses being chosen within the faculties and remaining discipline-based;
- to give greater visibility to courses already dealing in one way or another with this issue (43 lecture courses and seminars are identified in the three faculties designated by the *LIEGE* project to take part in such a laboratory: *Lettres* [Arts], Social and Political Sciences, Theology and Science of Religions) and to create synergies capable of establishing this interfaculty laboratory as a gender studies research cluster in French-speaking Switzerland (LIEGE 1998, p. 5).

Since gender studies constitutes a body of specific knowledge, the development of gender studies also involved the institutionalisation and recognition of academic programmes in this area. A first qualification in gender studies was set up between the Universities of Geneva and Lausanne in 1998 (a *DEA – Diplôme d'Études Approfondies*, a postgraduate diploma). A doctoral school session was organised in 1999, bringing together researchers from the Universities of Basel, Bern/Freiburg, Lausanne/Geneva and Zurich and laying the foundation for doctoral schools in gender studies, both French-speaking and German-speaking, constituting a 'pilot project' co-financed by the universities and the *Swiss University Conference* (Widmer and Schulz 2005).

Collaborating in all these structures, the project was thus clearly set in the line of work on gender (Scott and Varikas 1988) and not that of the 'women's issues' that are at the heart of women's studies. The latter paradigm was nonetheless the one invoked when the constitution of such a laboratory was justified by the requests made, from 1995 – the year of the *Fourth World Conference on Women* in Beijing (4–15 September) – by the Women's Committee of the Rectorate for the creation in the University of Lausanne of "an interfaculty department for teaching and research on the men-women issue" (LIEGE 1998, p. 1). The demands of the students and lecturers in the mobilisations of 1997 for teaching in gender studies (Pannatier 2005, p. 10) were also mentioned in this project but they stress the more political dimension of such an interfaculty laboratory.

3.3 The Creation of *LIEGE*: Between Bottom-up and Top-down Action

LIEGE (Interuniversity – and no longer *Interfaculty – Laboratory for Gender Studies)* was finally created on 1 May 2001 with the aid of funding from the first *Federal Equal Opportunities Programme 2000–2003*, and its history was marked from the outset by the tension between feminist activism and the need to play the academic and institutional game. Its birth was thus the result of a local configuration not only favourable to the establishment of such courses but also to the new awareness at a national level. It does not, however, entirely follow the same chronological logic as that which marked the institutionalisation of gender studies in other European countries, where "everywhere women's studies have been a bottom-up initiative, in contrast to equal opportunity policies, which have resulted from top-down public policies" (ANEF 2014, p. 20). In Switzerland, the question of women in science came late to the agenda, and it was precisely this delay in observing the rarity of women in professorial posts (fewer than 7 per cent in 2000), combined with a strong internationalisation of higher education, that had the effect of generating very active policies to improve the Swiss situation.

The first *Federal Equal Opportunities Programme* drove forward a series of actions to increase the number of women among academic staff, in particular by offering support individually to certain women (mentoring, nursery places, funding, etc.) to counter what was still primarily seen as the result of "the problem of women in science" (Garforth and Kerr 2009, p. 391). This perspective ignored the organisational aspect (Fassa and Kradolfer 2010; Marry 2010) and attributed the low numbers of potential women academics (students and assistants) to their 'delay', to unfamiliarity with the academic milieu and its rules, and to the problem of the work-life balance. At the local level, the clear will of the Rectorate of the University of Lausanne responded to the pressure of the feminist movement that had emerged in the student demonstrations of 1997 and had organised debates leading to the demand for a "chair in feminist teaching" (Pannatier and Roux 2006, p. 112). Presented as a "*collective mentoring* project bringing together people interested in gender questions across the whole of Switzerland" (Pannatier 2005, p. 9, original emphasis), *LIEGE* made clear its determination to maintain its links with a social movement strongly critical of the university institution and the neo-liberal turn of public policies in the late 1990s. Gaël Pannatier, the coordinator of *LIEGE* from the start, and Patricia Roux, a professor of gender studies from 2000 and the initiator of this interconnecting of feminist researchers, present this network as the site "of other modes of operation and [the opening up] of other spaces for discussion and reflection than those usually practiced in universities. In principle, therefore, *LIEGE* had an ambitious aim, which was to play a part in reducing the social inequalities produced in and by the hierarchical relations that structure the academic world." (Pannatier and Roux 2006, p. 113, authors' emphasis)

At the outset *LIEGE* constituted just under 100 people; in 2005 it had more than 450 members. *LIEGE* responded to the initial objectives of bringing together in a network people interested in the problematic of social gender relations, whether or not they belonged to the academic world, and providing a research cluster in gender studies in French-speaking Switzerland. The community group approach adopted by the creators of *LIEGE* thus seemed to be inspired by the experience of British feminists and aimed to establish a gender studies research cluster based on a broader collective of women interested in thinking and research on social gender relations.

3.4 The Institutionalisation of Gender Studies at the University of Lausanne and the End of the *LIEGE*[8] Interuniversity Network

In 2008, *LIEGE* merged with *Gender Campus*[9] as regards the gender studies research and information network. This is now national and open to the more vocational *Hautes Écoles Spécialisées* (Universities of Applied Sciences). In parallel, a new teaching and research entity of the Faculty of Social and Political Sciences, the *Centre for Gender Studies-LIEGE*, was set up in the framework of a faculty reorganisation, "the main mission of the Centre [being] to stimulate, promote and host research integrating a gender perspective in the University of Lausanne". This stabilisation, decided in February 2008 by the Directorate of the University of Lausanne, had both good and bad consequences. On the one hand, it strengthened gender studies because it made clear the recognition given to the professional accountability of the academic members of the network. In line with this good appraisal, it transformed this area of studies into a quasi-discipline in which the management of the university could show some exceptional skills compared with other tertiary institutions, thus complying with the rules of competitiveness of the knowledge economy. But on the other hand, this move was accompanied by a clear disciplinisation that made it impossible to respond to the social demands of the external members to the academic world in a participative way. Thus, willingly or not, this governance transformed the openness of gender studies to civil society.

---

8 The term *LIEGE* now designates the "interactive platform for members of the *Haute École Spécialisée de Suisse occidentale* [University of Applied Sciences and Arts of Western Switzerland] interested in gender studies and questions of equality" (Gender Campus 2017a, authors' emphasis). Although it shares the database of the national network *Gender Campus*, this platform only addresses people working in the *Hautes Écoles Spécialisées* – a sector of higher education differentiated from the universities by its directly vocational dimensions. It has experienced the same movements that we have observed in the University of Lausanne: an attempt to institutionalise teaching on gender in specific places and branches of education and the networking of researchers in this area. It should be noted that the funding of its activities is no longer assured for the future.

9 *Gender Campus* describes itself on its website as "The platform for information, communication and networking of gender studies and of equal opportunities at Swiss universities" (Gender Campus 2017b). This platform also gives a national dimension to the theme of gender studies and aims to bring interested knowledge-workers together at a national level. A regular (bilingual) newsletter is sent to its members, with news about national and international events, calls for papers, and professional and training opportunities.

The changes concerned the nature of the relationship it had with feminists outside academia and its proximity with the social problems it formerly addressed. As a consequence, the external members of the network soon deserted it because of its now exclusive setting in the world of higher education.

The historical and obsolete reference to *LIEGE* disappeared with a new faculty reorganisation in 2015, and the *Centre for Gender Studies* is now linked to only one faculty. To this clear movement of institutionalisation – and relative closure of the *Centre for Gender Studies* on itself and the faculty to which it is attached – corresponded a movement in the opposite direction which testified to the determination to retain the inter-, trans- or antidisciplinary[10] vocation of gender studies, since the actors of the creation and development of a new interfaculty platform focused on gender were also mostly members of the *Centre for Gender Studies*, a disciplinary research unit entirely comparable to other research units organised around a specific field of knowledge.

Thus in 2013, an interfaculty platform in gender studies, the *PlaGe (Plateforme en Études Genre)*, was (re)created in the University of Lausanne to revitalise the networking activities that had lost some of their vigour with the creation of the *Centre for Gender Studies-LIEGE*. Interdisciplinary reflection remains its objective and the construction of synergies at a local and purely university level. It aims to go beyond inter- or transdisciplinarity and manifest the vivacity of the gender perspective and its potential for insolence in the face of the established disciplines. In November 2016, the site had a membership of 105 researchers and reported 69 courses (33 at the bachelor's level and 36 at the master's level) given in the various faculties, which had at least a partial perspective on gender studies. This panoply was, however, not uniformly spread across the faculties: most of these offers came from just two faculties (Social and Political Sciences and Arts and Humanities). Analysis of the annual reports of the *Plateforme en Études Genre* shows that it is mainly focused on the visibility and fertility of the gender perspective, and that it has only been able to play a secondary role in the development of research and the setup of interdisciplinary courses in gender studies. It seems, however, to be able to some degree to reconnect with the 'cheekiness' of the initial proposals of the *LIEGE* network, since it recently enabled a working group to create synergies among researchers working on sexualities. Perhaps it can be the starting point

10 Darbellay (2016, p. 370) depicts this last positioning as highly questionable; he describes it as throwing "the production of knowledge into the abyss and into the antidisciplinary chaos. Chaos is still the most favorable ground for the resurgence of new disciplinary tribes and is more rarely the sign of the birth of a new and peaceful world between disciplines". Nonetheless, his point shows the disruptive and innovative dynamics that 'cheeky knowledge' can bring into a sometimes too quiet and too respectful realm.

for a new process of production of 'cheeky knowledge', given that some works on social gender relations have been strongly toned down to meet the demands of an academic world in which the norms of excellence – at least those that provide the basis for academic careers – remain cast in the modern division of knowledge. It is too early to say, just as one cannot know whether this initiative will or will not lead to the institutionalisation of a specific academic structure.

It can thus be concluded that the initial balancing of gender studies between activism and discipline remains relevant nowadays, since there is still a need today on the one hand to present credentials of the disciplinary scientificity of knowledge about social gender relations and on the other hand to develop 'insolent' knowledge, whose insolence is only measured with reference to other fields of knowledge.

4 Feminism, Social Demand and the Disciplinisation of Gender Studies

The few markers we have laid down so far show that while the courses set up in some faculties, mainly social and political sciences and arts, have enabled the students to complement the teaching in their major discipline by choosing a colouring linked to the study of social gender relations, the reorganisations imposed by the Bologna process have required gender studies to assert its scientificity and its conformity with the disciplinary fields. It seems, however, that the process of disciplinisation and institutionalisation is now being held back by a change in social demand, which approaches knowledge in gender studies as a welcome complement to other knowledge, but one that is unlikely to lead to a vocational opportunity. Because of the growing competition among universities, the number of major options for the master's in social science has been reduced and the gender major has disappeared; the teaching inspired by this perspective is now offered in a broader way. The students enrolled in the gender studies doctoral programme of the *West Switzerland University Conference* are often also enrolled in another doctoral programme more directly attached to a conventional discipline. It seems to us that these new configurations are akin to the reasons given to explain the decline in the number of people following the gender courses of the Open University (Kirkup and Whitelegg 2013).

So, however strong the inter-, trans-, or even antidisciplinarity aspiration that lay behind gender studies, it has to be observed that the traditional discipline-based organisation of the university has helped to partially neutralise the initial intention, and it may be thought that while doing a master's in gender studies still sometimes leads people to question the relevance of disciplinary divisions, this happens more rarely than in the past, with this self-critique not always readily extending to gender studies itself. This difficult reflexivity was central to the debates – both programmed and unexpected – that took place during the organisation in September 2012 of the 6th International French-speaking Feminist Studies Congress, an event which brought together in the University of Lausanne more than 600 researchers from four continents. The topic chosen for the conference concerned one of the currently most-debated issues in gender studies, the intersectionality of relations of domination. The title, *Intertwining of Power Relations: Discrimination and Privileges of Gender, Race, Class and Sexuality*, and the call for papers reasserted the strong relationship that has existed between feminist social movements and academic research. Overall the conference was a success since it allowed many in-depth exchanges on the theoretical and activist questions linked to this topic. But it also saw contestation of the 'white-washing' of intersectional thinking as an effect of the institutionalisation of gender studies and of what Bilge (2016) describes as the annexation by gender studies of a question that incorporates an activist praxis and so lies on the margin of academic feminism.

5 Comparison with Other 'Studies': Area Studies and Cultural Studies

The new academic governance that we are now experiencing, with the growing recourse to "institutional and public accountability with regard to money and productivity" (Joseph 2010, p. 332) lowers political accountability with regard to more social justice. This is the case not only for gender studies, but also for other fields such as area studies or cultural studies, as will be seen below with the examples of area studies in Switzerland and cultural studies at the University of Arizona (Joseph 2010).

Like gender studies, area studies is in general weakly institutionalised as such in Swiss universities, but it has to be noted that the number of teachers and researchers active in these fields is much higher than the small number of structures dedicated to them. The strength of the disciplinary anchorage thus tends to mask the extent of the work produced and the number of people engaged in these fields of research. Before starting our analysis, we must recall that the importance of area studies for military and defence issues has not been as central in Switzerland (with its long tradition of neutrality and development aid) as in the US. Nevertheless, the significant budget cuts in area studies all around the world during the past 20 years, and the reconfiguration of this field into other structures (global studies, international studies, etc.), has also had an impact in Switzerland.

5.1 Area Studies

The distinction between area studies and discipline-based studies is inherited from divisions of the world that date from the colonial era: area studies was then understood as covering everything that was 'exotic' or different.[11] As a consequence, being interested as a researcher in European regions implied pursuing a career in economics, sociology, etc., whereas the study of extra-European topics in Africa, Latin America, etc., led to a career in area studies. It follows that area studies generally appeals to inter- or transdisciplinarity, or at least requires knowledge of the methods and mobilisation of knowledge derived from several disciplines in order to approach the region studied (Quality Assurance Agency for Higher Education 2008). It is moreover widely accepted that area studies helps call into question a dominant disciplinary thinking constructed on the model of the Western world being taken for granted (Bates et al. 1993) and that the specificities that characterise it influence both the practice and the results of research.

As regards area studies in Switzerland at the institutional level, for a short time the Geneva Centre for the Training of African Managers, created in 1962 and renamed the African Institute of Geneva the following year, offered training centred on Africa. When it became the Graduate Institute of Development Studies in 1973, its African focus shifted to development in general, but for a long time it remained the main centre for African studies in Switzerland. After an attempt in the late 1990s to create a *Curriculum of African Studies*, consisting of two coordinated multidisciplinary networks, one for German-speaking and the other for French-speaking Switzerland, the Swiss Science Council abandoned this coordination project for area studies, and African studies was not mentioned in the *Message of 25 November 1998 on the Encouragement of Training, Research and Technology in the Period 2000–2003* (Conseil Fédéral 1998, no pagination) because of its institutional and structural weakness. Like African studies, Latin-American studies was a subject of great interest especially in the 1970s, but did not develop as an institutionalised field of research. However, since the turn of the century, various structures have been created or reactivated. Thus, the *Swiss Latin-American Centre* of the University of Saint Gallen, after ceasing its activities in 1992, reopened in 2007. More recently, since the academic year 2009–2010, the *Center for Global Studies* of the

11 This section takes over some elements of the text published by Künzler et al. (2016).

University of Bern has offered a master's in Latin-American studies. The University of Zurich set up a *Centre of Competence on Latin America* in 2016. There was also a new impulse in African studies in the same period, leading to the positioning of Basel as a centre of competence in this area and the creation of an interdisciplinary master's in African studies in 2002. Since 2012, a similar ambition has emerged at the University of Geneva (Mayor et al. 2013), and a master's in African studies, based in the *Global Studies Institute*, is being developed.

So it seems that the interest in and development of global studies at the turn of the century, in line with the need for a better understanding of globalisation and internationalisation processes, have enabled area studies to regain relevance at the institutional level. The redefinition of 'areas' – and of the paradigm of area studies – in the new context of globality happened at the cost of changes that neglected some regions or (re)configured the research questions. Regrouped under the banner of globality/globalisation, it has enjoyed a degree of revitalisation: "The first college programmes to be called 'global studies' were formed in the mid-1990s, and within a decade there were hundreds." (Juergensmeyer 2014, p. XIV) As in other countries, at the University of Bern, the University of Geneva, the École Polytechnique Fédérale de Lausanne, etc., the work produced in area studies in the framework of global studies seems more in tune with the *zeitgeist*, since it reinserts research that previously appeared localised to a single region into the phenomena of transnationalism, multiculturalism, networks and international flows (of goods, people and knowledge). And it has to be noted that not all area studies arouse the same interest, since while BRIC (Brazil, Russia, India and China) have become essential countries to study, Africa and Latin America, like other Asian or Oceanic regions, are little studied. The need for new knowledge also shows clearly that research and teaching are profoundly linked to developments in international politics and economic exchanges and the increased competition among universities due to the new forms of the academic governance. If area studies developed during the Cold War as a 'strategic' field to acquire knowledge (largely financed in the US through the federal government) about 'other' regions of the world, today the new political order affects researchers in area studies by asking them to shift the focus of their research onto global and transnational issues (Berger 2006).

5.2 Cultural and Gender Studies at Arizona in the Face of Managerial Demands

Joseph's (2010) thorough and reflexive analysis of the place of cultural studies in her institution helps us understand why gender studies, which was seen as a pioneer in interdisciplinarity, does not benefit from the supplement of legitimacy that is now attached to practices of interdisciplinary research. Having been appointed to the committee in her university which decided on budget allocations, she analysed the demands made on academics, observing that in the framework of the new conditions of the production of science, interdisciplinarity implies applied research whose products can be easily commodified and its outputs entered into balance sheets. This distance taken from the nostalgic positions that we have described earlier makes it possible to understand how the Bologna process valorises interdisciplinarity differently depending on whether it is practised in the 'hard' or life sciences or is articulated with the new "domains of specialised hybrid knowledge" (Perrig-Chiello and Darbellay 2004, p. 35) of cultural studies or gender studies. It also explains how the integration of work stemming from gender studies by equality policies, particularly through mainstreaming, is not always accompanied by valorisation of the modes of knowledge acquisition proposed by gender studies (a situated position), and still less by the 'insolence' they have imposed in the face of the established disciplines. On this point she concurs with the conclusions of Perrig-Chiello and Darbellay (2004, p. 36) on the difference between specialised fields depending on whether they are or are not close to the now recognised sciences:

> "These aggregated disciplines present states of development that are differentiated in terms of their disciplinary self-definition, their academic institutionalisation, and their scientific and social recognition, above all for reasons of economic priorities and training policy."

But Joseph's (2010) conclusions are more self-critical and optimistic and her analysis is less internalistic as regards the capacity for insolence of inter-, trans-, or even antidisciplinarity studies, since she proposes nothing less than to take seriously the necessities of accountability and push them to their limits. Adopting the tools of new public management so as to make visible the goods created by education for the benefit of communities would, in her view, make it possible to turn them against the people who propose a development of knowledge driven purely by the need to transform knowledge into economic gain.

Her heterodox position is refreshing because it proposes to pervert the instruments that managerial power imposes on universities and their researchers in order to show to what extent the accounting process now under way (systematic measures of the performances of institutions and researchers) neglects what is produced by researchers who work in fields that have no immediately applied perspectives. In addition, she sketches some cross-paths (Fassa 2013) through which the actions of the 'femocrats' (Bereni 2009; Jacquot 2009), of feminism – academic or not – and of social movements challenging the organisation and management of higher education (cf. for example the *Maple Spring* in Quebec) can be reconciled. Nevertheless, this policy requires researchers in these hybrid fields to practice self-reflexivity and abandon a nostalgic position that prevents them from "engag[ing] in a broader contestation over the scope and goals of higher education" (Joseph 2010, p. 343).

6 Difficult Validation and Institutionalisation of Inter- or Transdisciplinary Knowledge

From its inception, the institutionalisation of gender studies has articulated different kinds of tensions, which for some people stem from the relationship of universities with the outside world and for others from the organisation of higher education itself:

1. a tension between an activist social demand aimed at the emancipation of women as a dominated group, and the construction of 'scientific' knowledge on specific situations of domination;
2. a tension between knowledge already established in disciplines and based on specific methodologies and questioning of those same disciplines as factors of reproduction of the relation of domination between men and women;
3. a tension between a traditional pedagogy which prolongs the scholastic form (Vincent 1994), the hierarchical relations that it vehicles and underpins, and the aim of constructing more democratic relations at the heart of the university teaching relationship.

Examining the place of gender studies in universities therefore seems to be an interesting way into understanding to what types of social demands interdisciplinary approaches now respond, and how. Inspired by the sociology of education, in particular British studies of the relationship between curricula and the sociology of knowledge (Bernstein 1971; Young 1971), we have tried in this article to examine the ways in which the institutionalisation of gender studies translates various social demands in Castel's (2002) sense and intervenes on curricula to disturb them, but ultimately takes away some of their potential for subversion and opening onto a future that does not reproduce the present and its inequalities. Based on the Lausanne example, we have tried to articulate the transformations linked to the changes in demands for gender equality and those that can be attributed to changes in the universities themselves. We have drawn on this example to reflect on these tensions and sketch the beginnings of some answers as to the place that can be occupied by knowledge that disturbs the traditional modes of operation in an institution that is subjected to the logics of the market (Dardot and Laval 2009) and which must demonstrate its transparency and its good governance (Paradeise and Thoenig 2011; Musselin 2009).

In comparison, area studies, which also generally appeals to inter- or transdisciplinarity, seems harshly judged when it comes to the evaluation of quality and performances:

> "Ironically enough, even though it is precisely collaboration between different fields that can lead to astonishing breakthroughs, multidisciplinary research only gets moderate scores on traditional quality indicators." (Royal Netherlands Academy of Arts and Sciences 2013, p. 16)

It is also observed that area studies is subject to pressures aimed at restricting its research to 'applied' questions, or, in other words, to make a "Nietzschean shift away from philosophy (scholarship) into technology (practical relevance)" (Macamo 2014 quoted in Künzler et al. 2016, p. 64). And yet area studies, as the *Schweizerische Asiengesellschaft* has also observed, has "the essential function of developing competences in cultural diversity, otherness and intercultural understanding" and therefore has as its "main challenge the development of fundamental research in phase with society" (Schweizerische Asiengesellschaft 2016, p. 47).

Joseph's (2010) reflexive reading of the changes demanded of her cultural studies department at the University of Arizona has served as an anchorage point for reflection on the institutionalisation of 'cheeky knowledge' and on the changes that the standardisation of degree courses implied by the Bologna reform has imposed on "specialised domains with a hybrid character" (Perrig-Chiello and Darbellay 2004, p. 35). Comparison among these different inter- or transdisciplinary domains suggests that social resistance and the new scientific objects that are proposed are now tending to be weakened under the joint influence of the fragmentation of social demand and the process of globalisation, paving the way for a return to normal of the definition of the academic disciplines.

Thus, gender studies at Lausanne – which were part of and which was driven by the social contestation in 1997 and challenged in 2012 by another mode of social contestation – has followed an itinerary which, throughout its short history, has been marked by the fundamental tension which articulates knowledge for emancipation – set, according to Crenshaw (1991), in individual and collective experience of domination and struggle against that oppression – with institutionalisation as an academic quasi-discipline of knowledge-derived reflections and those contextualised practices. We are thus faced, to paraphrase Stacey (2000, p. 1190), with a glass that is both half empty and half full. Full, because institutionalisation has brought recognition of reflections on the oppression of women as ideas that cannot be ignored in the production of knowledge. Empty, because that same institutionalisation has partly neutralised the radical political impact of the feminist practices – since all practice bears knowledge – that gave rise to those reflections, and has helped rigidify categories that gender studies sought to deconstruct and question.

Acknowledgement

We are grateful to Damien Michelet, coordinator of the *Interfaculty Gender Studies Platform (PlaGe)* at the University of Lausanne and of the French-speaking Swiss network *Gender Campus*, for his attentive reading and his constructive, informed and positive comments.

All the translations from French were done by Richard Nice, whom we would like to thank very much for doing a wonderful job.

References

Association Nationale des Études Féministes (ANEF). 2014. *Le Genre dans l'Enseignement Supérieur et la Recherche. Livre Blanc.* Paris: La Dispute.

Bates, Robert Hinrichs, Valenti-Yves Mudimbe and Jean O'Barr. 1993. *Africa and the Disciplines. The Contributions of Research in Africa to the Social Sciences and Humanities.* Chicago and London: The University of Chicago Press.

Bereni, Laure. 2009. Quand la Mise à l'Agenda Ravive les Mobilisations Féministes. *Revue Française de Science Politique* 2 (59): 301–323.

Berger, Anne. 2006. Traversées de Frontières: Postcolonialité et Études de "Genre" en Amérique. *Labyrinthe* 24 (2): 10–37.

Bernstein, Basil. 1971. On the Classification and Framing of Educational Knowledge. In *Knowledge and Control: New Directions for the Sociology of Education*, ed. by Michael F.D. Young, 47–69. London: Collier-Macmillan.

Bilge, Sirma. 2016. Plaidoyer pour une Intersectionnalité Critique Non-Blanchie. In *L'Intersectionnalité: Enjeux Théoriques et Politiques*, ed. by Marta Roca i Escoda, Farinaz Fassa and Éleonore Lepinard, 75–102. Paris: La Dispute.

Burawoy, Michael. 2003. L'Étude de Cas Élargie. Une Approche Réflexive, Historique et Comparée de l'Enquête de Terrain. In *L'Enquête de Terrain*, ed. by Daniel Cefaï, 425–464. Paris: La Découverte, MAUSS.

Castel, Robert. 2002. La Sociologie et la Réponse à la Demande Sociale. In *À Quoi Sert la Sociologie?*, ed. by Bernard Lahire, 67–77. Paris: La Découverte.

Chaperon, Sylvie. 2002. L'Histoire Contemporaine des Sexualités en France. Vingtième Siècle. *Revue d'histoire* 75 (3): 47–59.

Conseil Fédéral. 1998. *Message relatif à l'encouragement de la formation, de la recherche et de la technologie pendant les années 2000–2003 du 25 novembre 1998, FF 1999 269.* Berne: Conseil Fédéral.

Crenshaw, Kimberle. 1991. Mapping the Margins: Intersectionality, Identity Politics, and Violence against Women of Color. *Stanford Law Review* 6 (43): 1241–1299.

Darbellay, Frédéric. 2014. Rethinking Inter- and Transdisciplinarity: Undisciplined Knowledge and the Emergence of a New Thought Style. *Futures* 65: 163–174.

Darbellay, Frédéric. 2016. From Disciplinarity to Postdisciplinarity: Tourism Studies Dedisciplined. *Tourism Analysis* 21: 363–372.

Dardot, Pierre, and Christian Laval. 2009. *La Nouvelle Raison du Monde. Essai sur la Société Néolibérale.* Paris: La Découverte.

Fassa, Farinaz. 2013. La Recherche en Suisse: Quand le Genre Interroge les Critères de l'Excellence Scientifique. *Mouvements* 4 (76): 156–169.

Fassa, Farinaz. 2016a. *Filles et Garçons Face à la Formation. Les Défis de l'Égalité.* Lausanne: PPUR.

Fassa, Farinaz. 2016b. Politiques d'Égalité des Chances dans les Universités Suisses. Bilan Provisoire d'un Pilotage Décentralisé. In *Les Femmes dans le Monde Académique. Perspectives Comparatives*, ed. by Rebecca Rogers and Pascale Molinier, 167–179. Rennes: PUR.

Fassa, Farinaz, and Sabine Kradolfer. Eds. 2010. *Le Plafond de Fer de l'Université. Femmes et Carrières.* Zurich: Seismo.

Fassa, Farinaz, Valérie Rolle and Chiara Storari. 2014. Politiques de l'Égalité à l'École Obligatoire. Des Ambivalences qui Diluent les Rapports Sociaux de Sexe. *Swiss Journal of Sociology* 2 (40): 37–52.

Garforth, Lisa, and Anne Kerr. 2009. Women and Science: What's the Problem? *Social Politics: International Studies in Gender, State and Society* 3 (16): 379–403.

Gender Campus. 2017a. *Policy of the University of Applied Sciences and Arts.* https://www.gendercampus.ch/fr/hochschulen/netzwerke/liege-hes-so/über-uns. Accessed: February 15, 2017.

Gender Campus. 2017b. *Welcome.* https://www.gendercampus.ch/EN. Accessed: February 15, 2017.

Haraway, Donna. 1991. Situated Knowledges: The Science Question in Feminism and the Privilege of Partial Perspective. *Feminist Studies* 14 (3): 575–599.

Harding, Sandra, and Kathryn Norberg. 2005. New Feminist Approaches to Social Science Methodologies: An Introduction. *Signs: Journal of Women in Culture and Society* 30 (4): 2009–2015.

Jacquot, Sophie. 2009. La Fin d'une Politique d'Exception. *Revue Française de Science Politique* 59 (2): 247–277.

Joseph, Miranda. 2010. Accounting for Interdisciplinarity. In *Interdisciplinarity and Social Justice: Revisioning Academic Accountability*, ed. by Joe Parker, Ranu Samantrai and Mary Romero, 321–352. Albany: State University of New York Press.

Joye-Cagnard, Frédéric, Raphaël Ramuz, Philippe Sormani, Martin Benninghoff, Gaële Goastellec and Jean-Philippe Leresche. 2008. *Évaluation de l'Instrument "Projets de Coopération et d'Innovation" (2004–2007). Rapport Final.* Berne: Conférence Universitaire Suisse.

Juergensmeyer, Mark. 2014. *Thinking Globally: A Global Studies Reader.* Berkeley: University of California Press.

Kirkup, Gill, and Elizabeth Whitelegg. 2013. The Legacy and Impact of Open University Women's/Gender Studies: 30 Years On. *Gender and Education* 25 (1): 6–22.

Künzler, Daniel, Anne Mayor, Sabine Kradolfer and Thomas Herzog. 2016. Prise de Position sur les Area Studies de la Société Suisse d'Études Africaines, la Société Suisse Moyen-Orient et Civilisation Islamique et la Société Suisse des Américanistes. In *Swiss Academies Reports* 11 (2): 57–70.

Laboratoire Interuniversitaire en Études Genre (LIEGE). 1998. *Projet de Création d'un Laboratoire Interfacultaire en Études Genre (LIEGE), Lausanne.* [Document addressed by the Gender Studies Working Party to the Rectorate of the University of Lausanne, 21 December 1998]. (unpub.).

Macamo, Elísio. 2014. *Solving Problems or Raising Issues: Area Studies and the Problem of Relevance.* Paper presented at the Workshop *Assessing Quality and Performance in Area Studies* at the University of Freiburg on 14 November 2014. Ms. (unpub.).

Marry, Catherine. 2010. Le Plafond de Verre dans le Monde Académique: l'Exemple de la Biologie. In *Le Plafond de Fer de l'Université. Femmes et Carrières*, ed. by Farinaz Fassa and Sabine Kradolfer, 173–193. Zurich: Seismo.

Mayor, Anne, Daniel Künzler, Didier Péclard, Yvan Droz and Veit Arlt. 2013. *Les Études Africaines dans les Universités de Suisse Romande et de Bâle. Rapport de la Société Suisse d'Études Africaines (SSEA-SGAS).* http://www.sagw.ch/dms/africa/publikationen/Rapport-Etudes-africaines_final. Accessed: September 13, 2016.

Musselin, Christine. 2009. Les Réformes des Universités en Europe: des Orientations Comparables, mais des Déclinaisons Nationales. *Revue du MAUSS* 33 (1): 69–91.

Pannatier, Gaël. 2005. *Réseau de Mentoring Collectif en Étude Genre. Rapport d'Activités et Perspectives (2001–2005).* Lausanne: LIEGE-Université de Lausanne, Conférence Universitaire Suisse.

Pannatier, Gaël, and Patricia Roux. 2006. Institutionnalisation des Études Féministes en Suisse. Le Défi de l'Intégration et du Maintien d'une Dimension Critique. In *Transmission: Savoirs Féministes et Pratiques Pédagogiques*, ed. by Soline Blanchard, Jules Falquet and Dominique Fougeyrollas, 105–117. Paris: Cahiers du CEDREF.

Paradeise, Catherine, and Jean-Claude Thoenig. 2011. Réformes et Ordres Universitaires Locaux. In *Gouverner l'Éducation par les Nombres?* ed. by Georges Felouzis and Siegfried Hanhart, 33–52. Bruxelles: De Boeck.

Perrig-Chiello, Pasqualina, and Frédéric Darbelley. 2004. La Vieillesse est Féminine – Qui s'en Soucie? La Recherche en Études Genre et en Gérontologie entre Auto-Définition Disciplinaire et Exigence Interdisciplinaire. *Nouvelles Questions Féministes* 1 (23): 31–42.

Quality Assurance Agency for Higher Education. 2008. *Area Studies.* Gloucester: QAAHE.

Rehmann, Irene. 2004. *Helsinki Group: Women and Science – Review of the Situation in Switzerland.* Berne: Office Fédéral de l'Éducation et de la Science.

Revenin, Régis. 2007. Les Études et Recherches Lesbiennes et Gays en France (1970–2006). *Genre & Histoire* Automne (1). http://genrehistoire.revues.org/219. Accessed: February 7, 2017.

Royal Netherlands Academy of Arts and Sciences. 2013. *Towards a Framework for the Quality Assessment of Social Sciences.* Amsterdam: KNAW.

Schweizerische Asiengesellschaft. 2016. Leistungs- und Qualitätsevaluation in den Asien- und Orientwissenschaften. In *Swiss Academies Reports* 11 (2): 41–48.

Scott, Joan, and Eléni Varikas. 1988. Genre: une Catégorie Utile d'Analyse Historique. *Cahiers du GRIF* 37 (1): 125–153.

Stacey, Judith. 2000. Is Academic Feminism an Oxymoron? *Signs: Journal of Women in Culture and Society* 25 (4): 1189–1194.
Vincent, Guy. 1994. *L'Éducation Prisonnière de la Forme Scolaire? Scolarisation et Socialisation dans les Sociétés Industrielles.* Lyon: Presses Universitaires.
Widmer, Maya, and Patricia Schulz. 2005. *Les Études Genre en Suisse.* Berne: Fonds National Suisse, Bureau Fédéral de l'Égalité entre Femmes et Hommes.
Young, Michael F.D. Ed. 1971. *Knowledge and Control.* London: Collier-Macmillan.

Gender Equality as a Boon and a Bane to Gender Studies in the Conditions of the New Academic Governance

Heike Kahlert

Abstract

In this article the author argues that the strong link between gender studies and gender equality policies that is well-established in EU policies is both a boon and a bane in the conditions of the new academic governance in German academia. This argument is based on case studies on the significance and consideration of gender studies in university development processes that were conducted in Germany. First, the author examines how and in what conditions gender studies are taken into consideration in university development processes, especially when universities can profit from gender studies in order to fulfil the legal requirement to put gender equality into practice. Second, she shows what constellations of factors and actors support or hinder the development of gender studies in universities and how these mechanisms function in practice. Thirdly, she discusses how the relationship between gender studies and gender equality policies is shaped in the organisational practices of the universities analysed in the case studies and how the partly implicit connection of gender studies with gender equality policies is made explicit. The result is that gender studies profits from the legal pressure to put gender equality into action but suffers from the disqualification as non-academic because of its link with gender equality.

Keywords

Gender Equality, Gender Studies, New Academic Governance, Case Studies, Germany

1 Gender Equality Policies and Gender Studies in Global University Transformations

The research system and universities in particular are currently contested institutions. As the sites of the production of useful and usable knowledge for society as the institutions that hold the monopoly on the acquirement and allocation of academic qualifications, universities are of great importance for emerging late-modern knowledge societies and their outstanding position within the global context. Globalisation is accompanied by the politically intended, widespread transformations of universities and research, which are promoted in the academic system through the introduction of market principles and conditions in the form of 'new public management' (e.g. Ferlie et al. 2009). These transformations are linked with the 'new governance' (Schimank 2007) and lead to the creation of 'entrepreneurial universities' (Clark 1998). In doing so, not only are internationalisation, initiatives of excellence and the Bologna process promoted, but new management instruments are also introduced, such as target agreements, global budgets, performance-oriented funding, rankings, and evaluations of universities and research (cf. Binner et al. 2013; Nickel 2011; Lewis 2013; Paradeise et al. 2009). One strong tendency resulting from this is the 'marketisation' and 'metrification' of research, scientific organisations and scholars in all disciplines. The research content, moreover, only seems to be relevant if the knowledge it involves or produces is important for economic and sometimes also social development. Under these conditions, critical knowledge as such, for example, the knowledge that comes from gender studies, is often marginalised.

Universities are thus at the centre of these transformations stemming from the new academic governance. In this process their organisational scope has expanded through deregulation and a growing autonomy of universities which have become more or less disentangled from tight state regulation. At the same time, the demands that universities as organisations are confronted with are changing, for example, with respect to the efficient use of resources and the demand to overcome pressing societal challenges.

Besides the implementation of new public management, the question of gender equality is also on the agenda. Of course, this question is anything but new and has already been problematised since the 1980s in Western societies with regard to the democracy deficit, as it is a question that concerns the participation of women in all public spheres, including politics and academia. However, in light of the market rules, at least in the German context which is the focus of this article, gender equality has become an economic question, following the premise that all available so-called human potential should generally be used optimally, thus including hitherto underrepresented so-called female potential. Gender equality policies in universities and research that are aimed at achieving this goal seem to have an enhanced status, at least in research systems where male dominance is especially striking. This is the case, for example, in the German system of higher education and research, where gender equality policies are widely institutionalised in universities and research, for example, in the form of laws, gender equality officers and affirmative action plans. The state puts considerable pressure on the academic system to increase the proportion of female researchers and especially professors and to put gender equality into action.

Yet the *gender equality policies* use a double strategy that comprises person-centred special activities that favour women and the organisation-centred practice of gender mainstreaming. Gender equality policies are aimed at the organisational level. Ideally, efforts to increase the participation of women in science and academia, in particular in top positions, and of gender-equal organisational development in universities and research should go hand in hand. However, at least in German academia, affirmative action and gender mainstreaming are de facto often practiced as alternatives. The promotion of gender studies can form a part of equality policies because it is a feminised field: at every status level of gender studies women make up the majority working in this field, while men are the minority. Therefore, the promotion of gender studies also contributes to the promotion of female scholars, though the so-called glass ceiling works in gender studies as well.

Gender studies aims at the transformation of content, epistemic practices and forms of production of academic knowledge itself and produces knowledge on gender-related questions that do not only concern inequality issues. Gender studies is situated on the epistemic level, which will be discussed below.

In what follows I will argue that, in the conditions of the new academic governance in the German system of higher education and research, gender studies is primarily promoted mainly because of its link to gender equality policies. This link is simultaneously a boon and a bane to gender studies: it serves not only to implement gender studies in universities as an instrument of gender equality policies but also to disqualify gender studies as non-academic.

In order to understand this argument, it is important to take into account that, in contrast to the EU gender equality strategy which considers gender studies to be a part of gender equality policies, in the German context gender equality policies and gender studies are somehow considered to be opposites (cf. Niedersächsisches Ministerium für Wissenschaft und Kultur 1994; Lüdke et al. 2005; Riegraf and Plöger 2009; Wissenschaftliche Kommission Niedersachsen 2013; Kahlert 2015). Gender equality activists often see the promotion of gender studies as part of their political work and as reflecting observations and findings from knowledge production in the academic field of gender studies. In contrast, gender studies scholars are mostly sceptical about the strong links between their academic knowledge production and gender equality policies. They point to the variety of fields and topics of gender studies and opt for neutrality and distance of their knowledge production from political usability.[1]

With respect to the latest developments in gender equality policies in the conditions of the new academic governance, there exist a number of empirical studies that focus primarily on the organisation- and person-centred level of promoting women's equality with men (cf. e.g. Kahlert 2003; Kamphans 2014; Löther and Vollmer 2014; Schacherl et al. 2015; Weber 2017; Löther and Riegraf 2017). However, there are knowledge deficits with respect to the current significance, implementation and promotion of gender studies under these governance conditions. Questions that remain open are what significance is given to gender studies in light of the implementation of new public management in universities and research and how the new governance structures influence the situation and promotion of gender studies. In this article, I will discuss three connected questions which will help to fill in these gaps in knowledge: how and under what conditions is gender studies given consideration in university development processes? What constellations and actors can be identified as supporting or hindering the development of gender studies in universities and how do they do this? How significant are organisational gender equality policies for establishing and developing gender studies?

This article is based on empirical case studies that are part of a research project on these questions conducted under my leadership.[2] Firstly, I will present an outline of the epistemic field of gender studies and its specific institutionalisations in the German system of higher education and research. In the next section I will outline the new academic governance that shapes the frame of the empirical discussions, and will then introduce the methodology and data of the empirical case studies that were conducted at German universities and that looked at the significance and consideration of gender studies in university development processes. Drawing on these empirical data, I will first examine how and in what conditions gender studies

1 Because of the limited space in this article, I cannot reflect on the question of why in the German context especially gender studies scholars regard their activities as the opposite of or remote from gender equality policies.

2 The project *Gender Research and the New Academic Governance*, which this article is based on, was funded by the Federal Ministry of Education and Research with the promotional reference 01FP1306 and was conducted at the University of Hildesheim in Germany. The responsibility for the content of this publication lies with the author. More information can be found online at http://www.genderforschung-governance.de/en/.

is considered in university development processes, and I will secondly show what constellations and actors support or hinder the development of gender studies in universities and how these mechanisms function in practice. On the basis of this analysis, I will thirdly discuss how the relationship between gender studies and gender equality policies is shaped in the organisational practices of the studied universities. Finally, I will comprehensively discuss the results.

2 The Academic Field in Focus: Gender Studies in the German System of Higher Education and Research

Gender studies is characterised by at least three features: having gender, gender relations or gender orders as its objective; having critical reflexivity; and being inter- or transdisciplinary (Kahlert 2014, p. 147–148). Gender studies distinguishes itself by a specific epistemic perspective reflecting the significance of the gendered embeddedness in social structures for the production of knowledge. Gender studies' "self-concept as critique of science"[3] (Kahlert 2014, p. 148) results from the impetus to challenge androcentric modes of knowledge production concerning omissions and normativities. This activity is accompanied by the "development of new knowledge" (Kahlert 2008, p. 57) by exploiting themes and perspectives that until now have been excluded from the disciplinary canon or were marginalised.

There is no consensus in the German academic system or even within the scientific community of gender studies itself about whether gender studies is a new discipline of its own or not. In this respect, it is possible to differentiate between three typical and simultaneously existing standpoints. Following these ideal types, gender studies can be considered an inter- or transdiscipline, a part of the traditional disciplines, or a discipline in its own right, each with specific political and organisational strategies of institutionalisation and promotion (cf. Kahlert 2005). As has been shown, there are competing discussions about the disciplinary status of gender studies from an epistemological point of view (cf. Hark 2005). At the same time, the model of institutionalisation that is put into action, such as professorships, study programmes and/or academic centres for gender studies at individual universities, often depends on pragmatic decisions concerning the question of which model seems to be the most successful or politically feasible.

In this article, I consider all the different epistemological, political and organisational pluralities of gender studies' conceptualisations and models of institu-

3 All translations from German to English have been done by the author.

tionalisations in the academic system. This means that all academic perspectives, disciplinary orientations and specific models of institutionalisations of gender-related research are included. Thus, the term 'gender studies' is used here as an umbrella term for the different streams, directions and organisational models of research and teaching on questions of sex and/or gender, gender relations, and gender orders.

In the 1980s, the path of gender studies into the system of higher education and research in West Germany was mainly paved by the interplay between actors in women's social movements[4] and state support. Universities and research were challenged from the 'bottom up' and the 'top down' to epistemically and organisationally integrate gender studies. At the same time, in doing so, a powerful frame of legitimacy was shaped through gender equality with respect to the participation and representation of women in science and academia which was and is legally required and has since then to be put into action organisationally. In the German context, federal states' laws force scientific organisations to implement gender equality officers, affirmative action plans and gender equality measures. With this direction of impact, gender studies in the German system of higher education and research was, especially in its beginnings, politically promoted as a contribution to enforcing justice and equality between women and men (cf. e. g. Hagemann-White 1995), for example, through the additional resources (positions, money for research, teaching and administration) provided by the research ministries of the federal states. Thus, gender studies can in a certain way also be considered a part of state feminism. In the system of higher education and research in the former East Germany, there were no comparable developments. After reunification, however, gender studies programmes at former East German universities were also demanded by an emerging academic women's movement, but since the 1990s state policies globally has changed in the conditions of the new academic governance, and the institutionalisation of gender studies is now left to the universities.

In its self-description, gender studies appreciates the gender perspective as having strong transformative potential for science and the humanities and society into account. A frequently used argument in gender and research policy contexts is that gender studies contributes to the assertion of gender equality and therefore to

4 As in many other Western countries, according to gender studies the academic women's movement in West Germany was influenced by Anglo-American developments. However, with respect to the institutionalisation of gender studies, the main strategy was to integrate gender issues into existing disciplines, programmes and units, such as doing gender mainstreaming, and not to found special programmes and centres. Since the 1990s this strategy has been complemented by struggles for special gender studies programmes and interdisciplinary academic centres for gender studies because the integration strategy did not prove to be very successful.

the development of the academic system and different societal institutions as such. In this argument, gender studies and gender equality policies are closely linked. At the same time, there are many theoretical reflections in the field of gender studies that question these links with respect to the stated closeness of gender studies to political and societal practices. These theoretical reflections also strongly support the epistemological ideal of science and the humanities which should be pure and free from considerations about usefulness and usability (cf. Holland-Cunz 2005).

Recent analyses of the significance of gender studies for university development focus on the questions of the institutionalisation and professionalisation of gender studies, for example, through professorships; study programmes on the bachelor's, master's and doctoral level; and interdisciplinary academic centres for gender studies (cf. e.g. Bock 1998; ZtG 2004). Additionally, there are some studies on the institutionalisation of gender studies at universities in the individual federal states of Germany (cf. e.g. on Saxony-Anhalt: Bomke and Heinzel 1997; on Hesse: Teubner and Herbert 1997; on Lower Saxony: Wissenschaftliche Kommission Niedersachsen 2013). What characterises many of these studies is their documentary style; in addition, there is a lack of empirical data that reflect the situation in the 2010s. Studies that analyse the significance of gender studies for current university development processes in the conditions of the new academic governance and take aspects of organisational cultures and structures into account are rare (however, for study programmes on the bachelor's, master's and doctoral level, cf. Malli et al. 2015; Oloff and Rozwandowicz 2015).

Quantifiable indicators of the institutionalisation of gender studies in German universities are full professorships, study programmes or study focal points on the bachelor's, master's and doctoral level, and interdisciplinary academic centres for gender studies. The professorships are especially important because these are the only academic positions in Germany that are permanent, whereas all other academic positions are limited to a maximum term of three to five years and thus do not guarantee continuity. The *Margherita von Brentano Centre* at the Free University of Berlin is collecting data on these indicators, but not all data are publicly available. In addition, with respect to the topic of this article, data limitations must be taken into account, as the *Margherita von Brentano Centre* only counts professorships, study programmes and academic centres that make the gender focus visible in their names. In the German system of higher education and research, however, there are also professors who are doing research on gender issues but do not have a specialised professorship in this area, and there are study programmes and academic centres that include gender studies issues in their work without reflecting this in their names. Therefore, it is not easy to describe the academic field of gender studies in numbers.

On 10 July 2016, there were a total of 150 professorships for gender studies in different disciplines at German universities, and 138 were occupied (Margherita-von-Brentano-Zentrum 2016a). As of 20 April 2016, this collection of data documented the existence of 6 bachelor's and 11 master's study programmes and comparable structured study focal points, as well as 12 certificate and similar study programmes, and one doctoral study programme for gender studies at German universities (Margherita-von-Brentano-Zentrum 2016b). Finally, the data show that as of 5 April 2016, 49 academic centres for research and teaching in the field of gender studies had existed at German universities since 1979, but 11 of these centres no longer existed at that date (Margherita-von-Brentano-Zentrum 2016c). This might sound like a very successful institutionalisation of gender studies in the German system of higher education and research. However, compared with the fact that the German academic landscape in 2016 was made up of around 400 universities and universities of applied science and 46,344 professorships,[5] the number of professorships and study programmes for gender studies is quite small.

The achieved status of the establishment of gender studies is valued differently by its protagonists, either as a success story of permeating universities step by step (Krais 2010, p. 25) or as a history of wearing out engaged actors in stable or even resisting structures (Bock 2002, p. 124). De facto, in this discussion one has to take into account not only experiences from perspectives of organisational cultures and developments within organisational structures at universities, but also political reforms like the Bologna process or the *German Universities Excellence Initiative*. Under these conditions, the significance of the gender perspective and especially the integration of gender studies as a special kind of academic knowledge in the current transformation processes going on in the system of higher education and research is mostly viewed with scepticism (cf. e.g. Baer 2005; Hark 2005; Holland-Cunz 2005; Kahlert 2005; Hark 2013). However, until now these partially contrasting appraisals have not yet been examined empirically. So far, the research results introduced here contribute to close this gap, namely empirical results on the current significance, implementation and promotion of gender studies under conditions of the new academic governance in Germany.

5 The latest data are from 2015 (cf. Statistisches Bundesamt 2017).

3 Conceptual Frame: The New Academic Governance

The conceptual frame of this research lies within the orientation of universities and research to ideological ideas of a new managerialism and the organisational strategies of new public management that started to spread into the public sector in the 1980s. The main elements of this new academic governance are an orientation towards the market, efficiency, competition, a focus on clients and strengthening the management. These elements find their expression in organisational governance which shifts from an orientation towards input to an orientation towards output (cf. Nickel 2011; Paradeise et al. 2009; Lewis 2013). Universities are supposed to perform more, for example more research, documented by success rates in third-party funding and publications, and more teaching, documented by exams taken successfully by their students, *and* they are expected to present their performance results to the public. It seems obvious that this leads to a great deal of pressure to produce, which impacts the scientific organisations and the people working in academia. Individually, the German system of higher education and research, which does not include permanent academic positions beyond professorships, also forces the next generation of academics in particular into geographical and vertical career mobility in order to achieve one of the rare permanent professorships (cf. Becker and Tippel 2013; Leemann and Boes 2012; Wissenschaftsrat 2014).

In the course of the new academic governance, the reputation of universities and individual researchers becomes increasingly important for positioning and significance in a globalising academic landscape. Thereby, academic reputation and appreciation are mainly documented by research performance which is supposed to be produced by networks of research institutions or at least networks of researchers. Within this system the disciplines where research per se is done in teams profit most, for example, the natural, life and engineering sciences. One main consequence is a permanent performance metrification that is applied to research institutions as a whole (e.g. universities, research institutes), organisational areas (e.g. faculties, institutes), and individual researchers. This metrification impacts institutional strategies as well as individual working styles and career planning.

Thus, external grants and funding agencies like the German Research Foundation (DFG) or the European Research Council (ERC) are generally gaining more importance. What is specific to the German system of higher education and research is also that already-obtained third-party funding counts as a central performance indicator and has become a key unit in the measurement of research performance, whereas publications resulting from this research are often not considered so important (cf. e.g. Gerhards 2013; Jungbauer-Gans and Gross 2012). For example, the amount of third-party funding is used for target agreements between the university management and individual professors and influences a professor's pay and pension. Internationally, publications are more important, especially those in international high-impact journals (cf. e.g. Jungbauer-Gans and Gross 2012; Leemann and Boes 2012).

Thus, the new academic governance has to be analysed on three interconnected levels in order to explore the dynamics of transforming universities and research in a comprehensive manner (cf. Lewis 2013):

- On the *structural* level, it is necessary to analyse the research funding system as a main force determining the development of research and academia.
- On the *intermediate* level, it is necessary to explore university development processes where structural and individual aspects merge.
- On the *individual* level, it is necessary to focus on the structural and organisational conditions of an individual scholar's research work.

This kind of widely conceived analysis of the situation and perspectives of gender studies in the conditions of the new governance in the German system of higher education and research is the focus of the research project[6] underlying this article. However, presenting all the results of that research would be beyond the scope of this article.[7] Therefore, the focus here is on the intermediate level, where governance phenomena are observed on the organisational level. In the following empirical analysis, I will reflect on the significance of gender studies in university development processes. The case studies that were conducted for this purpose at universities serve as an analysis of the social practice. They focus on the questions of how gender studies is established and developed further in the conditions of the new academic governance in the German system of higher education and research, and of what mechanisms of support and barriers or even resistance gender studies encounters on its paths in and through the university.

6 Cf. footnote 2.

7 The research project this article is based on includes other parts that focus on both other levels of analysis (cf. footnote 2). On the structural level, the analysis focused on how public research funding takes gender studies into account. On the individual level, the project considers first how gatekeepers in research policy, research funding, gender research and the societal public appraise the significance of gender studies, and second how the new academic governance influences the career strategies of the next generation of academics on the pre- and postdoctoral levels.

4 Methodology and Data

The following empirical results are based on a case study design analysing five universities from five different federal states in Germany.[8] The cases (Table 1) were selected with the aim of making contrasting comparisons and the sample was constructed on the basis of six criteria:[9] the type of organisation and its disciplinary profile, geopolitical location, the size and age of the university, the institutionalisation of gender studies (in professorships, study programmes and academic centres), gender equality, and reputation. Most of the data on these criteria were obtained from existing relevant rankings, for example, that of the German Research Foundation, and from collections of data on the institutionalisations of gender studies (as mentioned above) or gender equality.

Table 1 Overview of the universities used in the analyses

Case	Characteristics
A	• Large university offering all disciplines • Founded between 1810 and 1967 • Research-oriented • Strong in third-party funding for research • Many institutionalisations of gender studies • In the top group in gender equality
B	• Large university offering many disciplines • Founded after 1967 • Research-oriented • Strong in third-party funding for research • Several institutionalisations of gender studies • In the upper-middle group in gender equality

8 To achieve this aim it was first necessary to identify the universities from an overview by the *German Rector's Conference*, which on 3 November 2013 (the date when we had to decide about the sample) consisted of 393 universities for all 16 federal states. Finally, the basis for the case selection consisted of 81 universities from all over Germany. The theoretically built sample represents around a third of all federal states and 6.17 per cent of all German universities. Agnes Raschauer supported the preparation and execution of the case studies and the analysis of data from the fieldwork.

9 After the universities to be analysed were selected according to these criteria, each rectorate was asked for a written agreement to participate in the study before starting the fieldwork. However, not all the universities selected wanted to participate in the study. Therefore, we had to modify the originally planned sample.

Case	Characteristics
C	• Medium-sized university (focusing on social sciences and humanities) • Founded after 1967 • Research-oriented • Strong in third-party funding in one research area • Several institutionalisations of gender studies • In the upper-middle group in gender equality
D	• Medium-sized university offering all disciplines • Founded in the Middle Ages/early modern era before 1810 • Research-oriented • Strong in third-party funding in one research area • Several institutionalisations of gender studies • In the bottom group in gender equality
E	• Large university offering all disciplines (focusing on natural and engineering sciences) • Founded between 1810 and 1967 • Research-oriented • Strong in third-party funding for research • Few institutionalisations of gender studies • In the middle group in gender equality

From a methodological point of view, the case studies consist of a mixture of document and website analyses and qualitative interviews.

The selection of documents to be analysed in the case studies was based on web analyses of the selected universities and the governance structures of each federal state and on information from actors. The analyses consist, among other things, of the current university laws of each federal state, the target agreements between the federal state and the university, the constitution of each university (*Grundordnung*), university development plans, the university reports for the *Research-Oriented Standards on Gender Equality* of the German Research Foundation,[10] gender equality reports, and affirmative action plans.

10 In December 2007 the Executive Committee of the German Research Foundation (DFG) established a committee of experts to draw up research-oriented standards on gender equality. The proposed standards were discussed at the DFG's General Assembly on 2 July 2008, where the majority of the member institutions spoke in favour of the draft, voluntarily committing themselves to implementing the standards. Between 2009 and 2013 a working group established by the DFG's General Assembly evaluated the gender equality concepts of their member institutions, supported their implementation, and monitored the progress of their implementation. Since 2014 the DFG has asked the member institutions annually, among others, about the proportion of women there are in each of all stages of an academic career (cf. DFG 2017).

Additionally, a total of 32 qualitative interviews were conducted, with at least six actors per case study, who were selected using theoretical sampling. The group of interviewees per university consists of two representatives from the management (rectorate and deans), two scholars from different fields of gender studies, a representative involved in organisational gender equality policies (e.g. gender equality officers or members of gender equality committees), and a representative of the research ministry of the given federal state. For the internal perspective, members of different faculties were included in order to obtain greater insight into the different organisations.

All the interviews took place between February and November 2014. The interviews were digitally recorded, transcribed and anonymised. For the purpose of data protection, no mention will be made here of any information from which it would be possible to identify the interviewees. The universities will only be named with letters (A – E) and the interviewees will additionally be characterised only by their function (management, research, gender equality and research ministry).

For the data analyses, a qualitative content analysis was conducted based on Mayring (e.g. 2000, 2010) and the technique of "structuration (deductive use of categories)" (Mayring 2010, p. 66) was used. Based on literature reviews concerning data content, a system of categories was developed with which to explore the empirical material from a theory-driven perspective.

The following sections of this article focus on the organisational activities, patterns of legitimation, and mechanisms of support and resistance that promote or hinder the consideration of gender studies in university development processes. The research questions are:

- How and under what conditions are gender studies considered in university development processes?
- What constellations and actors can be identified as supporting or hindering the development of gender studies in universities and how do they do this?
- How significant are organisational gender equality policies for establishing and developing gender studies?

5 Taking Gender Studies in University Development Processes into Account

In all five case studies the significance of gender studies in university development processes depends crucially on whether gender studies is recognised as an advantage for the organisation as such, for example, to strengthen the university's profile, and whether it appears to generate a significant amount of third-party funding. In all cases, the interviews with the gender studies scholars reveal that they are confronted with the demand to apply for bigger (network) research projects, to build an adequate research infrastructure and to make the university more visible. According to the interviews, however, this is not because gender studies is valued as an important academic field, but because the request to acquire a large amount of third-party funding is critical to all disciplines and academic fields. If gender studies, according to these aims, seems to offer little promise of achieving this objective, it is considered to be of little relevance for the given university's development, and this is so even in those cases where the analysed documents state this in a different way.

The case studies differ with respect to whether and to what extent the university actively supports the development of gender studies, for example, with resources such as positions and money. This can be seen from the documents and from the interviews.

The document analyses reveal that in all the case studies the extension of gender studies is considered an objective in the university's development. Thereby, the organisations explain their intention to promote the integration of gender perspectives in study programmes and teaching duties, and primarily their plan to promote gender research. From an organisational point of view, gender studies primarily attains importance if it is considered an element with which to build the university's profile, which works by receiving extra money. However, according to the documents, in only three cases (A, C and D) did the universities declare that they would spend extra money on this. In these three cases, gender studies is either presented in the documents as a unique selling proposition of the university (case D) or as an element in its organisational profile (cases A and C). And while in cases C and D the extra money allotted for this objective is described in the documents as gender equality resources, university A indicates it would spend substantial financial resources to support teaching and research and to extend the organisational structures for gender studies.

For universities A and C, different interviewees state that not only is gender studies made visible but also plays a role in policies for hiring professors and structural planning. Only in case A is the university's profile-building in relation to gender studies de facto coupled with the provision of resources and presented as a central element in the university's development. Here gender studies is mentioned in the analysed documents in direct reference to its significant reputation across locations and its quality. In this case gender studies is also integrated into organisational decision-making, as the interviews show, for example, by giving responsibility for gender studies to one member of the rectorate or to an in-house academic committee or with the promotion of the gender equality officer and of actors who defend gender studies in the academic self-administration. University C indeed acknowledges that it takes a positive view of gender studies as a focus on its university profile, but it does not de facto match this support for gender studies with the provision of adequate resources, although funding is promised in its documents. In light of a general lack of resources, the stated significance of this academic area could be weakened. In this case, doing gender studies is also an additional focus of its activists. In the conditions of the new governance, all gender studies scholars, like other professionals in academia, have a heavy workload. If gender studies has to be performed in addition to other academic work, there may be no work capacity left over to perform gender studies.

In university D the situation looks ambivalent. There gender studies is anchored in documents on the central university's development and according to the documents is supposed to be expanded. Although gender studies has been institutionalised at this university in the form of a professorship and/or an academic centre, which is unique for the federal state this university is in, according to the scholars interviewed it is not assigned any importance by the rectorate in the university's development. Gender studies does not seem to be one of the strategic focal points of this university, and it is not taken into account in the practice of hiring professors. On the one hand, the declaration of support for gender studies in the university's development documents is not reflected in organisational practices, but gender researchers and the gender equality officer interpret even this statement of support for gender studies as a positive development. On the other hand, the interviewee from the research ministry describes gender studies as consistent with the research interests of this federal state (case D) but makes clear that the ministry will only spend money on the institutionalisation of gender studies in the case that the given university is ready for accepting gender studies as necessary for its development:

> "If they themselves managed to say that the university directly profits from gender studies, surely the willingness within the university would be greater to spend more on this, another position and so on. This is how the game works." (Research ministry/ case D).

Case studies B and E are different from these three examples. At university B, gender studies is not a focal point of the organisational profile and because of this it is also not relevant for staff development; in addition, gender studies is not given substantial financial support. However, this university follows a model of institutionalisation where different areas and units of the university are responsible for the development of gender studies. The development of gender studies is oriented towards organisational targets and thus connected with the university's strategy. Therefore, gender studies is presented as an important topic for this university but it does not count as a main field of research in the organisational research strategy. And for university E, where almost no forms of institutionalised gender studies exist and gender equality policies are also not very well-established, the interviewees doubt that gender studies could be important for the university's development. While the extension of gender studies is mentioned in the university development documents as an aim and while the documents name concrete projects in order to put this into practice, organisational practices simultaneously reflect a lack of priority given to gender studies.

To sum up, all the case studies impressively show that the integration of gender studies in the speech of the documents, for example, in target agreements, university development plans, affirmative action plans and gender equality concepts, does not necessarily indicate the de facto significance of gender studies as an important academic area in the university's development. In the universities analysed, according to the interviews with gender studies scholars, the declarations of support for gender studies in the organisational documents are not necessarily translated into organisational practice. Action must and does not follow talk.

6 Enhancing and Hindering Constellations for the Consideration of Gender Studies in Universities

With respect to the promotion of gender studies, all the case studies show the important role played by individuals who are responsible for integrating gender studies into university development documents and into daily organisational practices. For example, the creation of organisational structures such as academic centres and the integration of gender studies into curricula or organisational strategy documents depend mainly on an individual person. However, at least for universities D and E, where gender studies is not a focal point of the university's organisational profile, and as a result of this is also not relevant for staff development and is not given substantial financial support, it is obvious that the ongoing activities of single individuals are alone not enough to advance the organisational significance of gender studies and encourage adequate measures.

The case studies show, however, some conditions and actors that are conducive to the progress of gender studies at universities. These conditions consist of the relationships between co-operation, influential actors and external resources.

Institutionalised and informal *relationships of co-operation* are crucial to the organisational promotion of gender studies. Professors with a good reputation and good networks who represent the interests of gender studies in committees and informally prepare decisions also belong to this enhancing group that promotes the advance of gender studies, as do gender studies activists at the universities who participate in strategy discussions, support gender studies, and clarify the relevance of this academic area for the university's development (case A). Additionally, the interviewees describe co-operation with administrative units in the universities that are responsible both for the integration of gender in research applications (cases B and D) or for checking study programmes to ensure the gender dimension is taken into consideration (case A). Finally, two gender studies scholars from different universities emphasise how important co-operation across different research contexts is within their universities (cases A and C).

In the case studies, three groups of actors appear particularly important in supporting the development of gender studies, and these are gender equality activists, rectorates and deans' offices, and federal state ministries.

In all the case studies *gender equality activists* play an exceptionally important role in supporting gender studies.

> "I participate in different working groups, including those relating to the organisation's consitution (*Grundordnung*). […] This then impacts other parts of the organisation's constitution, from general regulations to changes within the study system to bachelor's and master's degrees, to specific rules and examination rules, right through to evaluations. I participate in all of these committees and see to the integration of a gender-specific perspective." (Gender equality/case C)

Besides the promotion of gender studies being taken into account as part of professional responsibilities (cases A, C and D), the institutionalisation of co-operative relationships also seems to be important (cases A and B). In the best-case scenario, the support is mutual: it is not only gender equality actors who can promote gender studies but also gender equality policies that can profit from the knowledge produced about social issues oriented towards gender studies.

Furthermore, in the case studies *rectorates and deans* are also identified as contributing to the promotion of gender studies (cases A, B and C). In all the cases, the goodwill, interest, and engagement of university and faculty leaders are identified as helping promote gender studies. Faculties and their leaders can also function as co-operation partners.

Finally, some interviewees highlight the role of support for gender studies in universities through responsible *federal state ministries*. In two universities their influence was important for the creation and continuation of organisational structures for gender studies (cases B and D).

In two universities, interviewees furthermore emphasised that *external (federal) funds* for gender studies had been instrumental in the support for gender studies (cases A and B). Hence gender studies is locally revaluated through third-party funding. This points to the general significance of external research funding in the conditions of the new academic governance.

Conversely, the case studies also reveal the conditions and actors that to some extent delay and hinder the development of gender studies at universities, and the conflicting interests and competition that affect this academic area as well as the degradation it suffers from.

Almost all the case studies illustrate that gender studies is involved in *in-house conflicting interests* and in a *competition* for professorships or other identified resources (cases A and C), both between gender studies scholars (cases D and E) and between gender studies scholars and scholars from other disciplines. When this occurs, resistance to the development of gender studies emerges and develops centrally over the distribution of resources (cases A and D), or the insufficient provision of resources to develop this academic field is identified as the overriding problem (cases C and D). Furthermore, the interviews show that conflicts occur between the leaders which have the effect of hindering the development of gender studies (case D).

> "And I think the reason lies in the fact that it was not only the proportion of women, or that we eventually needed a professorship for gender studies in the (social scientific) discipline, but what is eventually at stake is the question of disciplinary identities. [...] That is something where I recognise clearly where the borders are." (Gender equality/case A)

Resistance to gender studies is mainly exercised through the *degradation of this academic research field*. On the one hand, the legitimacy of gender studies is called into question. In these cases, gender studies is, among other things, deemed ideological, non-academic or old-fashioned (cases D and E). On the other hand, in certain disciplinary contexts the academic relevance of gender studies is denied (cases A and B).

> "I would say that it is still a research field which is situated in politically contentious terrain, where in certain academic fields it still has to struggle for academic legitimacy

and to produce a legitimate and socially necessary research orientation and research focus. It is not self-evident. Not at all." (Research/case A)

"We were very alone. This means that we were confronted with the wind blowing into our faces from different directions. They found us ridiculous and useless, and a lot of people were against funding us." (Research and gender equality/case D)

It is evident from the interviews that the main actors in this resistance are not only professors from fields other than gender studies (cases A, C, D and E) but also the rectorates and deans' offices (cases D and E). That means that resistance mainly comes from academic peers.

These results make clear how and to what extent the promotion of gender studies in the universities depends on personal support from academic leaders, not only the rectorate and the deans but also peers. If they are in favour of gender studies the development of the field is supported; if they are not in favour of gender studies the field suffers from problems in its development.

7 Gender Equality (Policies) as a Frame for Promoting Gender Studies

A closer look at the case studies shows that in all five universities analysed, gender studies is not mentioned as a field of knowledge that needs to be supported as such but is primarily rhetorically positioned within the context of gender equality policies. In all the documents having to do with university development that were analysed, the expansion of gender studies is seen as one way of putting gender equality into action, meaning as part of political – not academic – activities demanded by the state. To give some examples: gender studies are presented as proof of the university's orientation towards gender equality (case D) or as an option to analyse gender equality measures (cases A, C and D). With the expansion of gender studies, the universities want to promote the next generation of female academics (cases B, D and E) and strengthen the proportion of female professors (cases B and E). The documents present a form of organisational governance concerning gender studies that is not primarily aimed at implementing a new discipline (in all its breadth and depth), but rather at fulfilling the legal requirement to implement a gender equality mission. Gender equality (politics) therefore is a must-have in academia, even if it is not recognised by the universities, and gender studies seems to be a possible instrument with which to reach this aim. However, there are no hints in the documents that gender studies is necessary in the academic production of knowledge as such.

The interviews draw a similar picture in which gender studies and the extension of gender equality policies are also strongly linked. At one university, the interviewees argue that their strong orientation towards gender equality promotes the organisational extension of gender studies and that both areas co-operate in a productive manner in order to push for organisational change (case A). At another university, problems with the implementation of gender equality were deemed to be linked to an atmosphere that is characterised as hindering the development of gender studies (case E). And at a third university, the existence of gender studies is mentioned as being proof of the university's orientation towards gender equality, which is otherwise comparatively weak (case D).

In every group of interviewees at the universities a strong association was made between gender equality policies and gender studies:

> "I believe that also the structures of discriminating women and gender studies are quite similar. [...] And I also believe [...] that gender equality policies very strongly need gender studies." (Gender equality/case A)

Gender equality policies and gender studies are not equated with each other within the organisations analysed. Both seem to need each other. However, in some universities there is a competition between gender studies and gender equality policies over resources which are generally given to gender-related measures, regardless of whether they are aimed at gender equality in the sense of promoting women, or whether they are designed to promote gender-related research (and/or teaching).

In all case studies, a strong link between gender studies and gender equality policies is prevalent: a strong anchoring of gender equality in the documents and the social practice of university development goes hand in hand with adequate consideration of gender studies (cases A and B and partially also C). Gender equality policies and gender studies are strongest at those universities where co-operative relations between both areas have been institutionalised (cases A and B). On the contrary, if the university is not as well-positioned with respect to gender equality, the same also applies to gender studies, despite any existing institutionalisation measures (case D). However, moderately developed gender equality is not inevitably mirrored adequately by gender studies (case E). It is apparent from the case studies that gender studies is stronger in those universities with strong gender equality policies. If there are no strong gender equality policies, gender studies is also weak.

In all the cases analysed, actors in the field of gender equality play a fundamental role in the support of gender studies in university development processes. In some universities, these actors emphasise that they see the promotion of gender studies as part of their professional responsibilities (cases A, C and D), meaning as an element of gender equality policies. And, vice versa, the development and implementation of gender equality policies can also profit from gender studies, because gender studies fulfils important academic functions for gender equality policies and work. Gender studies provides academic knowledge for gender equality programmes and measures and develops the methodological equipment for planning and implementing gender equality projects. Gender studies also documents and evaluates the results of gender equality measures. Gender studies' methods and results make the professionalisation of gender equality efforts possible, which is one reason why the interviewees evaluate gender studies as indispensable to the development of gender equality work.

At the same time, the significance of gender studies for gender equality policies and work does not advance the academic acceptance of gender studies in universities. On the contrary, it prompts its marginalisation and degradation as not being an academic (enough) field. The interviewees working in the field of gender studies in particular are often confronted with the degradation of their research, a general suspicion about their being ideological, and antifeminist objections. It is as though being female, which is still not as much a matter of course as being male (in academia), and also working in the field of gender studies is (still?) too much for the German university and research landscape. Additionally, the gender studies scholars interviewed reject the one-sided reduction of their research to the production of knowledge for gender equality policies and work and point to the variety of their research topics, which are not always linked to (in)equality issues. Only in a few cases, especially within the social science field of gender studies, does gender studies directly serve gender-equality-related knowledge.

8 Discussion and Conclusions

The case studies demonstrate that gender studies plays a part in university development processes even though not necessarily in the organisational units or with the organisational significance that its protagonists envision. How successful gender studies is in these games depends essentially on its involvement in the necessary power networks, including the connected support of powerful actors, for example from the rectorates, the deans' offices and/or from professorial colleagues from other fields, who provide – or refuse to provide – material resources (positions, money, rooms) and non-material resources (academic appreciation) for the development of gender studies. Linking the promotion of gender studies with gender equality targets appears to be a strategic instrument with which to add authority to the demand of considering gender studies in university development processes and the associated in-house allocation struggles. In this way, legal specifications for gender equality can be used as an influential and externally justified instrument of power. Thus, it is not surprising that in all the universities analysed gender studies is, according to the university development documents, taken into account, mostly in connection with the (voluntary) commitment of research institutions to gender equality and the legal duty to do so.

However, the integration of gender studies, for example in target agreements, university development plans and gender equality concepts, is no guarantee for its de facto significance for university development processes. Therefore, remarkable discrepancies exist between the intentions declared in the documents to promote gender studies and the actual realisation of these intentions on different organisational levels, especially within faculties. Generally, it is not necessarily possible to conclude from targets and measures of university development anything about the practice within an organisation (cf. Krücken 2008; Ridder 2009). With regard to the integration of gender studies in university development, the analyses show that for the successful translation into organisational practice the consideration of gender studies must be called for continuously. In promising cases, the highlighting of this need is institutionalised and executed by organisational units. The discrepancy between the results of the document analyses and the statements of the interviewees also proves that the anchoring of gender studies in the documents of university development must be coupled with equivalent practices in the organisational management, for example, through their integration into governance instruments and combination with systems of incentives and sanctions.

In all the universities analysed, gender studies' paths into and through the university and the strengthening of gender studies within the organisation is channelled and supported by gender equality (work). Gender equality actors or co-operation between activists from gender equality (work) and the field of gender studies and to some extent also co-operation with the research ministries of the federal states prove to be conducive to the development of local gender studies. The case studies show that, with regard to institutionalising efforts, this is advantageous because gender studies can profit from the legal duty of universities and federal ministries to produce and enforce gender equality and justice (cf. Kahlert 2008). However, this link is rather counterproductive for the recognition of gender studies as a respected academic field: the societal relevance that is ascribed to gender studies because of its contribution to gender equality (cf. Krais 2010) and its politically necessary strategic closeness either hinders the academic recognition of gender studies or contributes to disqualifying it as non-academic.

Furthermore, the academic degradation of gender studies is a consequence of increasing competition for resources and reputation between academic areas in the conditions of the new governance (cf. Ferlie et al. 2009). In the conditions of increasing competition between disciplinary areas, gender studies is forced to participate in allocation struggles (cf. Hark 2013). The case studies prove that within the framework of the new academic governance, gender studies activists directly negotiate with rectorates and faculty leaders and thereby (are forced to) use an economic logic and economic arguments. In doing so, gender studies can be strategically successful if it contributes to the profile of the university and is advantageous to it within the context of competition with other universities (cf. Kahlert 2007). In the conditions of the new academic governance, this requires large-scale and publicly visible research activities, for which gender studies is not well prepared owing to its disciplinary status and disciplinary orientation. Gender studies' isolated forms of institutionalisation, its unclear disciplinary status and the small size of the field prove to be rather counterproductive insofar as it is unable to build alliances with other disciplines, institutions, and/or actors.

Finally, the results of the case studies show that the frequently posed question in existing research literature about whether new possibilities for a stronger anchoring of gender studies can be opened up through organisational transformations in universities (cf. Becker et al. 2006; Pache 2004) cannot unequivocally be answered. The analyses rather suggest that this depends on the conditions that shape the implementation of local university reforms. The processes of transformation that are occurring with the new academic governance are reflected differently in universities. On the one hand, context-related spaces can open up, but on the other hand, exclusions can also take place. These developments also, but not exclusively, concern the field of gender studies.

However, in all the cases analysed external financial support has been and is supportive for gender studies. If gender studies scholars succeed in receiving third-party funding, primarily for larger research projects and/or networks, and thereby are promoting the profile of their university and its visibility in the public, gender studies is strategically accepted and institutionally welcomed. However, that does not generally mean that the support for gender studies continues when the third-party funding is over. In this regard, gender studies shares the same fate as other disciplines, primarily in the social sciences and the humanities which are also pressured by the conditions of the new academic governance to legitimise their direct usability and utilisation. However, gender studies is different from these disciplines because of its partly implicit and partly unwelcome connection with gender equality policies. With regard to the political pressure that, at least in the German academic system, impacts universities and research and calls for the enforcement of gender equality, it can be stated that the interconnection with gender equality described herein proves to be a strategic advantage that protects gender studies in the conditions of the new academic governance and not only enables it to survive, but also to develop.

References

Baer, Susanne. 2005. Geschlechterstudien/Gender Studies: Transdisziplinäre Kompetenz als Schlüsselqualifikation in Wissensgesellschaften. In *Quer denken – Strukturen verändern. Gender Studies zwischen den Disziplinen*, ed. by Heike Kahlert, Barbara Thiessen and Ines Weller, 143–162. Wiesbaden: VS Verlag für Sozialwissenschaften.

Becker, Ruth, Bettina Jansen-Schulz, Beate Kortendiek and Gudrun Schäfer. 2006. Gender-Aspekte bei der Einführung und Akkreditierung gestufter Studiengänge. *Journal Netzwerk Frauenforschung NRW* (21): 21–32.

Becker, Ruth, and Cornalia Tippel. 2013. Akademische Nomadinnen? Zum Umgang mit Mobilitätserfordernissen in akademischen Karrieren von Frauen. In *Einfach Spitze? Neue Geschlechterperspektiven auf Karrieren in der Wissenschaft*, ed by Sandra Beaufaÿs, Anita Engels and Heike Kahlert, 204–230. Frankfurt/Main, New York: Campus.

Binner, Kristina, Bettina Kubicek, Anja Rozwandowicz and Lena Weber. Eds. 2013. *Die unternehmerische Hochschule aus der Perspektive der Geschlechterforschung. Zwischen Aufbruch und Beharrung*. Münster: Westfälisches Dampfboot.

Bock, Ulla. 1998. Am Ausgang des Jahrhunderts. Zum Stand der Institutionalisierung von Frauenstudien an deutschen Universitäten. *Feministische Studien* 16 (2): 103–117.

Bock, Ulla. 2002. Zwanzig Jahre Institutionalisierung von Frauen- und Geschlechterforschung an deutschen Universitäten. *Feministische Studien* 20 (1): 113–125.

Bomke, Heidrun, and Friederike Heinzel. 1997. *Frauenforschung in Sachsen-Anhalt. Erste Dokumentation 1997*, ed. by Kultusministerium des Landes Sachsen-Anhalt und Leitstelle für Frauenpolitik des Landes Sachsen-Anhalt. Magdeburg: Kultusministerium des Landes Sachsen-Anhalt/Leitstelle für Frauenpolitik des Landes Sachsen-Anhalt.

Clark, Burton R. 1998. *Creating Entrepreneurial Universities: Organizational Pathways of Transformation*. Paris, Oxford: IAU and Elsevier Science.

DFG. 2017. *Forschungsorientierte Gleichstellungsstandards der DFG*. http://www.dfg.de/foerderung/grundlagen_rahmenbedingungen/chancengleichheit/forschungsorientierte_standards/. Accessed: May 26, 2017.

Ferlie, Ewan, Christine Musselin and Gianluca Andresani. 2009. The Governance of Higher Education Systems: A Public Management Perspective. In *University Governance, Western European Comparative Perspectives*, ed. by Catherine Paradeise, Emanuela Reale, Ivar Bleiklie and Ewan Ferlie, 1–19. Dordrecht: Springer.

Gerhards, Jürgen. 2013. *Der deutsche Sonderweg in der Messung von Forschungsleistungen*. Berlin: Berlin-Brandenburgische Akademie der Wissenschaften.

Hagemann-White, Carol. 1995. *Frauenforschung – der Weg in die Institution. Ideen, Persönlichkeiten und Strukturbedingungen am Beispiel Niedersachsens*. Bielefeld: Kleine.

Hark, Sabine. 2005. *Dissidente Partizipation. Eine Diskursgeschichte des Feminismus*. Frankfurt/Main: Suhrkamp.

Hark, Sabine. 2013. Widerstreitende Bewegungen. Geschlechterforschung in Zeiten hochschulischer Transformationsprozesse. In *Die unternehmerische Hochschule aus der Perspektive der Geschlechterforschung. Zwischen Aufbruch und Beharrung*, ed. by Kristina Binner, Bettina Kubicek, Anja Rozwandowicz and Lena Weber, 194–208. Münster: Westfälisches Dampfboot.

Holland-Cunz, Barbara. 2005. *Die Regierung des Wissens. Wissenschaft, Politik und Geschlecht in der "Wissensgesellschaft"*. Opladen: Barbara Budrich.

Jungbauer-Gans, Monika, and Christiane Gross. 2012. Veränderte Bedeutung meritokratischer Anforderungen in wissenschaftlichen Karrieren. *die hochschule. journal für wissenschaft und bildung* 21 (2): 245–259.

Kahlert, Heike. 2003. *Gender Mainstreaming an Hochschulen. Anleitung zum qualitätsbewussten Handeln*. Opladen: Leske + Budrich.

Kahlert, Heike. 2005. Wissenschaftsentwicklung durch Inter- und Transdisziplinarität: Positionen der Frauen- und Geschlechterforschung. In *Quer denken – Strukturen verändern. Gender Studies zwischen den Disziplinen*, ed. by Heike Kahlert, Barbara Thiessen and Ines Weller, 23–60. Wiesbaden: VS Verlag für Sozialwissenschaften.

Kahlert, Heike. 2007. Emanzipatorisches Wissen im Schatten des Neoliberalismus: Ökonomisierung der Kritik oder Kritik der Ökonomisierung? In *Ökonomien der Geschlechter. Jahrbuch der Frauen- und Geschlechterforschung in der Erziehungswissenschaft 3*, ed. by Eva Borst and Rita Casale, 45–59. Opladen, Farmington Hills/MI: Barbara Budrich.

Kahlert, Heike. 2008. Der Beitrag der Frauen- und Geschlechterforschung zur Modernisierung der Universität. *Österreichische Zeitschrift für Soziologie* 33 (3): 43–64.

Kahlert, Heike. 2014. Geschlechterforschung. In *Wörterbuch der Soziologie*. 3rd Completely Revised Edition, ed. by Günter Endruweit, Gisela Trommsdorf and Nicole Burzan, 147–152. Konstanz: UVK (UTB).

Kahlert, Heike. 2015. Spannungsvolle Verflechtungen: Gender Mainstreaming ist Hochschulreform – Genderforschung ist Wissenschaftsentwicklung. *Zeitschrift für Sozialistische Politik und Wirtschaft (spw)* 39 (6): 17–23.

Kamphans, Marion. 2014. *Zwischen Überzeugung und Legitimation. Gender Mainstreaming in Hochschule und Wissenschaft*. Wiesbaden: Springer VS Verlag für Sozialwissenschaften.

Krais, Beate. 2010. Das Projekt "Gleichstellung in der Wissenschaft". Anmerkungen zu den Mühen der Ebenen. In *Subversion und Intervention. Wissenschaft und Geschlechter(un)ordnung*, ed. by Carola Bauschke-Urban, Marion Kamphans and Felizitas Sagebiel, 23–45. Opladen, Farmington Hills/MI: Barbara Budrich.

Krücken, Georg. 2008. Zwischen gesellschaftlichem Diskurs und organisationalen Praktiken: Theoretische Überlegungen und empirische Befunde zur Wettbewerbskonstitution im Hochschulbereich. In *Perspektiven der Hochschulforschung*, ed. by Karin Zimmermann, Marion Kamphans and Sigrid Metz-Göckel, 165–175. Wiesbaden: VS Verlag für Sozialwissenschaften.

Leemann, Regula Julia, and Stefan Boes. 2012. Institutionalisierung von "Mobilität" und "Internationalität" in wissenschaftlichen Laufbahnen: Neue Barrieren für Frauen auf dem Weg an die Spitze? In *Einfach Spitze? Neue Geschlechterperspektiven auf Karrieren in der Wissenschaft*, ed. by Sandra Beaufaÿs, Anita Engels and Heike Kahlert, 174–203. Frankfurt/Main, New York: Campus.

Lewis, Jenny M. 2013. *Academic Governance. Disciplines and Policy.* New York/NY, Abingdon: Routledge.

Löther, Andrea, and Birgit Riegraf. Eds. 2017. *Gleichstellungspolitik und Geschlechterforschung. Veränderte Governance und Geschlechterarrangements in der Wissenschaft.* Opladen: Barbara Budrich.

Löther, Andrea, and Lina Vollmer. Eds. 2014. *Gleichstellungsarbeit an Hochschulen. Neue Strukturen – neue Kompetenzen.* Opladen, Berlin, Toronto: Barbara Budrich.

Lüdke, Dorothea, Anita Runge and Mechthild Koreuber. Eds. 2005. *Kompetenz und/oder Zuständigkeit. Zum Verhältnis von Geschlechtertheorie und Gleichstellungspraxis.* Wiesbaden: VS Verlag für Sozialwissenschaften.

Malli, Gerlinde, Susanne Sackl-Sharif and Elisabeth Zehetner. 2015. *Nach Bologna. Gender Studies in der unternehmerischen Hochschule. Eine Untersuchung in Österreich und der Schweiz.* Online-Monographie. Graz: Universität Graz (UniPub). http://unipub.uni-graz.at/obvugroa/download/pdf/478245?originalFilename=true. Accessed: March 18, 2016.

Margherita-von-Brentano-Zentrum. 2016a. *Professuren mit einer Voll- oder Teildenomination für Frauen- und Geschlechterforschung/Gender und Diversity an deutschen Universitäten – insgesamt und systematisiert nach Bundesländern und Hochschulen.* http://www.mvbz.fu-berlin.de/service/datensammlungen/professuren/tabellarische_zusammenfassungen/tabelle_1_dt_universitaeten.html. Accessed: October 16, 2016.

Margherita-von-Brentano-Zentrum. 2016b. *Studiengänge/Studienschwerpunkte.* http://www.mvbz.fu-berlin.de/service/datensammlungen/studiengaenge/index.html. Accessed: October 16, 2016.

Margherita-von-Brentano-Zentrum. 2016c. *Zentren.* http://www.mvbz.fu-berlin.de/service/datensammlungen/zentren/index.html. Accessed: October 16, 2016.

Mayring, Philipp. 2000. Qualitative Inhaltsanalyse. *Forum Qualitative Sozialforschung* 1 (2): Art. 20. http://www.qualitative-research.net/index.php/fqs/article/view/1089/2383. Accessed: March 18, 2016.

Mayring, Philipp. 2010. *Qualitative Inhaltsanalyse. Grundlagen und Techniken.* 11th Updated and Revised Edition. Weinheim, Basel: Beltz.

Nickel, Sigrun. 2011. Governance als institutionelle Aufgabe von Universitäten und Fachhochschulen. In *Autonomie und Verantwortung, Governance in Schule und Hochschule*, ed. by Thomas Brüsemeister and Martin Heinrich, 123–143. Münster: Monsenstein und Vannerdat.

Niedersächsisches Ministerium für Wissenschaft und Kultur. Ed. 1994. *Frauenförderung ist Hochschulreform – Frauenforschung ist Wissenschaftskritik. Bericht der niedersächsischen Kommission zur Förderung von Frauenforschung und zur Förderung von Frauen in Lehre und Forschung.* Hannover: Niedersächsisches Ministerium für Wissenschaft und Kultur.

Oloff, Aline, and Anja Rozwandowicz. 2015. "… weil eben alles in Bewegung war." Gender Studies in der neuen Universität. *Zeitschrift für Kulturwissenschaften* 9 (1): 23–35.

Pache, Ilona. 2004. Zu konzeptionellen Chancen und kapazitären Risiken. Studienreform und Geschlechterstudien an der HU. In *Geschlechterstudien im deutschsprachigen Raum. Studiengänge, Erfahrungen, Herausforderungen. Dokumentation der gleichnamigen Tagung vom 4.–5. Juli 2003*, ed. by Zentrum für transdisziplinäre Geschlechterstudien an der Humboldt-Universität zu Berlin, 149–152. Berlin: trafo.

Paradeise, Catherine, Emanuela Reale, Ivar Bleiklie and Ewan Ferlie. Eds. 2009. *University Governance: Western European Comparative Perspectives*. Dordrecht: Springer.
Ridder, Hans-Gerd. 2009. Universitäten zwischen Eigensinn und strategischer Orientierung. In *Management von Universitäten. Zwischen Tradition und (Post-)Moderne*, ed. by Heike Welte, Manfred Auer and Claudia Meister-Scheytt, 107–119. München, Mering: Rainer Hampp.
Riegraf, Birgit, and Lydia Plöger. Eds. 2009. *Gefühlte Nähe – Faktische Distanz: Geschlecht zwischen Wissenschaft und Politik. Perspektiven der Frauen- und Geschlechterforschung auf die "Wissensgesellschaft"*. Opladen, Farmington Hills/MI: Barbara Budrich.
Schacherl, Ingrid, Melanie Roski, Maresa Feldmann and Birgit Erbe. 2015. *Hochschule verändern. Gleichstellungspolitische Innovationen im Hochschulreformprozess*. Opladen, Berlin, Toronto: Barbara Budrich.
Schimank, Uwe. 2007. Die Governance-Perspektive: Analytisches Potential und anstehende konzeptionelle Fragen. In *Educational Governance: Handlungskoordination und Steuerung im Bildungssystem*, ed. by Herbert Altrichter, Thomas Brüsemeister and Jochen Wissinger, 231–260. Wiesbaden: VS Verlag für Sozialwissenschaften.
Statistisches Bundesamt. 2017. *Hauptberufliches wissenschaftliches und künstlerisches Personal 2015*. Wiesbaden: Statistisches Bundesamt. https://www.destatis.de/DE/ZahlenFakten/GesellschaftStaat/BildungForschungKultur/Hochschulen/Tabellen/PersonalGruppen.html. Accessed: May 26, 2017.
Teubner, Ulrike, and Gabriele Herbert. 1997. *Frauen- und Geschlechterforschung in der Lehre an hessischen Hochschulen*, ed. by Hessisches Ministerium für Wissenschaft und Kunst. Wiesbaden: Hessisches Ministerium für Wissenschaft und Kunst.
Weber, Lena. 2017. *Die unternehmerische Universität: Chancen und Risiken für Gleichstellungspolitiken in Deutschland, Großbritannien und Schweden*. Weinheim, Basel: Beltz Juventa.
Wissenschaftliche Kommission Niedersachsen. 2013. *Geschlechterforschung – Bericht und Empfehlungen*. Hannover: Wissenschaftliche Kommission Niedersachsen.
Wissenschaftsrat. 2014. *Empfehlungen zu Karrierezielen und -wegen an Universitäten*. Accessed: March 18, 2016.
ZtG (Zentrum für transdisziplinäre Geschlechterstudien an der Humboldt Universität zu Berlin). Ed. 2004. *Geschlechterstudien im deutschsprachigen Raum. Studiengänge, Erfahrungen, Herausforderungen. Dokumentation der gleichnamigen Tagung vom 4. bis 5. Juli 2003*. Berlin: trafo.

Gender Studies in the Czech Republic: Institutionalisation Meets Neo-liberalism Contingent on Geopolitics

Blanka Nyklová

Abstract

In the article, I focus on some of the intersections of geopolitical location and the position of gender studies as a discipline in the Czech Republic. The first section depicts the functioning of the higher education and research systems in the Czech Republic and the establishment of gender studies and its institutionalisation. The second section then looks at the intersection of geopolitics and neo-liberalism and how it affects local gender studies. Based on 27 semi-structured interviews with scholars and activists, and observations and practice as a gender studies researcher at the *Centre for Gender and Science*, I explore how a specific geopolitical setting impacts the field of gender studies and scholars navigating it. I argue that gender studies as a discipline has profited from the massification of higher education, which many see as part of neo-liberal higher education reforms. At the same time, research into gender-related issues has been assisted by the incorporation of gender, e. g. in the European Research Area and in other EU policies. This positioning of gender studies is at least partly problematic as it both strengthens the local focus on institutionalised (rather than grassroots) activities and may undermine the perceived local relevance of the discipline that resonates with early post-1989 anti-feminist discourse that has not been effectively challenged so far.

Keywords

Neo-liberal Reforms of Academia, Czech Feminist Scene, Gender Studies

1 Introduction

In this article, I explore consequences of geopolitical location of the field of gender studies in the Czech Republic that are linked to the overarching topic of this book, i. e. the broadly defined neo-liberal reforms of research and higher education institutions and their impact on the state of local gender studies as of the 2010s. As often described in the literature, neo-liberalism is a term used so often to mean so many different things that it faces the threat of losing any meaning at all (Boas and Gans-Morse 2009; Birch 2015). In the article, I generally use 'neo-liberalism' to mean the application of economic/market values to realms previously governed by different values/logic (Brown 2015; Žarkov 2015; Bourdieu 1998). In the particular setting of higher education and research, this may mean a focus on making sure that education serves to build skills that graduates will be able to sell as part of their labour (Prudký et al. 2010) rather than guaranteeing that higher education leads to the development of the understanding of one's political location in society and the world and the corollary responsibilities. This has always been especially central to democracy as citizens need to understand the repercussions of the political decisions they make and higher education has been understood as the guarantee of such skills, and namely of critical thinking (Brown 2015). By 'neo-liberalisation' I mean processes that lead to the introduction and acceptance of this kind of logic. These processes may be formal – when reforms of academic work assessment, bureaucratisation, incentives for massification of higher education and audit culture are introduced – as well as informal, when these reforms are accepted, taken for granted and embodied by academics.

Geopolitically speaking, the focus on neo-liberalism has mostly flourished in Anglophone settings (most recently Gill and Donaghue 2016; Gill 2010; Brown 2015; Pereira 2016). However, as it affects and is affected by political structures, its impact and forms vary greatly with geopolitical location (Pereira 2014a).[1] I analyse an intersection of different geopolitical forces in the field of gender studies in the Czech Republic, a setting not exactly marked by a 'march through the institutions'.

My interpretation of the influences and pressures faced by those involved in teaching gender studies and doing research in the field in the Czech Republic in the 2010s is based on a combination of an analysis of a set of local academic texts that reflect the local situation of gender studies,[2] 27 semi-structured interviews

1 Cf. also the special issue 1/2017 of the *Gender and Research* journal.

2 Cf. Vodrážka (1999, 2003); Saxonberg (2011); Uhde et al. (2006); Linková (2006); Václavíková-Helšusová (2006); Havelková and Oates-Indruchová (2014); Oates-Indruchová (2008a, 2008b, 2011a, 2016); Šmausová (2011); Kampichler (2006); Martin (2008); Cen-

conducted in 2011–2012 with representatives of what I came to call the Czech feminist scene (Nyklová 2013), and observations and conversations with gender experts forming the *Gender Expert Chamber* established in early 2015.[3] The set of texts then represents most of the prominent authors who tend to return to pondering the state of the gender studies field in the Czech Republic. These data are furthermore complemented by my observations as a researcher at the *Centre for Gender and Science*, a department of the Institute of Sociology of the Czech Academy of Sciences. Semi-structured interviews allowed me to combine the advantages of accounts provided by research participants with the possibility to concentrate primarily on topics of research interest (Flick 2006; Denzin 2009). Research participants comprised scholars, most of whom were engaged in teaching their respective specialisation in gender studies, besides grassroots activists and non-governmental organisation (NGO) members. The interviews centred on issues such as the local and geopolitical position of local feminist activities, self-positioning vis-à-vis other people active in feminism, relation to feminist theory and personal paths to feminism, as well as other topics. Using discourse analysis (following Flick 2006, p. 324–326; Rose 2013) the transcribed interviews were originally used to assess the theories informing the scene. For the present study, I reread especially the interviews with research participants employed by an academic institution[4] with a special emphasis on their views regarding their geopolitical positioning within gender studies both locally and globally. Given the relatively small scale of the scene (the *Gender Expert Chamber* has about 100 members), the sets of scholars represented by the *Gender Expert Chamber*, the *Centre for Gender and Science*, the texts and the interviews partly overlap.

Based on the analysis of the described sources, I present here an assessment of the influences that affect the position of gender studies in academia in the Czech

trum Genderových Studií: Historie Centra (2013); Kapusta-Pofahl (2002); Pavlík (2004); Lorenz-Meyer (2004).

3 I was the head of a working group that established the *Gender Expert Chamber* between 2014 and 2015 and as of 2017 serve as its vice-president. The *Chamber* is a professional organisation uniting gender experts in the Czech Republic. All members of the executive committee are engaged in research and teaching gender studies, and about 2/3 of those in the working group are engaged in research/university teaching (cf. Gender Expert Chamber of the Czech Republic 2016).

4 There were 15 academics with institutional backing and one independent researcher in the sample. Out of these, two worked abroad as of 2017, nine at a university and five at a research institution. Please note that those employed at a research institution often engage in lecturing at a university, while those at universities are obliged to engage in research where at least in some instances, the requirements regarding research output have increased as of the 2010s.

Republic with a special emphasis placed on geopolitical influences. I start by first summarising the general developments in the area of research and higher education in the Czech Republic with an emphasis on reforms inspired by neo-liberalism. Then, I turn to the specific developments regarding gender studies. I finish by discussing the need addressed by the present book to contextualise our study of neo-liberal reforms in order to understand its sometimes rather disparate repercussions, and not only for the field of gender studies.

2 Higher Education and Research Reforms

Since gender studies has been an institutionalised discipline in the Czech Republic since the 1990s, key developments in the academic setting need to be outlined before we move on to describing their impact on the discipline. In the early 1990s, public higher education institutions[5] gained high degrees of autonomy, except economic one as they are funded from the state budget via the Ministry of Education, Youth and Sports, partly depending on the number of students they teach. The new stress on and quick introduction of academic freedoms together with largely independent decision-making by newly established academic senates was a reaction to the political control imposed on higher education by the government prior to 1989.[6] The first pieces of legislation on higher education and research adopted in the early 1990s specifically focused on opening up research opportunities also for higher education institutions as until then they were reserved for the Czechoslo-

5 When basic conditions are met, the education is free. After 1989, private higher education facilities also started to be founded. According to Soukromevysokeskoly.cz (2017) there are ca. 50 private higher education facilities, mostly offering economic or arts-oriented bachelor's programmes, although three of these facilities offer education up to the PhD level. According to the framework programme of development of higher education (Ministerstvo školství, mládeže a tělovýchovy 2015), private higher education facilities cater to ca. 15 per cent of the student population, and they mostly focus on professional training in the form of relatively short courses. Private higher education facilities are not included in the present study. Besides providing higher education, higher education institutions are also expected to take part in research. Publicly funded research institutions (mainly the Czech Academy of Sciences) cannot grant any diplomas. Competitive funding is first and foremost an issue affecting public research institutions, although higher education institutions are also expected to contribute to research output and it is to be stressed in the future (Ministerstvo školství, mládeže a tělovýchovy 2015).

6 The main areas of control concerned the banning of certain disciplines (e.g. sociology) and restrictions on who could teach and be taught at higher education institutions.

vak Academy of Sciences that later became the Czech Academy of Sciences in the Czech Republic. Attempts at strengthening the collaboration of higher education with the Czech Academy of Sciences were not very successful as higher education institutions had established a monopoly on granting PhD degrees already in 1990; in practice this started to be respected only with a new law in 1999; the idea was to build a higher "Western-type" education system (Prudký et al. 2010, p. 88). In terms of research capacity and topics, a key change occurred with the establishment of a grant agency, first an internal one at the Czech Academy of Sciences that was intended as a parallel to the "Anglo-Saxon model" (Prudký et al. 2010, p. 88). The establishment of the Grant Agency of the Czech Republic in 1993 meant the opening up of research capacities of higher education institutions. The thing to note here is the acknowledgment of a 'Western' and even 'Anglo-Saxon' model to follow, a recurring factor in the transformation of many segments of Czech (and Slovak) society in the early 1990s that went largely unchallenged.

Soon the system of public higher education started to be affected by institutional isomorphism with a tendency to follow a single, prestigious organisational model inspired by the Humboldtian one (Šima and Pabian 2017). This model centres on the combination of research activities and teaching and de facto defines research and publications as an essential condition for high-quality teaching (Šima and Pabian 2013; Prudký et al. 2010). Research into higher education teachers' expectations has repeatedly shown that they widely embrace it (Prudký et al. 2010; Dvořáčková et al. 2014). This has caused great tensions in expectations both on the side of teachers and students with the onset of massification and universalising of higher education, which peaked in the Czech Republic in the early 2000s when the original student/teacher ratio of 9,7 to 1 in 1989 rose to 19 to 1 in 2007 (Prudký et al. 2010, p. 65). One of the results of rapidly growing student numbers supported by the system of public higher education funding, which also depends on the number of students enrolled (the more students a programme attracts, the more money it is awarded), was a growth in the number of faculties, departments and new specialisations at established universities, i.e. the inevitable diversification of the student body met with a diversification of available content. These developments also led to substantial changes to available academic career paths.

The onset of massification meant that even inexperienced scholars got a chance to get a foothold in academic institutions, even if only as contract teachers. The following positions are available in a university-based academic career: lectors (academic titles not required, assist and provide non-academic training such as in sports or laboratory tasks), assistants (often PhD students; at the peak of massification, the fastest-growing position marked by temporary contracts and a high teaching workload not easily compatible with expected research output), research assistants (PhD or former equivalent academic title holders with a high teaching and research workload who are not only expected to become readers/associate professors but also frequently work on temporary contracts that can be prolonged for up to nine years without a permanent position), readers/associate professors (key for the accreditation process of the respective programme; permanent contracts are the norm starting on this level) and full professors who represent just about 12 per cent of the academics (Prudký et al. 2010; Tenglerová 2015).

This shows that massification and universalising of higher education do not necessarily result in higher employment security for academics but may in fact simply lead to the hiring of more contract teachers who hope to get a more stable position in the long term. In terms of wages, women academics' median monthly salary is EUR 1,194 pre-tax, while men academics' median monthly salary is EUR 1,441 pre-tax (Czech Statistical Office 2015) when using the 2015 average exchange rate (Czech National Bank 2016), which is relevant for the present study as we focus on gender studies, a highly feminised discipline. Statistics for higher education academics show that the highest number of academic employees comprises research assistants,[7] i.e. employees who often do not have a permanent contract. All these factors combined suggest that precarity can be seen as present, especially in the lives of those who bear the greatest amount of teaching.

At the same time, higher education pedagogy has been – and continues to be – a highly neglected subject in the Czech setting (Dvořáčková et al. 2014; Šima and Pabian 2016), which brought about unexpected challenges for both the teachers and the students when inexperienced contract teachers were expected to maintain extensive teaching workloads. Unless they have had the capacity and will to independently develop teaching methods suitable for the new setting, they started to opt out of academic careers, leaving the field altogether/turning their attention to research, or pragmatically focusing on academic career development. In the given setting marked by mechanistic output-oriented research evaluation policies (Linková and Stöckelová 2012; Linková 2017) this means striving to attain the positions of reader/associate and then full professor as these positions are the only ones that may at many higher education institutions grant some level of stability, i.e. a permanent or long-term contract. This is caused by the method of periodic re/accreditation of programmes with emphasis on the numbers of associate and full professors. The conditions under which one can apply to become an associate/full professor vary greatly across the board, yet publications dominate over teaching quality and other aspects of academic life (Dvořáčková et al. 2014; Šima and Pabian 2013;

7 They comprise 8,075.4 out of a total of 29,863.7 as of 2015. For details see the Czech Statistical Office (2016a).

Šima and Pabian 2017). The combination of the importance of the right informal networks for one's career, the stress on publications and the in/formal power of various stakeholders in higher education may mean that even a workplace with a high publication output and wide international cooperation and exchange may also face cancellation as absolute student numbers start to drop.[8]

If we compare the situation with public institutions primarily aimed at conducting research, i.e. mainly the Czech Academy of Sciences, we can see that the employment conditions are frequently more precarious than in the case of higher education institutions (Tenglerová 2015). The main reason for this situation is the dependence of this sector on grant (competitive) funding, which can be said to have gotten out of hand as many researchers are forced to apply for grants even for projects that would previously – until the mid-1990s – have been paid from institutional resources. This development has been linked with the increasing reliance on external rather than internal assessment, a process in line with the New Public Management logic that stresses managerial practices application in all areas of public life, including academia (Linková and Stöckelová 2012). Linková and Stöckelová (2012) link the new stress on external (managerial) assessment with efforts to first depoliticise science and research heavily politicised before 1989 and then in the early 2000s repoliticise them with an explicit focus on their profitability and direct applicability. Until 1999, assessment of science and research was conducted internally by individual research institutes with the Czech Academy of Sciences (and namely natural scientists working there) pushing for a national assessment system based on criteria applied to natural sciences. The national assessment system was launched in 2004 together with an explicit turn towards stressing output, innovations and research and development over 'science' (Linková 2017; Linková and Stöckelová 2012), i.e. changes that are in line with the logic of neo-liberalisation outlined in the introduction. When the national system underwent an international audit, the consortium condemned what it saw as an unprecedented shift towards turning competitive funding into at least 60 per cent of public research institutions' budgets (Arnold 2011) while applying an assessment policy that encourages "opportunistic" behaviour on the side of the scientists and institutions (Arnold et al. 2011, p. 13).[9]

The assessment of academic and research performance is not only limited to public research institutions but also affects universities. The distinction in the impact is that at universities, high-ranking positions still carry relative job security,

8 For the total numbers of students in higher education, see the Czech Statistical Office (2016b).

9 Starting in 2017, a new evaluation methodology will be applied, but it is too early to assess its impact. For details (in Czech) see Úřad vlády České republiky (2017).

which is starting to be a thing of the past at research institutions due to the stress on competitive funding and the instability of institutional funding (Arnold 2011). An aspect not to miss in this summary is the political motivation of most of these changes, including their models.

The 'West' as well as 'Anglo-Saxon' and generally English-speaking countries started to be treated as unquestioned etalons of academic merit and the desirable model of how both higher education institutions, and science and research as such should operate (Linková et al. 2008; Linková 2013; Linková 2017; Linková and Stöckelová 2012; Stöckelová 2012; Šima and Pabian 2013; Šima and Pabian 2017). While none of the referenced authors denies a need for transforming both the systems, what they point out is the fact that a) many of the changes had been at least planned before 1989 and b) the actual shape of the changes fits the radical shift in geopolitical orientation following the collapse of the Communist Party government in 1989 Czechoslovakia. Thus, the need to reshape the system was mainly associated with a necessity to depoliticise it via removing some of the staff with political allegiances, introducing peer-review and autonomous assessment criteria, granting academic freedoms and self-governance in the case of higher education institutions, and reassessing the desired strands and disciplines to be pursued (Linková and Stöckelová 2012; Prudký et al. 2010). This need was of course political in its own respect, but a political focus on science and research in all realms where it is done explicitly resurged in the early 2000s with a new government embracing neo-liberalism and its stress on profitability. The evaluation methodology, internationally deplored only eight years into its operation, was introduced at a time when massification of higher education reached the next stage of universalising higher education. I now turn to the actual impact of these trends on the establishment of gender studies in the Czech Republic.

3 Establishment of Gender Studies at Czech Higher Education and Research Institutions

Gender studies as a field of scientific enquiry and university education did not exist in Czechoslovakia before 1989. This is not to say, however, that discourse on gender was absent in Czechoslovak society in all forms; even the pre-WWII feminist discourses still had some influence on the developments between 1948 and 1989 (Oates-Indruchová 2016; Havelková and Oates-Indruchová 2014; Nečasová 2011). The establishment of gender studies as a fully fledged academic discipline occurred on several fronts at once. It needs to be highlighted that the origins of efforts to make the study of gender relations in the fast-transforming Czech society came from a conglomerate of activists and social scientists (primarily sociologists) gathered around the *Gender Studies NGO*[10] in Prague. The summary overview of the developments below centres on the establishment of gender studies as a research discipline as well as a subject of higher education.

3.1 Establishment of Gender Studies as a Research Discipline

Gender studies as a scientific and academic discipline was established in the Czech Republic in the early 1990s together with pro-women and later openly feminist activism, the aspects of which have been researched from various perspectives.[11] To summarise the developments, activism and academic explorations of gender relations as well as of issues more typically of interest to women's studies have walked hand in hand throughout the 1990s. As especially political scientists have noted, the establishment of NGOs and possibly also of a women's movement were expected and encouraged by the international community. This was so because they were seen as part and parcel of the establishment of a civil society that was, in turn, understood as crucial for a sustainable democracy (Císař 2008). Thus, the support and flourishing of gender-oriented groups in the 1990s needs to be understood as part of the transition process with a clearly set end-point: the establishment of a Western-type democracy contingent on market capitalism. This very contingency that was not questioned by the local political representation and the role assigned to market capitalism was identified as a serious epistemological and ontological problem for local feminist and gender-oriented activism (Kapusta-Pofahl et al. 2005;

10 The *Gender Studies NGO* (cf. Gender Studies, o.p.s. 2017b) was founded in 1991 at the flat of Czech sociologist Jiřina Šiklová. It started to formalise with the first funding in 1992 when it also launched the first series of lectures at the Faculty of Arts of Charles University in Prague. In the first stage, the functioning of a library operated by the *NGO* was crucial and so were educational activities organised by the centre for the general public and the narrow expert public. With the establishment of gender studies as a discipline and a switch to EU funding, the organisation started to predominantly focus on issues such as work-life balance and the labour market, which is its main focus as of 2016 (Gender Studies, o.p.s. 2013). As of 2016, the *NGO* also cooperates with the gender studies master's programme at the Faculty of Humanities, and it is possible for the students to intern at the *NGO*.

11 Cf. Čermáková et al. (2000); Hašková et al. (2006); Vodrážka (1999); Císař and Vráblíková (2010); Císař (2008); Havelková and Oates-Indruchová (2014); Oates-Indruchová (2004); Oates-Indruchová (2011a); Kapusta-Pofahl et al. (2005); True (2003).

Ghodsee 2004; True 2003). A similar critique of hinging a local type of democracy on an in-practice unattainable 'Western' ideal was offered by those questioning the logic and repercussions of undemocratically directing the local developments by institutions such as the World Bank and the International Monetary Fund, de facto leading to a neo-liberal political system (Buden 2010; Buden 2013; Shields 2012).

The proliferation of neo-liberalism has arguably also informed the key research focus on funding as the most researched influence on the shape of gender-oriented, feminist and pro-women activities (cf. Kapusta-Pofahl et al. 2005; Hašková 2005). This type of interest peaked around the accession of the Czech Republic to the EU, which was marked by a renewed focus on gender as a category that appeared in the *acquis communautaire* even in the public discourse where it met with opposition that was expressed, e.g. in the fact that the anti-discrimination act was approved by the Czech Republic only in 2009 after fierce political opposition, especially from former President Václav Klaus (Gender Studies, o.p.s. 2009).

One of the results of efforts to establish gender studies in the Czech Republic as well as to transform studies in social relations into an apolitical, neutral field was the creation of a new department named *Gender & Sociology* at the Institute of Sociology of the Czech Academy of Science as early as 1990 (Sociologický ústav AV ČR, v.v.i. 2017). The *Gender & Sociology* department started to focus on basic topics and statistics related to the positions of various groups of men but mostly women in Czech society. As of 2017, the department focuses on four key areas: gender and the labour market, the sociology of private life, feminist critiques of inequality, and the politics of care. One of the most important contributions to building gender studies expertise is the publishing of the only gender studies academic journal in the Czech Republic: *Gender and Research*, which began in 2000.[12] Since 2006, the journal has been turned into a biannual peer-reviewed edition and, as of 2017, it is represented in the Scopus database. The department together with the journal have been instrumental and still represent the core research centre on issues relevant both to gender and specifically women's studies in the Czech Republic.

In 2001, a project focused on women scientists and gender equality in science was awarded to the department. In 2015, the project was eventually turned into an independent research department, which should have ideally meant a greater degree of stability. As a project, it both significantly contributed to the budget of the Institute of Sociology in the form of relatively high overhead contributions. However, this did not translate into institutional positions for the members of the department with the exception of the chief investigator of the project, Dr Marcela Linková. With the establishment of the independent department, this situation

12 For the journal's website, see the Institute of Sociology (2017).

partly changed; however, the amount of institutional positions open to some 10 members of the team was still only 1.5. This means that most of the members of the team have to work on short-term contracts (the maximum length for any member of the department has been three years) that may or may not be prolonged based on the team's success in obtaining competitive funding and an individual's ability to pass through the system of internal attestations. These are directly related to the above-described neo-liberalising, a scientometrics-based reform of the whole system of public science and research and therefore focused especially on the publication output, while civic engagement and involvement in popularisation activities is expected but not comparably valued.

This is especially threatening for the department because it has a double focus. It engages both in research into the intersection of gender and science and technology studies and in activities that strive to achieve an infrastructural change towards greater gender equality in Czech science and research, which is marked by a strong emphasis on a masculinised model of a straightforward career of a care-less and disembodied academic worker (Linková and Červinková 2013). The key issue here is that only one part of the work gets any academic credit, although especially activities aimed at implementing change towards greater gender equality take up substantial portions of the energy and time of team members. Moreover, up until 2017, most of the projects undertaken by the team targeted infrastructural change, which forced the team to somehow fit research into the projects not primarily focused on research. This meant in reality that the research conducted was largely unpaid.

Research institutions are by far not the sole source of gender-related research in the Czech Republic. A substantial amount of work originates from individual researchers, centres, programmes and departments established at higher education institutions (Linková 2006; Hašková et al. 2006).

3.2 Establishment of Gender Studies at Higher Education Institutions

As mentioned above, gender-relevant research is not only conducted by research centres and vice-versa: even those engaged primarily in research often have a short-term contract for teaching one or two courses at a university. Research conducted at gender studies programmes is substantial not only in the lacking funding for academic work at academic institutions, but also because there are researchers who use a gender lens in their work who come from departments scattered across Czech universities with no gender programmes (for an overview, see Nyklová 2014). Thus, even disciplines such as history and philosophy are affected by the gender perspective at least in some instances. This being said, the establishment of the *Gender & Sociology* department is important as it documents the local strong association of gender studies with sociology (Oates-Indruchová 2011). At the same time, it pronounced very early on the need to establish a relatively independent institutional form of the discipline. This is not to say that there were no debates on whether gender studies should form an independent discipline or strive to inform other disciplines without necessarily becoming institutionally independent. These debates can be seen as reflected in the curricula of the two universities offering a degree in gender studies (Masarykova Univerzita in Brno and Charles University in Prague) as well as in the fact that in many instances, gender studies is promoted by academics from different disciplines at institutions with no specific gender studies centre/programme.

In terms of the higher education system, gender studies was first taught at several universities in the format of travelling lectures by the *Gender Studies NGO* based in Prague. The *NGO* "played a key role in introducing education on gender topics to Czech universities with the first series of lectures launched at the Faculty of Social Sciences at Charles University in 1992" (Gender Studies, o.p.s. 2013, no pagination). Although the lectures were approved by the respective universities, they were never integrated into the institutionally backed curriculum and were fully funded by the *NGO*. This meant, among other things, that the formal curriculum was left intact, and it was up to the higher education institutions' academic leadership to decide whether or not the lectures could take place at the respective institution and whether or not students would be given any credits for attending. What we can see here is a stark contrast between the formal support for activism defined as substantial for the establishment of a Western-type democracy and the lack thereof for the discipline of gender studies from formal higher education institutions.

This was definitely not because of a lack of scholars invested in this line of research. The first relatively successful attempt at institutionalising a gender studies programme with the end goal of setting up a master's degree in the discipline came with the foundation of the *Centre for Gender Studies* at the Faculty of Arts at Charles University in Prague in 1998, which was also initiated by the *Gender Studies NGO* (Lorenz-Meyer 2004; Pavlík 2004). The attempt was only partly successful as it was highly dependent on the good will of the faculty's dean (this became clear when the dean changed). The new dean refused to abide by the promises of his predecessor and instead of appointing the historically first Czech full professor of gender studies (a *sine qua non* of the formal establishment and accreditation of any master's programme at the time in the Czech Republic), he made several decisions that led to the *Centre*'s transition to another faculty (Pavlík 2004; Linková 2006).

This faculty was the Faculty of Humanities where the first Master's programme in gender studies in the Czech Republic was accredited in 2005. This was largely possible due to the cooperation between Dr Hana Havelková and most of the core members of the *Centre for Gender Studies*. Dr Havelková had taught a series of classes on feminist theories at the bachelor's degree level at the Faculty of Humanities for several years and had striven to establish an independent programme. When the situation around the *Centre for Gender Studies* escalated, establishing a master's at the Faculty of Humanities was made possible due to her contact with the members of the centre. Although it seemed clear the transfer would mean the end of the *Centre*, it did not close down and as of 2017 offers several courses mostly in the areas of film and literary criticism and history of science at the Faculty of Arts, whose management supports this line of research as research is also a substantial part of the *Centre for Gender Studies'* activities. Nevertheless, the *Centre* cannot grant any degrees as had been originally envisioned.

The first bachelor's programme in gender studies was launched in 2004/2005 in Brno. Unlike in the case of the Prague master's programme, which forms an independent department, students in Brno always have to combine their studies in gender with a different discipline, such as social work or sociology, and the programme falls under the Department of Sociology. This is partly because the founders of the programme see it as only meaningful as a transdisciplinary endeavour while institutional negotiations also play a role (Masarykova Univerzita 2017). I believe the very outline of the local history of the discipline shows some of the academic opposition and permanent threat under which the programmes and the academic field of gender studies find themselves, which unavoidably affects those engaged in teaching gender studies.

Besides the two programmes, there are subdivisions and specialised programmes or at least lectures on gender offered at almost all public universities in the Czech Republic. For instance, the Faculty of Philosophy and Arts at the University of West Bohemia offers several courses and subspecialisations in gender studies (Katedra Antropologie FF ZČU 2014) while PhD candidates in philosophy at the University of Ostrava are expected to specifically focus on feminism in their research (Ostravská Univerzita 2017). A valuable resource on where one can study and engage in gender studies is the database of graduation theses maintained by the *Gender Studies NGO*. As of September 2016, 3,926 theses were entered with a sharp surge after the introduction of the two gender studies programmes.[13]

13 While between 1992 and 2004 1,124 theses were entered, between 2005 and 2006 alone, there were 584 (Gender Studies, o.p.s. 2017a).

There are two aspects of the foundation of both the higher education programmes that need to be highlighted. The first one concerns the geopolitical situation, the second one the local reception of feminist and gender-centred discourses both in the public discourse and specifically at higher education and research institutions, which is further exacerbated by the aforementioned levels of precarity. I turn to these two issues in the following section.

4 Positioning Gender Studies: Geopolitics, Location and Neo-liberalism

This final section[14] of the article strives to point out the synergies and overlaps between the local functioning and influences of geopolitical power inequalities and effects of the neo-liberal reforms in academia.

4.1 Gender Studies in the Light of Geopolitics

The two university gender studies programmes at the bachelor's- and master's-degree level at Masaryk University in Brno and Charles University in Prague described above are, as of 2017, the only two places where it is possible to gain a degree in the field. As of 2017, it was not possible to earn a PhD in gender studies in the Czech Republic, which is in itself rather paradoxical, given the existence of two research departments at the leading public research institution. While there is a clear and well-documented dominance of sociological approaches to the study of gender in the Czech Republic, only the department of sociology at Masaryk University offers at least a bachelor's degree in the field. The two sociology departments that can be found at the Faculty of Arts and Faculty of Social Sciences of Charles University do not offer even a specialisation in gender studies as of 2017, and the teaching of the perspective is left to potential interest on the part of the teachers, but the discipline is not integrated into the curriculum.

This is not a simple omission but an expression of a widely shared negative stance on issues related to gender studies and broadly to feminism. The feeling that the discipline is not acknowledged by colleagues at both research centres and at their respective faculties and departments was shared by most of my research participants. Similarly, opposition and resistance to the critiques offered by the *Centre for*

14 Parts of this section appeared in Nyklová (2014).

Gender and Science are very frequent and mostly come from the institutions the department has to work with, such as the ministries, which readily disregard the output of years of research and policy suggestions (Tenglerová 2011) but also from within the Institute of Sociology. Some of those most critical of the conservative academic culture as regards gender studies are not members of any gender-oriented team but rather navigate a university environment hostile to their perspective and work. One research participant commented that she had heard the following remark regarding her own name on an election notice board: "Oh, it's her, she does gender. I would rather vote for the communist, then."[15]

Despite such accounts about the anti-feminist Czech environment, compared with the beginning of the 1990s when an *NGO* had to not only engage in activism targeting the general public and the state, but also engage in research and education, the steps made may indeed be easily understood as a sign of democratisation expected of all Central and Eastern European countries after 1989/1990. This means the institutionalisation and gradual specialisation of different parts of the activities are in line with the theory of transitology generally applied to Central and Eastern Europe after 1989. Czech sociologist Jiří Večerník (1999, p. 34) defines transition as the "path from a totalitarian regime to a democratic one and from a directive economy to a market one". As such, it has been approached from different angles, although arguably the most prevalent approaches focus on its economic (Stiglitz 1999; Fischer and Sahay 2000; Mlčoch 2001; Vliegenthart 2010) and political and social aspects (Welsh 1994; Wolchik 1995; Shields 2012; Večerník 2002). The end-point set out differently across the studies seems to comprise the establishment of a functioning democratic market capitalist society that is a member of international economic and political organisations and that shares the values and direction of countries believed to be on the winning side of the Cold War discourse (Cerwonka 2008).

The discourse of transition still seems to affect the local geopolitical imagination and understanding of the world (i. e. whose models are to be followed) and is used by various actors in political negotiations. Thus, the fact that gender studies is an established discipline to the west of Czech borders was an argument used when striving to establish the discipline locally as the research participants, some of whom were among the founding members of the discipline at the various sites, explained. It is not a strategy limited to the Czech Republic as other studies have shown (Pereira 2014a).

Such an approach to advocating the relevance and salience of gender studies and their subject topics clearly has several drawbacks. Firstly, it tends to solidify the perceived geopolitical power inequality and turns concepts such as the East/

---

15 All the Czech to English translations in the text were done by the author.

West binary into solid entities. It thereby obscures the fact that in many respects, the Czech Republic is part of the 'global north' and should, including its gender studies scholars and activists, act accordingly and that the categories are highly situational (Kolářová 2010; Horký 2008; Vodrážka 2003). Secondly, the focus on the role models – i. e. Western countries – tends to limit cooperation across Central and Eastern European countries as one of the research participants pointed out: "My experience with academic work in Central Europe is that we do not really communicate, cooperate … we do not quote or read one another." Thirdly, the power hierarchy may start to be seen as a given, which is something many of the research participants did, and this specifically concerned those engaged in academia: "Eastern and Central Europe are only good as sources of empirical data but not for critical inspiration," or to put it more bluntly: "We provide the data, they the theory." A similar approach or resignation to the global power inequality within academia was voiced by the following researcher in her early thirties:

> "When you write for abroad, the things you can usually present are the results from local research because how would they respond to a Czech creating a theory of feminism, post-socialism or globalism? That would not be acceptable anyway. There are inequalities. … We can de facto no longer have ambitions to make a breakthrough with a theory. I would have to leave and create something there, not publish something only in English from here."

Geopolitically speaking, the EU framework was strongly emphasised around the accession period of the respective 'new' member countries (Kapusta-Pofahl et al. 2005; Hašková 2005; Hašková and Uhde 2009; Saxonberg 2011), and its relevance as of the 2010s is hardly disputable. The Czech Republic took part in the Bologna process (Cerwonka 2009; Hemmings 2006), which impacted both higher education institutions mostly focused on practically oriented professional education (Víznerová and Nyklová 2016) and the permeability of universities in the social sciences and the humanities. In this respect, the concept of opening political opportunities (Saxonberg 2011; Císař and Vráblíková 2010; Císař 2008) is invoked, stressing the importance of EU policies and *acquis communautaire* for the success of advancing feminist issues in Central and Eastern European countries. The problem here is that it ignores the possible contradictory effects of institutionalising gender studies (Ghodsee 2004; Stratigaki 2004), such as a stress on formal hierarchies. Moreover, the concept may obscure the accounts of rejection of the gender perspective in various venues, including universities, while universities may on the outside even use the existence of similar research/pedagogy to boost their image in specific settings.

Nevertheless, especially cooperation within the EU was sometimes welcomed with enthusiasm and in some respect was credited with the introduction of certain topics in the local environment: "Although it is dictated from above, it is positive. … Sometimes nothing happens without such an impulse." This quote especially relates to one of the issues faced by local gender studies and feminism. It is the idea that feminist issues, ideas and solutions are imported into the Czech Republic. This makes them irrelevant to many of those contributing to the Czech public discourse, including numerous representatives of Czech academia.[16]

Czech feminists and gender scholars have long lamented what they understand to be the myth of imported feminism, although some of them helped establish it in the first place (Oates-Indruchová 2016). In fact, when the location and its geopolitical meaning are used in order to push for, e.g. the establishment of a discipline, it is a double-edged sword that we need to recognise. On the one hand, it is a common strategy stemming from and taking advantage of the transitology discourse prevalent in the Czech Republic throughout the 1990s that still lingers and may be used to push for change. With the Czech Republic's EU accession, it slightly changed and started to involve the study of EU legislation, policies and frameworks that could be used for similar purposes. Already here, though, the other edge of the sword becomes visible. In terms of argumentation, this discursive feature may be relatively easily turned around in order to portray issues such as domestic violence and especially sexual harassment as imports that are locally irrelevant and even harmful.

In terms of academia, a perfect example of such an approach was presented in the case of a student association at Charles University in Prague. The feminist student organisation, the *Feminist Society of Charles University*, illustrates the consequences of the opposition to the discipline and focus of gender studies. On 12 March 2016, the students associated with the *Feminist Society of Charles University* organised a protest march, pointing out the need to join forces against fascism. The goal of the march was to counter the repeated attempts by nationalistic extremists to claim the status of protectors of women, mostly in relation to the so-called European migration/refugee crisis; the march was a reaction to the local nationalistic response to street sexual harassment incidents on New Year's Eve in Germany. The participants were able to paint and phrase their own banners, so one read 'A dead chauvinist [equals] a good chauvinist', which immediately prompted the Charles University rector's office to call on the student body to disassociate from the university and to stop using the university name as part of the *Feminist Society's* name. The person responsible for the banner as well as the *Society* promptly apologised and wanted

16 To give a recent example, the rector of the University of South Bohemia in České Budějovice, Tomáš Machula, sees gender studies as a discipline "that only generates people for NGOs, which sponge off public money" (Perknerová 2017).

to start a dialogue with the rector's office but was answered with a threat of legal prosecution of individual student members unless they stopped using the university's name. In the end, the *Society* dropped 'Charles University' from its name, but when its representatives eventually managed to meet with the deputy rector, they were not only patronised but also told that all the banners, stances and opinions of the student body pose a problem to the university leadership (Nyklová 2016). Thus, the students who were voicing their political opinion and taking part in international feminist activism were silenced not only based on the fact they were acting in a political manner but also specifically because of the ideals they were promoting and their feminist core. Becoming politically conscious and active based on that consciousness, generating and wanting to develop a political subjectivity, and especially engaging with feminist issues is not supported in the given setting and may serve as a basis for persecution.

4.2 Neo-liberalism as Part and Parcel of Local Geopolitical Influences

What then is the link between geopolitics and neo-liberalism? Apart from the general introduction and embracing of a neo-liberal logic within the framework of transition as it was implemented locally, it has also specifically affected the discipline of gender studies in at least two ways: massification of higher education and its repercussions, and uneven impact on research funding and assessment.

Firstly, it is no coincidence that long-standing efforts of individuals highly invested in gender-relevant research, pedagogy and activism reached fruition in the same time period as the massification and universalising of Czech higher education institutions. The massification itself may be understood as part of neo-liberalisation, for it strives to trigger a knowledge society that would guarantee economic prosperity and that inevitably leads to changing the very functioning and standards of higher education (Šima and Pabian 2013). The push towards massification and its actual materialisation created the need for a diversification of study tracks and programmes, which in turn created the needed window of opportunity for gender studies. It needs to be noted that this would not have happened had it not been for researchers active in gender studies ever since 1989. As of 2017, when the peak of universalising has been reached and the number of academic staff has started to subside, there is a new pressure being exerted on the programmes.

The Prague-based master's programme lists 10 academics as its core faculty, out of whom three are associate professors (Katedra Genderových Studií 2016), while the Brno-based bachelor's programme has six faculty members, out of whom two are associate professors (Masarykova Univerzita 2016). Both the departments also use contract teachers, often to teach practice-oriented courses as the state and non-governmental sectors are among the possible employers of the graduates: the Prague programme even mentions gender mainstreaming as a field of practice for its graduates and the focus on employability is very much present on the Brno programme's website as well, as it presents successful graduates and their stories. In both cases then it is possible to discern one of the effects of neo-liberalisation of university studies as explicit emphasis is put on the practical applicability and employability of the prospective graduates.

Secondly, in the case of gender studies at research institutions, we can see an uneven impact of the newly introduced and fiercely criticised assessment criteria. These have led to a push towards the convergence of academic cultures, e.g. via perpetuating the ideals of where relevant academic research is to be published (Stöckelová 2012) and in what language (Bennett 2013). However, in the case of gender studies as a research discipline, it seems that academic merit measured within audit culture is somehow never enough. The discipline is also becoming a frequent target of attacks, e.g. from within the Institute of Sociology when excellent results of an international audit are questioned and understood as the result of 'friendship' with one of the auditors in what Maria do Mar Pereira calls "corridor talk" (Pereira 2014b, p. 14). This means in practice that even excellent results according to the assessment system do not guarantee stability and recognition given the local conservative academic culture.

5 Concluding Remarks

The main goal of the article was to highlight the complex intersections of neo-liberal reforms and geopolitics, and their joined impact on gender studies in the Czech Republic. To finish using an example of the complexities described in the sections above, let me elaborate on an above-mentioned example. The near-abolition of the *Centre for Gender Studies* after years of activity and great success at raising funds (Pavlík 2004) documents well the threat of precarity of gender studies in the Czech university setting and its dependence on higher education decision makers. Decision makers such as rectors and deans are technically mostly independent in the Czech higher education context, although they are in fact dependent on an intricate network of mostly informal relations, which creates a milieu not readily accessible and easy to understand (Šima and Pabian 2016; Prudký et al. 2010). Given the importance of student enrolment for Czech public university funding

(Šima and Pabian 2016), it is relatively easy for decision makers to exert pressure on programmes in gender studies to "prove their worth", as one academic put it at a meeting of the *Gender Expert Chamber* working group, while at the same time effectively obstructing their very 'worth' by, e. g. not approving applications for the development of a follow-up master's programme.

The neo-liberal reforms of higher education have not only arguably helped the establishment of gender studies but also affect the functioning of the discipline. Neo-liberal reforms of the assessment criteria especially stress publication output and do not assume the possibility of career breaks and affect gender studies both within higher education and at research institutions. At the latter, the situation is further affected by the availability of certain, strictly defined opportunities for international funding. These both encourage and limit the scope and focus of projects as geopolitical concerns are usually not a major focus; this can be seen when countries from across the EU are treated as high income, and framework programmes for the implementation of gender equality assume gender cultures not necessarily present/accepted in all parts of Europe (Vohlídalová and Linková 2017). These lacks and resistances then mean that although publication output and international connections actually thrive in the field of Czech gender studies, the assessment mixes here with other, informal (networks) as well as formal (academic titles) structures forming a very specific milieu.

As a result of the intersection of a neo-liberal audit culture with local discrediting of gender studies as foreign or outright ideological and unscientific, the fate of gender studies at both higher education and research institutions is rather precarious. Higher education management may stress both publications *and* appeal to students, and these demands may change rapidly and unexpectedly, leading to precarity of both individual positions (unless you are at least an associate professor) and whole programmes. By precarity here I mean an ongoing uncertainty about one's employment conditions, especially the lack of influence over the possibility to win a full (or similar) position that would be permanent or at least long term. The lack of influence means that one's professional qualities even if externally approved (by publication output, international networking, mobility and/or awards) do not seem to guarantee the stability of one's career, especially in the field of gender studies, where programmes may surprisingly easily share the fate of the *Centre for Gender Studies*.

It needs to be noted that local gender conservatism thrives, although many scholars are free to supervise theses researching gender relations and engaging feminist theories, and there is publicly funded research in gender studies. I believe this contradictory setting may well illustrate the prospects ahead of us all in a globally neo-liberalised academic world where collectives have been methodically destroyed

(Bourdieu 1998) together with the values they upheld, such as egalitarianism and solidarity. I do not want to highlight just the negative effects but rather wish to draw our research attention to a careful study of the mutual influences of neo-liberal reforms with different geopolitical locations and their perceptions.

References

Arnold, Erik. 2011. *Synthesis Report*. Brighton: Technopolis Limited. http://www.technopolis-group.com/wp-content/uploads/2011/09/1315-International-Audit-CR_Final-report_Synthesis.pdf. Accessed: February 15, 2017.

Arnold, Erik, Barbara Good, Fritz Ohler, Brigitte Tiefenthaler and Niki Vermeulen. 2011. *The Quality of Institutional Funding and Research Evaluation in the Czech Republic and Abroad*. Brighton: Technopolis Limited. http://www.technopolis-group.com/wp-content/uploads/2011/09/1315_CzAudit_FinalRep_3-Quality-of-Research_EM.pdf. Accessed: February 15, 2017.

Bennett, Karen. 2013. *Resistant Translation in the Global Knowledge Exchange: Can It Combat Epistemicide?* Keynote Speech given at an Interdisciplinary Conference *Rethinking Domination and Hegemony in Translation*, Bangor University, September 5–6, 2013. (unpub.).

Birch, Kean. 2015. Neoliberalism: The Whys and Wherefores… and Future Directions. *Sociology Compass* 9 (7): 571–584.

Boas, Taylor C., and Jordan Gans-Morse. 2009. Neoliberalism: From New Liberal Philosophy to Anti-Liberal Slogan. *Studies in Comparative International Development* 44 (2): 137–161.

Bourdieu, Pierre. 1998. Utopia of Endless Exploitation. The Essence of Neoliberalism. *Le Monde Diplomatique*, December. http://mondediplo.com/1998/12/08bourdieu. Accessed: February 14, 2017.

Brown, Wendy. 2015. *Undoing the Demos: Neoliberalism's Stealth Revolution*. New York: Zone Books.

Buden, Boris. 2010. Children of Postcommunism. *Radical Philosophy* 159 (Jan/Feb): 18–25. http://www.identitymove.eu/assets/pdf/boris%20buden.pdf. Accessed: May 14, 2017.

Buden, Boris. 2013. *Konec postkomunismu: od společnosti bez naděje k naději bez společnosti*. Prague: Rybka.

Centrum Genderových Studií. 2013. *Centrum Genderových Studií: Historie Centra*. http://gender.ff.cuni.cz/historie.html. Accessed: May 15, 2017.

Čermáková, Marie, Hana Hašková, Alena Křížková, Marcela Linková, Hana Maříková and Martina Musilová. 2000. *Relations and Changes of Gender Differences in the Czech Society in the 90s*. Praha: Sociologický ústav AV ČR.

Cerwonka, Allaine. 2008. Traveling Feminist Thought: Difference and Transculturation in Central and Eastern European Feminism. *Signs: Journal of Women in Culture and Society* 33 (4): 809–832.

Cerwonka, Allaine. 2009. Higher Education "Reform", Hegemony, and Neo-Cold War Ideology. Lessons from Eastern Europe. *Cultural Studies* 23 (5–6): 720–735.

Císař, Ondřej. 2008. *Politický Aktivismus v České Republice. Sociální Hnutí a Občanská Společnost v Období Transformace a Evropeizace*. Brno: Centrum pro studium demokracie a kultury.
Císař, Ondřej, and Kateřina Vráblíková. 2010. The Europeanization of Social Movements in the Czech Republic: The EU and Local Women's Groups. *Communist and Post-Communist Studies* 43 (2): 209–219.
Czech National Bank. 2016. *Kurzy devizového trhu – Měsíční průměry*. Praha: Czech National Bank. http://www.cnb.cz/miranda2/m2/cs/financni_trhy/devizovy_trh/kurzy_devizoveho_trhu/prumerne_mena.jsp?mena=EUR. Accessed: September 10, 2016.
Czech Statistical Office. 2015. *A22 Number of Employees, Time Paid and Gross Monthly Earnings by CZ-ISCO Major Group and Sub-Group and by Sex*. Praha: Czech Statistical Bureau. https://www.czso.cz/documents/10180/32846295/11002616A22.pdf/91cbc71e-5e1b-4281-b267-1f3c295d7fbe?version=1.0. Accessed: September 10, 2016.
Czech Statistical Office. 2016a. *University Education – Employees, Teachers*. https://vdb.czso.cz/vdbvo2/faces/en/index.jsf?page=vystup-objekt&pvokc=&katalog=30848&pvo=VZD10&z=T. Accessed: February 15, 2017.
Czech Statistical Office. 2016b. *University Education – Students*. https://vdb.czso.cz/vdbvo2/faces/en/index.jsf?page=vystup-objekt&pvo=VZD11&pvokc=&katalog=30848&z=T. Accessed: February 15, 2017.
Denzin, Norman K. 2009. *The Research Act: A Theoretical Introduction to Sociological Methods*. New Brunswick: Aldine Transaction.
Dvořáčková, Jana, Petr Pabian, Simon Smith, Tereza Stöckelová, Karel Šima and Tereza Virtová. 2014. *Politika a Každodennost Na českých Vysokých školách: Etnografické Pohledy Na Vzdělávání a Výzkum*. Praha: Sociologické nakladatelství.
Fischer, Stanley, and Ratna Sahay. 2000. *The Transition Economies After Ten Years*. Cambridge: National Bureau of Economic Research. http://www.nber.org/papers/w7664. Accessed: May 15, 2017.
Flick, Uwe. 2006. *An Introduction to Qualitative Research*. 3rd Edition. London: Sage Publications.
Gender Expert Chamber of the Czech Republic. 2016. *Genderová expertní komora* ČR. http://gekcr.cz/en/. Accessed: September 10, 2016.
Gender Studies, o.p.s. 2009. *Česká republika má antidiskriminační zákon!* http://www.feminismus.cz/cz/clanky/ceska-republika-ma-antidiskriminacni-zakon. Accessed: February 15, 2017.
Gender Studies, o.p.s. 2013. *Historie Gender Studies, o.p.s.* http://genderstudies.cz/gender-studies/historie.shtml?x=237046. Accessed: September 9, 2016.
Gender Studies, o.p.s. 2017a. *Databáze studentských prací*. http://genderstudies.cz/gender-studies/diplomky.shtml. Accessed: September 15, 2016.
Gender Studies, o.p.s. 2017b. *Gender Studies*. http://en.genderstudies.cz/. Accessed: May 23, 2017.
Ghodsee, Kristen R. 2004. Feminism-by-Design: Emerging Capitalisms, Cultural Feminism and Women's Nongovernmental Organizations in Post-Socialist Eastern Europe. *Signs: Journal of Women in Culture and Society* 29 (3): 727–753.
Gill, Rosalind. 2010. Breaking the Silence: The Hidden Injuries of Neo-Liberal Academia. In *Secrecy and Silence in the Research Process: Feminist Reflections*, ed. by Róisín Ryan-Flood and Rosalind Gill, 228–244. New York: Routledge.

Gill, Rosalind, and Ngaire Donaghue. 2016. Resilience, Apps and Reluctant Individualism: Technologies of Self in the Neoliberal Academy. *Women's Studies International Forum* 54: 91–99.

Hašková, Hana. 2005. Vliv evropské integrace na ženské občanské organizace v ČR. *Gender, Rovné Příležitosti, Výzkum* 6 (2): 37–42.

Hašková, Hana, Alena Křížková and Marcela Linková. Eds. 2006. *Mnohohlasem. Vyjednávání ženských Prostorů Po Roce 1989.* Praha: Sociologický ústav AV ČR.

Hašková, Hana, and Zuzana Uhde. 2009. *Women and Social Citizenship in Czech Society: Continuity and Change.* Prague: Sociologický ústav AV ČR.

Havelková, Hana, and Libora Oates-Indruchová. 2014. *The Politics of Gender Culture under State Socialism. An Expropriated Voice.* London, New York: Routledge.

Hemmings, Clare. 2006. Ready for Bologna? The Impact of the Declaration on Women's and Gender Studies in the UK. *European Journal of Women's Studies* 13 (4): 315–323.

Horký, Ondřej. 2008. Gender a Rozvoj. Co Nás Rozděluje, Co Nás Spojuje. *Gender, Rovné Příležitosti, Výzkum* 9 (2): 10–21.

Institute of Sociology CAS. 2017. *Gender and Research. Academic Journal.* http://www.genderonline.cz/en. Accessed: February 15, 2017.

Kampichler, Martina. 2006. Reflexe k tématu genderových studií na pozadí feministického rozvoje. Příklady z Masarykovy univerzity v Brně a Universität Wien (Univerzity Vídeň). *Gender, Rovné Příležitosti, Výzkum* 7 (2): 1–6.

Kapusta-Pofahl, Karen. 2002. "Who Could Create a Czech Feminism?" Challenging Assumptions in the Process of Creating Relevant Feminisms in the Czech Republic. *Anthropology of East Europe Review* 20 (2): 61–68.

Kapusta-Pofahl, Karen, Hana Hašková and Marta Kolářová. 2005. "Only a Dead Fish Flows with the Stream": NGO Formalization, Anarchofeminism, and the Power of Informal Associations. *Anthropology of East Europe Review* 23 (1): 38–52.

Katedra Antropologie FF ZČU. 2014. *Struktura oboru.* http://www.antropologie.org/cs/struktura-oboru-0. Accessed: September 8, 2016.

Katedra Genderových Studií. 2016. *Lidé.* http://gender.fhs.cuni.cz/KGS-10.html. Accessed: September 10, 2016.

Kolářová, Marta. 2010. Od globálního sesterství k transnacionálnímu feminismu: výzvy ženskému hnutí ve formě kulturních odlišností a nerovností mezi ženami. *Gender, Rovné Příležitosti, Výzkum* 11 (1): 30–40.

Linková, Marcela. 2006. Co si neuděláš, to nemáš, aneb ženský aktivismus, produkce znalosti a gender. In *Mnohohlasem. Vyjednávání ženských prostorů po roce 1989,* ed. by Hana Hašková, Alena Křížková and Marcela Linková, 143–164. Praha: Sociologický ústav AV ČR.

Linková, Marcela. 2013. V pasti dějin: křižovatky feminismu a neoliberalismu v evropské politice genderové rovnosti ve vědě. In *Nejisté Vyhlídky: Proměny Vědecké Profese Z Genderové Perspektivy,* ed. by Alice Červinková, Marcela Linková, Kateřina Cidlinská and Marta Vohlídalová, 148–173. Praha: Sociologické nakladatelství.

Linková, Marcela. 2017. Czech Research Landscape: Shifts in the Organization of Research After 1989. In *Gender and Neoliberalism in Czech Academia,* ed. by Marta Vohlídalová, and Marcela Linková, in print. Praha: SLON.

Linková, Marcela, and Alice Červinková. 2013. "Vlastní laboratoř": akademické trajektorie a gender v současných biovědách. *Gender, Rovné Příležitosti, Výzkum* 14 (1): 15–26. http://www.genderonline.cz/uploads/90ad1ebe5e19555dd25eecf4966dead5dc744f79_linkova-cervinkova-vlastni-laborator.pdf. Accessed: May 14, 2017.

Linková, Marcela, and Tereza Stöckelová. 2012. Public Accountability and the Politicization of Science: The Peculiar Journey of Czech Research Assessment. *Science and Public Policy* 39 (5): 618–629.
Linková, Marcela, Dunja Mladenić, Elzbieta H. Oleksy, Mária Palasik, Ester Papp, Magdaléna Piscová and Daniela Velichová. 2008. *Reclaiming a Political Voice: Women and Science in Central Europe*. Praha: SOÚ. http://www.zenyaveda.cz/files/re-claimingvoice-wsdfinal-eng.pdf. Accessed: May 14, 2017.
Lorenz-Meyer, Dagmar. 2004. Passionate Engagements. Challenges in Institutionalising, Teaching and Doing Gender Studies at the Centre for Gender Studies in Prague. In *Ročenka katedry/Centra Genderových Studií* 03/04, ed. by Blanka Knotková-Čapková, 22–39. Praha: Univerzita Karlova v Praze, Fakulta Humanitních studií.
Martin, Megan. 2008. The Growth of Czech Feminism: Analyzing Resistance Activities Through a Gendered Lens. *Gender, Rovné Příležitosti, Výzkum* 2008 (1): 37–44.
Masarykova Univerzita. 2016. *Vyučující*. http://gender.fss.muni.cz/cs/lide/vyucujici. Accessed: September 10, 2016.
Masarykova Univerzita. 2017. *Vyberte si druhý obor*. http://gender.fss.muni.cz/cs/studium/vyberte-si-druhy-obor. Accessed: September 9, 2016.
Ministerstvo školství, mládeže a tělovýchovy. 2015. *Rámec rozvoje vysokého školství do roku 2020*. http://www.vzdelavani2020.cz/images_obsah/dokumenty/ramec_vs.pdf. Accessed: May 15, 2017.
Mlčoch, Lubomír. 2001. Deset Lekcí Z Deseti Let české Transformace. *Finance a úvěr* 51 (4): 193–205.
Nečasová, Denisa. 2011. *Buduj Vlast – Posílíš Mír!: ženské Hnutí v českých Zemích 1945–1955*. Brno: Matice moravská.
Nyklová, Blanka. 2013. Krajinou Současného českého Feminismu. *Gender, Rovné Příležitosti, Výzkum* 14 (1): 52–62.
Nyklová, Blanka. 2014. *Czech Feminist Scene: Theoretical Inclinations, Stances, and Controversies*. Dissertation. Prague: Charles University.
Nyklová, Blanka. 2016. Feministická společnost (kontra) UK. *Newsletter* 3. www.genderaveda.cz/files/newsletter-brezen2016.pdf. Accessed: May 14, 2017.
Oates-Indruchová, Libora. 2004. Transforming and Emerging: Discourses of Gender in the Czech Culture of the Transition Period. In *Representing Gender in Cultures*, ed. by Elzbieta H. Oleksy and Joanna Rydzewska, 107–117. Frankfurt/Main: Peter Lang.
Oates-Indruchová, Libora. 2008a. Feminismus v akademii: aktivismus v akademii – angažovanost feministického výzkumu – témata – jazyk rovných příležitostí. Část I. Jak chápete pojem angažovanosti či aktivismu? (Jaká jsou specifika ve vědě a neakademickém prostředí?). *Kontext: Časopis pro gender a vědění* 2008 (1): 1–10. http://www.genderaveda.cz/files/feminismus-v-akademii-1.pdf. Accessed: May 14, 2017.
Oates-Indruchová, Libora. 2008b. Feminismus v akademii: aktivismus v akademii – angažovanost feministického výzkumu – témata – jazyk rovných příležitostí. Část II. Je, nebo není feministický přístup k vědeckému bádání specifický ve vztahu k angažovanosti/aktivismu? *Kontext: Časopis pro Gender a Vědění* 2008 (1): 1–11. http://www.genderaveda.cz/files/feminismus-v-akademii-2.pdf. Accessed: May 14, 2017.
Oates-Indruchová, Libora. 2011. Tak pěkně od začátku: o vztahu sociologie a kategorie genderu. In *Tvrdošíjnost myšlenky. Od feministické kriminologie k teorii genderu*, ed. by Libora Oates-Indruchová, 76–86. Praha: SLON.

Oates-Indruchová, Libora. 2016. Unraveling a Tradition, or Spinning a Myth? Gender Critique in Czech Society and Culture. *Slavic Review* 75 (4): 919–943.

Ostravská Univerzita. 2017. *Nabízené studijní obory pro přijímací řízení.* http://ff.osu.cz/vyber-si-studijni-obor/?obor=1784. Accessed: May 15, 2017.

Pavlík, Petr. 2004. O stěhování oboru aneb gender a moc v praxi. In *Ročenka katedry/Centra Genderových Studií* 03/04, ed. by Blanka Knotková-Čapková, 40–44. Praha: Univerzita Karlova v Praze, Fakulta Humanitních studií.

Pereira, Maria do Mar. 2014a. The Importance of Being "Modern" and Foreign: Feminist Scholarship and the Epistemic Status of Nations. *Signs: Journal of Women in Culture and Society* 39 (3): 627–657.

Pereira, Maria do Mar. 2014b. Toxic Corridor Talk: The Dismissal of Feminist Research in Everyday Academic Life. *Newsletter of the Feminist and Women's Studies Association (UK and Ireland)* 62 (May): 14.

Pereira, Maria do Mar. 2016. Struggling Within and Beyond the Performative University: Articulating Activism and Work in an "Academia without Walls". *Women's Studies International Forum* 54: 100–110.

Perknerová, Kateřina. 2017. *Rektor Jihočeské univerzity: Stačilo by, aby politici nešli do úplných kanálů.* http://www.denik.cz/z_domova/stacilo-by-aby-politici-nesli-do-uplnych-kanalu-kam-rada-z-nich-bohuzel-chodi-20170102.html. Accessed: May 15, 2017.

Prudký, Libor, Petr Pabian and Karel Šima. 2010. *Na Cestě Od Elitního K Univerzálnímu Vzdělávání 1989–2009.* Praha: Grada.

Rose, Gillian. 2013. *Visual Methodologies: An Introduction to Researching with Visual Materials.* Third Edit. London, Thousand Oaks: Sage.

Saxonberg, Steven. 2011. *With a Whimper, Not a Bang: The Increasing Acceptance of Feminism in Central Europe.* Lecture at University of Wisconsin, Madison (unpub.). Madison: University of Wisconsin. http://www.creeca.wisc.edu/images/events/posters/Fall2011/Saxonberg.pdf. Accessed: May 4, 2013.

Shields, Stuart. 2012. *The International Political Economy of Transition: Neoliberal Hegemony and Eastern Central Europe's Transformation.* RIPE Series in Global Political Economy. London, New York: Routledge.

Sociologický ústav AV ČR, v.v.i. 2017. *Gender & Sociologie.* http://www.soc.cas.cz/oddeleni/gender-sociologie. Accessed: May 15, 2017.

Soukromevysokeskoly.cz. 2017. *Katalog škol.* http://www.soukrome-vysoke-skoly.cz/. Accessed: June 6, 2017.

Stiglitz, Joseph. 1999. Whither Reform? – Ten Years of the Transition. In *Annual World Bank Conference on Economic Development*, ed. by Boris Pleskovic and Joseph Stiglitz, 27–56. Washington/D.C.: World Bank.

Stöckelová, Tereza. 2012. Immutable Mobiles Derailed: STS, Geopolitics and Research Assessment. *Science, Technology & Human Values* 37 (2): 286–311.

Stratigaki, Maria. 2004. The Cooptation of Gender Concepts in EU Policies: The Case of "Reconciliation of Work and Family". *Social Politics* 11 (1): 30–56.

Šima, Karel, and Petr Pabian. 2013. *Ztracený Humboldtův ráj. IdeologiejJednoty výzkumu a výuky ve vysokém školství.* Praha: SLON.

Šima, Karel, and Petr Pabian. 2017. Higher Education Policy Context. In *Gender and Neoliberalism in Czech Academia,* ed. by Marta Vohlídalová and Marcela Linková, in print. Praha: SLON.

Šmausová, Gerlinda. 2011. Proti tvrdošíjné představě o ontické povaze genderu a pohlaví. In *Tvrdošíjnost myšlenky. Od feministické kriminologie k teorii genderu*, ed. by Libora Oates-Indruchová, 179–194. Praha: SLON.

Tenglerová, Hana. 2011. Politiky nečinnosti: genderová rovnost v české vědní politice. *Gender, Rovné Příležitosti, Výzkum* 12 (1): 63–73. http://www.genderonline.cz/uploads/787600d-8c27097683eb92921293be25ca5da4cfa_politiky-necinnosti.pdf. Accessed: May 14, 2017.

Tenglerová, Hana. 2015. *Postavení žen v české vědě. Monitorovací zpráva za rok 2014*. Praha: Sociologický ústav AV ČR, v.v.i.

True, Jacqui. 2003. *Gender, Globalization, and Postsocialism: The Czech Republic After Communism*. New York: Columbia University Press.

Uhde, Zuzana, Hana Hašková, Hana Maříková and Alena Křížková. 2006. Diskurz spravedlnosti mezi aktivismem a vědou. *Sociologický časopis / Czech Sociological Review* 42 (5): 1013–1018.

Úřad vlády České republiky. 2017. *RVVI projednala zásady nového hodnocení výzkumu*. http://www.vyzkum.cz/FrontAktualita.aspx?aktualita=780879. Accessed: February 10, 2017.

Václavíková-Helšusová, Lenka. 2006. Genderová vědecká komunita vlastníma očima. In *Mnohohlasem. Vyjednávání ženských prostorů po roce 1989*, ed. by Hana Hašková, Alena Křížková and Marcela Linková, 167–180. Praha: Sociologický ústav AV ČR. http://www.genderaveda.cz/files/monohohlasem.pdf. Accessed: February 16, 2017.

Večerník, Jiří. 1999. Střední vrstvy v české transformaci / The Middle Classes in Czech Reforms. *Sociologický Časopis / Czech Sociological Review* 35 (1): 33–51.

Víznerová, Hana, and Blanka Nyklová. Eds. 2016. *Hledání Dynamické Rovnováhy: Tři Generace Výzkumnic Na VŠCHT Praha*. Praha: VŠCHT, SOÚ.

Vliegenthart, Arjan. 2010. Bringing Dependency Back In: The Economic Crisis in Post-Socialist Europe and the Continued Relevance of Dependent Development. *Historical Social Research* 35 (2): 242–265.

Vodrážka, Mirek. 1999. *Esej O Politickém Harémismu. Kritická Zpráva O Stavu Feminismu v Čechách*. Brno: Zvláštní vydání.

Vodrážka, Mirek. 2003. Diskursivní Smrt a Feminismus Bez Feminismu. *Aspekt*. http://archiv.aspekt.sk/desat.php?desat=46. Accessed: February 20, 2014.

Vohlídalová, Marta, and Marcela Linková. Eds. 2017. *Gender and Neoliberalism in Czech Academia*, in print. Prague: SLON.

Welsh, Helga A. 1994. Political Transition Processes in Central and Eastern Europe. *Comparative Politics* 26 (4): 379–394.

Wolchik, Sharon L. 1995. The Politics of Transition in Central Europe. *Problems of Post-Communism* 42 (1): 35–40.

Žarkov, Dubravka. 2015. On Intellectual Labour and Neoliberalism in Academia – Or, in Praise of Reviewers. *European Journal of Women's Studies* 22 (3): 269–273.

Author Information

Kadri Aavik, PhD, Lecturer in Sociology, Tallinn University, Estonia

Research areas and interests: Sociology of Gender; Intersectionality; Critical Studies of Men and Masculinities; Gender and Work; Feminist and Intersectional Qualitative Methodologies; Critical Animal Studies; Critical University Studies

Recent publications:

Aavik, Kadri. 2015. Resistance to Gender Equality at Work: Discursive Practices of Estonian Male Managers. In *Engaging Men in Building Gender Equality*, ed. by Michael Flood and Richard Howson, 182–192. Newcastle upon Tyne: Cambridge Scholars Press.

Aavik, Kadri. 2015. "The Most Important Decisions Are Made in the Sauna": The Role of Social Capital in Creating Intersectional Privilege in the Career Narratives of Estonian Male Managers. *NORMA: International Journal for Masculinity Studies* 10 (1): 39–54.

Aavik, Kadri. 2017. The Vulnerability of Gender Equality Mechanisms in the Post-socialist Academia: "Doing Neoliberalism" in Estonian Universities. In *Gender in/and the Neoliberal University: Transnational Processes and Localised Impacts.* Gender, rovné příležitosti, výzkum [Gender and Research], Special Issue 18 (1), ed. by Blanka Nyklová, Birgit Riegraf and Kadri Aavik, 130–153. Prague: Czech Academy of Sciences.

Aavik, Kadri, and Dagmar Kase. 2015. Challenging Sexism While Supporting Speciesism: The Views of Estonian Feminists on Animal Liberation and its Links to Feminism. *Journal for Critical Animal Studies* 13 (1): 92–127.

Emília Araújo, Assistant Professor at the Institute of Social Sciences, University of Minho, Portugal; Project Principal Investigator *Mobiscience: Portuguese Researchers Trajectories and Movement of Knowledge*

Research areas and interests: Culture and Techno-science; Time, Gender and Academic Mobility

Recent publications:

Araújo, Emília. 2016. Uma abordagem sobre o tempo de (para) na ciência e academia [An Approach about Time from (for) Science and Academia]. *Sociologia Online* 12, 110–136.

Araújo, Emília, and Victor Barros. 2017. "Modo deadline": uma análise sobre o tempo das mulheres académicas. *Revista Tempos e Espaços em Educação* 10 (22): 173–186.

Araújo, Emília, and Monica Franch. 2017. Apuntes sobre la pertinencia heurística del concepto de "tiempo en abundancia" para el análisis del tiempo de desempleo desde una perspectiva de género [Notes on the Heuristic Relevance of the Concept of "Time in Abundance" for the Analysis of Unemployment Time from a Gender Perspective]. *ARBOR Ciencia, Pensamiento y Cultura* 193 (784): 1–17.

Araújo, Emília, Margarida Fontes and Sofia Bento. Eds. 2013. *Para um debate sobre a fuga de cérebros / To a Debate on Brain Drain*. Braga: Centro de Estudos de Comunicação e Sociedade (CECS).

Martins, Moisés de Lemos, Maria Manuel Baptista, Emília Araújo and Larissa Latif. 2016. Ciência e conhecimento: políticas e discursos [Science and Knowledge: Policies and Speeches]. *Revista Lusófona de Estudos Culturais* 3 (2): 7–17.

Mariana Prandini Assis, PhD Candidate in Politics, New School for Social Research, United States of America

Research areas and interests: Feminist Political and Legal Theory; Transnationalism; Human Rights; Legal Mobilization; Social Movements; Gender Studies

Recent publications:

Assis, Mariana Prandini. 2017. Violence Against Women as a Translocal Category in the Jurisprudence of the Inter-American Court of Human Rights. *Direito & Práxis* 8 (2): 1507–1544.

Assis, Mariana Prandini, and Ana Carolina Ogando. 2014. Confronting Sexual Violence While Fueling the Apparatuses of the Neoliberal State? Ambiguities of an Emancipatory Project. *Labrys: Estudos Feministas* 25. https://www.labrys.net.br/labrys25/recherches/mariana.htm.

Kaneti, Marina, and Mariana Prandini Assis. 2016. (Re)branding the State: Humanitarian Border Control and the Moral Imperative of State Sovereignty. *Social Research: An International Quarterly* 83 (2): 295–325.

Seabra, Joana Emmerick, and Mariana Prandini Assis. 2016. Transforming from the Margins: A Proposal for Mapping Latin American Critical Feminist Social Thought. *Direito & Práxis* 7 (13): 465–493.

Amélia Augusto, PhD, Assistant Professor, University of Beira Interior (UBI), Portugal; Researcher at the Centre for Research and Studies in Sociology (CIES-IUL); Member of the UBI's Commission for Gender Equality

Research areas and interests: Sociology of Health; Gender and Health; Gender and Technology; Gender Inequality

Recent publications:

Augusto, Amélia. 2013. Género e Saúde. In *Saúde, Medicina e Sociedade. Uma visão sociológica*, ed. by Fátima Alves, 29–34. Lisboa: Pactor.

Augusto, Amélia. 2014. A construção social da infertilidade. In *Saúde no Prisma da Sociologia. Olhares Plurais*, ed. by Maria Engrácia Leando and Baltazar Ricardo Monteiro, 268–281. Viseu: Psicosoma.

Augusto, Amélia. 2015. Comentário: da medicalização à biomedicalização da vida. In *Novos Temas de Saúde, Novas Questões Sociais*, ed. by Graça Carapinheiro and Tiago Correia, 83–98. Lisboa: Mundos Sociais.

Sales Oliveira, Catarina, and Amélia Augusto. 2017. El gender mainstreaming en la academia portuguesa. *Ciencia, Técnica y Mainstreaming Social* (1): 17–27.

Santos, Mário, and Amélia Augusto. 2016. "Se estava tudo bem, porque é que eu havia de ir a uma obstetra?" Identidade, risco e consumo de tecnologia médica no parto domiciliar em Portugal. *Sociologia, Problemas e Práticas* 82: 49–67.

Carla Cerqueira, PhD, Assistant Professor at University Lusófona in Lisbon, Portugal; Postdoctoral Grantee in Communication Sciences at the Communication and Society Research Centre (CECS), University of Minho, Portugal

Research areas and interests: Feminist Media Studies; Gender; Technologies; NGOs; Communication Strategies; Public Policies

Recent publications:

Cerqueira, Carla. 2017. Feminist Film Analysis. In *International Encyclopedia of Media Effects*, ed. by Patrick Rössler, Cynthia A. Hoffner and Liesbet van Zoonen. New Jersey: John Wiley & Sons. doi: 10.1002/9781118783764.wbieme0112.

Cerqueira, Carla, and Sara I Magalhães. 2017. Ensaio sobre cegueiras: cruzamentos intersecionais e (in)visibilidades nos media. *ex aequo* 35: 9–20.

Magalhães, Sara I., and Carla Cerqueira. 2015. Our Place in History: Young Feminists at the Margins. In *"Young Feminists" Doing Recognition & Reflexivity & (R)evolution*. Feminism & Psychology, Special Issue 25 (1), ed. by Rachel J. Liebert and Lucy Thompson, 39–44. Thousand Oaks: Sage.

Cerqueira, Carla, Sara I. Magalhães, Anabela Santos, Rosa Cabecinhas and Conceição Nogueira. 2014. *De outro género: propostas para a promoção de um jornalismo mais inclusivo*. Braga: LASICS/CECS.

Magalhães, Sara, Carla Cerqueira and Mariana Bernardo. 2012. Media and the (Im)permeability of Public Sphere to Gender. In *Democracy, Mass Media and Public Sphere*, ed. by Marta Nunes da Costa, 35–52. Vila Nova de Famalicão: Edições Húmus.

Farinaz Fassa, Dr, Professor of Sociology of Education at the University of Lausanne, Switzerland; Co-Director of the Observatory of Education and Training of the Institute of Social Sciences; Member of the Equality delegation of the University of Lausanne

Research areas and interests: Gender Theory, Education and Training; Higher Education, Inequalities, Equality and Equity in Careers

Recent publications:

Fassa, Farinaz. 2015. Excellence and Gender: Playing the Game of Scientific Excellence or Being Played by the Game? The Swiss Example. *Equality, Diversity and Inclusion: An International Journal* 34 (1): 37–54.

Fassa, Farinaz. 2016. *Filles et garçons face à la formation. Les défis de l'égalité*. Lausanne: Presses polytechniques et universitaires romandes (Le savoir suisse).

Fassa, Farinaz. 2016. Politiques d'égalité des chances dans les universités suisses. Bilan provisoire d'un pilotage décentralisé. In *Les femmes dans le monde académique. Perspectives comparatives*, ed. by Rebecca Rogers and Pascale Molinier, 167–179. Rennes: Presses universitaires de Rennes.

Fassa, Farinaz, and Sabine Kradolfer. 2013. The Gendering of Excellence Through Quality Criteria: The Case of the Swiss National Science Foundation Professorships in Switzerland. *Tertiary Education and Management* 19 (3): 189–204.

Roca I Escoda, Marta, Farinaz Fassa and Eléonore Lépinard. 2016. *L'intersectionnalité: enjeux théoriques et politiques*. Paris: La Dispute (le genre du monde).

Heike Kahlert, Dr habil., Professor and Chair of Sociology/Social Inequality and Gender at the Ruhr University Bochum, Germany; Affiliated Member of the Center for Feminist Social Studies (CFS) at Örebro University, Sweden

Research areas and interests: Transformations of Knowledge in Modernity; Gender Relations and Social Change in the Welfare State; Institutionalised Inequalities in the Educational System; Gender-Sensitive Organisational Development in the Public-Profit Sector

Recent publications:

Kahlert, Heike. 2012. The Simultaneity of Stability and Change in Gender Relations – Contributions from Giddens' Structuration Theory. *Studia Humanistyczne AGH/Humanistic Studies* 11 (2): 57–67.

Kahlert, Heike. 2014. Gender (In)Equality in Academic Career Promotion of Doctoral Students. In *Paths to Career and Success for Women in Science. Findings from International Research*, ed. by Britta Thege, Silvester Popescu-Willigmann, Roswitha Pioc and Sabah Badri-Höher, 37–62. Wiesbaden: Springer VS Verlag für Sozialwissenschaften.

Kahlert, Heike. 2015. Gender Equality Politics in Ageing Welfare Societies: The Case of the European Union. In *Institutionalizing Gender Equality. Historical and Global Perspectives*, ed. by Yulia Gradskova und Sara Sanders, 85–103. Lanham, Boulder, New York, London: Lexington Books.

Kahlert, Heike. 2015. Nicht als Gleiche vorgesehen. Über das "akademische Frauensterben" auf dem Weg an die Spitze der Wissenschaft. *Beiträge zur Hochschulforschung* 37 (3): 60–78.

Kahlert, Heike. 2017. Exzellenz im Mainstream der Wissenschaft – Gender auch? Frauen- und Geschlechterforschung in der unternehmerischen Universität. In *Zum Selbstverständnis der Gender Studies: Technik – Raum – Bildung*, ed. by Corinna Onnen and Susanne Rode-Breymann, 39–63. Opladen: Barbara Budrich.

Sabine Kradolfer, Dr, Equality Officer of the Swiss National Centre of Competence in Research LIVES *Overcoming Vulnerability: Life Course Perspectives* at the University of Lausanne, Switzerland

Research areas and interests: Intersections between Social Inequalities (Sex, Race, Class); Gender Equality in Academic Careers; Race and Ethnicity; Indigenous Peoples of Latin America

Recent Publications:

Kradolfer, Sabine. 2015. Switzerland. In *Garcia Working Papers – Academic Careers and Gender Inequality: Leaky Pipeline and Interrelated Phenomena in Seven European Countries*. Vol. 4, ed. by Farah Dubois-Shaik and Bernard Fusulier, 116–136. Trento: University of Trento.

Fassa, Farinaz, and Sabine Kradolfer. 2013. The Gendering of Excellence Through Quality Criteria: The Case of the Swiss National Science Foundation Professorships in Switzerland. *Tertiary Education and Management* 19 (3): 189–204.

Bataille, Pierre, Nicky Le Feuvre and Sabine Kradolfer. 2017. Should I Stay or Should I Go? The Effects of Precariousness on Career Aspirations of Postdocs in Switzerland. *European Educational Research Journal* 16 (2–3): 313–331.

Le Feuvre, Nicky, and Sabine Kradolfer (in collaboration with Maria Del Rio Carral, Farinaz Fassa, Gaële Goastellec and Michael Posse). 2015. Switzerland. In *Garcia Working Papers – Constructing Excellence: The Gap between Formal and Actual Selection Criteria for Early Career Academics*. Vol. 2, ed. by Channah Herschberg, Yvonne Benschop and Marieke van den Brink, 179–240. Trento: University of Trento.

Desiree Lewis, Dr, Professor in the Women's and Gender Studies Department at the University of the Western Cape, South Africa

Research area and interests: The Politics of South African and Global Feminisms; Gender Sexuality and Nationalism; Popular and Visual Culture; Critical Food Studies

Recent Publications:

Lewis, Desiree. 2017. Bodies, Matter and Feminist Freedoms: Revisiting the Politics of Food. *Agenda* 30 (3): 6–16.

Lewis, Desiree. 2015. "Another University Is Possible": Thoughts on Student Protests and Universities in Postcolonial Africa. *Los Angeles Review of Books*, December 9. https://lareviewofbooks.org/article/another-university-is-possible-thoughts-on-student-protests-and-universities-in-postcolonial-africa/.

Lewis, Desiree. 2015. Gender, Feminism and Food Studies. *African Security Review* 24 (4): 414–429.

Lewis, Desiree. 2017. Academy-Based Feminist Intellectuals and the Nexus of State, Globalization and Civil Society. In *The Role of Intellectuals in the State-Society Nexus*, ed. by Barry Gilder and Angela McCelland, 110–125. Johannesburg: Real African Publishers.

Raili Marling, PhD, Professor of English Studies, University of Tartu, Estonia
Research areas and interests: Gendered Discourses in the Public Sphere and Literature; Gendered Affects under Neoliberalism; Contradictions of Gender in the Post-socialist Context

Recent publications:

Marling, Raili. 2010. The Intimidating Other: Feminist Critical Discourse Analysis of the Representation of Feminism in Estonian Print Media. *Nora: Nordic Journal of Women's Studies* 18 (1): 7–19.
Marling, Raili. 2015. World Wide Web and the Emotional Public Sphere. In *Metamorphoses of (New) Media*, ed. by Julia Genz and Ulrike Küchler, 3–26. Newcastle: Cambridge Scholars Publishing.
Koobak, Redi, and Raili Marling. 2014. The Decolonial Challenge: Framing Post-Socialist Central and Eastern Europe within Transnational Feminist Studies. *European Journal of Women's Studies* 21 (4): 330–343.
Örtenblad, Anders, Raili Marling and Snježana Vasiljević. Eds. 2017. *Gender Equality in a Global Perspective*. New York, London: Routledge.

Louise Morley, AcSS, Professor of Education and Director of the Centre for Higher Education and Equity Research (CHEER), University of Sussex, United Kingdom
Research areas and interests: Gender; Leadership; Equity; Political Economy of Higher Education Internationally

Recent publications:

Morley, Louise. 2012. The Rules of the Game: Women and the Leaderist Turn in Higher Education. *Gender and Education* 25 (1): 116–131.
Morley, Louise. 2014. Lost Leaders: Women in the Global Academy. *Higher Education Research and Development* 33 (1): 111–125.
Morley, Louise. 2015. Troubling Intra-actions: Gender, Neo-liberalism and Research in the Global Academy. *Journal of Education Policy* 31 (1): 28–45.
Morley, Louise, and Barbara Crossouard. 2016. Gender in the Neoliberalised Global Academy: The Affective Economy of Women and Leadership in South Asia. *British Journal of Sociology of Education* 37 (1): 149–168.
Morley, Louise, and Barbara Crossouard. 2016. Rejection, Refusal, Reluctance, Revisioning: Women in Higher Education Leadership in South Asia. *Studies in Higher Education* 46 (5): 801–814.

Blanka Nyklová, PhD, Postdoctoral Researcher at the Czech Academy of Sciences, Institute of Sociology; Lecturer in Gender Studies at the Council on International Educational Exchange at Charles University Prague, Czech Republic
Research areas and interests: Czech Feminist Scene; Gender in Science; Institutional and Organisational Change; Feminist Pedagogy; Geopolitics of Gender Studies; Visual Studies

Recent publications:

Nyklová, Blanka. 2015. Through Feminist Eyes. In *Democratization Through Social Activism: Gender and Environmental Issues in Post-Communist Countries*, ed. by Katalin Fábián and Ioana Vlad, 71–94. Bucharest: Tritonic.

Nyklová, Blanka. 2017. Science on the Semi-periphery? Beyond Geopolitics. In *Gender and Neoliberalism in Czech Academia*, ed. by Marta Vohlídalová and Marcela Linková, in print. Praha: SLON.

Víznerová, Hana, and Blanka Nyklová. Eds. 2016. *Hledání dynamické rovnováhy: tři generace výzkumnic na VŠCHT Praha*. Praha: VŠCHT, SOÚ.

Maria do Mar Pereira, PhD, Associate Professor, Department of Sociology, University of Warwick, United Kingdom
Research areas and interests: Gender; Feminism; Ethnography; Higher Education; Science; Academia; Epistemology; Young People

Recent Publications:

Pereira, Maria do Mar. 2012. "Feminist Theory Is Proper Knowledge, But…": The Status of Feminist Scholarship in the Academy. *Feminist Theory* 13 (3): 283–303.

Pereira, Maria do Mar. 2014. The Importance of Being "Modern" and Foreign: Feminism and the Epistemic Status of Nations. *Signs: Journal of Women in Culture and Society* 39 (3): 627–657.

Pereira, Maria do Mar. 2015. Higher Education Cutbacks and the Reshaping of Epistemic Hierarchies: An Ethnographic Study of the Case of Feminist Scholarship. *Sociology* 49 (2): 287–304.

Pereira, Maria do Mar. 2016. Struggling Within and Beyond the Performative University: Articulating Activism and Work in an "Academia Without Walls". *Women's Studies International Forum* 54: 100–110.

Pereira, Maria do Mar. 2017. *Power, Knowledge and Feminist Scholarship: An Ethnography of Academia*. London: Routledge.

Cristiano Rodrigues, PhD, Assistant Professor of Political Science, Federal University of Minas Gerais, Brazil
Research areas and interests: Democratic Theory; Comparative Perspectives on Afro-Latin America; Social Movements Theory; Black Feminist Thought; Gender Studies

Recent Publications:

Rodrigues, Cristiano. 2014. Reforma Constitucional, Políticas Públicas e Desigualdades Raciais no Brasil e Colômbia: um (breve) apontamento analítico. *Revista de História Comparada (UFRJ)* 8 (1): 236–274.
Machado, Frederico Viana, and Cristiano Rodrigues. 2015. Movimentos Negros e LGBT no Governo Lula: desafios da institucionalização segmentada. In *Estado, Ambiente e Movimentos Sociais*, ed. by Frederico Viana Machado, Gustavo Martineli Massola and Maria Auxiliadora Teixeira Ribeiro, 22–45. Florianópolis: Abrapso, Edições do Bosque.
Rodrigues, Cristiano, and Marco Aurélio Prado. 2013. A History of the Black Women's Movement in Brazil: Mobilization, Political Trajectory and Articulations with the State. *Social Movement Studies* 12 (2): 158–177.

Catarina Sales Oliveira, PhD, Assistant Professor, University of Beira Interior (UBI), Portugal; Researcher at the Centre for Research and Studies in Sociology (CIES-IUL); President of the UBI's Commission for Gender Equality

Research areas and interests: Gender; Transports, Mobilities and Inequalities; Work and Organisations

Recent Publications:

Martins, Ana, Catarina Sales Oliveira and Manuel Loureiro. 2016. Assédio e capacidade para o trabalho. Um estudo exploratório numa universidade portuguesa [Mobbing and Working Capacity. An Exploratory Study in a Public University]. *International Journal on Working Conditions* 12 (Dec.): 35–53.
Monteiro, Alcides, Silvia Ferreira and Catarina Sales Oliveira. 2015. Applied Theatre, Gender Consciousness and Transformative Learning. In *Perspectives on Community Practices: Living and Learning in Community*, ed. by Sabina J. Krasovec and Damijan Stefanc, 209–218. Ljubljana: Ljubljana University Press.
Sales Oliveira, Catarina, and Amélia Augusto. 2017. El gender mainstreaming en la academia portuguesa. *Ciencia, Técnica y Mainstreaming Social* 2017 (1): 17–27.
Sales Oliveira, Catarina, and Nuno Jerónimo. 2016. Small but Focused: Women (Self) Empowerment in a Rural Village. In *Overcoming Gender Inequalities through Technology Integration*, ed. by Joseph Wilson and Nuhru Gapsiso, 93–122. Hershey: Information Science Reference.
Sales Oliveira, Catarina. 2015. (Auto)Mobilities and Social Identities in Portugal. *Sociologia, problemas e práticas* 77: 137–151.

Sigrid Schmitz, Dr, Professor of Gender & Science at the Department of History, Humboldt-University Berlin, Germany

Research areas and interests: Feminist Science Technology Studies; Brain Research; Neurocultures; Body Discourses; Feminist Epistemologies

Recent Publications:

Schmitz, Sigrid. 2012. The Neuro-technological Cerebral Subject: Persistence of Implicit and Explicit Gender Norms in a Network of Change. *Neuroethics* 5 (3): 261–274.

Schmitz, Sigrid. 2015. Gender in Science: Bis hierhin und wie weiter? Potenziale und Grenzen genderbezogener Interventionen in/mit den MINT-Fächern. In *Akademische Wissenskulturen und soziale Praxis. Geschlechterforschung zu natur-, technik- und geisteswissenschaftlichen Fächern*, ed. by Tanja Paulitz, Barbara Hey, Susanne Kink and Bianca Prietl, 228–250. Münster: Westfälisches Dampfboot.

Schmitz, Sigrid. 2016. Science. In *Handbook Gender: Sources, Perspectives, and Methodologies*, ed. by Renée C. Hoogland, 347–362. Massachusetts: Macmillan.

Schmitz, Sigrid, and Grit Höppner. Eds. 2014. *Gendered NeuroCultures. Feminist and Queer Perspectives on Current Brains Discourses*. Vienna: Zaglossus.

Pia Vuolanto, PhD, Postdoctoral Researcher, University of Tampere Research Centre for Knowledge, Science, Technology and Innovation Studies, Finland

Research areas and interests: Science and Technology Studies; Controversies in Science; Gender Research in Controversy; Gender Perspectives in Nursing; Nursing Science in Controversy; Development of Academic Nursing; Women in Science; Complementary and Alternative Medicine

Recent Publications:

Vehviläinen, Marja, Pia Vuolanto and Oili-Helena Ylijoki. 2010. Gender Equality in the Interface Organisations Between Science, Technology and Innovations. *Journal of Technology Management and Innovation* 5 (1): 64–74.

Vuolanto, Pia. 2015. Boundary Work and Power in the Controversy Over Therapeutic Touch in Finnish Nursing Science. *Minerva* 53 (4): 359–380.

Vuolanto, Pia. 2016. Academic Nursing: An Epitome of a Conflict-Prone Domain. In *Paradoxes of Conflicts*, ed. by Giovanni Scarafile and Leah Gruenpeter Gold, 109–122. Cham: Springer.

Vuolanto, Pia. 2017. The Universities' Transformation Thesis Revisited: A Case Study of the Relationship Between Nursing Science and Society. *Science and Technology Studies* 30 (2): 34–52.

Vuolanto, Pia, and Anne Laiho. 2017. The Gender Perspective in Nursing Research: A Theoretical Treasure Chest or a "Thorn" in the Side? *Minerva* 55 (3): 371–390. doi: 10.1007/s11024-017-9318-0.

MIX
Papier aus verantwortungsvollen Quellen
Paper from responsible sources
FSC® C105338

If you have any concerns about our products,
you can contact us on
ProductSafety@springernature.com

In case Publisher is established outside the EU,
the EU authorized representative is:
Springer Nature Customer Service Center GmbH
Europaplatz 3, 69115 Heidelberg, Germany

Printed by Libri Plureos GmbH
in Hamburg, Germany